kare kano

his and her circumstances

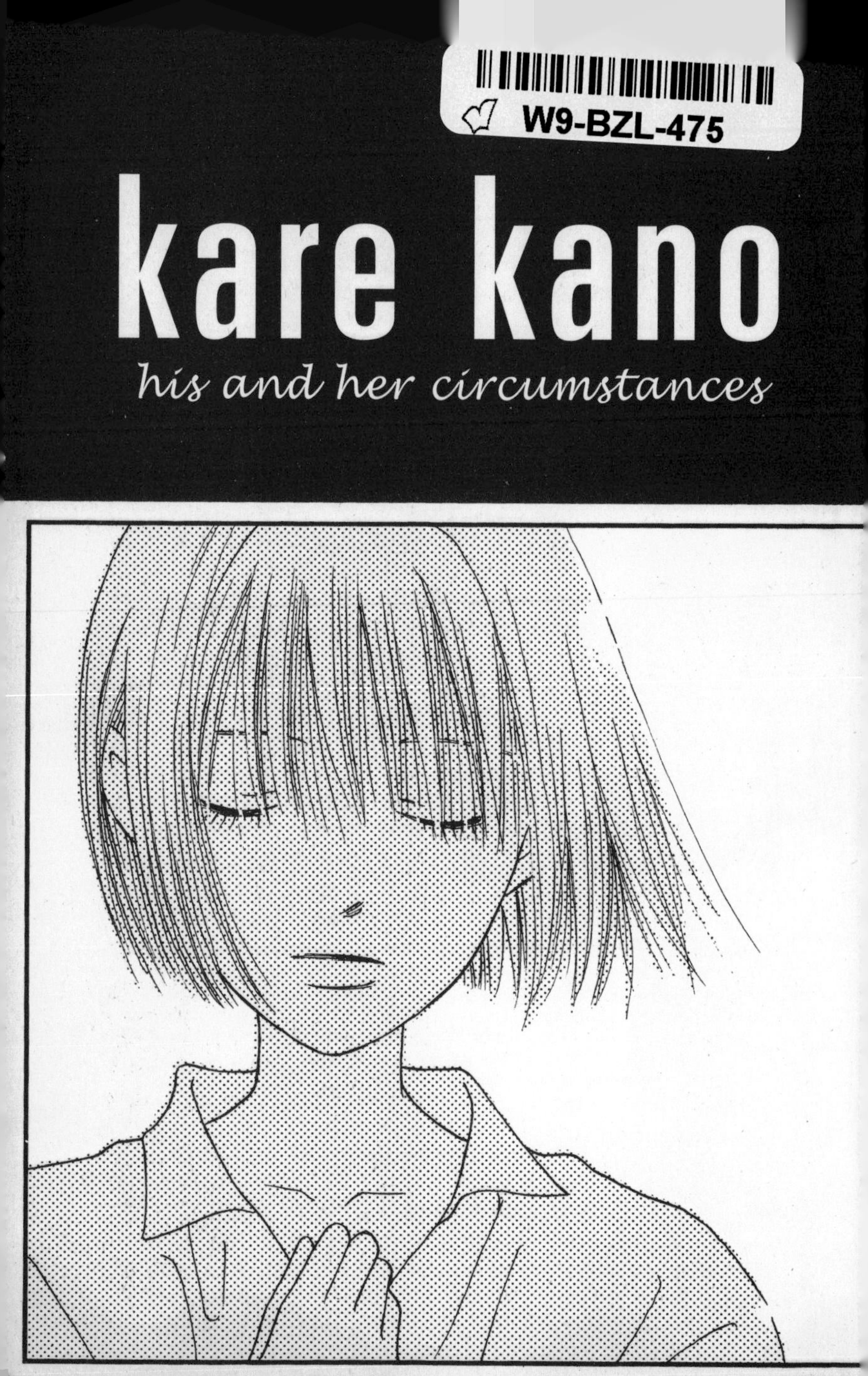

Kare Kano Vol. 14
Created by Masami Tsuda

Translation - Michelle Kobayashi
Retouch and Lettering - Samantha Yamanaka
Graphic Designer - Vicente Rivera, Jr.
Cover Artist - Gary Shum

Editor - Carol Fox
Digital Imaging Manager - Chris Buford
Pre-Press Manager - Antonio DePietro
Production Managers - Jennifer Miller and Mutsumi Miyazaki
Art Director - Matt Alford
Managing Editor - Jill Freshney
VP of Production - Ron Klamert
Editor-in-Chief - Mike Kiley
President and C.O.O. - John Parker
Publisher and C.E.O. - Stuart Levy

A **TOKYOPOP** Manga

TOKYOPOP Inc.
5900 Wilshire Blvd. Suite 2000
Los Angeles, CA 90036

E-mail: info@TOKYOPOP.com
Come visit us online at www.TOKYOPOP.com

ISBN: 1-59532-588-3

First TOKYOPOP printing: March 2005
10 9 8 7 6 5 4 3 2 1
Printed in the USA

kare kano

his and her circumstances

volume fourteen

by Masami Tsuda

HAMBURG // LONDON // LOS ANGELES // TOKYO

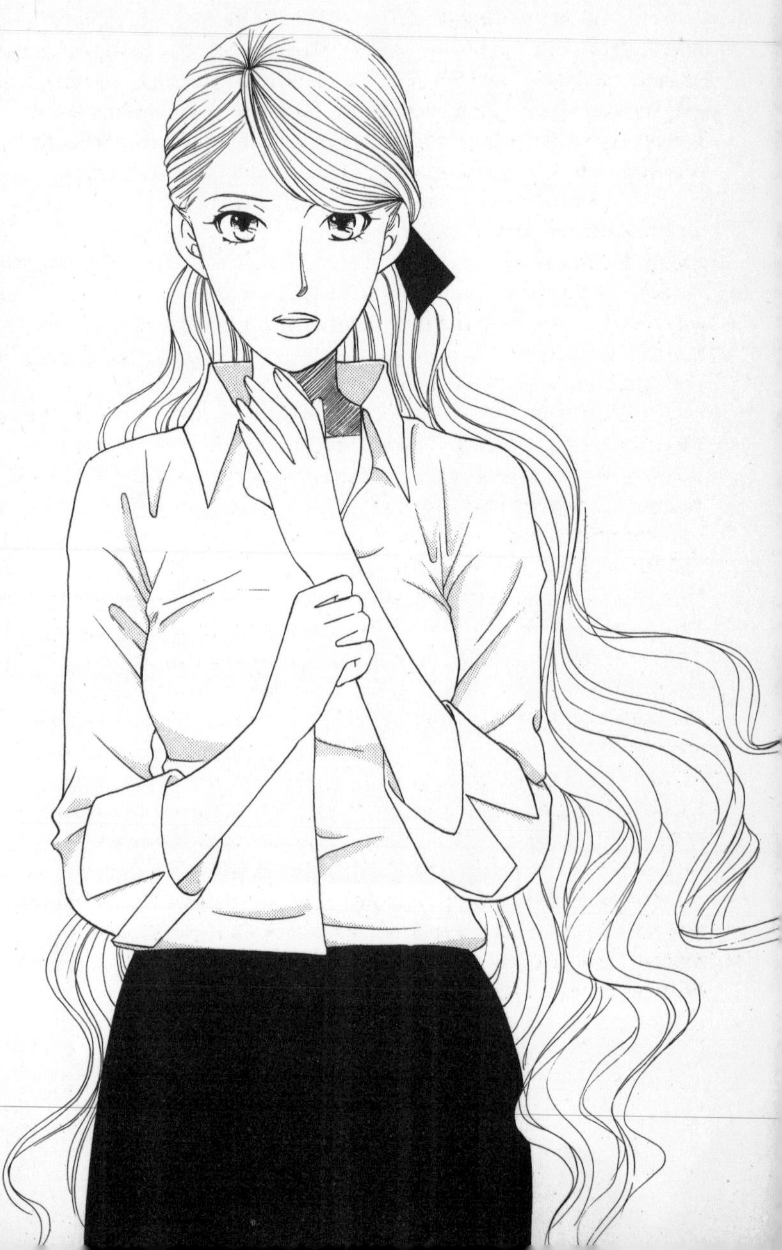

KARE KANO: THE STORY SO FAR

Yukino Miyazawa is the perfect student: kind, athletic and smart. But she's not all she seems. She is really the self-professed "queen of vanity," and her only goal in life is winning the praise and admiration of everyone around her. Therefore, she makes it her business to always look and act perfect during school hours. At home, however, she lets her guard down and lets her true self show.

When Yukino enters high school, she finally meets her match: Soichiro Arima, a handsome, popular, ultra-intelligent guy. Once he steals the top seat in class away from her, Yukino sees him as a bitter rival. Over time, her anger turns to amazement, when she discovers she and Soichiro have more in common than she ever imagined. As their love blossoms, they promise to stop pretending to be perfect and just be true to themselves.

But they have plenty of obstacles in their way. First, Hideaki, the school's token pretty boy, tries to come between them. Then Yukino and Soichiro's grades drop because they've been spending so much time together, and their teacher pressures them to break up. Once that's resolved, two more speed bumps are encountered on their road to romance. Maho, a jealous classmate, is convinced that Yukino is deceiving everyone and vows to turn everyone against her. Then an old friend of Soichiro's from junior high tries to steal Soichiro's affections. Somehow, Yukino and Soichiro's love manages to persevere—even after Soichiro spends the summer away at a kendo tournament. In fact, it makes their romance that much stronger.

Or does it? What Yukino doesn't realize is that although Soichiro's life with his adoptive family seems perfect, he once endured a very traumatic childhood…and the old demons are beginning to resurface. To Soichiro, achievement has not only meant praise for a job well done, but also revenge against his former family. And now Soichiro's success has attracted the attention of his birth mother, who suddenly wants him back in her life. For what purpose, he cannot yet tell…nor can he tell anyone he's been meeting with her.

kare kano
volume fourteen

TABLE OF CONTENTS

....

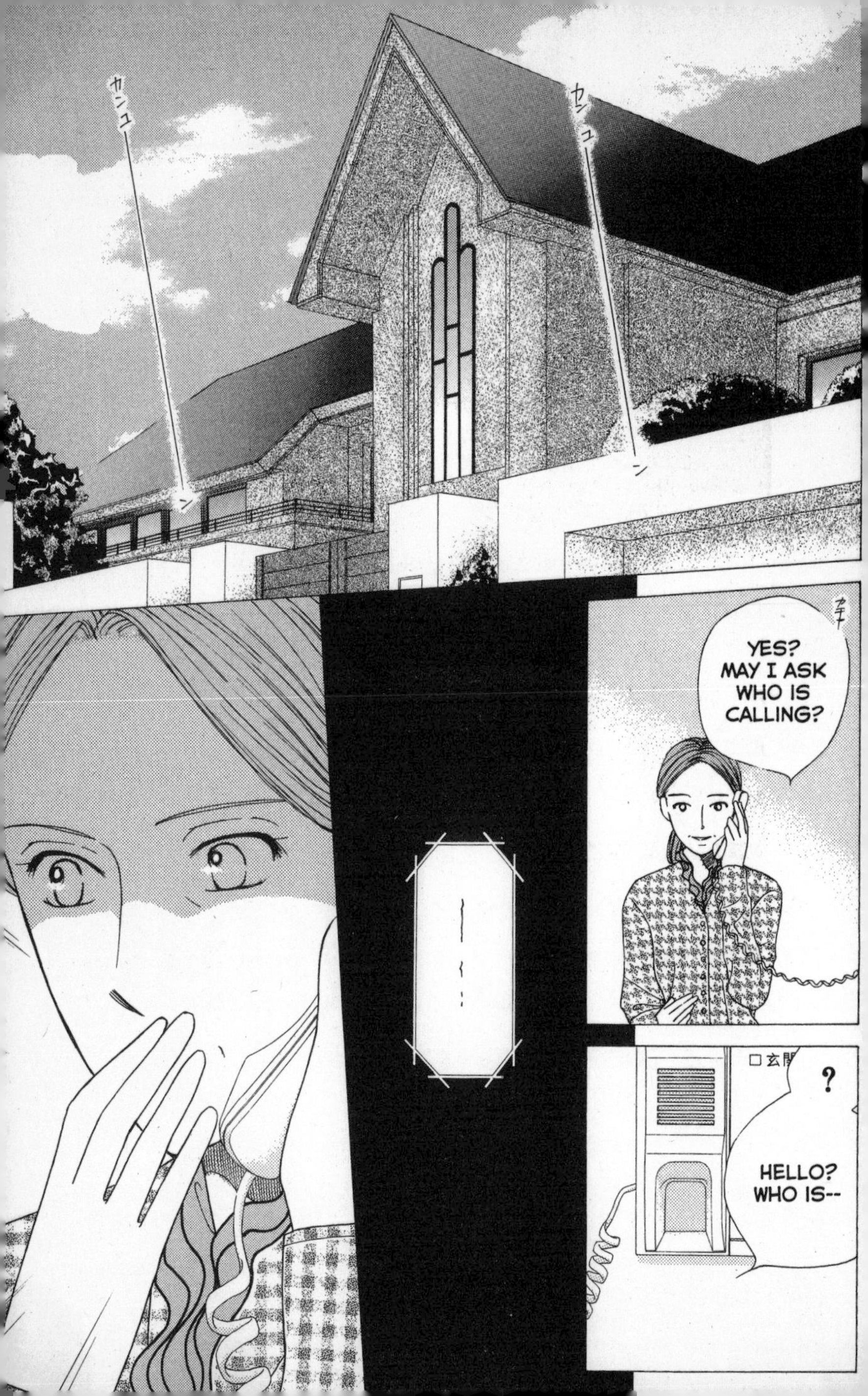
YES? MAY I ASK WHO IS CALLING?
玄関
?
HELLO? WHO IS--

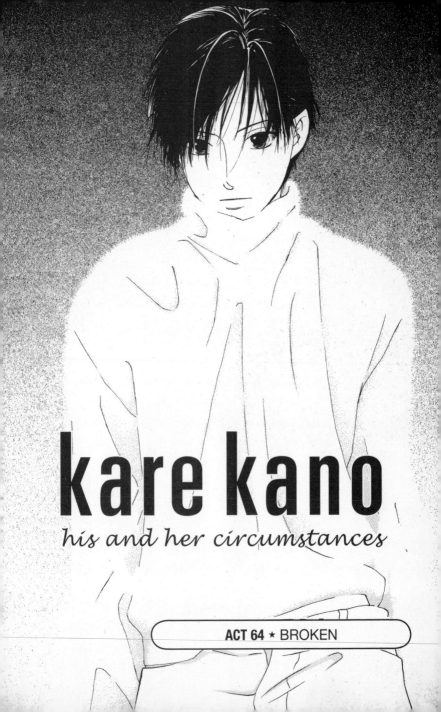

kare kano

his and her circumstances

ACT 64 ★ BROKEN

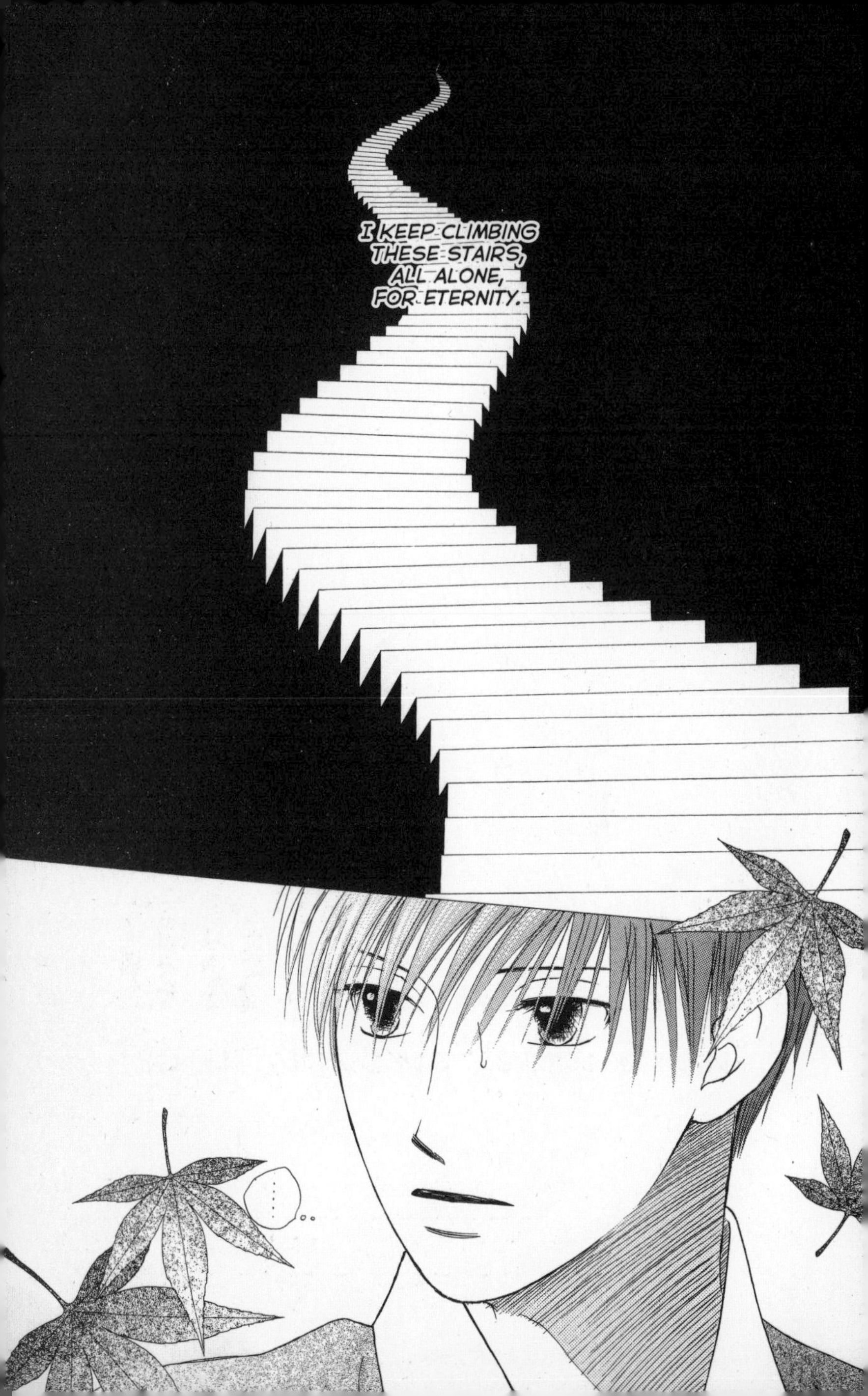
I KEEP CLIMBING THESE STAIRS, ALL ALONE, FOR ETERNITY.
......

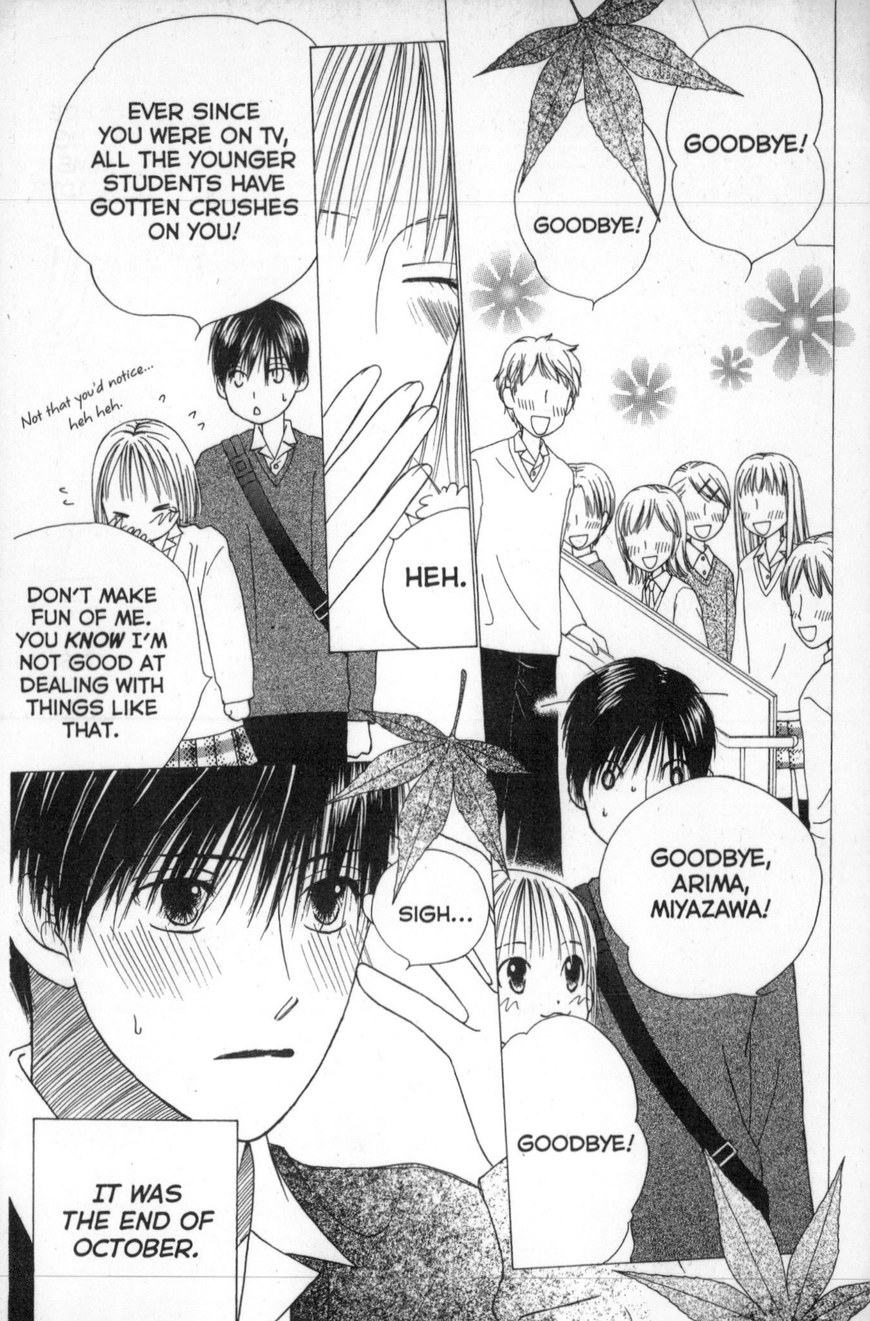
GOODBYE!
GOODBYE!
HEH.
EVER SINCE YOU WERE ON TV, ALL THE YOUNGER STUDENTS HAVE GOTTEN CRUSHES ON YOU!
Not that you'd notice... heh heh.
DON'T MAKE FUN OF ME. YOU *KNOW* I'M NOT GOOD AT DEALING WITH THINGS LIKE THAT.
GOODBYE, ARIMA, MIYAZAWA!
GOODBYE!
SIGH...
IT WAS THE END OF OCTOBER.

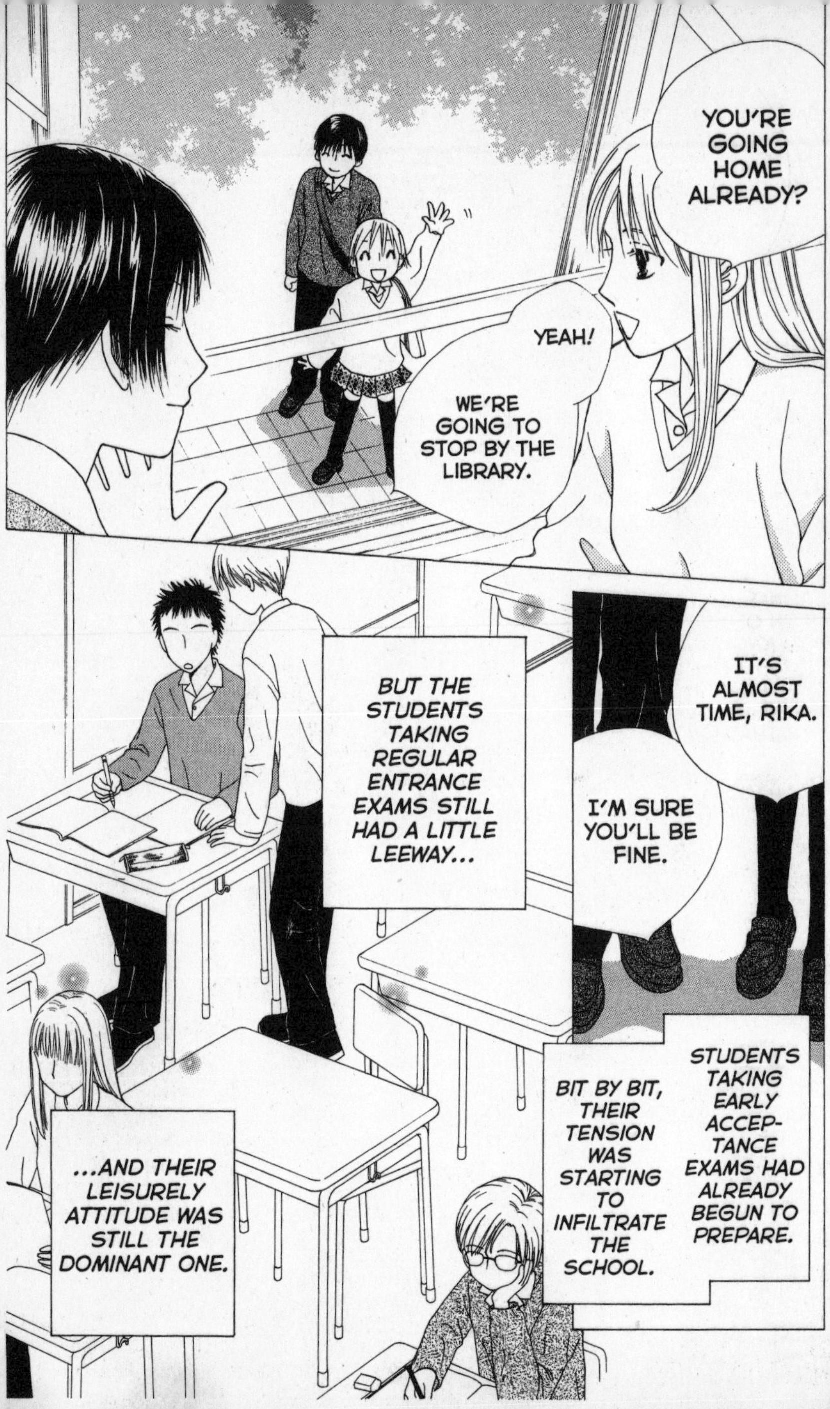
YOU'RE GOING HOME ALREADY?
YEAH!
WE'RE GOING TO STOP BY THE LIBRARY.
IT'S ALMOST TIME, RIKA.
I'M SURE YOU'LL BE FINE.
STUDENTS TAKING EARLY ACCEPTANCE EXAMS HAD ALREADY BEGUN TO PREPARE.
BIT BY BIT, THEIR TENSION WAS STARTING TO INFILTRATE THE SCHOOL.
BUT THE STUDENTS TAKING REGULAR ENTRANCE EXAMS STILL HAD A LITTLE LEEWAY...
...AND THEIR LEISURELY ATTITUDE WAS STILL THE DOMINANT ONE.

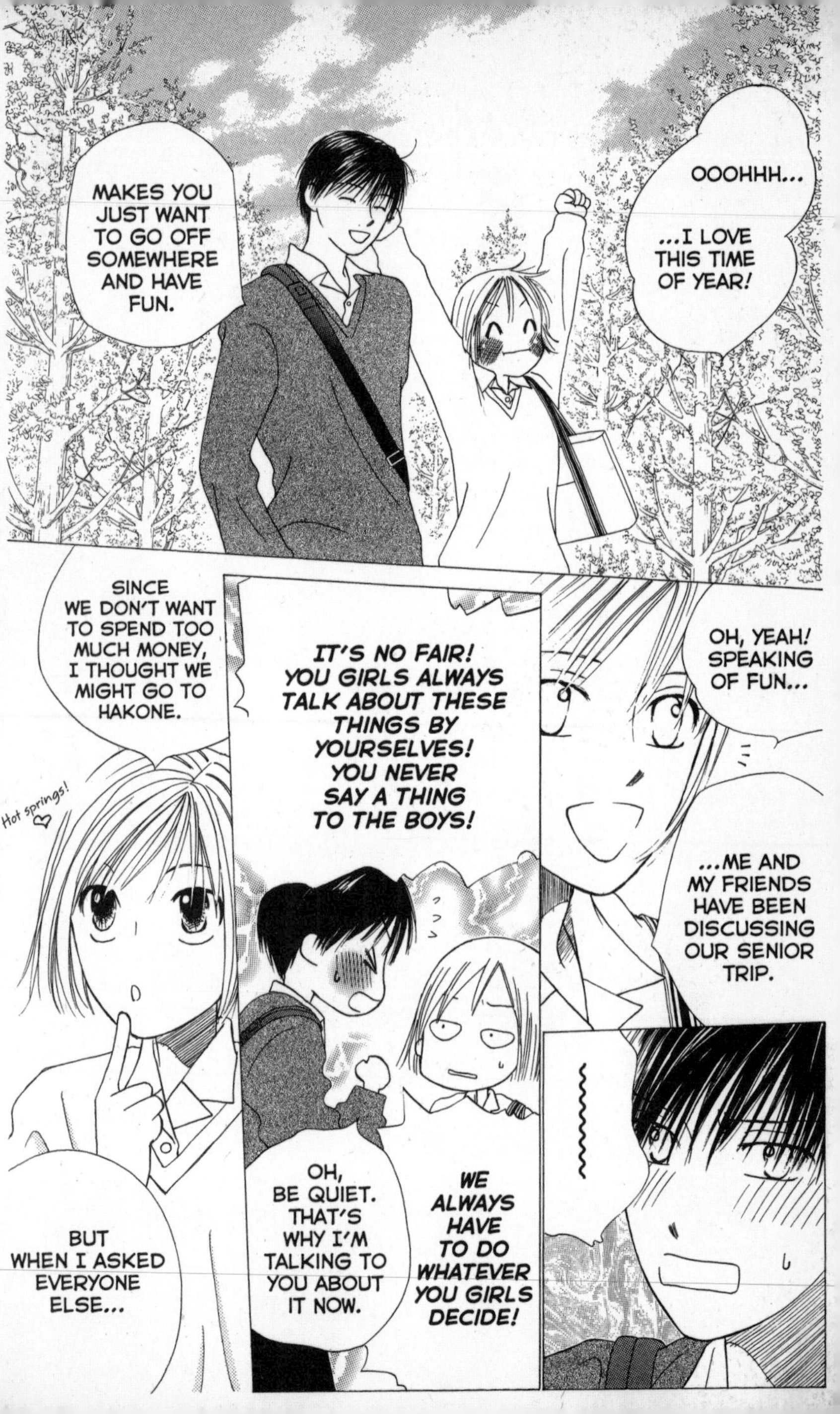
OOOHHH...
...I LOVE THIS TIME OF YEAR!
MAKES YOU JUST WANT TO GO OFF SOMEWHERE AND HAVE FUN.
OH, YEAH! SPEAKING OF FUN...
...ME AND MY FRIENDS HAVE BEEN DISCUSSING OUR SENIOR TRIP.
SINCE WE DON'T WANT TO SPEND TOO MUCH MONEY, I THOUGHT WE MIGHT GO TO HAKONE.
Hot springs!
BUT WHEN I ASKED EVERYONE ELSE...
...
IT'S NO FAIR! YOU GIRLS ALWAYS TALK ABOUT THESE THINGS BY YOURSELVES! YOU NEVER SAY A THING TO THE BOYS!
WE ALWAYS HAVE TO DO WHATEVER YOU GIRLS DECIDE!
OH, BE QUIET. THAT'S WHY I'M TALKING TO YOU ABOUT IT NOW.

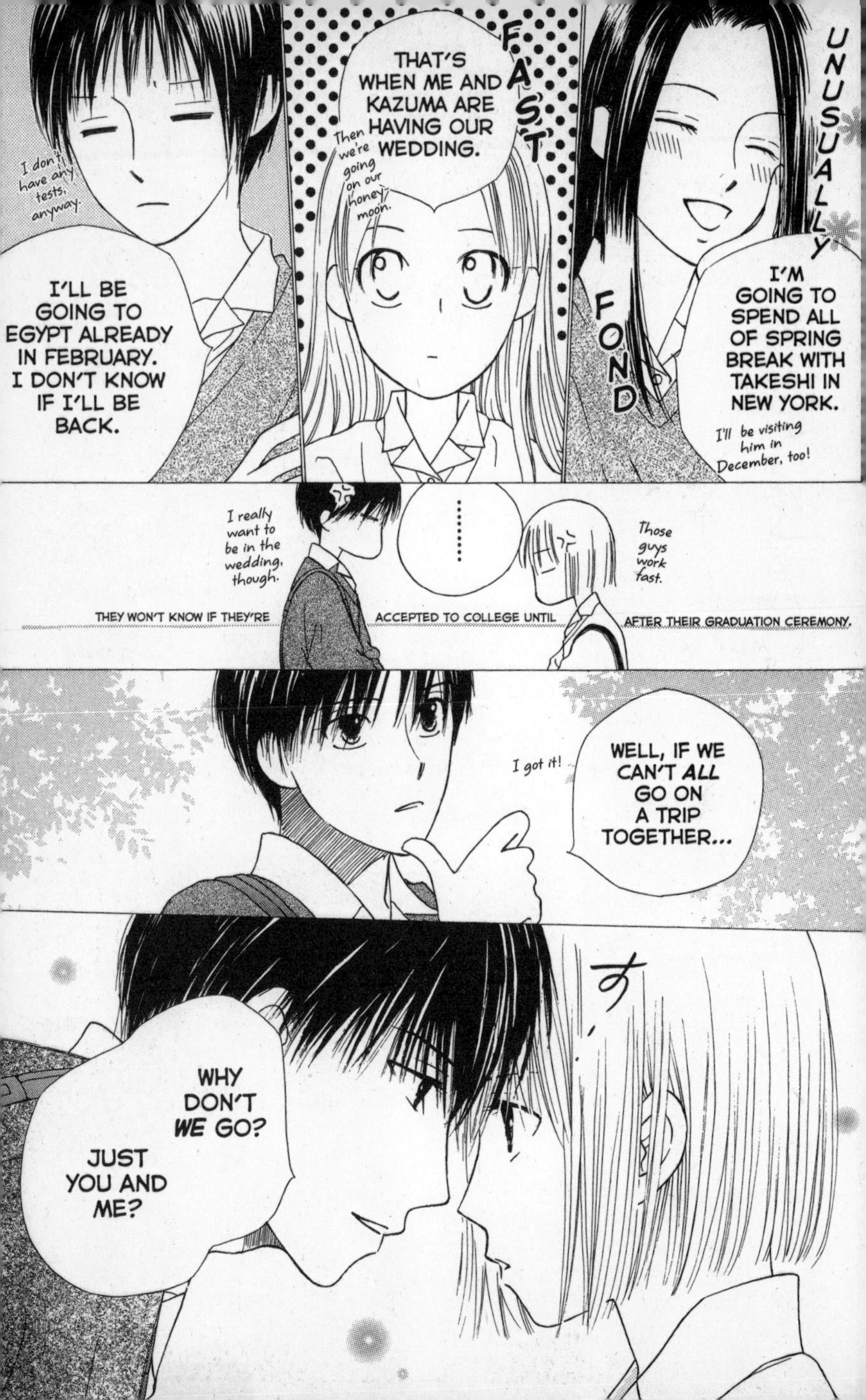
UNUSUALLY
FOND
I'M GOING TO SPEND ALL OF SPRING BREAK WITH TAKESHI IN NEW YORK.
I'll be visiting him in December, too!
FAST
THAT'S WHEN ME AND KAZUMA ARE HAVING OUR WEDDING.
Then we're going on our honey-moon.
I'LL BE GOING TO EGYPT ALREADY IN FEBRUARY. I DON'T KNOW IF I'LL BE BACK.
I don't have any tests, anyway.
Those guys work fast.
......
I really want to be in the wedding, though.
THEY WON'T KNOW IF THEY'RE ACCEPTED TO COLLEGE UNTIL AFTER THEIR GRADUATION CEREMONY.
I got it!
WELL, IF WE CAN'T ALL GO ON A TRIP TOGETHER...
す
WHY DON'T WE GO?
JUST YOU AND ME?

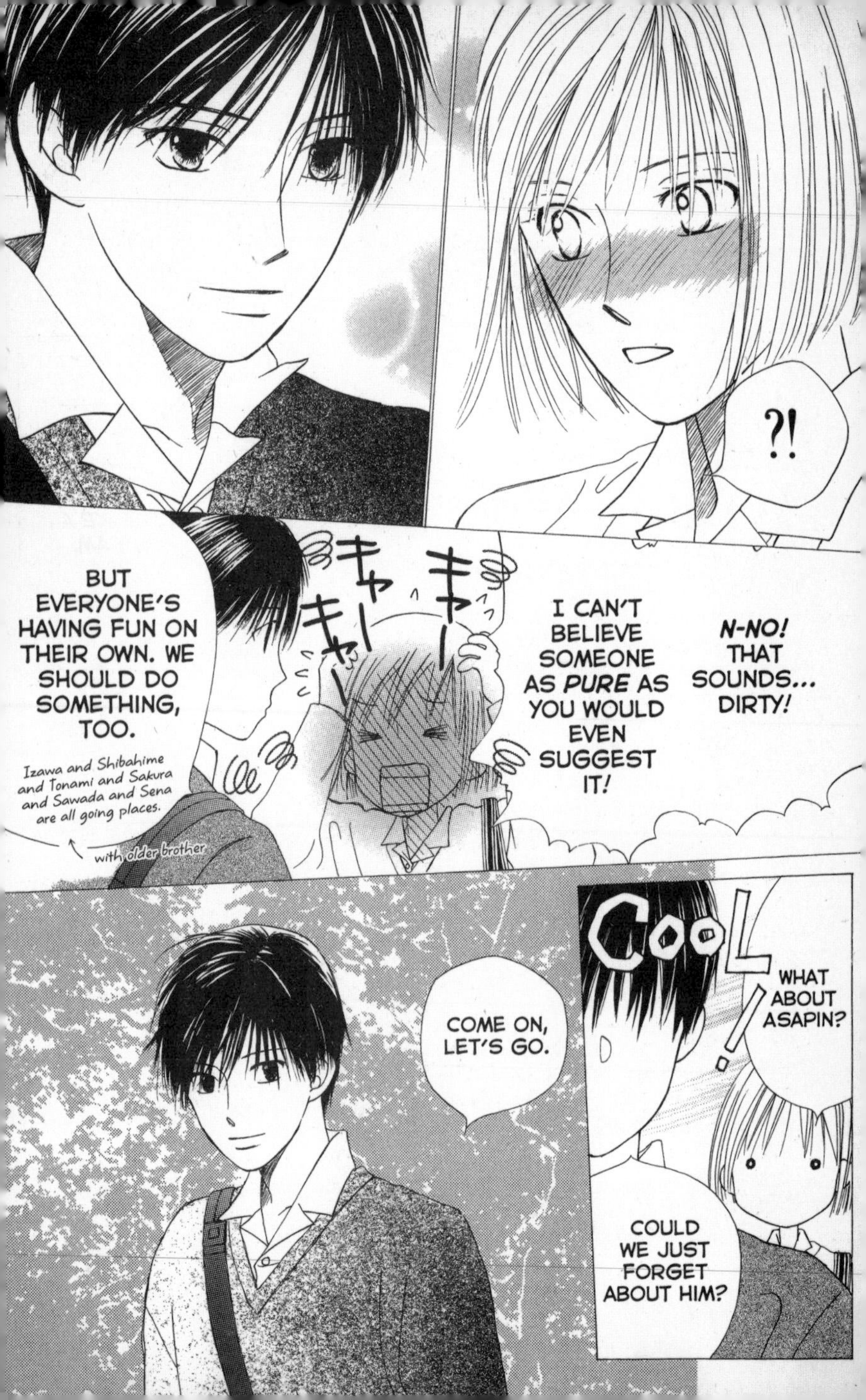

?!
N-NO! THAT SOUNDS... DIRTY!
I CAN'T BELIEVE SOMEONE AS PURE AS YOU WOULD EVEN SUGGEST IT!
キャー
キャーキャー
BUT EVERYONE'S HAVING FUN ON THEIR OWN. WE SHOULD DO SOMETHING, TOO.
Izawa and Shibahime and Tonami and Sakura and Sawada and Sena are all going places.
with older brother
COOL
WHAT ABOUT ASAPIN?
!
COULD WE JUST FORGET ABOUT HIM?
COME ON, LET'S GO.

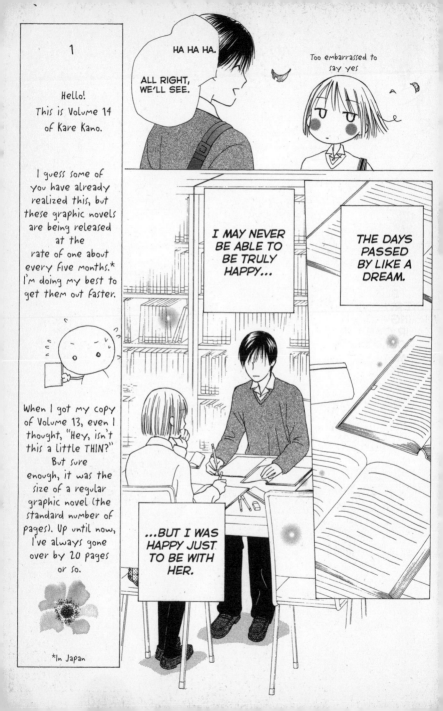

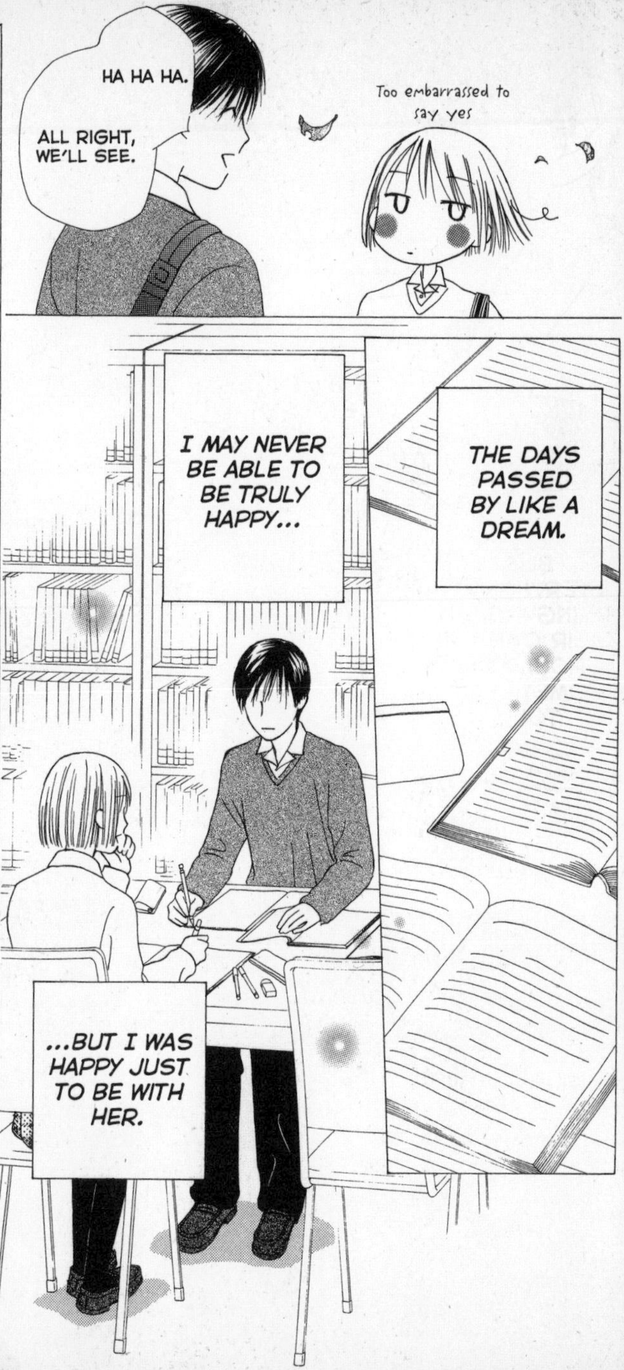
Too embarrassed to say yes
HA HA HA.
ALL RIGHT, WE'LL SEE.
THE DAYS PASSED BY LIKE A DREAM.
I MAY NEVER BE ABLE TO BE TRULY HAPPY...
...BUT I WAS HAPPY JUST TO BE WITH HER.

1

Hello! This is Volume 14 of Kare Kano.

I guess some of you have already realized this, but these graphic novels are being released at the rate of one about every five months.* I'm doing my best to get them out faster.

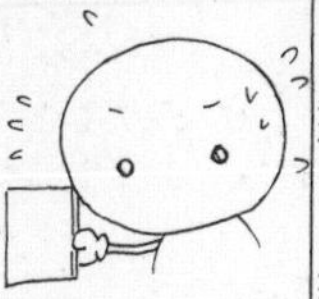

When I got my copy of Volume 13, even I thought, "Hey, isn't this a little THIN?" But sure enough, it was the size of a regular graphic novel (the standard number of pages). Up until now, I've always gone over by 20 pages or so.

*In Japan

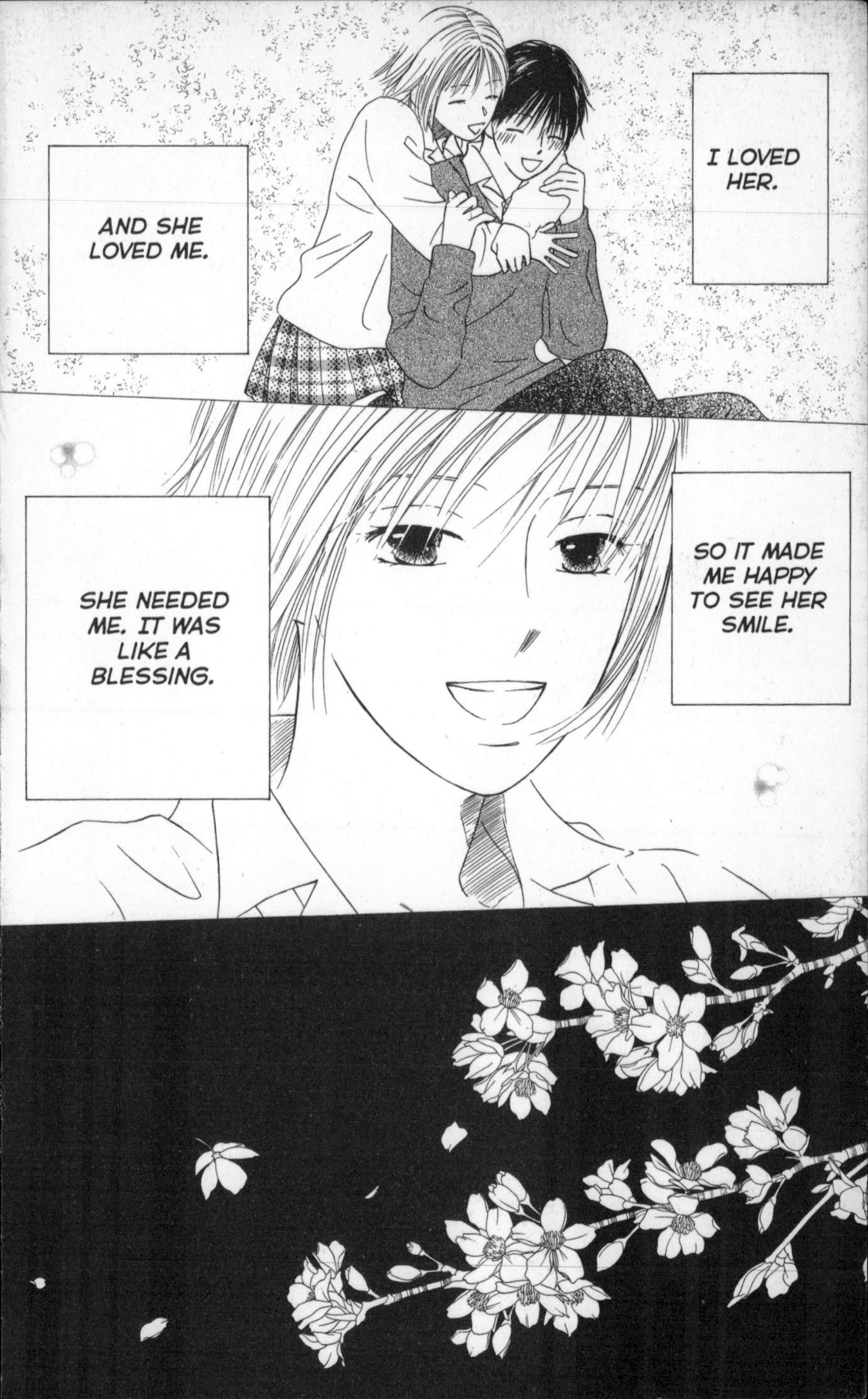
I LOVED HER.
AND SHE LOVED ME.
SO IT MADE ME HAPPY TO SEE HER SMILE.
SHE NEEDED ME. IT WAS LIKE A BLESSING.

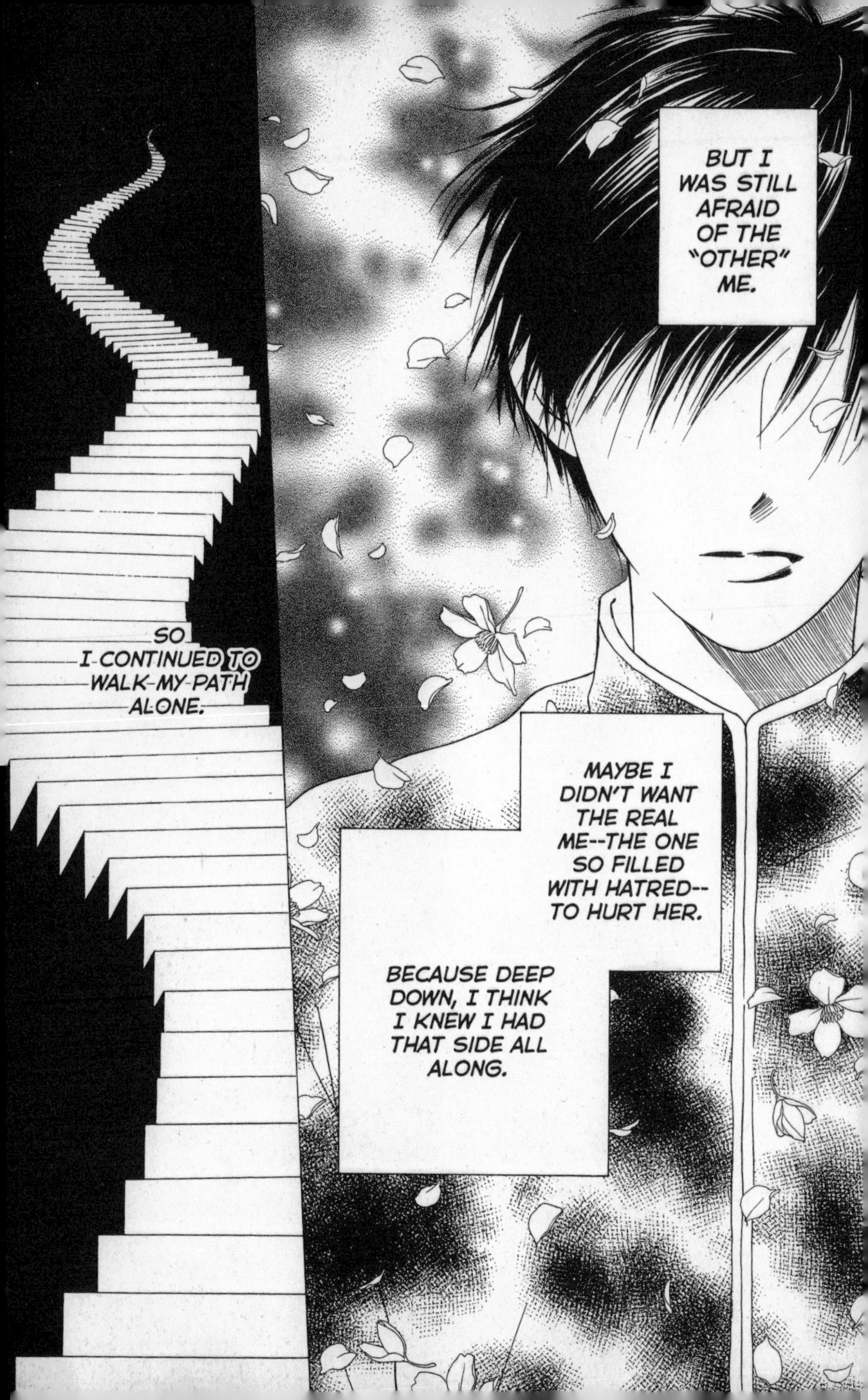
BUT I WAS STILL AFRAID OF THE "OTHER" ME.
MAYBE I DIDN'T WANT THE REAL ME--THE ONE SO FILLED WITH HATRED--TO HURT HER.
BECAUSE DEEP DOWN, I THINK I KNEW I HAD THAT SIDE ALL ALONG.
SO I CONTINUED TO WALK MY PATH ALONE.

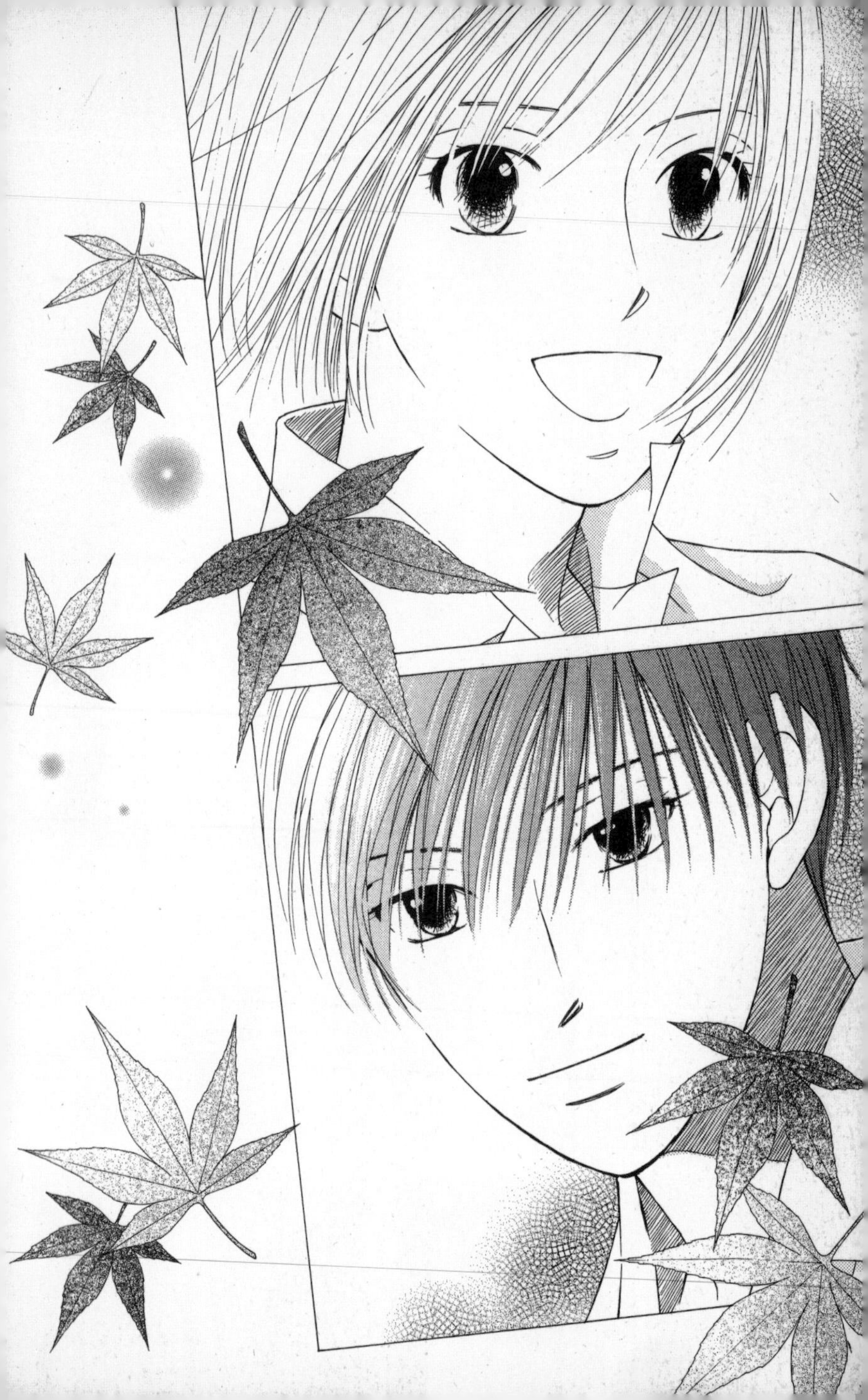

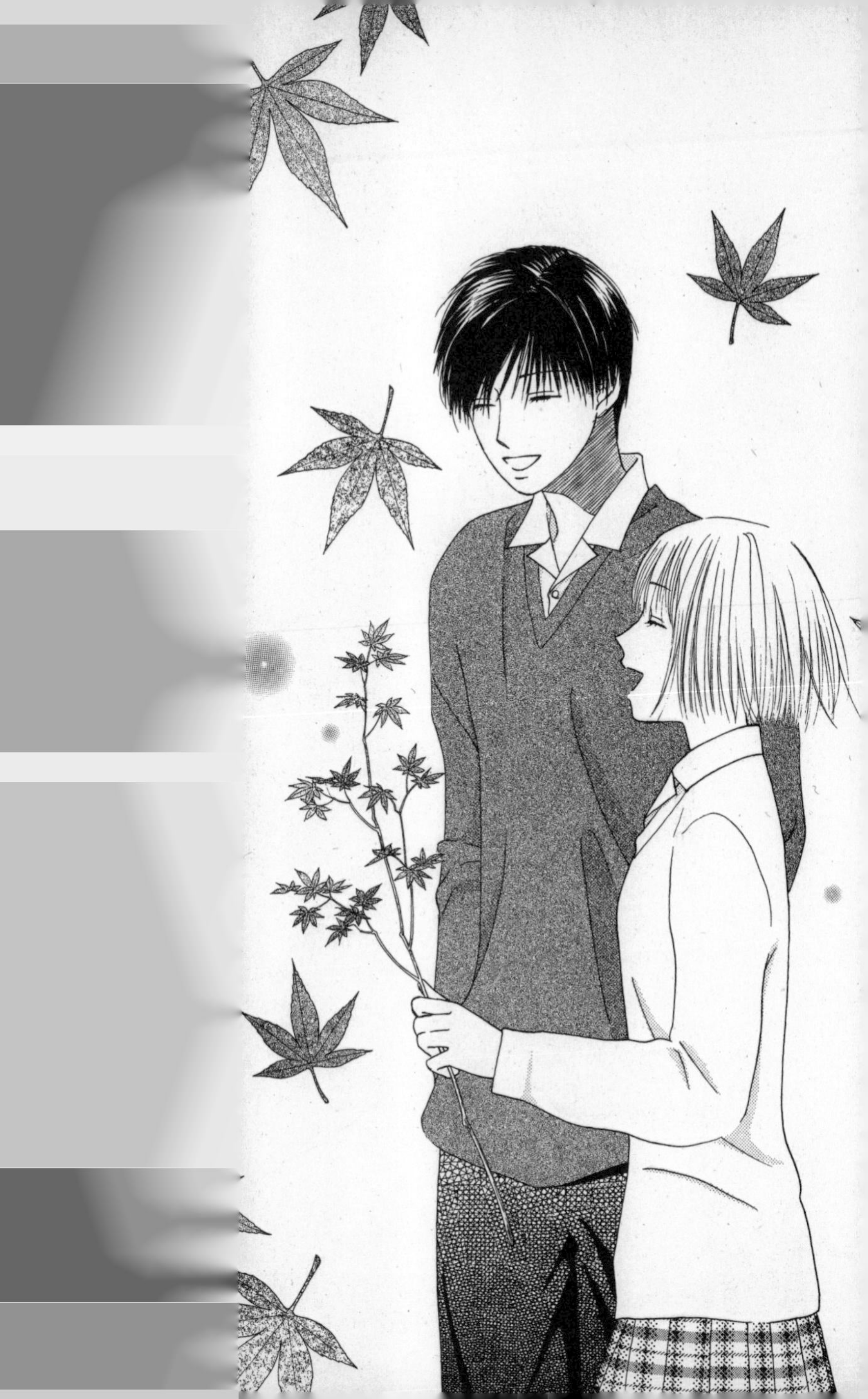

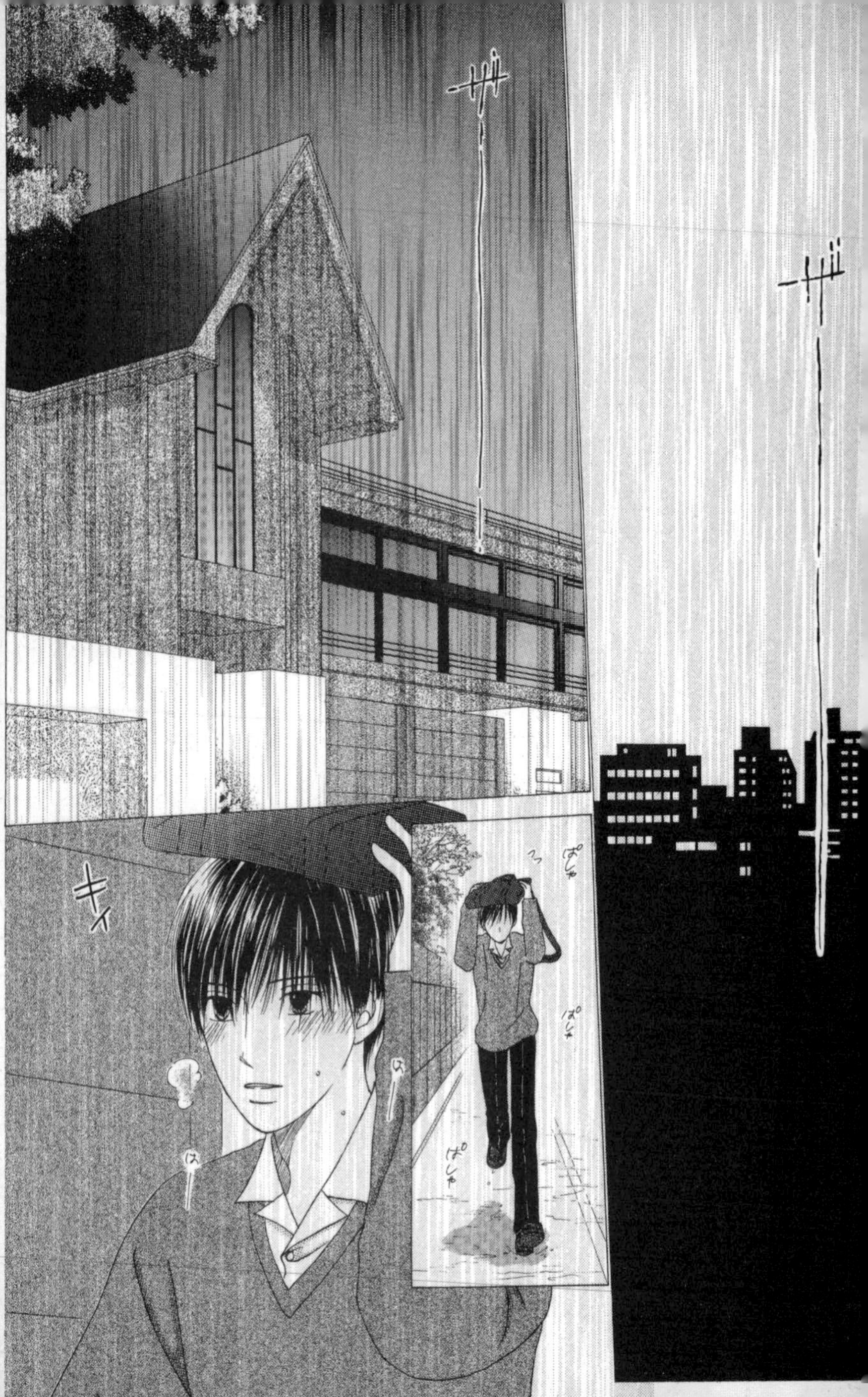
ぱしゃ
ぱしゃ
ぱしゃ
キイ
はー
は

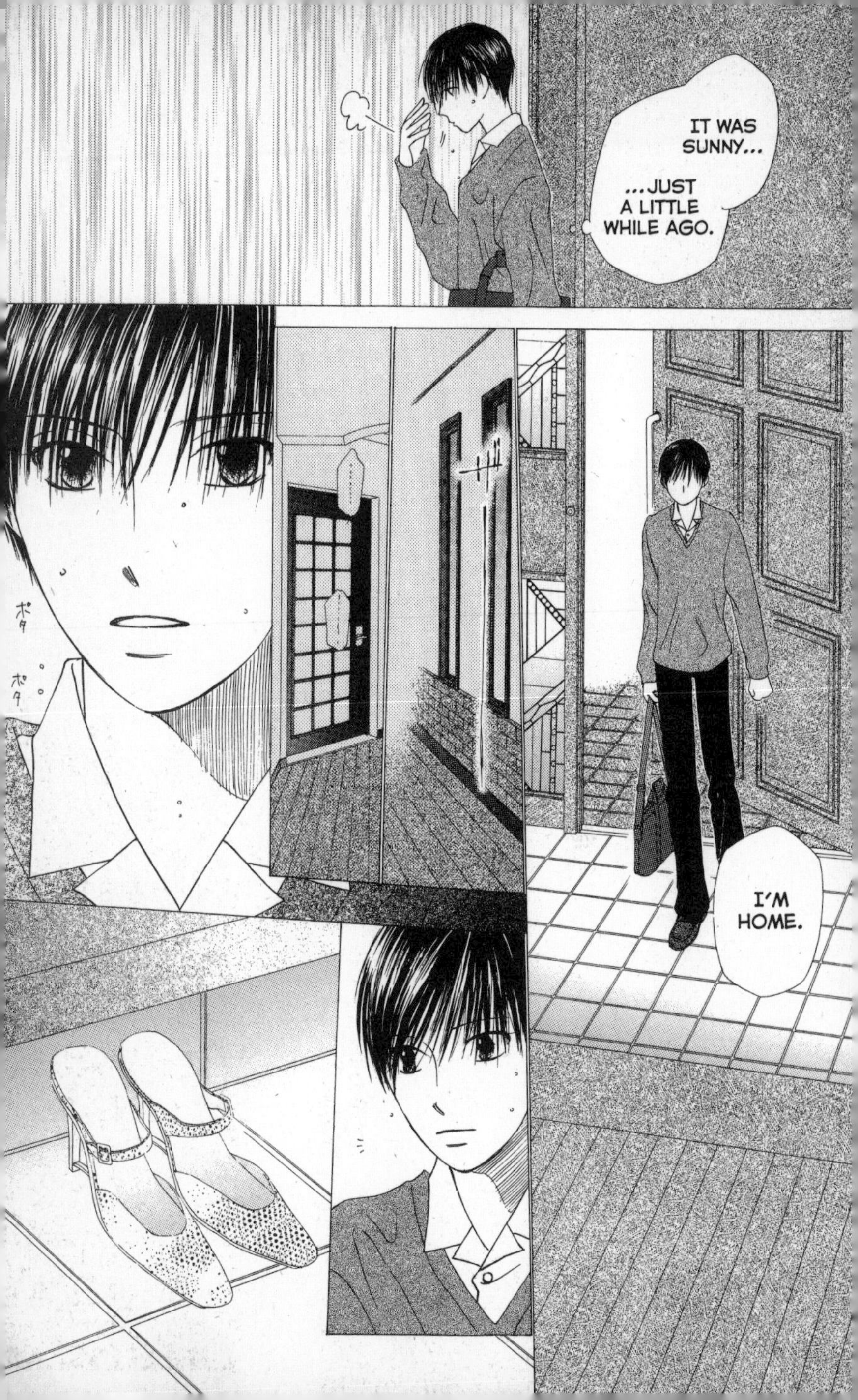
IT WAS SUNNY...
...JUST A LITTLE WHILE AGO.
I'M HOME.
ポタ
ポタ

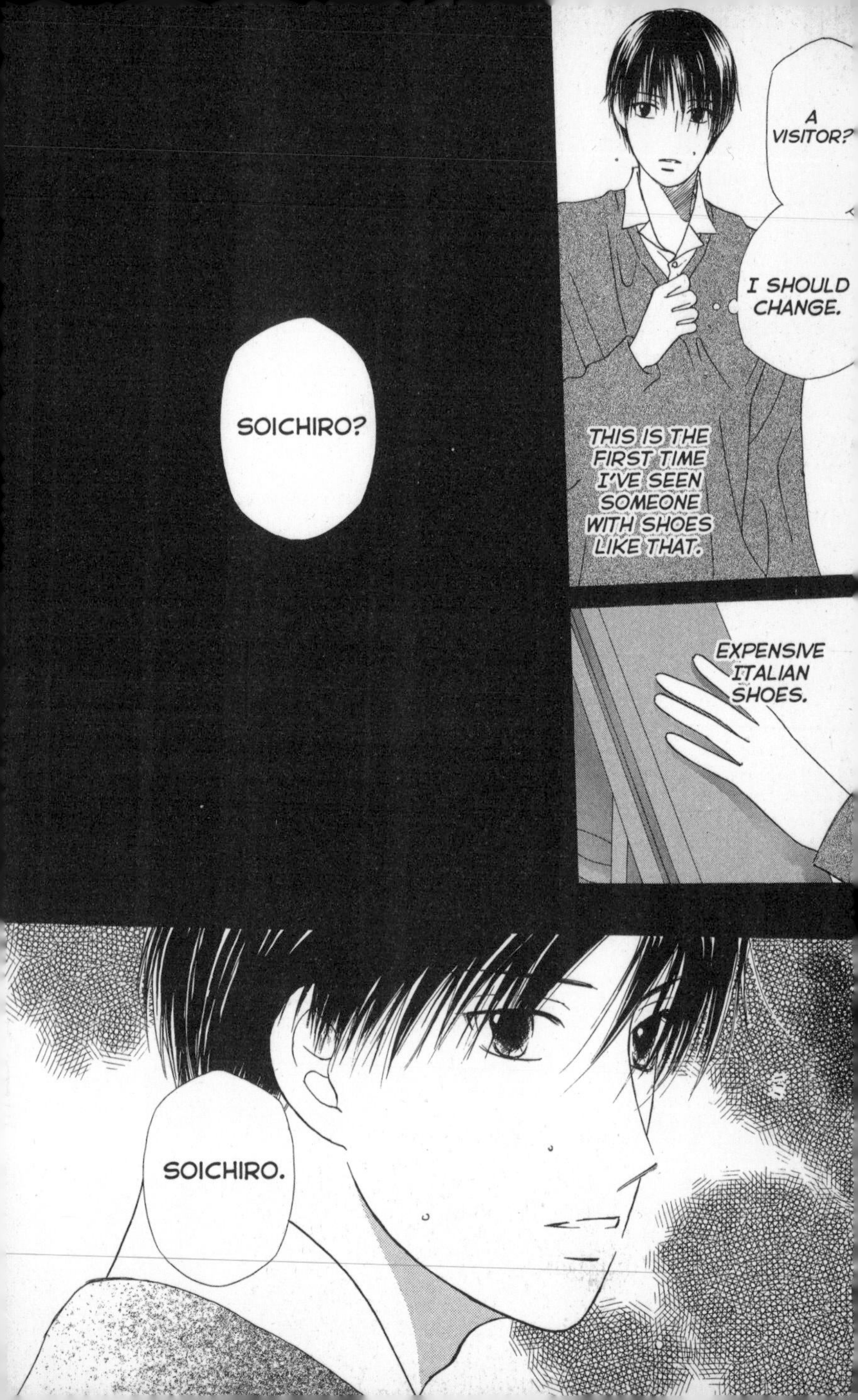
A VISITOR?
I SHOULD CHANGE.
THIS IS THE FIRST TIME I'VE SEEN SOMEONE WITH SHOES LIKE THAT.
EXPENSIVE ITALIAN SHOES.
SOICHIRO?
SOICHIRO.

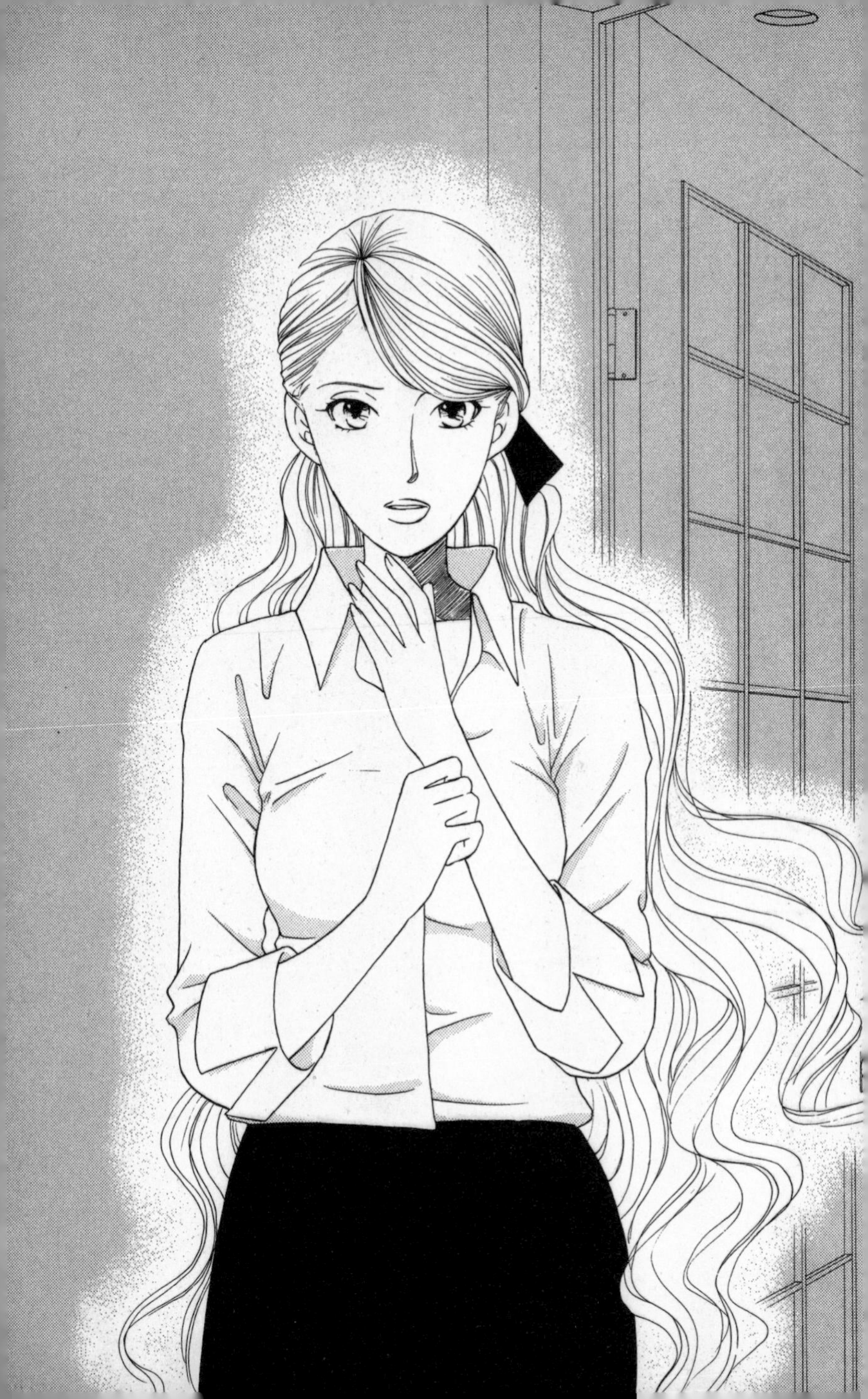

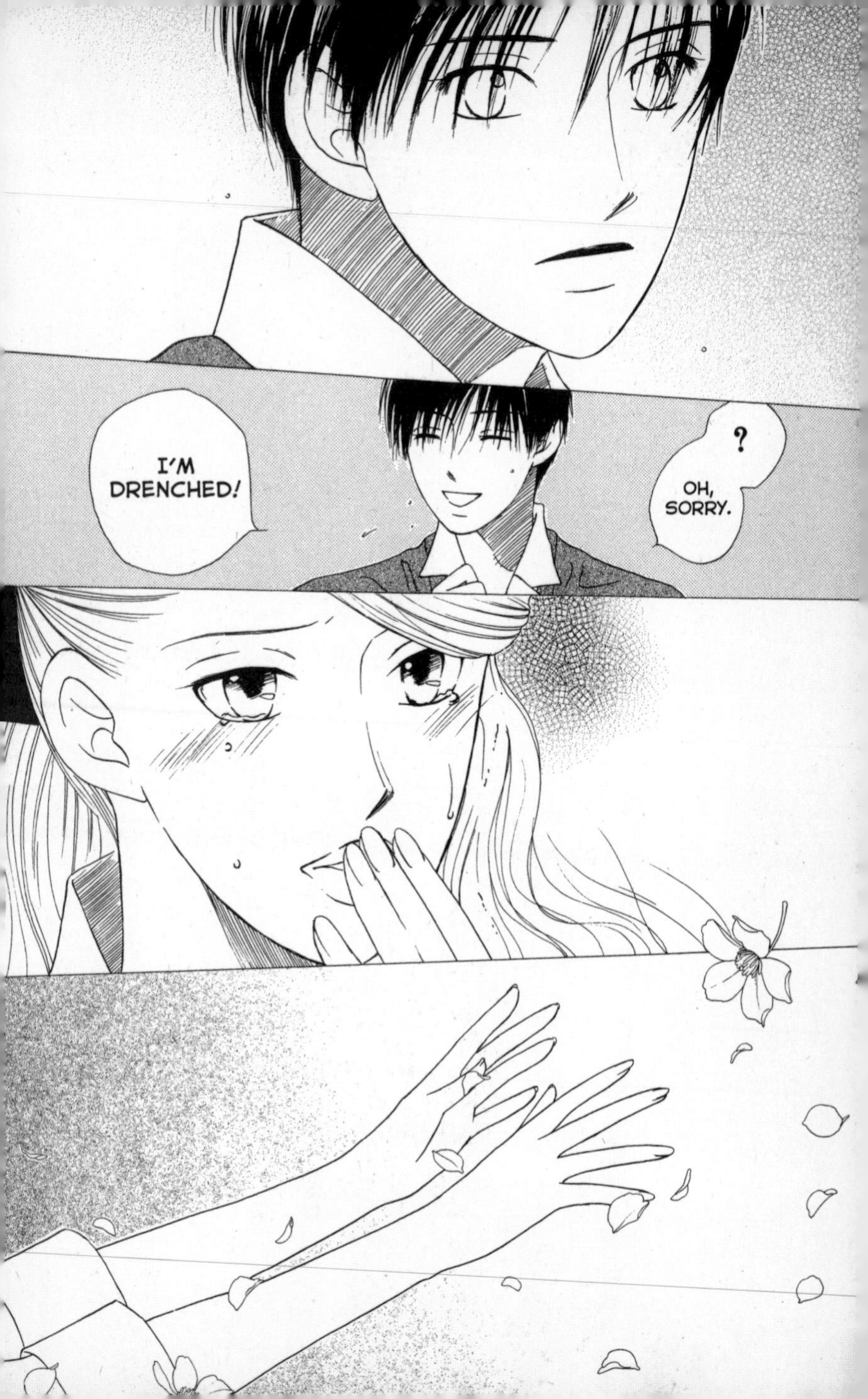
?
OH, SORRY.
I'M DRENCHED!

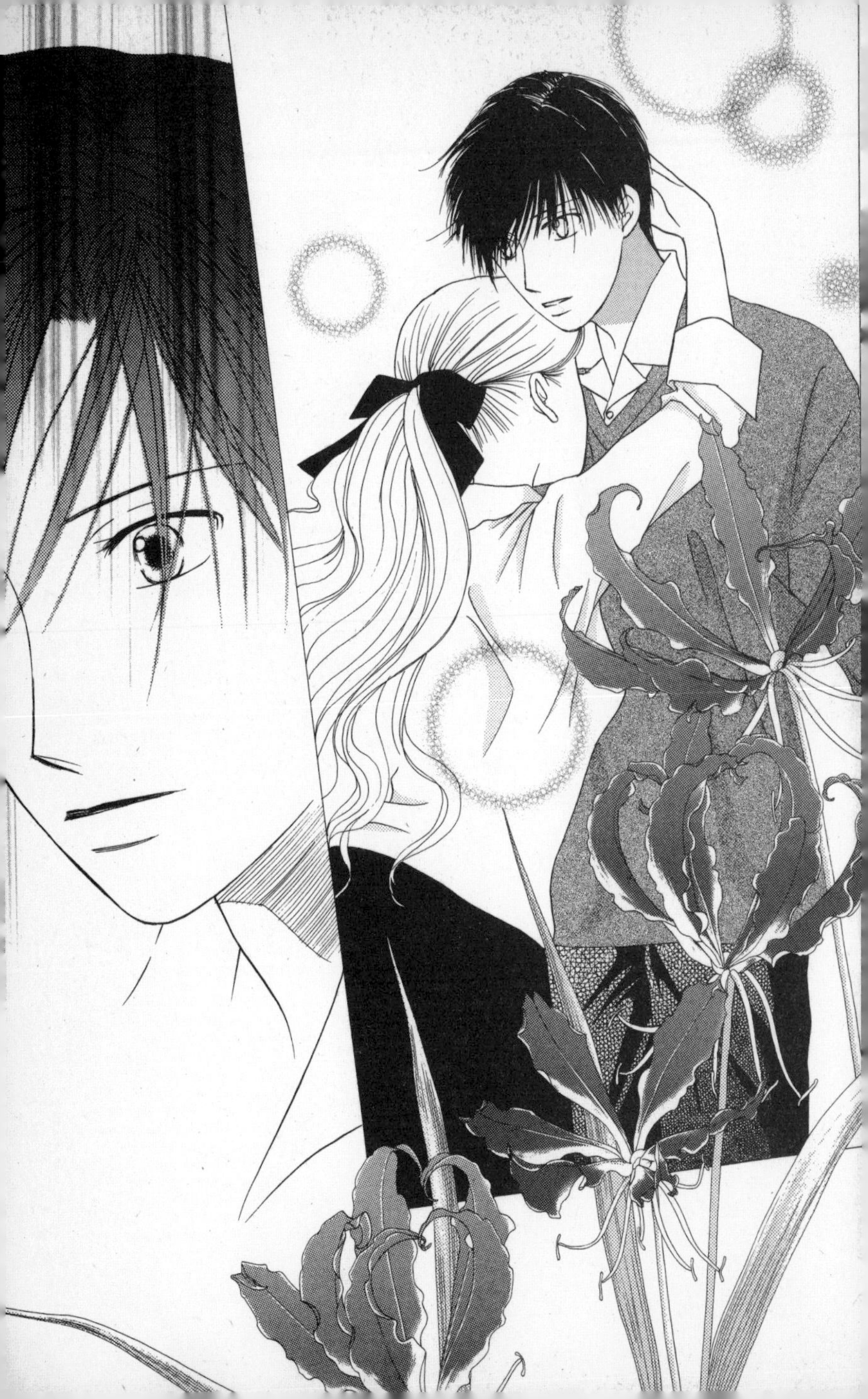

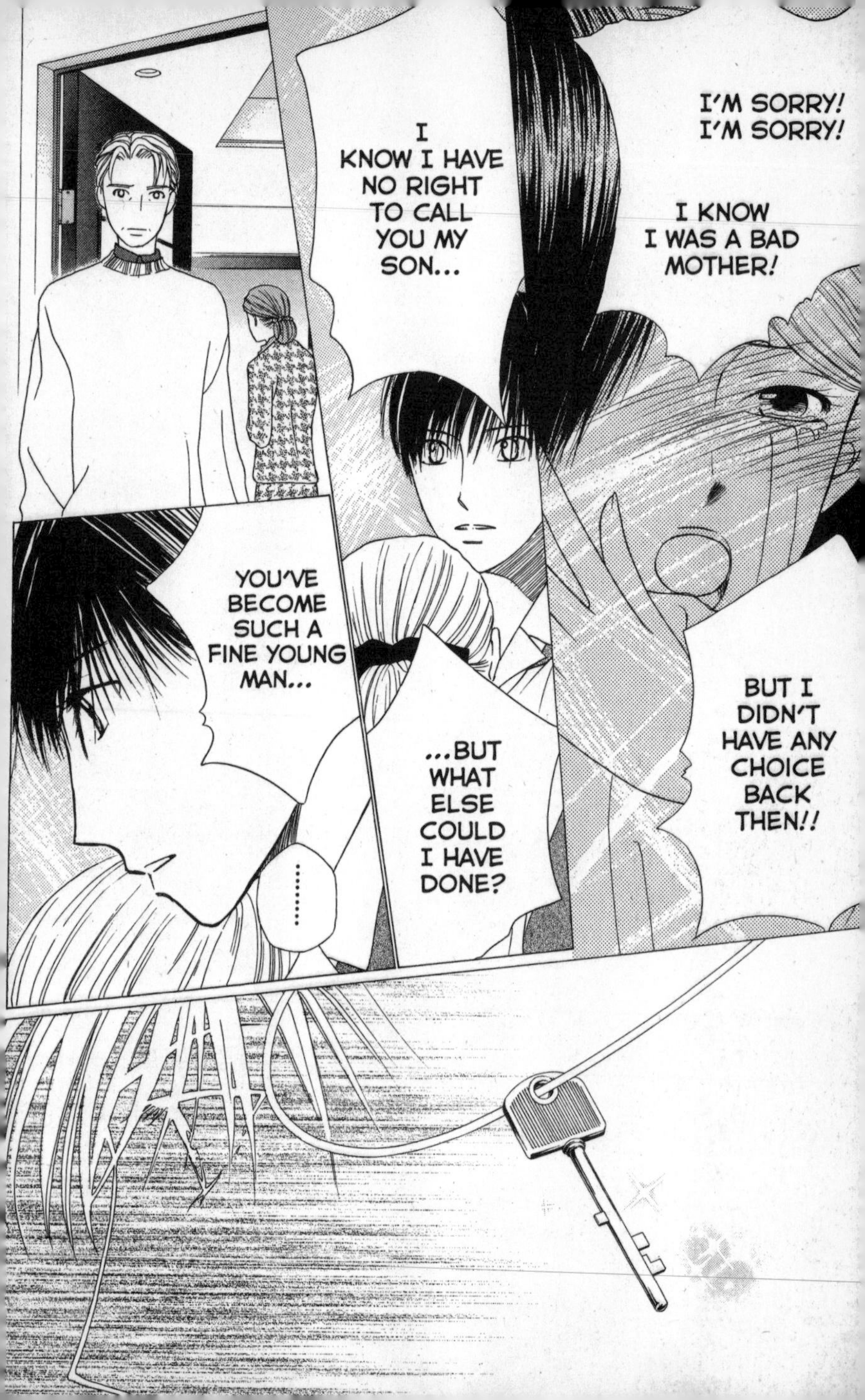
I'M SORRY! I'M SORRY!
I KNOW I WAS A BAD MOTHER!
BUT I DIDN'T HAVE ANY CHOICE BACK THEN!!
I KNOW I HAVE NO RIGHT TO CALL YOU MY SON...
...BUT WHAT ELSE COULD I HAVE DONE?
YOU'VE BECOME SUCH A FINE YOUNG MAN...
......

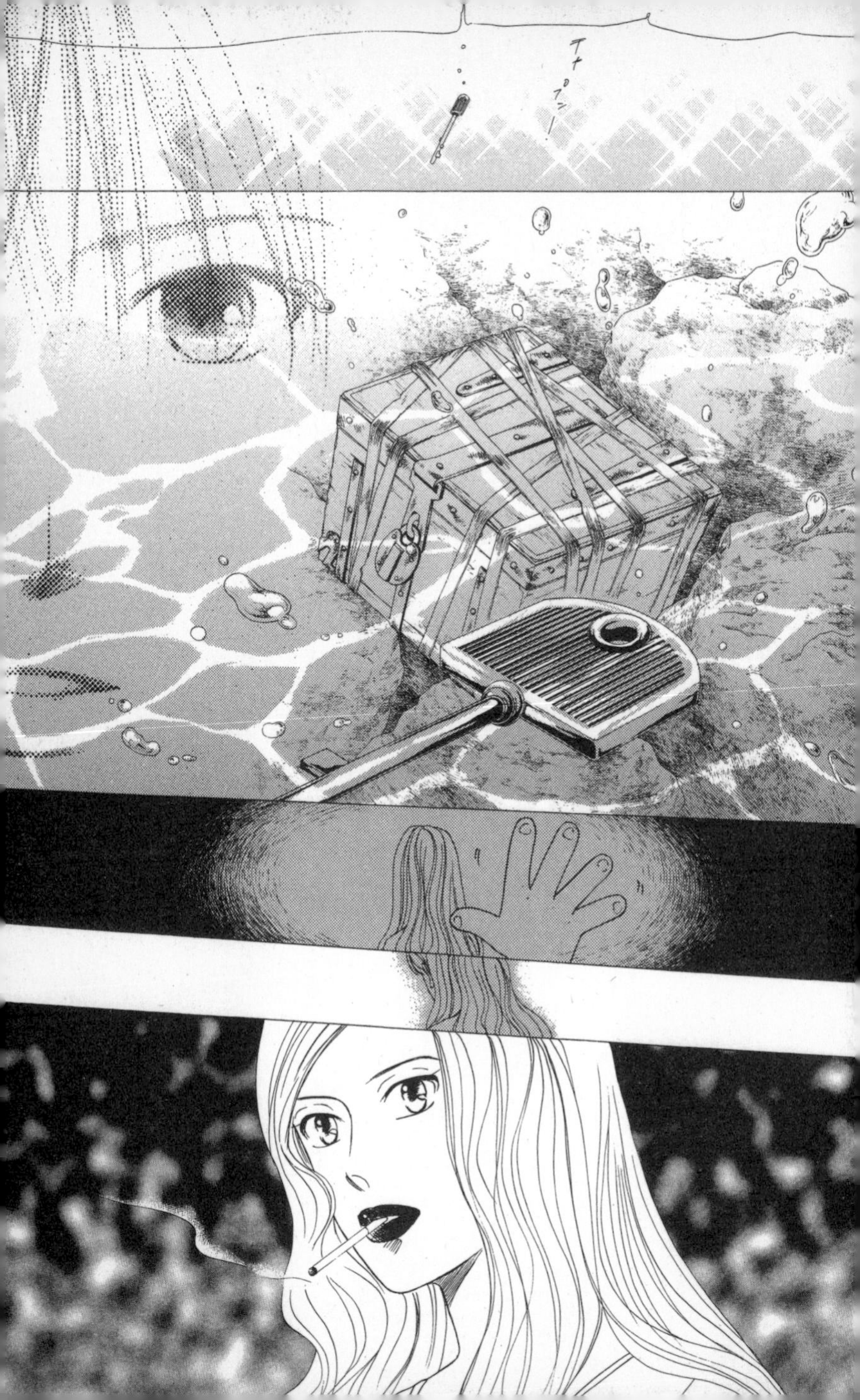
チャプンー

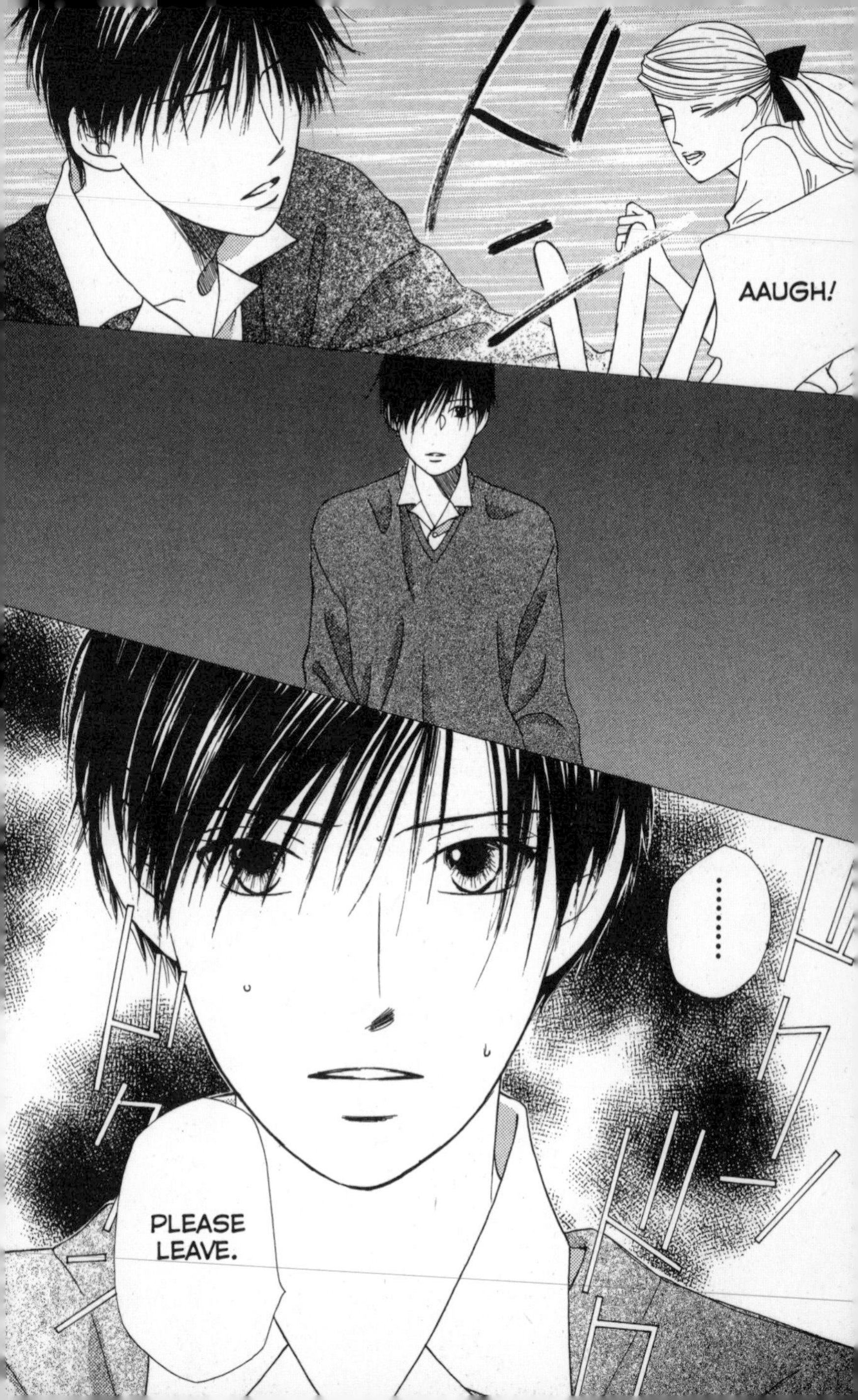
AAUGH!
....
PLEASE LEAVE.

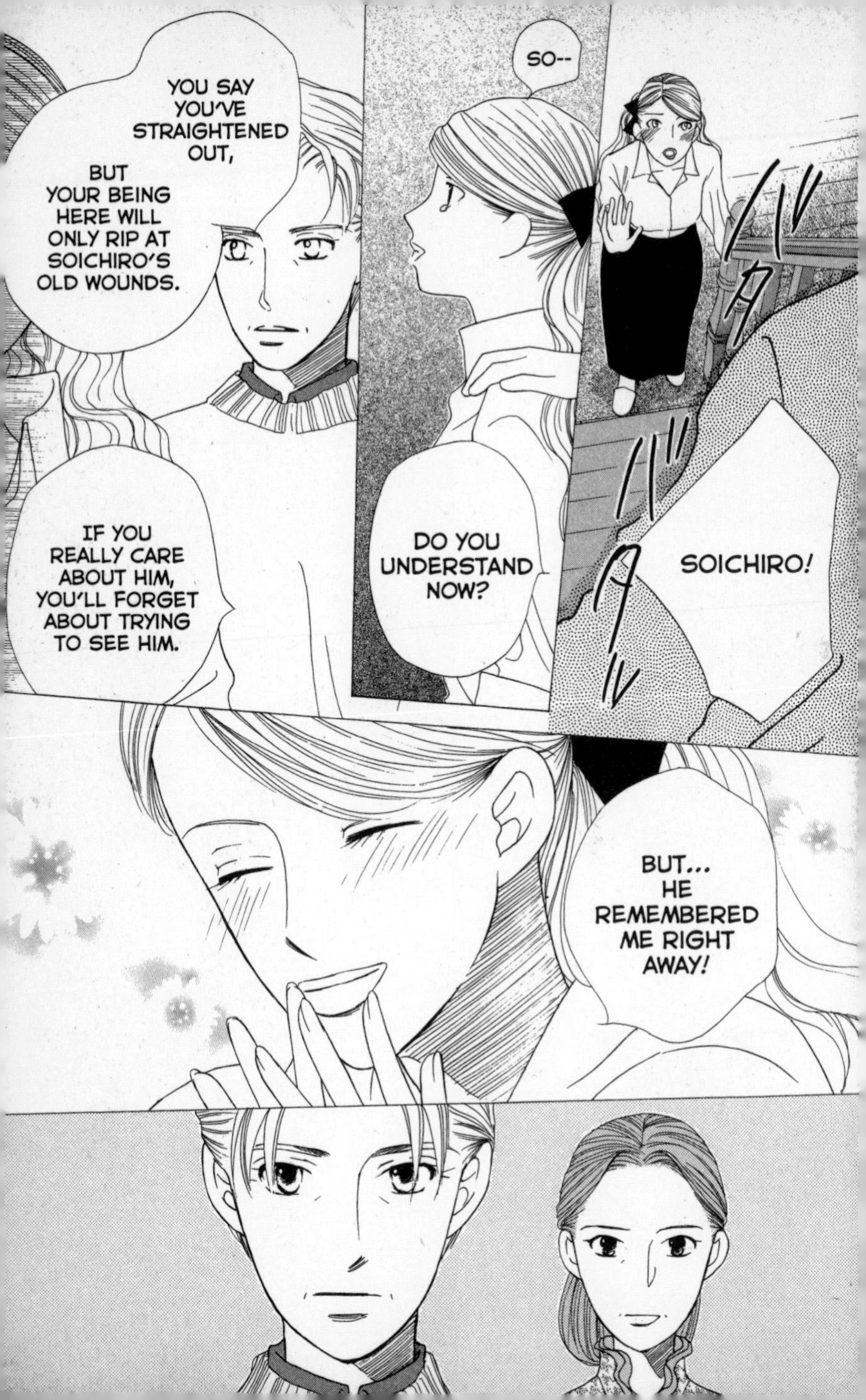
YOU SAY YOU'VE STRAIGHTENED OUT,
BUT YOUR BEING HERE WILL ONLY RIP AT SOICHIRO'S OLD WOUNDS.
IF YOU REALLY CARE ABOUT HIM, YOU'LL FORGET ABOUT TRYING TO SEE HIM.
SO--
DO YOU UNDERSTAND NOW?
SOICHIRO!
BUT... HE REMEMBERED ME RIGHT AWAY!

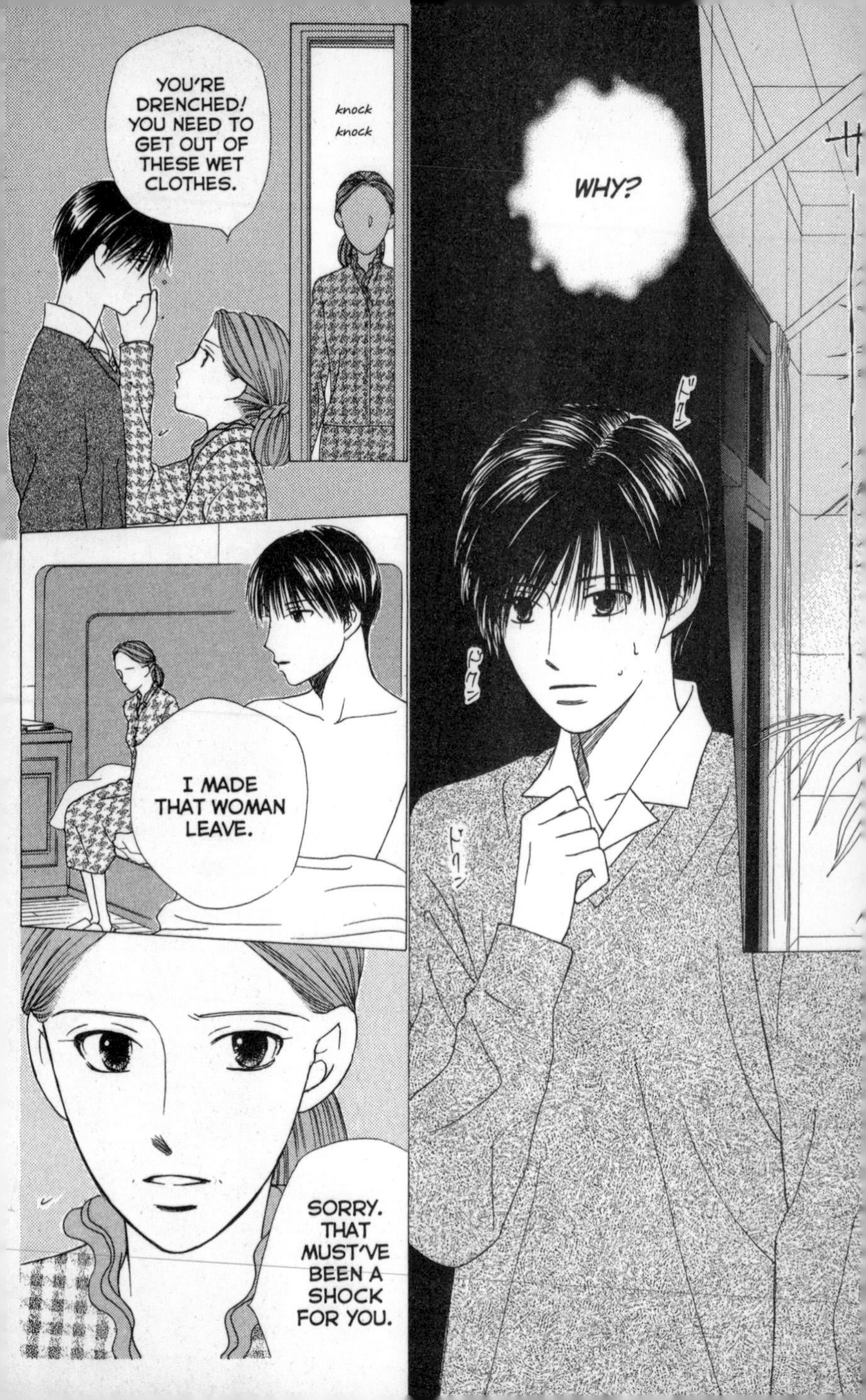
WHY?
knock
knock
YOU'RE DRENCHED! YOU NEED TO GET OUT OF THESE WET CLOTHES.
I MADE THAT WOMAN LEAVE.
SORRY. THAT MUST'VE BEEN A SHOCK FOR YOU.

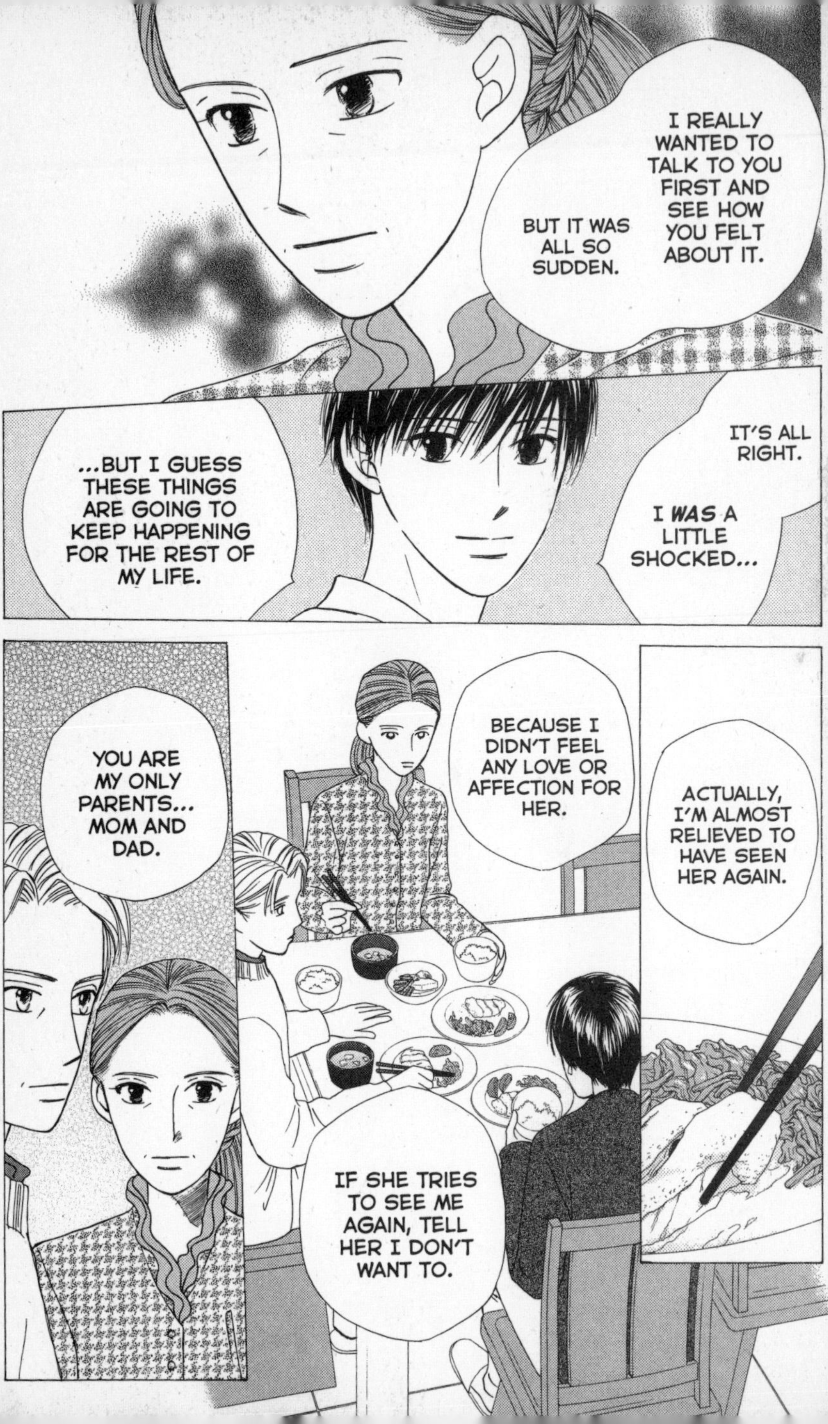
I REALLY WANTED TO TALK TO YOU FIRST AND SEE HOW YOU FELT ABOUT IT.
BUT IT WAS ALL SO SUDDEN.
IT'S ALL RIGHT.
I *WAS* A LITTLE SHOCKED...
...BUT I GUESS THESE THINGS ARE GOING TO KEEP HAPPENING FOR THE REST OF MY LIFE.
ACTUALLY, I'M ALMOST RELIEVED TO HAVE SEEN HER AGAIN.
BECAUSE I DIDN'T FEEL ANY LOVE OR AFFECTION FOR HER.
IF SHE TRIES TO SEE ME AGAIN, TELL HER I DON'T WANT TO.
YOU ARE MY ONLY PARENTS... MOM AND DAD.

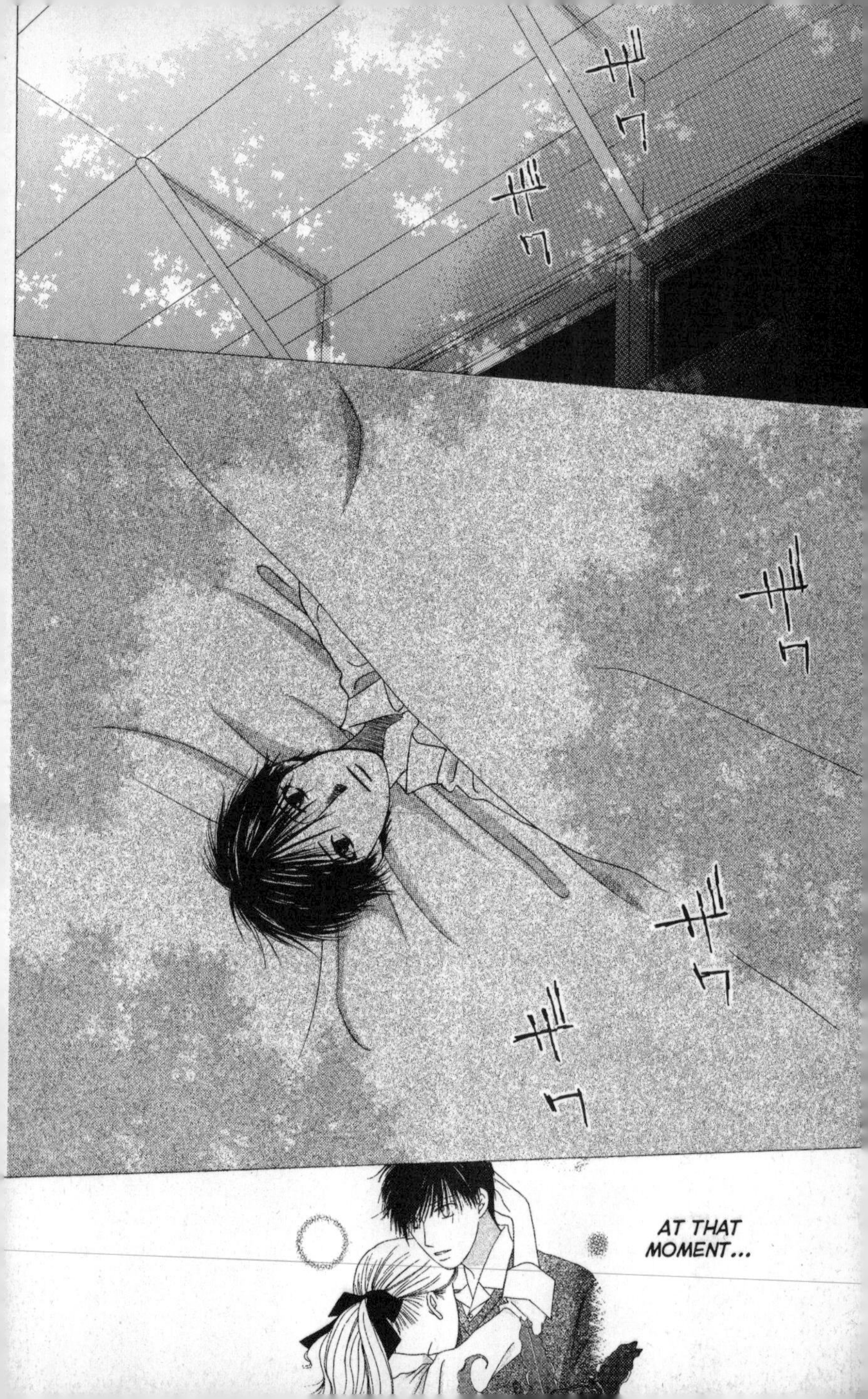
ザワ
ザワ
ザワ
ザワ
ザワ
AT THAT MOMENT...

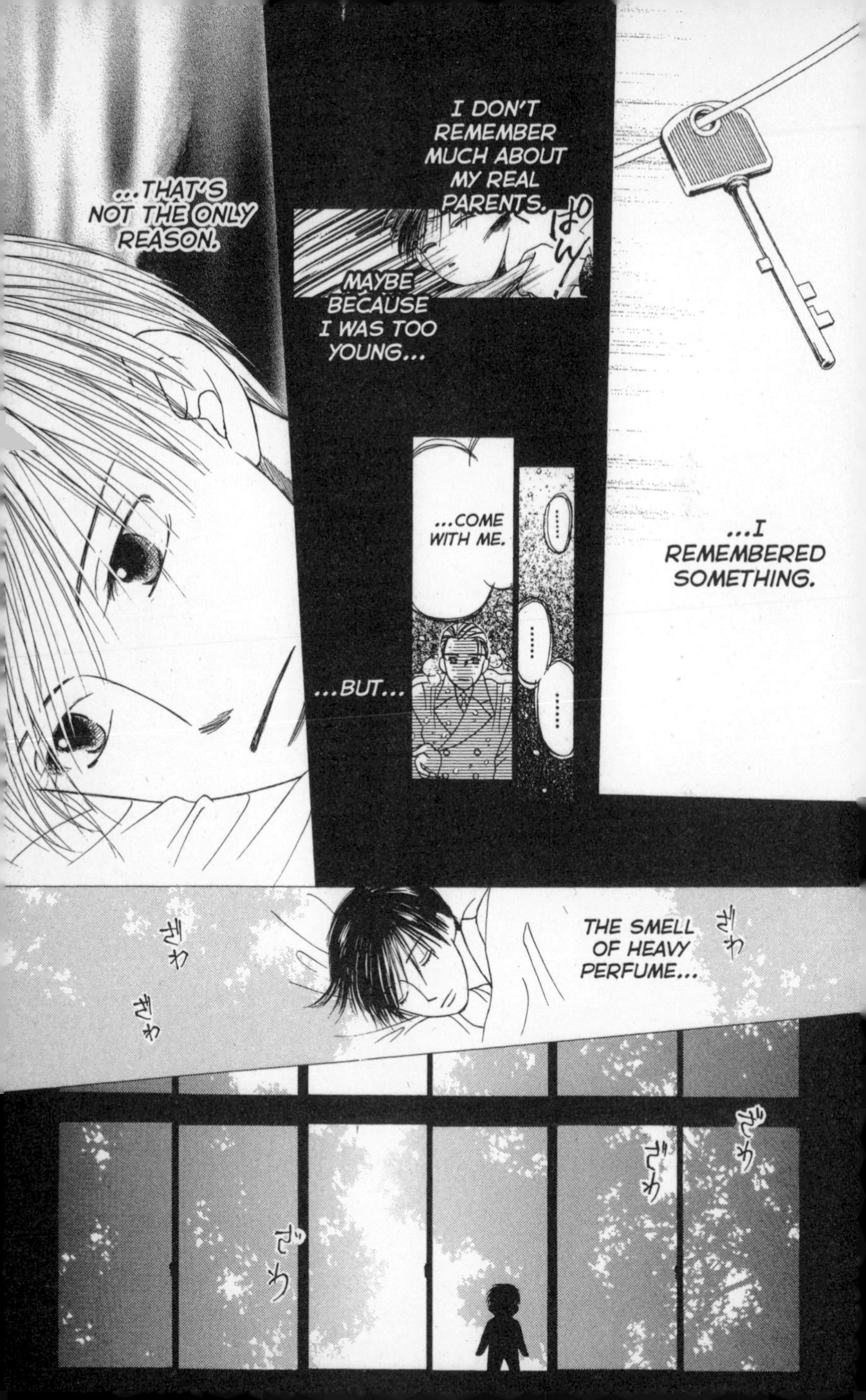
...I REMEMBERED SOMETHING.
I DON'T REMEMBER MUCH ABOUT MY REAL PARENTS.
ぱん!
MAYBE BECAUSE I WAS TOO YOUNG...
......
......
......
...COME WITH ME.
...BUT...
...THAT'S NOT THE ONLY REASON.
ざわ
THE SMELL OF HEAVY PERFUME...
ざわ
ざわ
ざわ
ざわ
ざわ

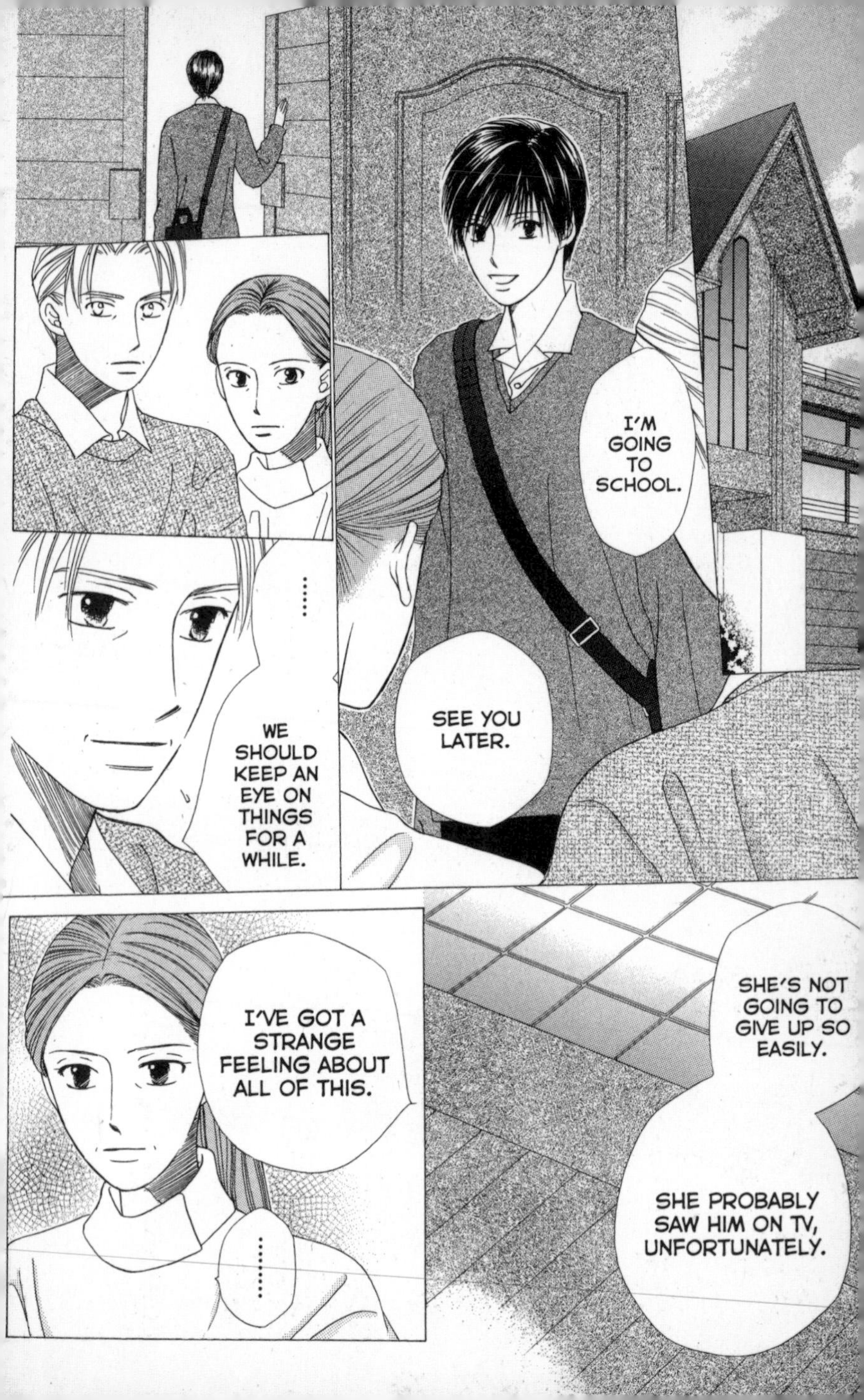
I'M GOING TO SCHOOL.
SEE YOU LATER.
......
WE SHOULD KEEP AN EYE ON THINGS FOR A WHILE.
SHE'S NOT GOING TO GIVE UP SO EASILY.
SHE PROBABLY SAW HIM ON TV, UNFORTUNATELY.
I'VE GOT A STRANGE FEELING ABOUT ALL OF THIS.
......

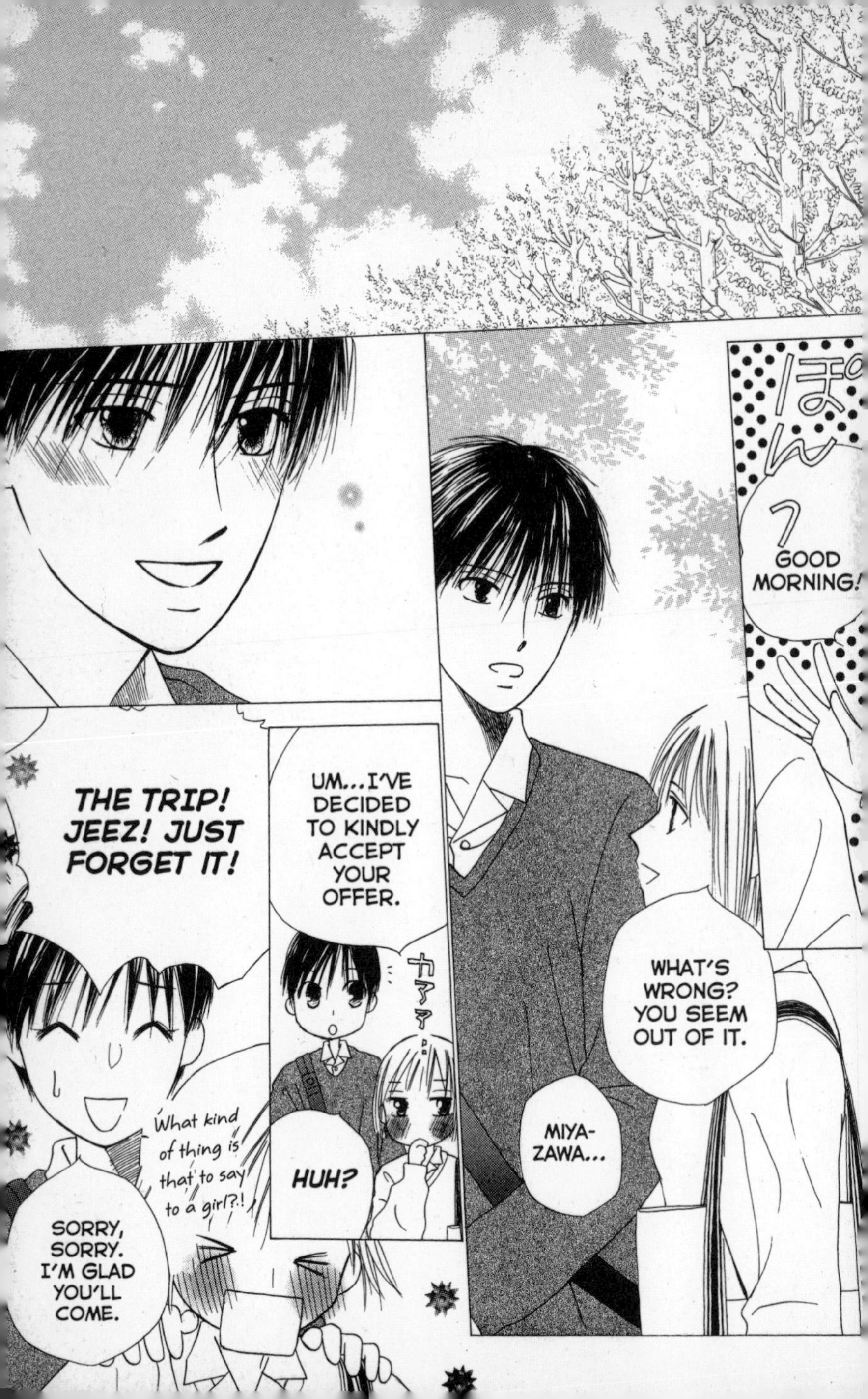
ぽん
GOOD MORNING!
WHAT'S WRONG? YOU SEEM OUT OF IT.
MIYA-ZAWA...
UM...I'VE DECIDED TO KINDLY ACCEPT YOUR OFFER.
カァァ
HUH?
THE TRIP! JEEZ! JUST FORGET IT!
What kind of thing is that to say to a girl?!
SORRY, SORRY. I'M GLAD YOU'LL COME.

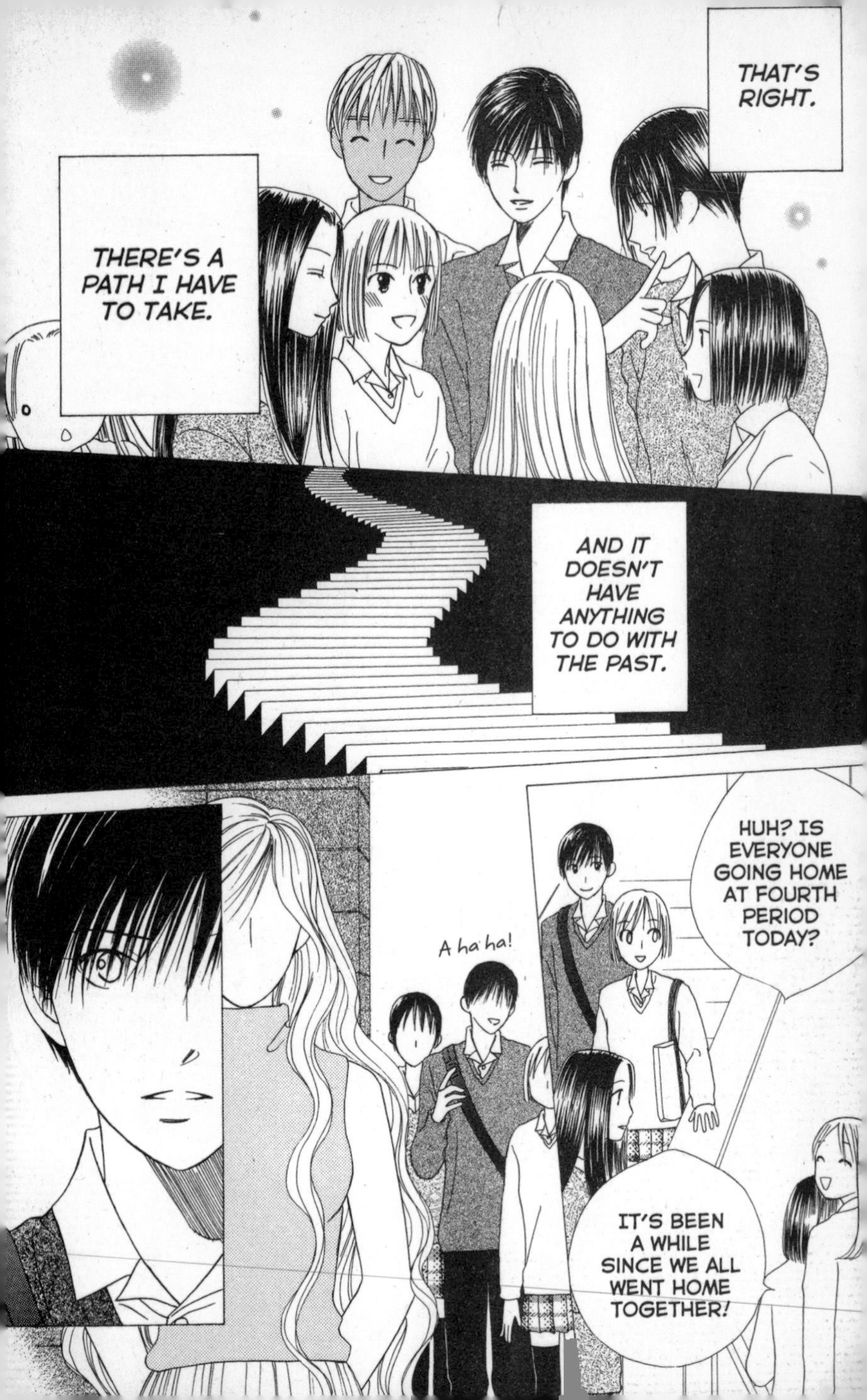
THAT'S RIGHT.
THERE'S A PATH I HAVE TO TAKE.
AND IT DOESN'T HAVE ANYTHING TO DO WITH THE PAST.
HUH? IS EVERYONE GOING HOME AT FOURTH PERIOD TODAY?
A ha ha!
IT'S BEEN A WHILE SINCE WE ALL WENT HOME TOGETHER!

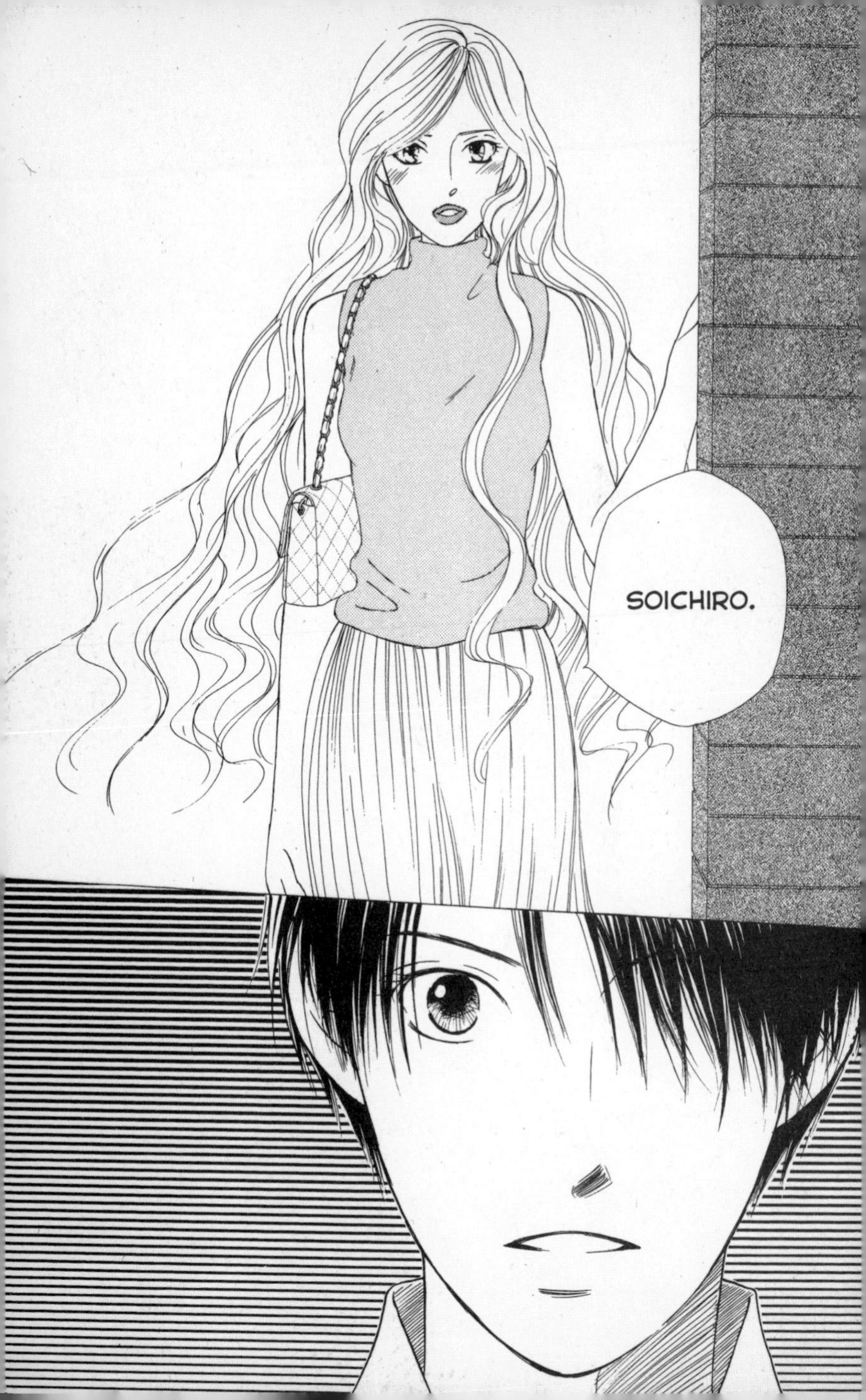
SOICHIRO.

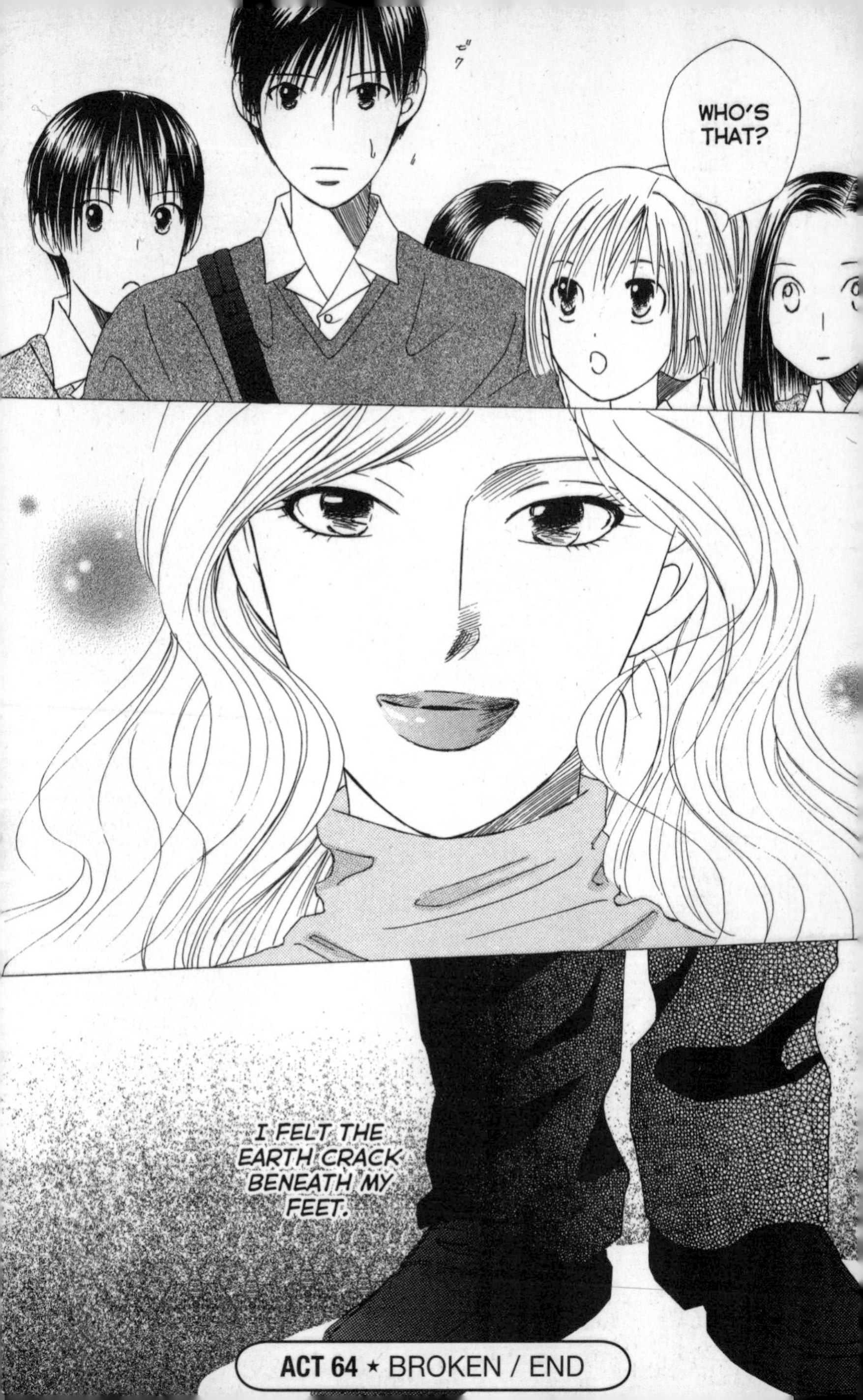
WHO'S THAT?
I FELT THE EARTH CRACK BENEATH MY FEET.
ACT 64 ★ BROKEN / END

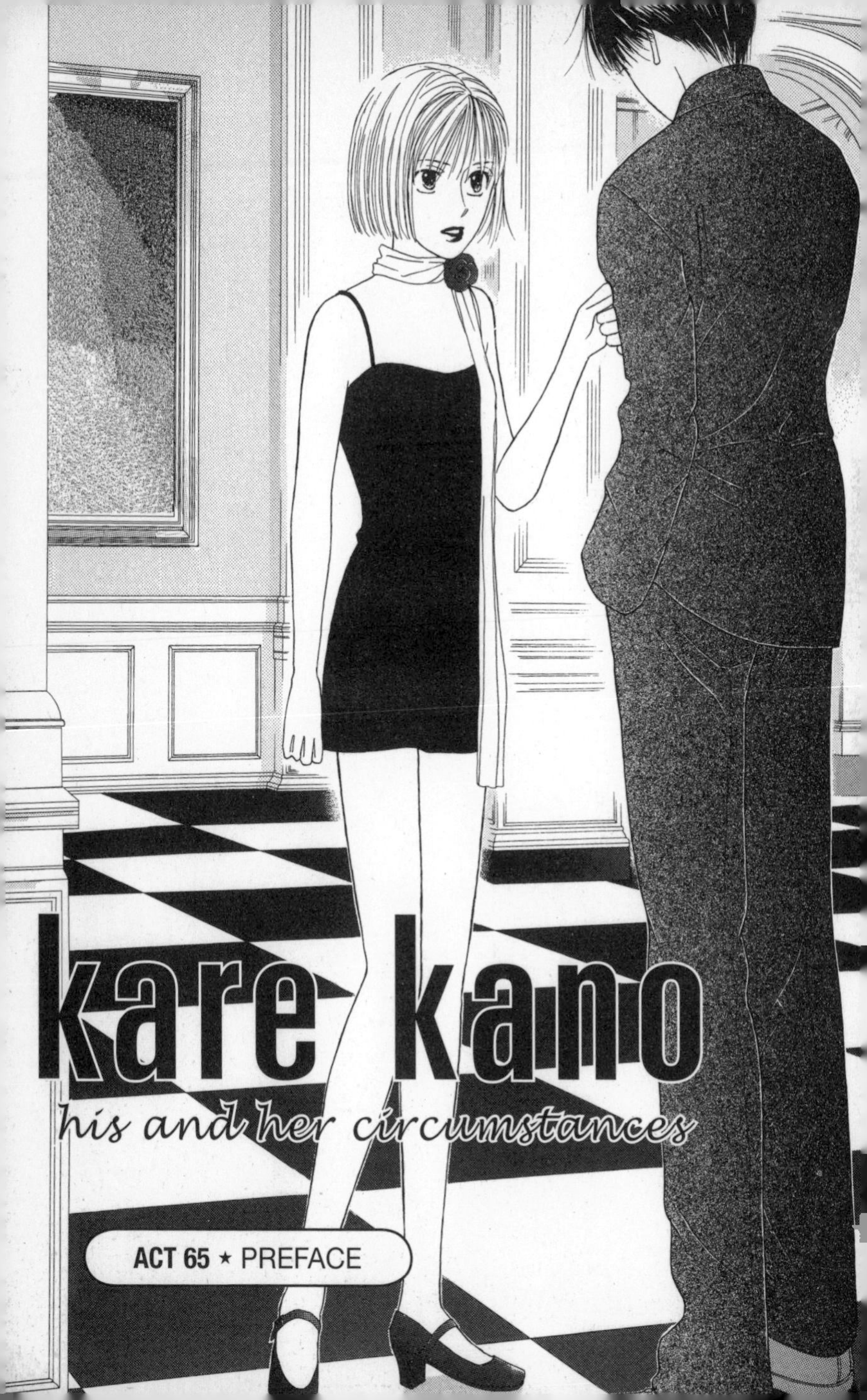
kare kano
his and her circumstances
ACT 65 ★ PREFACE

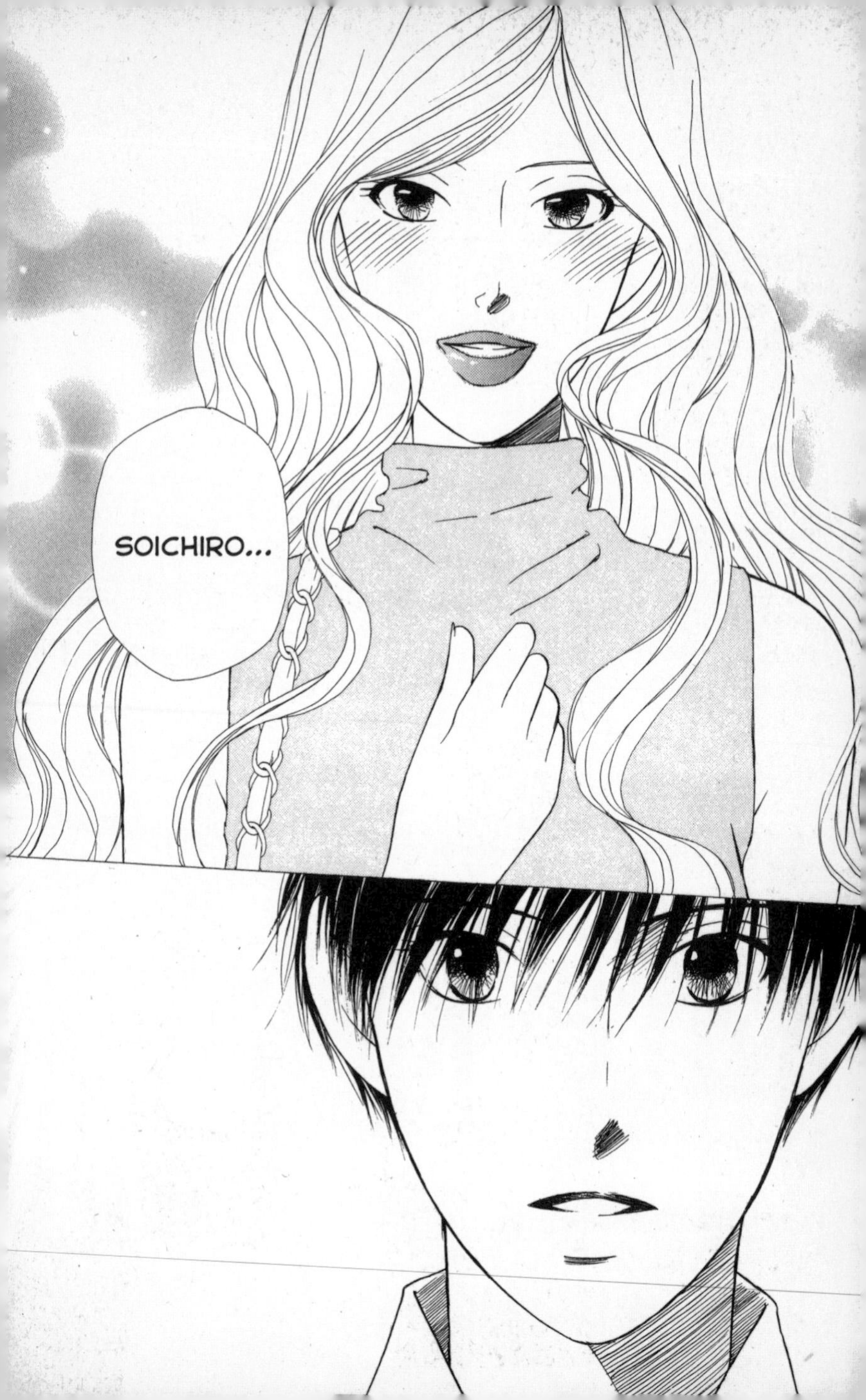
SOICHIRO...

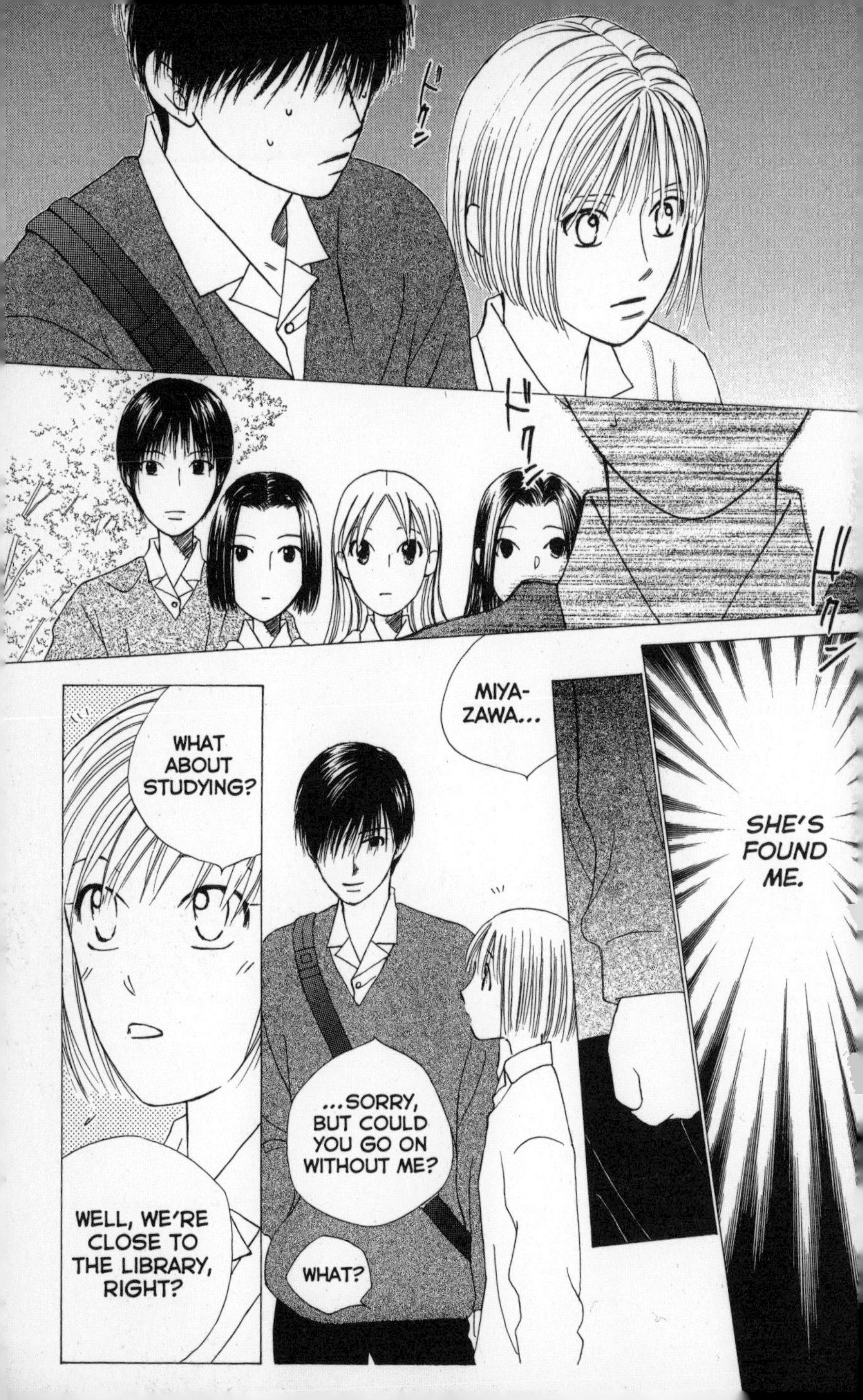

ドクン
ドク
ドクン
SHE'S FOUND ME.
MIYA-ZAWA...
...SORRY, BUT COULD YOU GO ON WITHOUT ME?
WHAT?
WHAT ABOUT STUDYING?
WELL, WE'RE CLOSE TO THE LIBRARY, RIGHT?

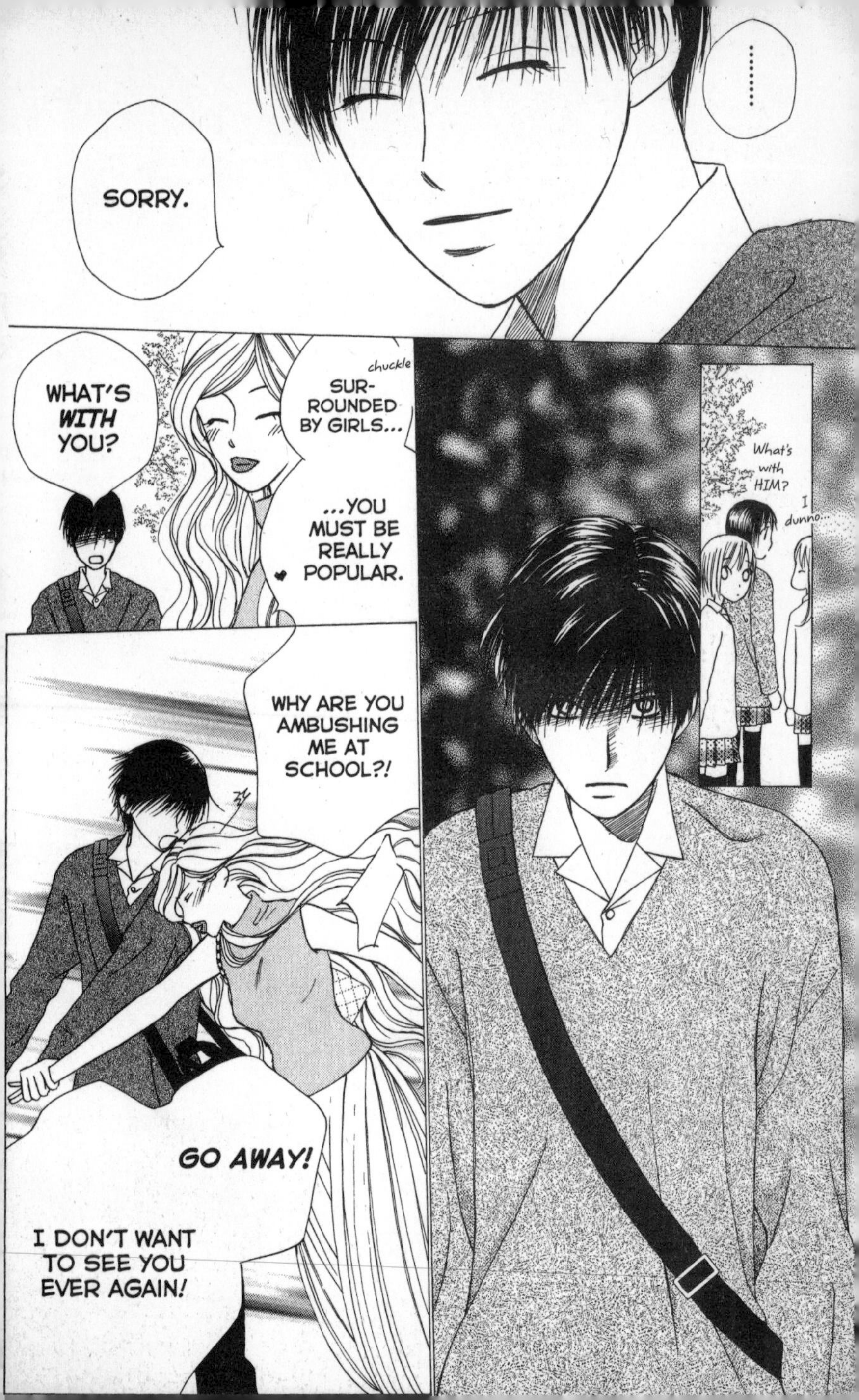

......
SORRY.
What's with HIM?
I dunno...
chuckle
SUR-ROUNDED BY GIRLS...
...YOU MUST BE REALLY POPULAR.
WHAT'S WITH YOU?
WHY ARE YOU AMBUSHING ME AT SCHOOL?!
GO AWAY!
I DON'T WANT TO SEE YOU EVER AGAIN!

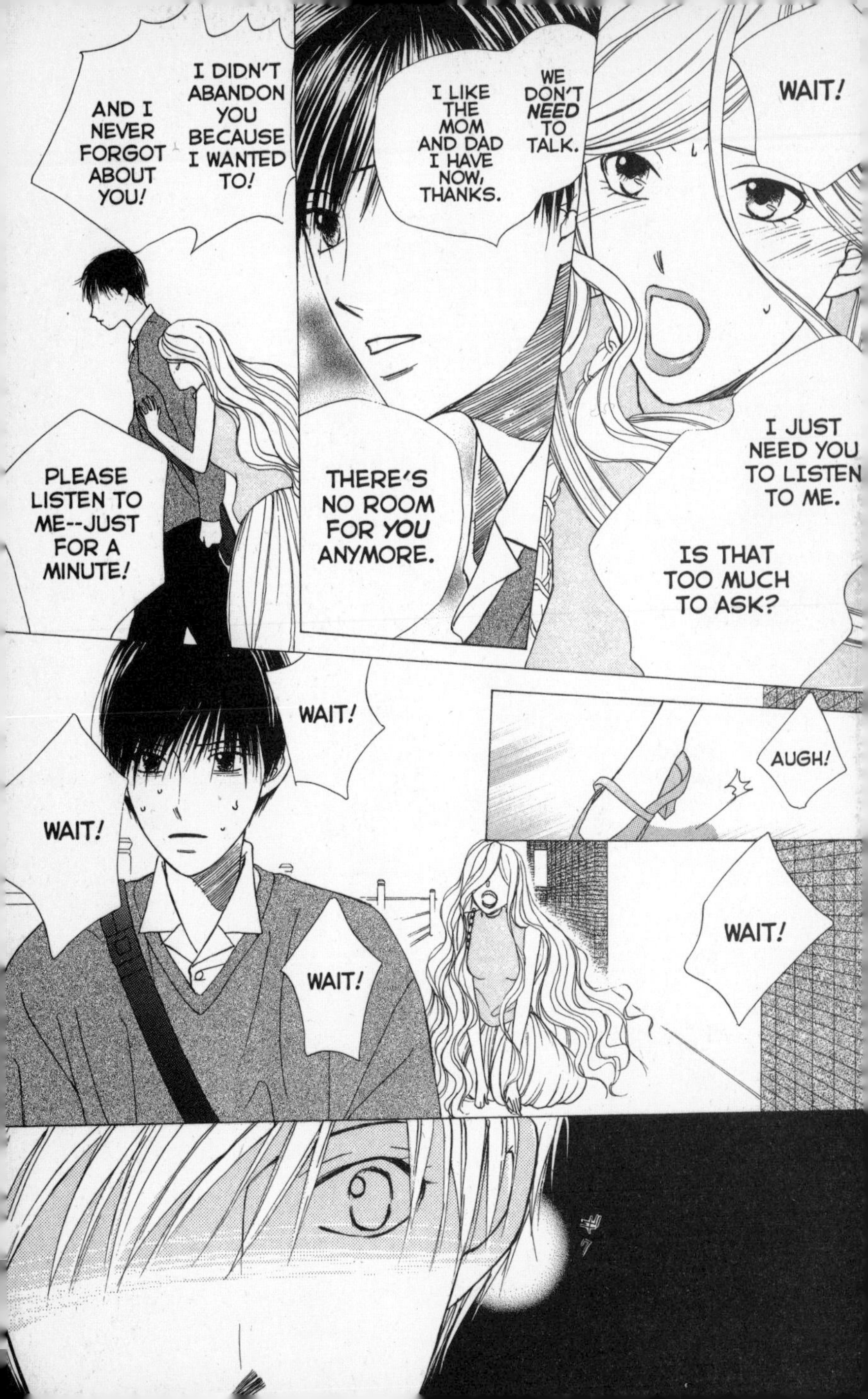
WAIT!
I JUST NEED YOU TO LISTEN TO ME.
IS THAT TOO MUCH TO ASK?
WE DON'T *NEED* TO TALK.
I LIKE THE MOM AND DAD I HAVE NOW, THANKS.
THERE'S NO ROOM FOR *YOU* ANYMORE.
I DIDN'T ABANDON YOU BECAUSE I WANTED TO!
AND I NEVER FORGOT ABOUT YOU!
PLEASE LISTEN TO ME--JUST FOR A MINUTE!
AUGH!
WAIT!
WAIT!
WAIT!
WAIT!

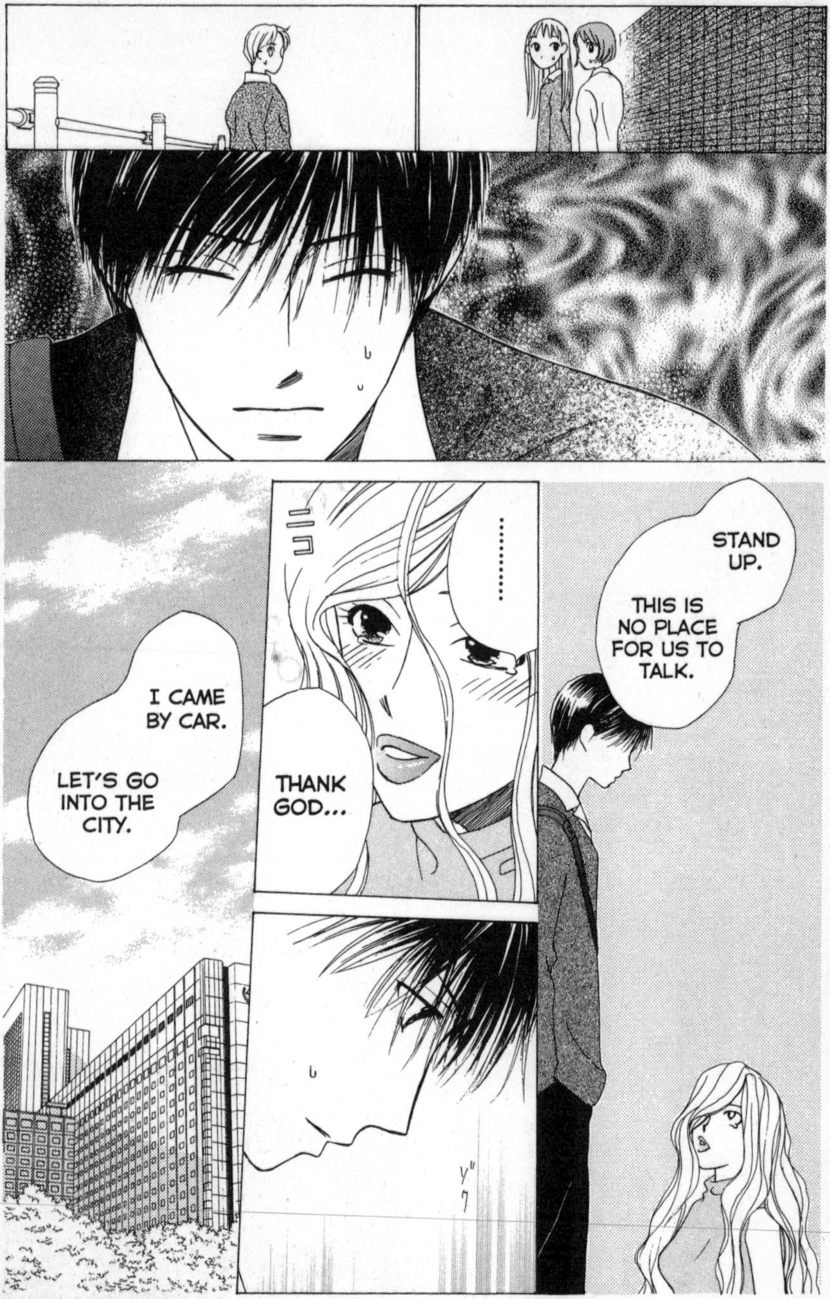
STAND UP.
THIS IS NO PLACE FOR US TO TALK.
ニコ
......
THANK GOD...
ゾク
I CAME BY CAR.
LET'S GO INTO THE CITY.

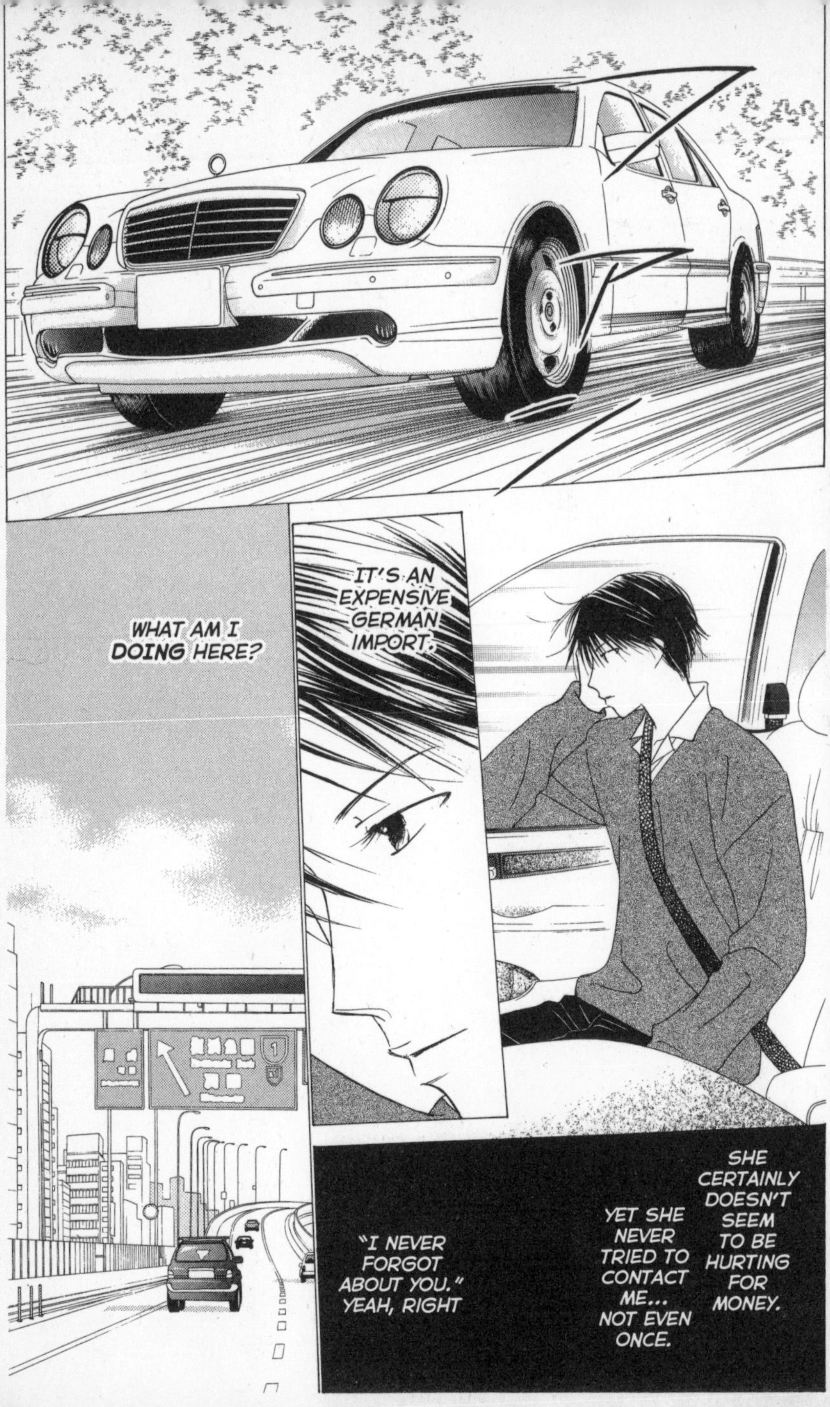
IT'S AN EXPENSIVE GERMAN IMPORT.
WHAT AM I DOING HERE?
SHE CERTAINLY DOESN'T SEEM TO BE HURTING FOR MONEY.
YET SHE NEVER TRIED TO CONTACT ME... NOT EVEN ONCE.
"I NEVER FORGOT ABOUT YOU." YEAH, RIGHT

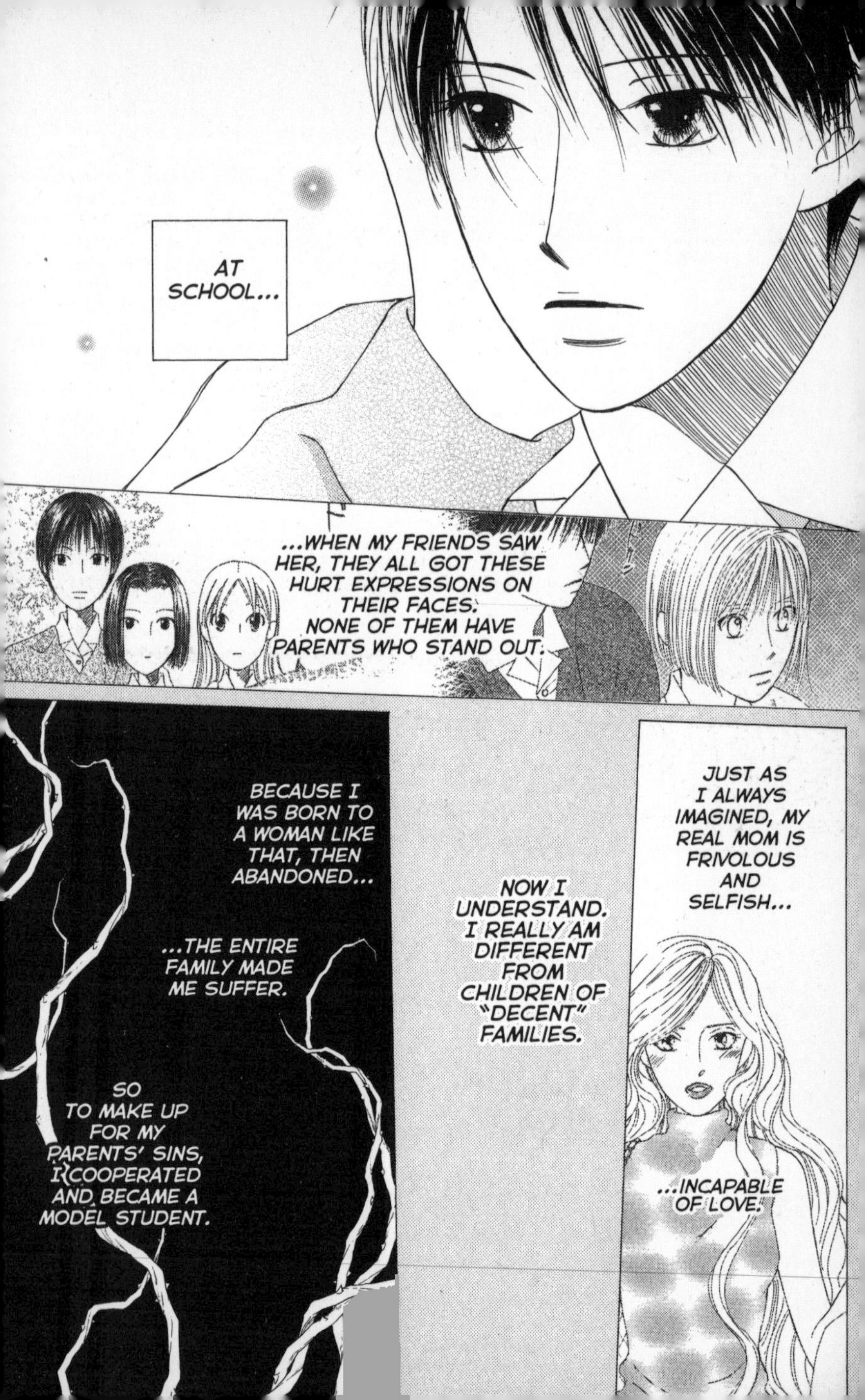
AT SCHOOL...
...WHEN MY FRIENDS SAW HER, THEY ALL GOT THESE HURT EXPRESSIONS ON THEIR FACES. NONE OF THEM HAVE PARENTS WHO STAND OUT.
JUST AS I ALWAYS IMAGINED, MY REAL MOM IS FRIVOLOUS AND SELFISH...
...INCAPABLE OF LOVE.
NOW I UNDERSTAND. I REALLY AM DIFFERENT FROM CHILDREN OF "DECENT" FAMILIES.
BECAUSE I WAS BORN TO A WOMAN LIKE THAT, THEN ABANDONED...
...THE ENTIRE FAMILY MADE ME SUFFER.
SO TO MAKE UP FOR MY PARENTS' SINS, I COOPERATED AND BECAME A MODEL STUDENT.

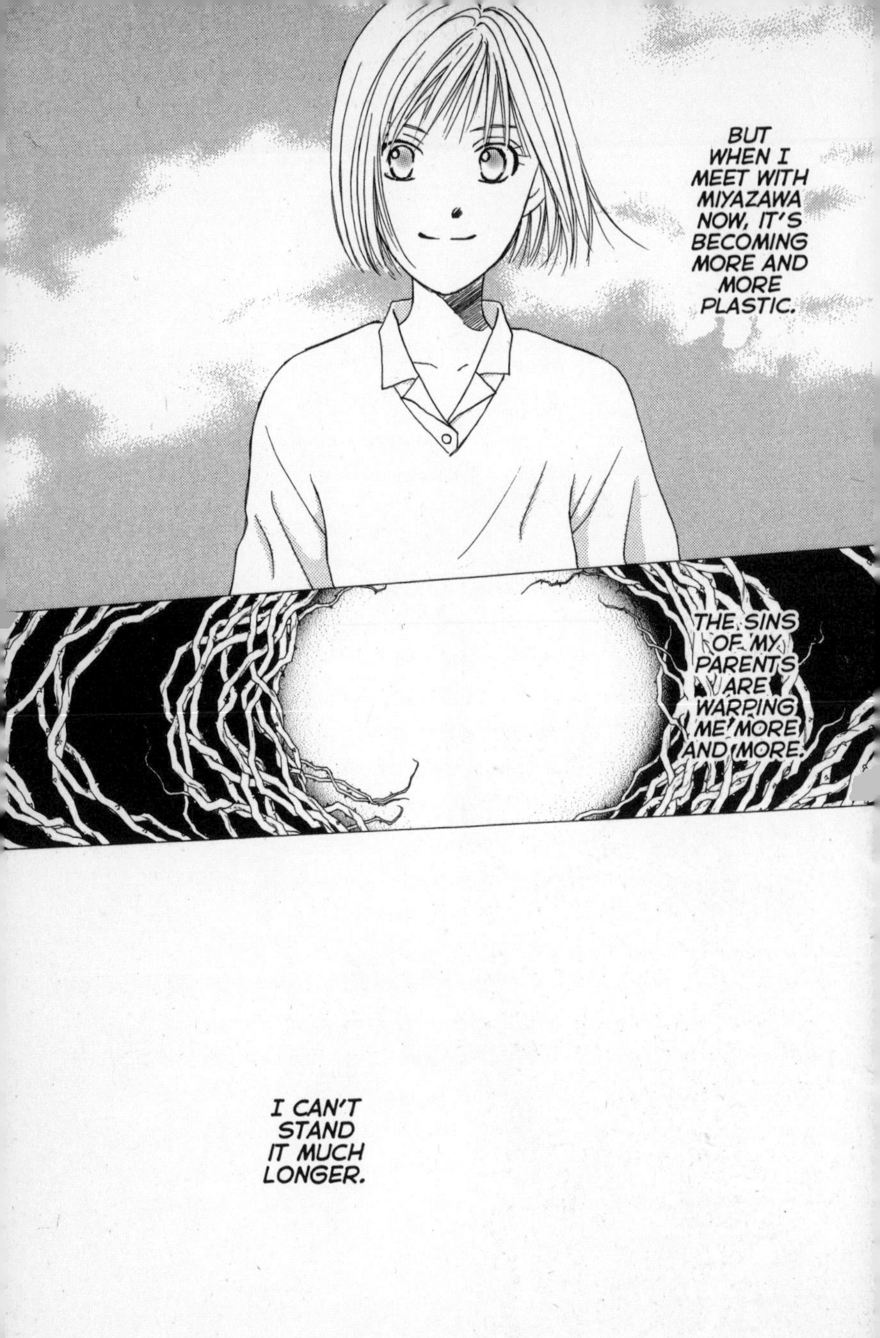
BUT WHEN I MEET WITH MIYAZAWA NOW, IT'S BECOMING MORE AND MORE PLASTIC.
THE SINS OF MY PARENTS ARE WARPING ME MORE AND MORE.
I CAN'T STAND IT MUCH LONGER.

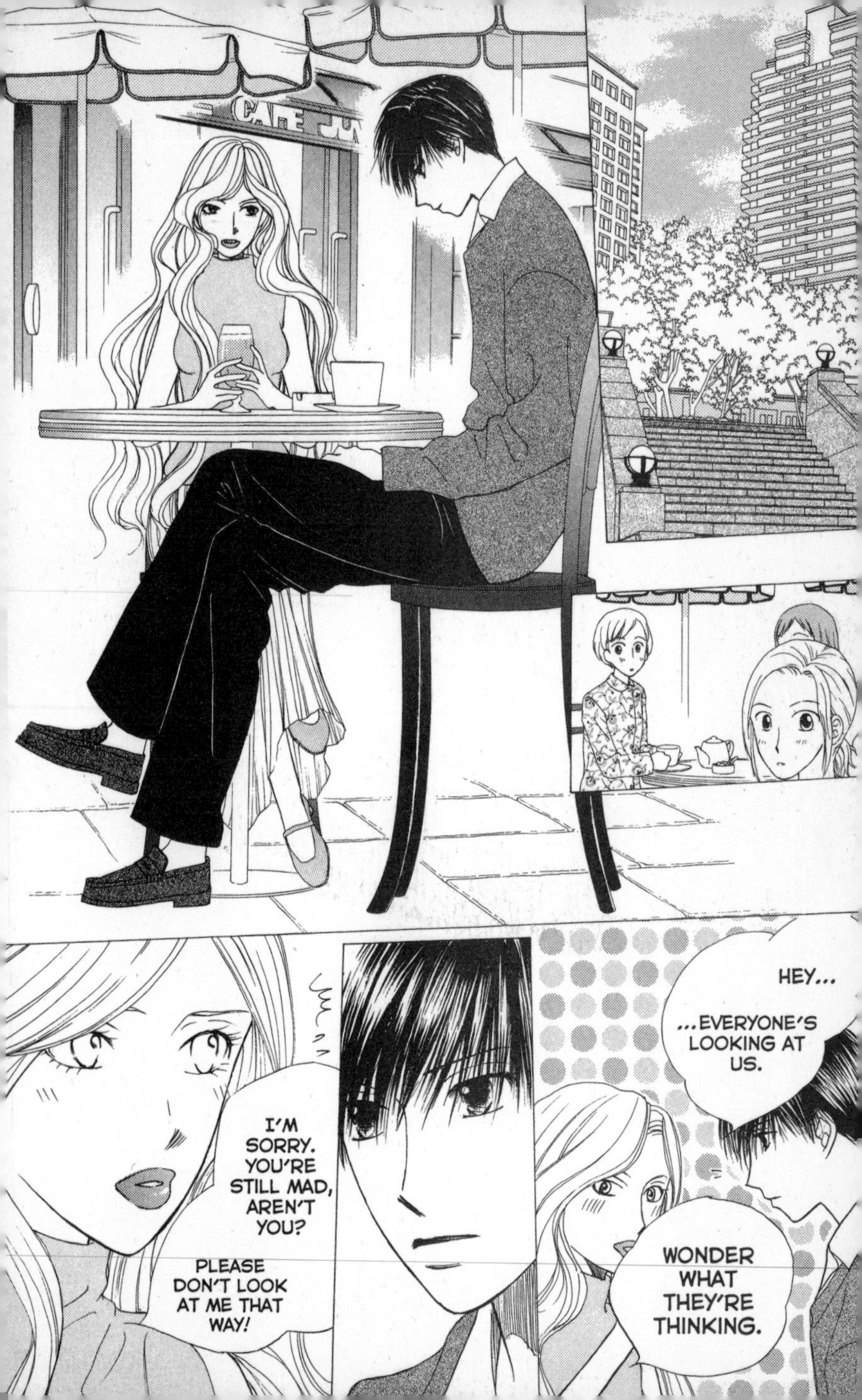
HEY...
...EVERYONE'S LOOKING AT US.
WONDER WHAT THEY'RE THINKING.
I'M SORRY. YOU'RE STILL MAD, AREN'T YOU?
PLEASE DON'T LOOK AT ME THAT WAY!

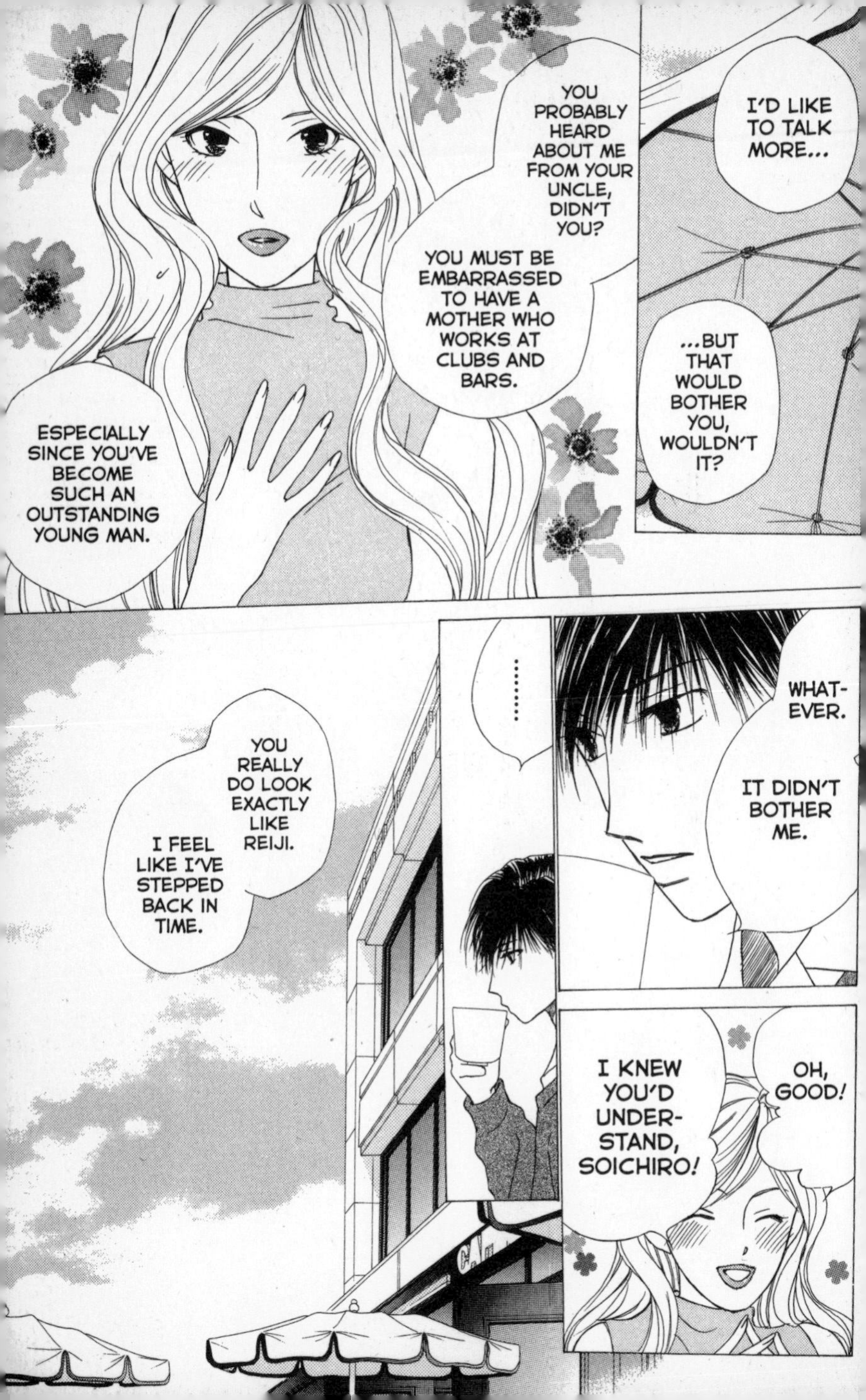
I'D LIKE TO TALK MORE...
...BUT THAT WOULD BOTHER YOU, WOULDN'T IT?
YOU PROBABLY HEARD ABOUT ME FROM YOUR UNCLE, DIDN'T YOU?
YOU MUST BE EMBARRASSED TO HAVE A MOTHER WHO WORKS AT CLUBS AND BARS.
ESPECIALLY SINCE YOU'VE BECOME SUCH AN OUTSTANDING YOUNG MAN.
WHAT-EVER.
IT DIDN'T BOTHER ME.
OH, GOOD!
I KNEW YOU'D UNDER-STAND, SOICHIRO!
......
YOU REALLY DO LOOK EXACTLY LIKE REIJI.
I FEEL LIKE I'VE STEPPED BACK IN TIME.

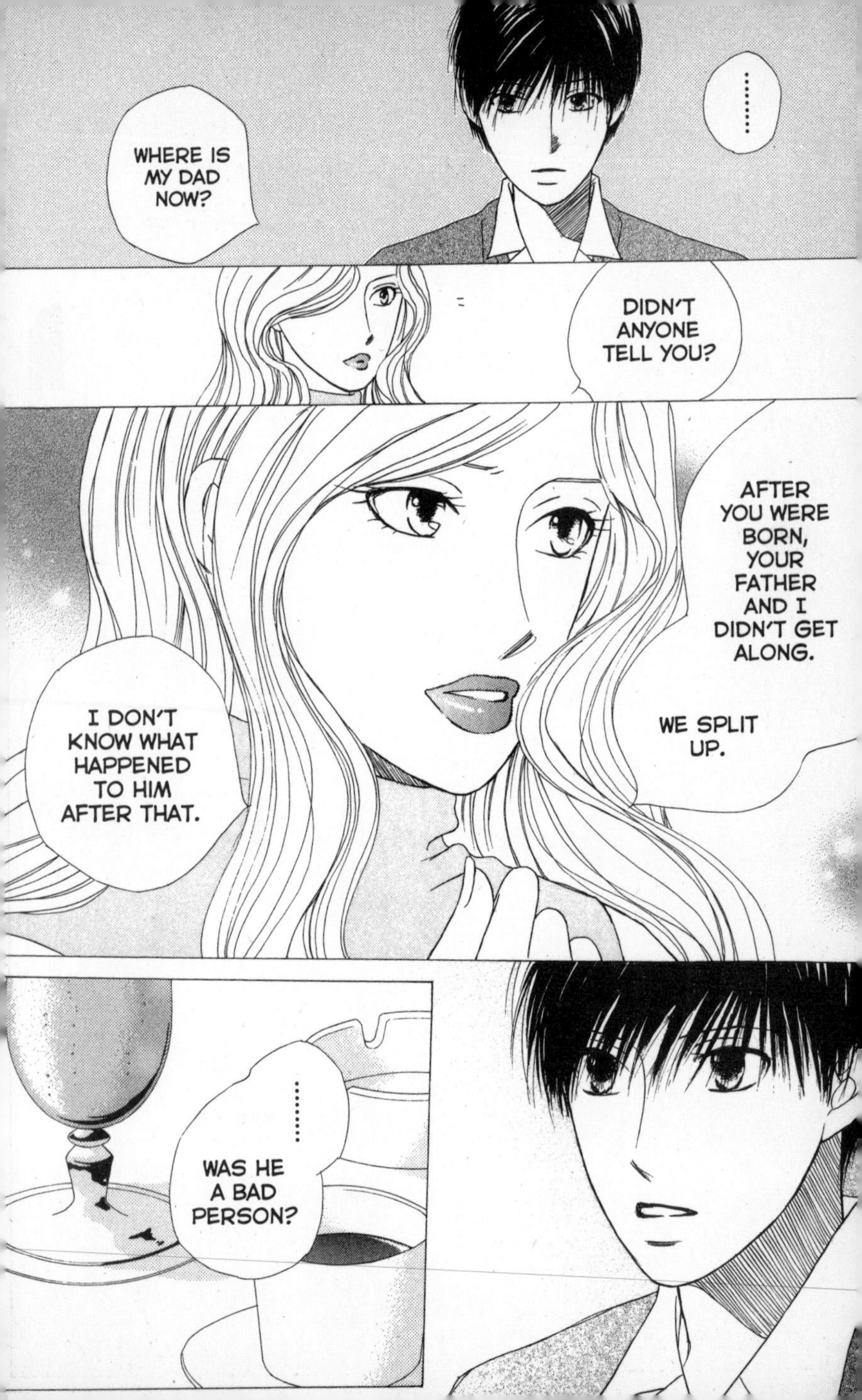
......
WHERE IS MY DAD NOW?
DIDN'T ANYONE TELL YOU?
AFTER YOU WERE BORN, YOUR FATHER AND I DIDN'T GET ALONG.
WE SPLIT UP.
I DON'T KNOW WHAT HAPPENED TO HIM AFTER THAT.
...... WAS HE A BAD PERSON?

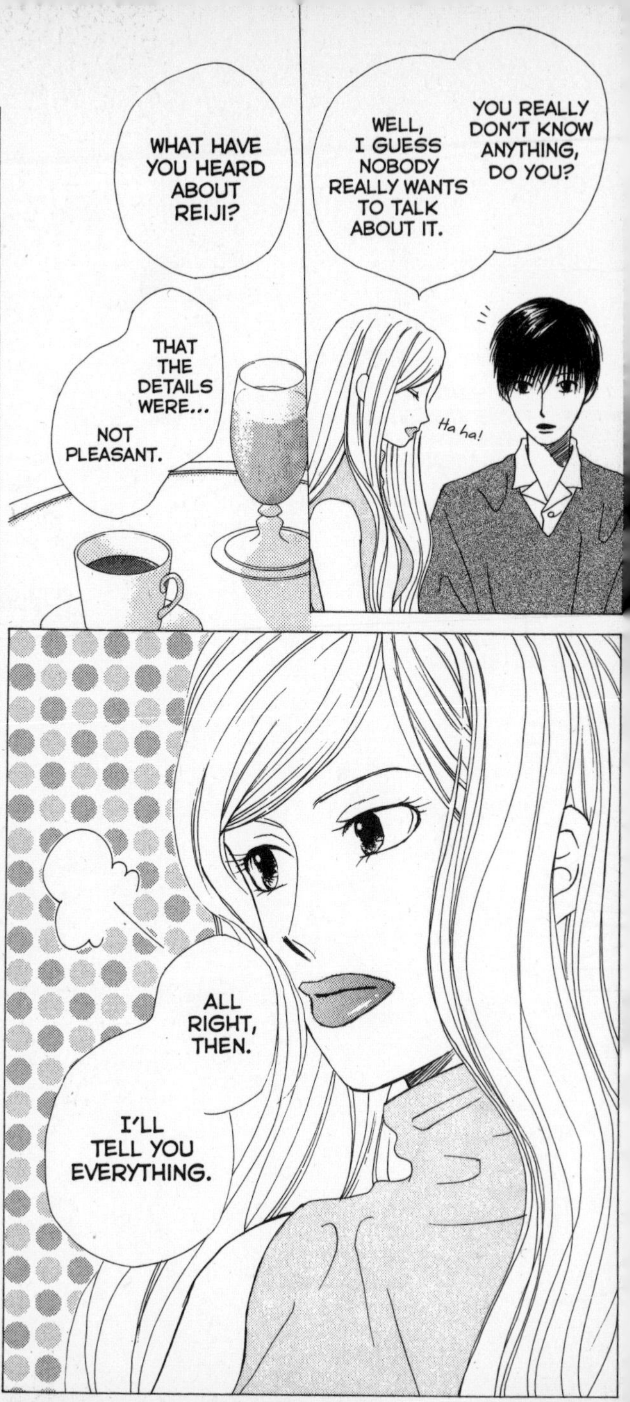
YOU REALLY DON'T KNOW ANYTHING, DO YOU?
WELL, I GUESS NOBODY REALLY WANTS TO TALK ABOUT IT.
Ha ha!
WHAT HAVE YOU HEARD ABOUT REIJI?
THAT THE DETAILS WERE...
NOT PLEASANT.
ALL RIGHT, THEN.
I'LL TELL YOU EVERYTHING.

2

The food I've been eating a lot of lately is...

"Five Grain" Rice!

Ah, the healthy life.

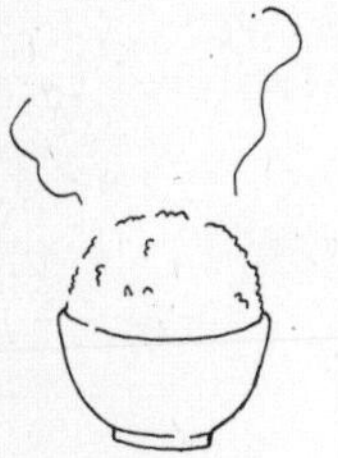

Whenever I eat at home, I always make a "five grain" blend of two parts whole rice and one part sprouted brown rice. I also add unpolished rice and red rice.

Sometimes I cook azuki beans...

sometimes I cook konbu...

I'm not particularly healthy, though.

I need to exercise.

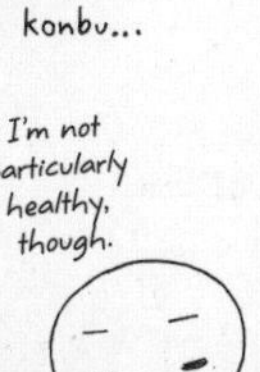

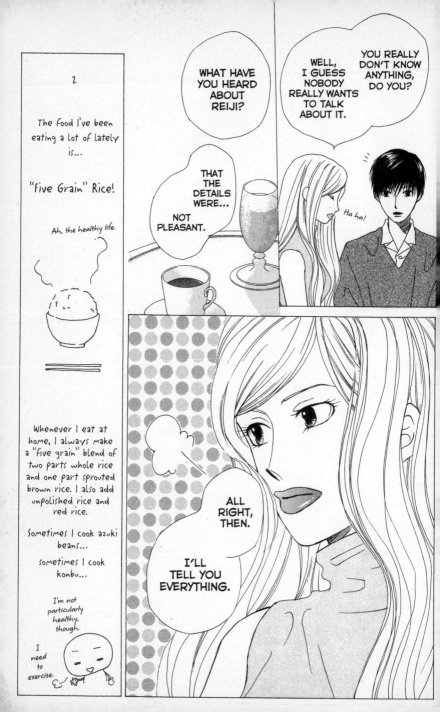

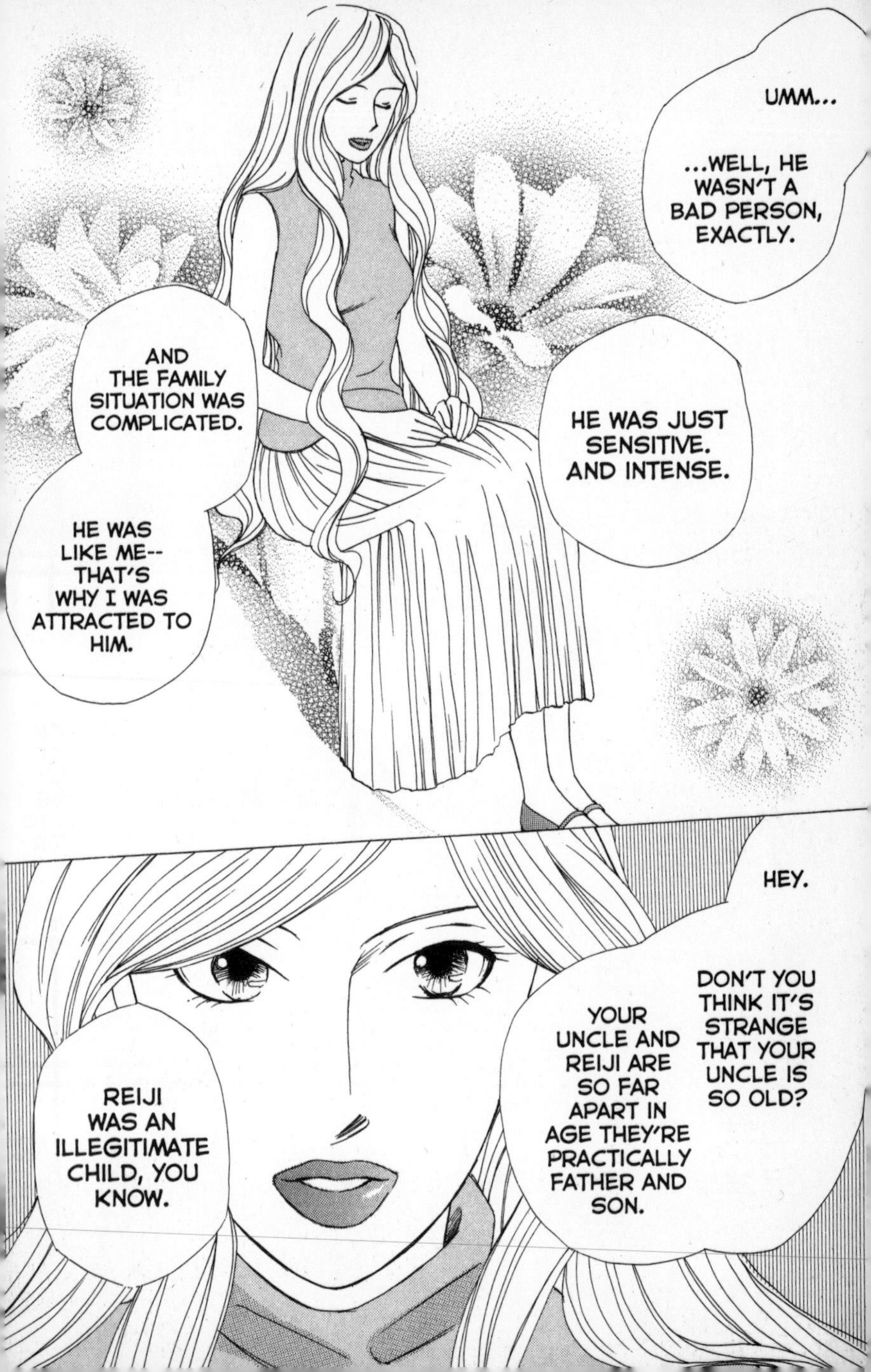
UMM...
...WELL, HE WASN'T A BAD PERSON, EXACTLY.
HE WAS JUST SENSITIVE. AND INTENSE.
AND THE FAMILY SITUATION WAS COMPLICATED.
HE WAS LIKE ME-- THAT'S WHY I WAS ATTRACTED TO HIM.
HEY.
DON'T YOU THINK IT'S STRANGE THAT YOUR UNCLE IS SO OLD?
YOUR UNCLE AND REIJI ARE SO FAR APART IN AGE THEY'RE PRACTICALLY FATHER AND SON.
REIJI WAS AN ILLEGITIMATE CHILD, YOU KNOW.

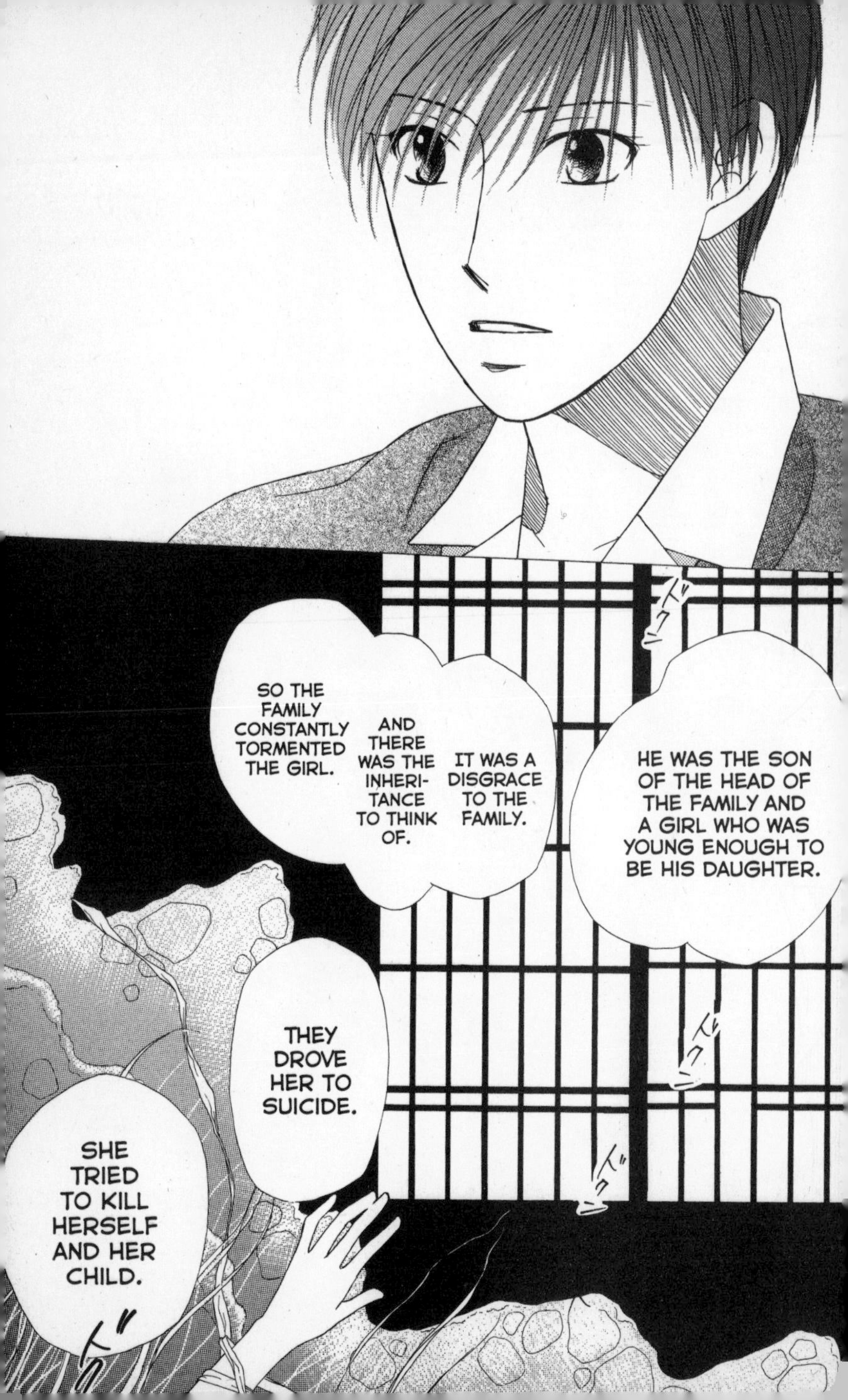
HE WAS THE SON OF THE HEAD OF THE FAMILY AND A GIRL WHO WAS YOUNG ENOUGH TO BE HIS DAUGHTER.
IT WAS A DISGRACE TO THE FAMILY.
AND THERE WAS THE INHERI- TANCE TO THINK OF.
SO THE FAMILY CONSTANTLY TORMENTED THE GIRL.
THEY DROVE HER TO SUICIDE.
SHE TRIED TO KILL HERSELF AND HER CHILD.

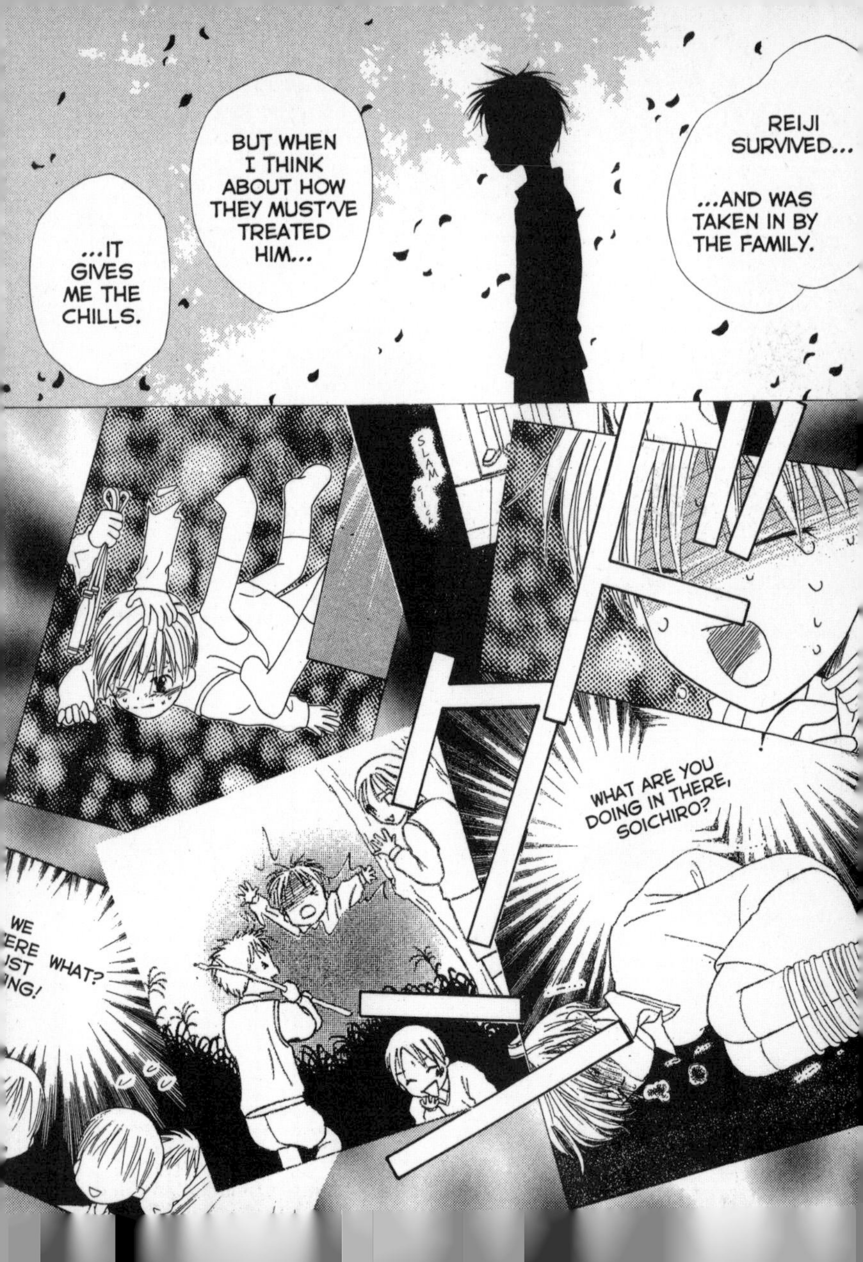
REIJI SURVIVED...
...AND WAS TAKEN IN BY THE FAMILY.
BUT WHEN I THINK ABOUT HOW THEY MUST'VE TREATED HIM...
...IT GIVES ME THE CHILLS.
SLAM
CLICK
WHAT ARE YOU DOING IN THERE, SOICHIRO?
WHAT?

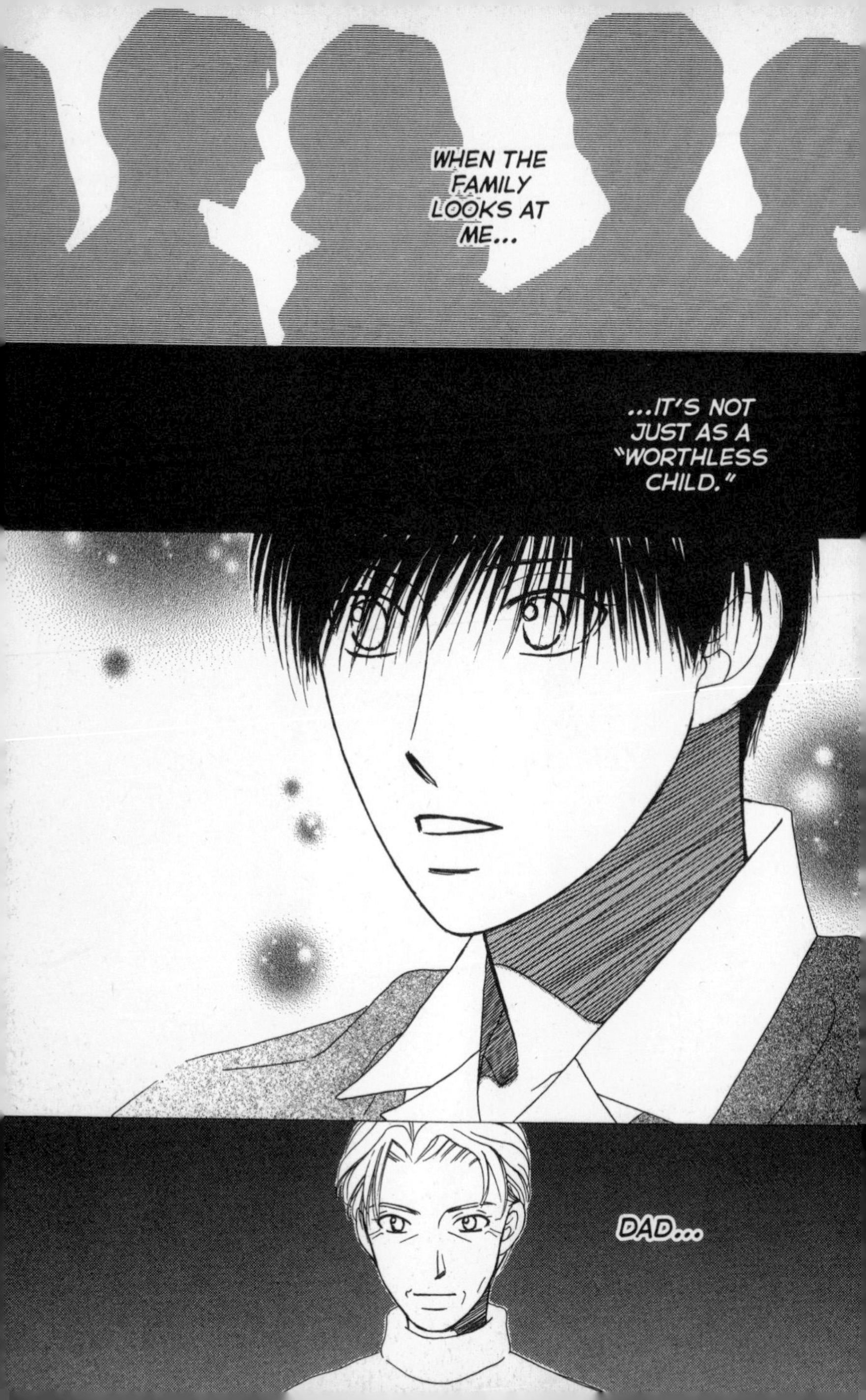
WHEN THE FAMILY LOOKS AT ME...
...IT'S NOT JUST AS A "WORTHLESS CHILD."
DAD...

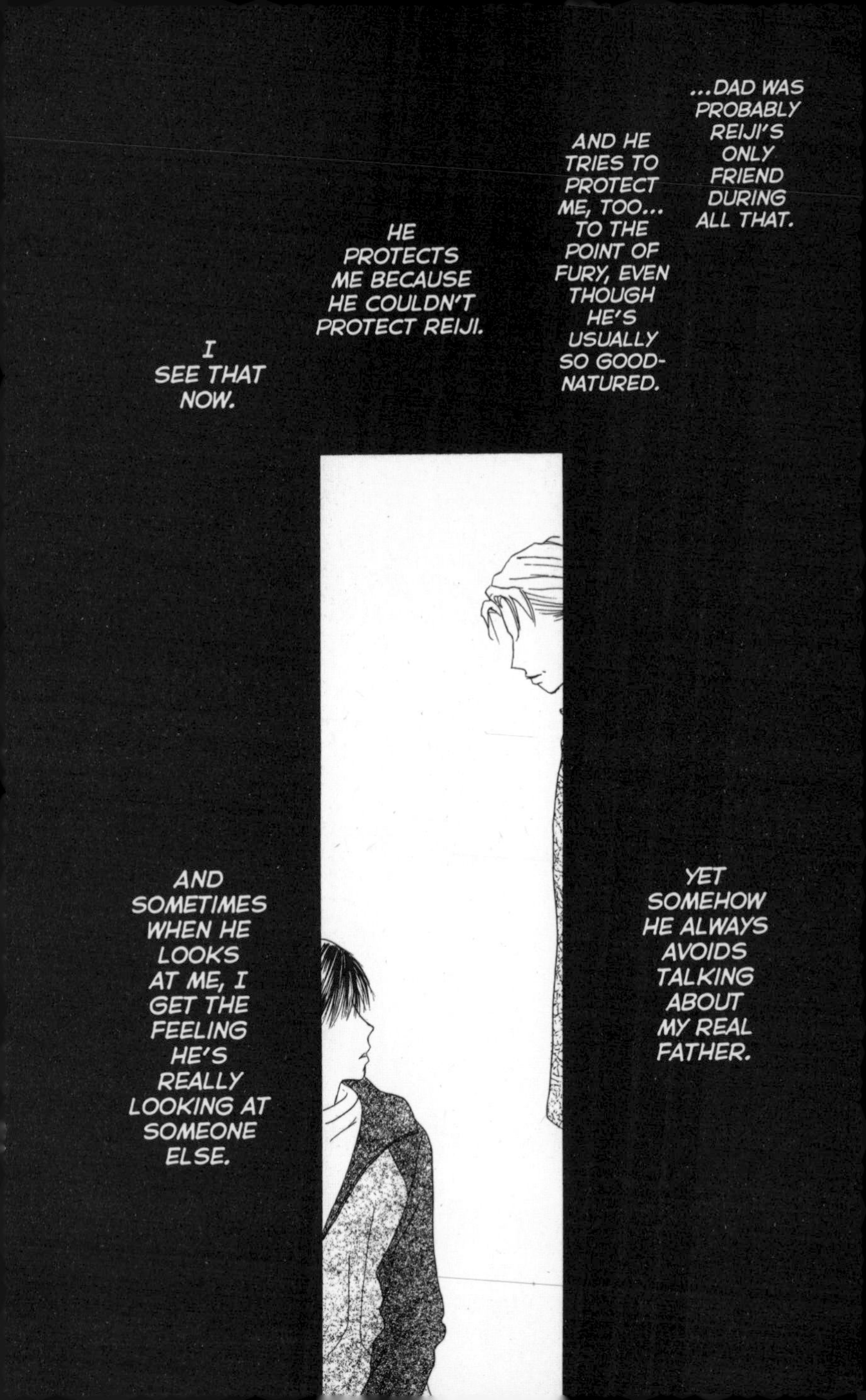
...DAD WAS PROBABLY REIJI'S ONLY FRIEND DURING ALL THAT.
AND HE TRIES TO PROTECT ME, TOO... TO THE POINT OF FURY, EVEN THOUGH HE'S USUALLY SO GOOD-NATURED.
HE PROTECTS ME BECAUSE HE COULDN'T PROTECT REIJI.
I SEE THAT NOW.
YET SOMEHOW HE ALWAYS AVOIDS TALKING ABOUT MY REAL FATHER.
AND SOMETIMES WHEN HE LOOKS AT ME, I GET THE FEELING HE'S REALLY LOOKING AT SOMEONE ELSE.

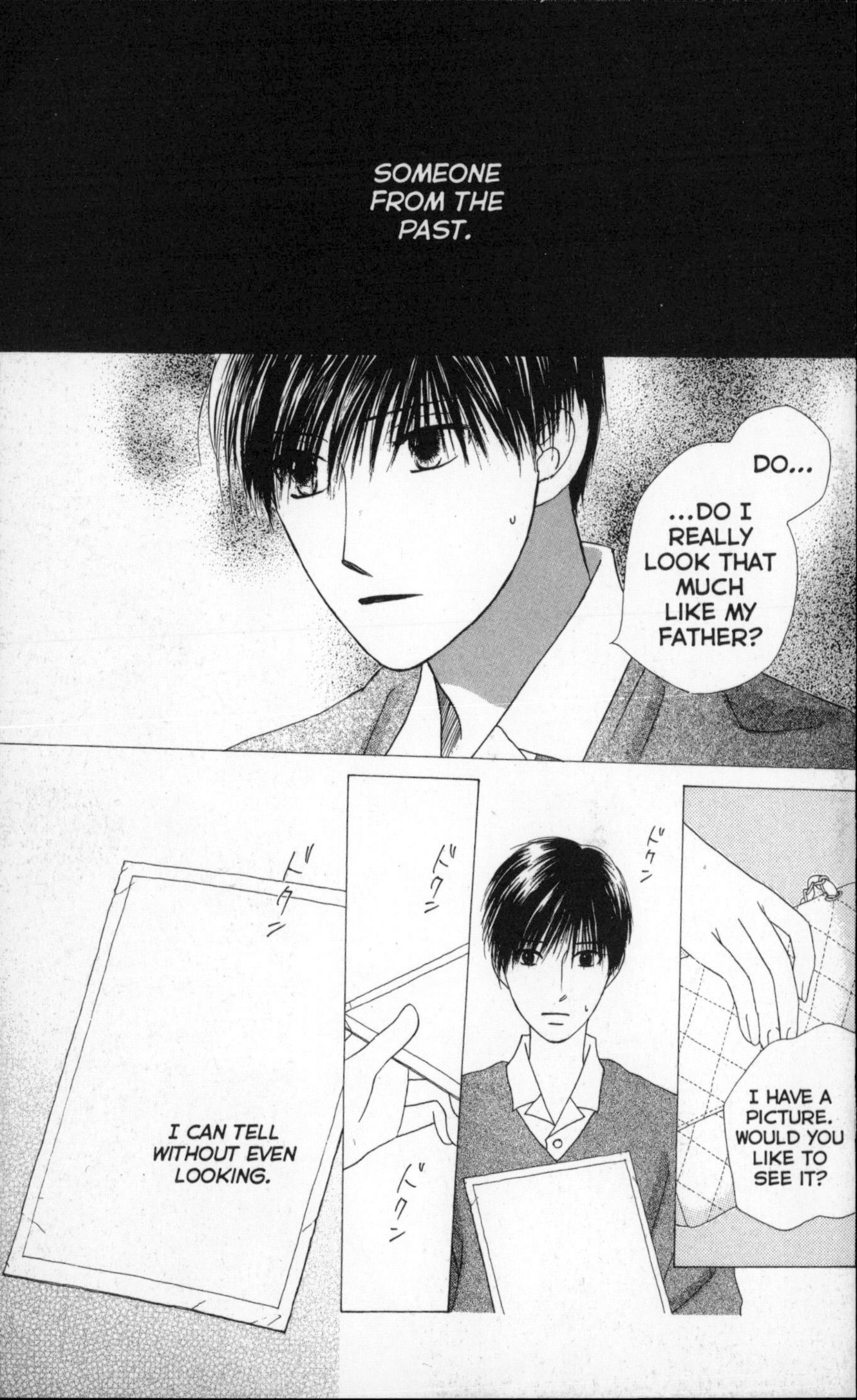
SOMEONE FROM THE PAST.
DO...
...DO I REALLY LOOK THAT MUCH LIKE MY FATHER?
I HAVE A PICTURE. WOULD YOU LIKE TO SEE IT?
ドクン
ドクン
ドクン
ドクン
I CAN TELL WITHOUT EVEN LOOKING.

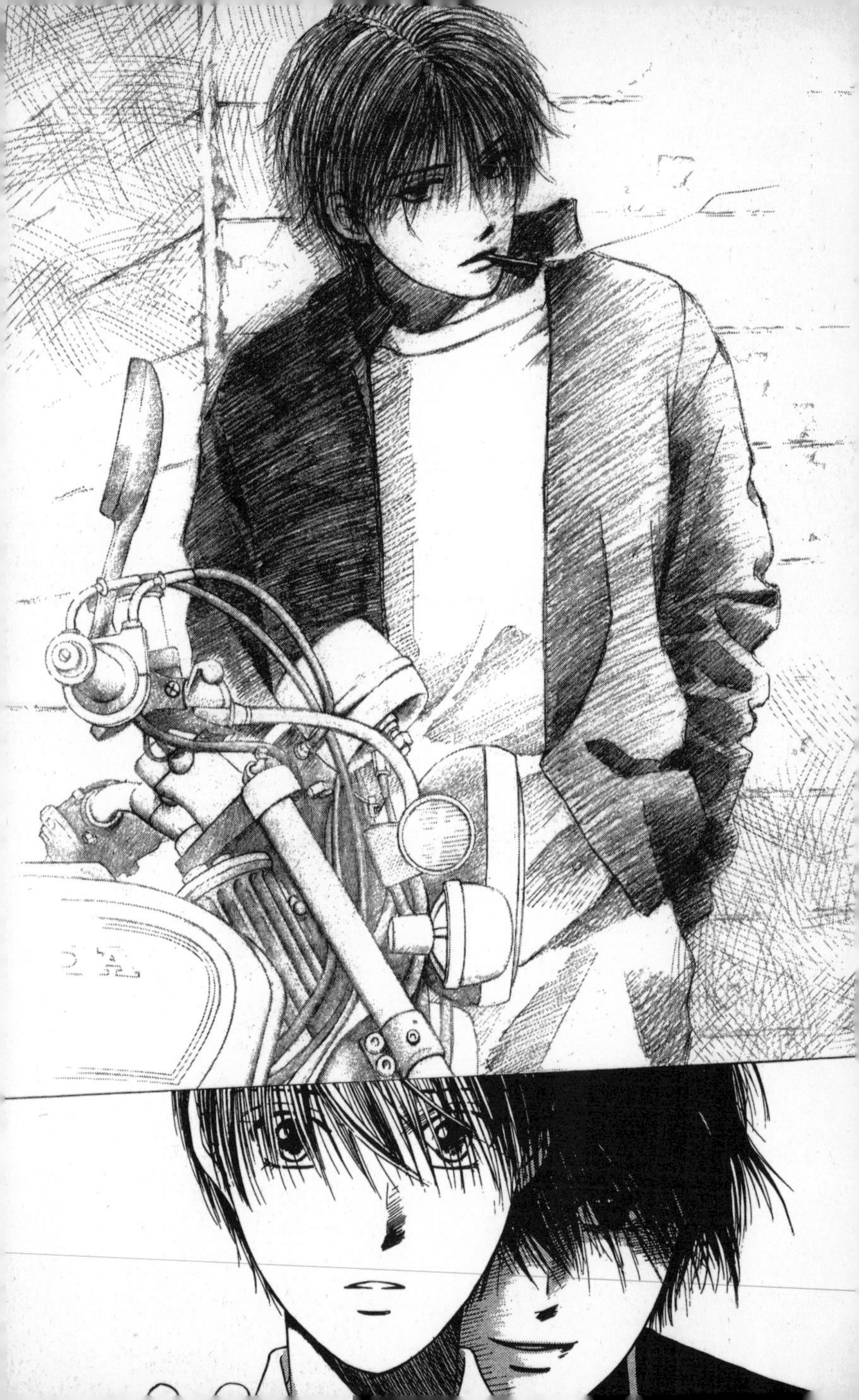

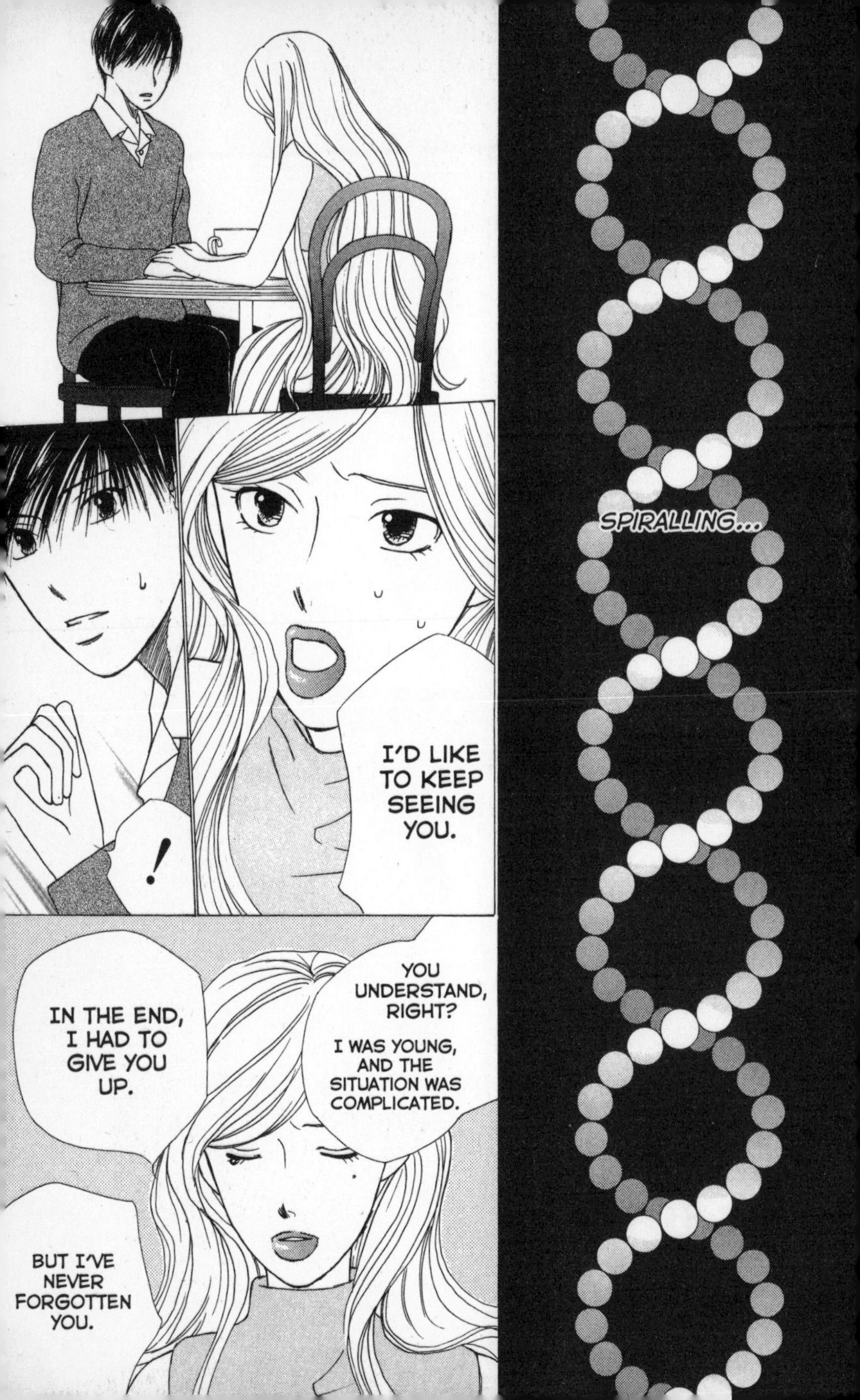
SPIRALLING...
I'D LIKE TO KEEP SEEING YOU.
!
YOU UNDERSTAND, RIGHT?
I WAS YOUNG, AND THE SITUATION WAS COMPLICATED.
IN THE END, I HAD TO GIVE YOU UP.
BUT I'VE NEVER FORGOTTEN YOU.

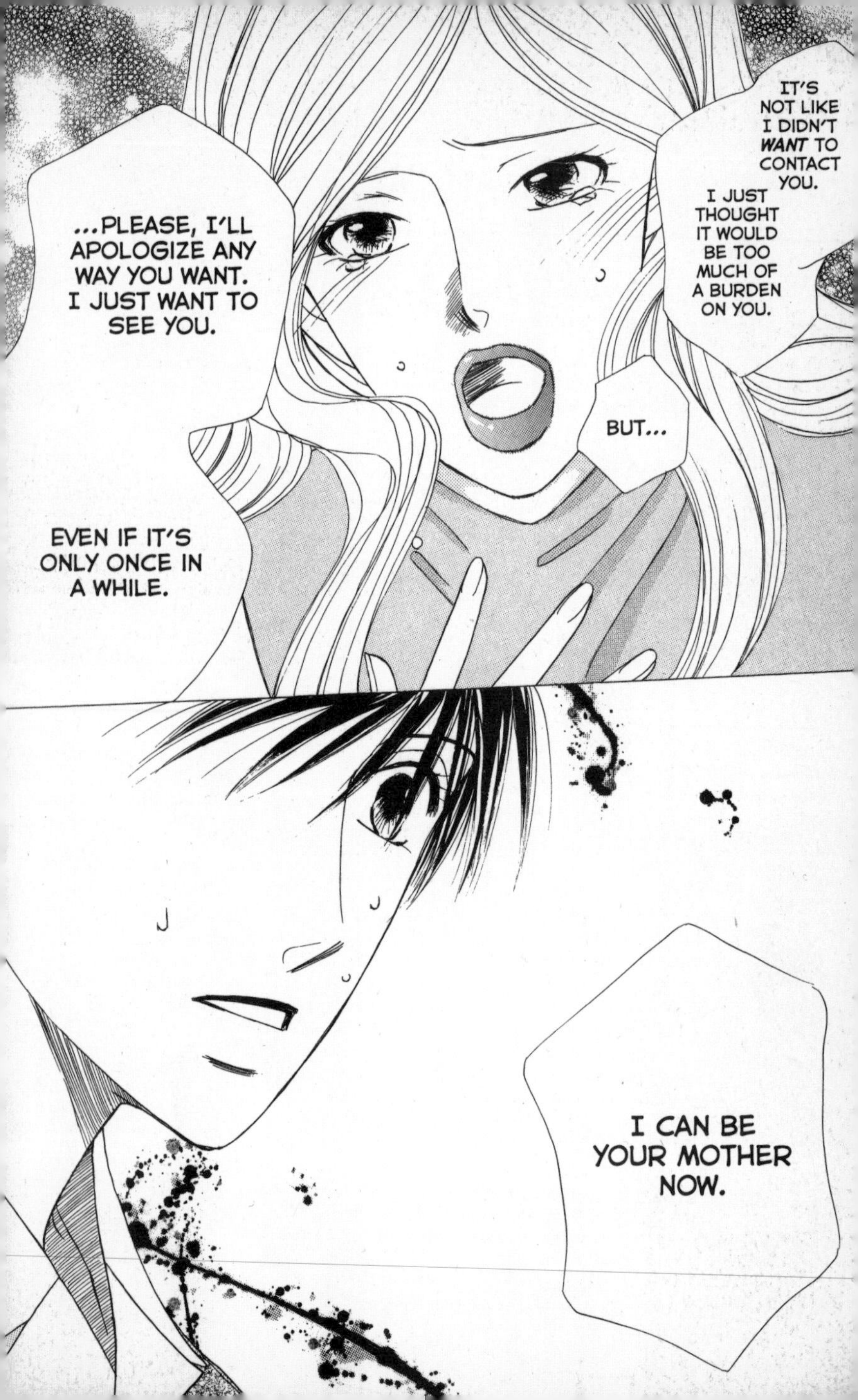
IT'S NOT LIKE I DIDN'T *WANT* TO CONTACT YOU.
I JUST THOUGHT IT WOULD BE TOO MUCH OF A BURDEN ON YOU.
BUT...
...PLEASE, I'LL APOLOGIZE ANY WAY YOU WANT. I JUST WANT TO SEE YOU.
EVEN IF IT'S ONLY ONCE IN A WHILE.
I CAN BE YOUR MOTHER NOW.

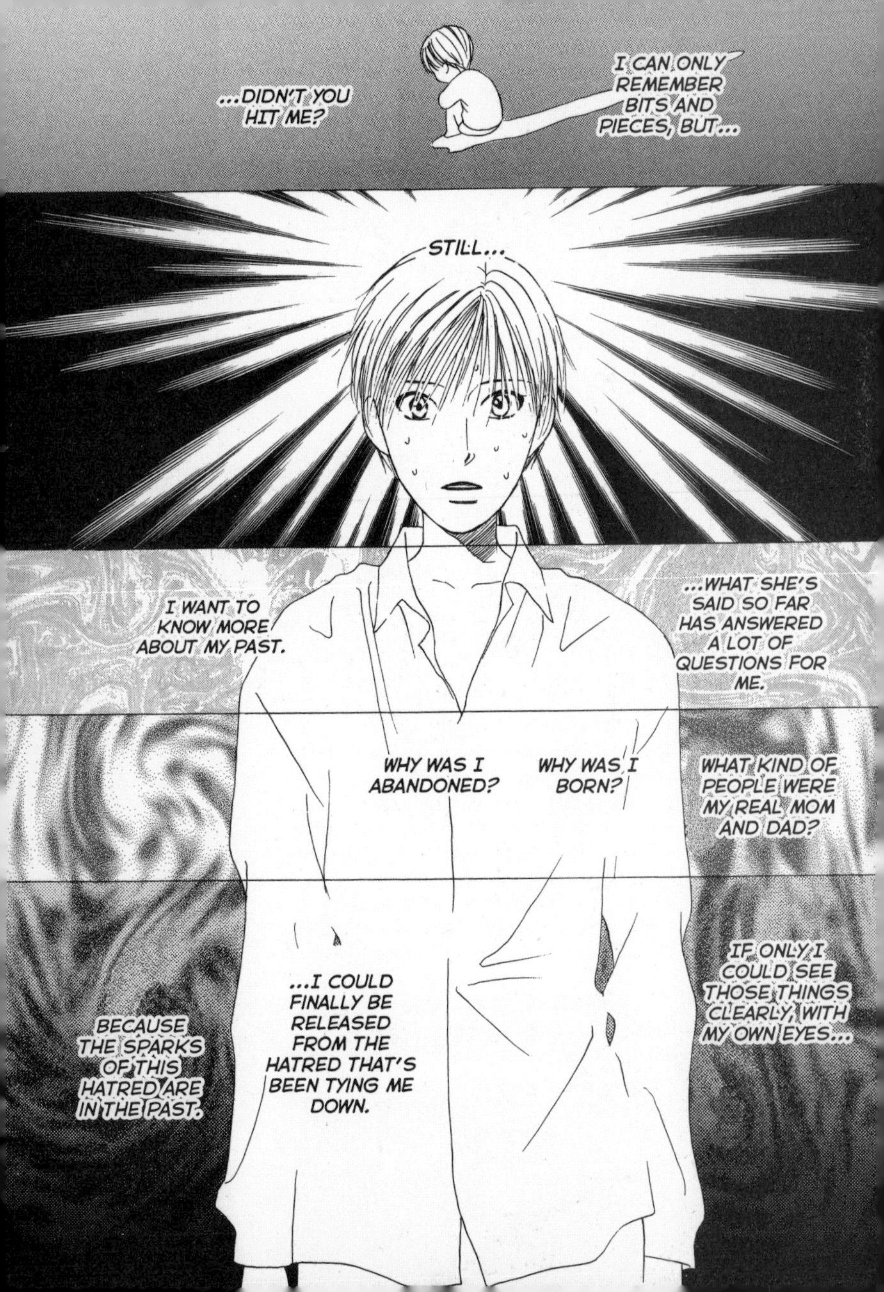
I CAN ONLY REMEMBER BITS AND PIECES, BUT...
...DIDN'T YOU HIT ME?
STILL...
...WHAT SHE'S SAID SO FAR HAS ANSWERED A LOT OF QUESTIONS FOR ME.
I WANT TO KNOW MORE ABOUT MY PAST.
WHAT KIND OF PEOPLE WERE MY REAL MOM AND DAD?
WHY WAS I BORN?
WHY WAS I ABANDONED?
IF ONLY I COULD SEE THOSE THINGS CLEARLY, WITH MY OWN EYES...
...I COULD FINALLY BE RELEASED FROM THE HATRED THAT'S BEEN TYING ME DOWN.
BECAUSE THE SPARKS OF THIS HATRED ARE IN THE PAST.

...AND I COULD HAVE A REAL, HONEST RELATIONSHIP WITH MIYAZAWA.

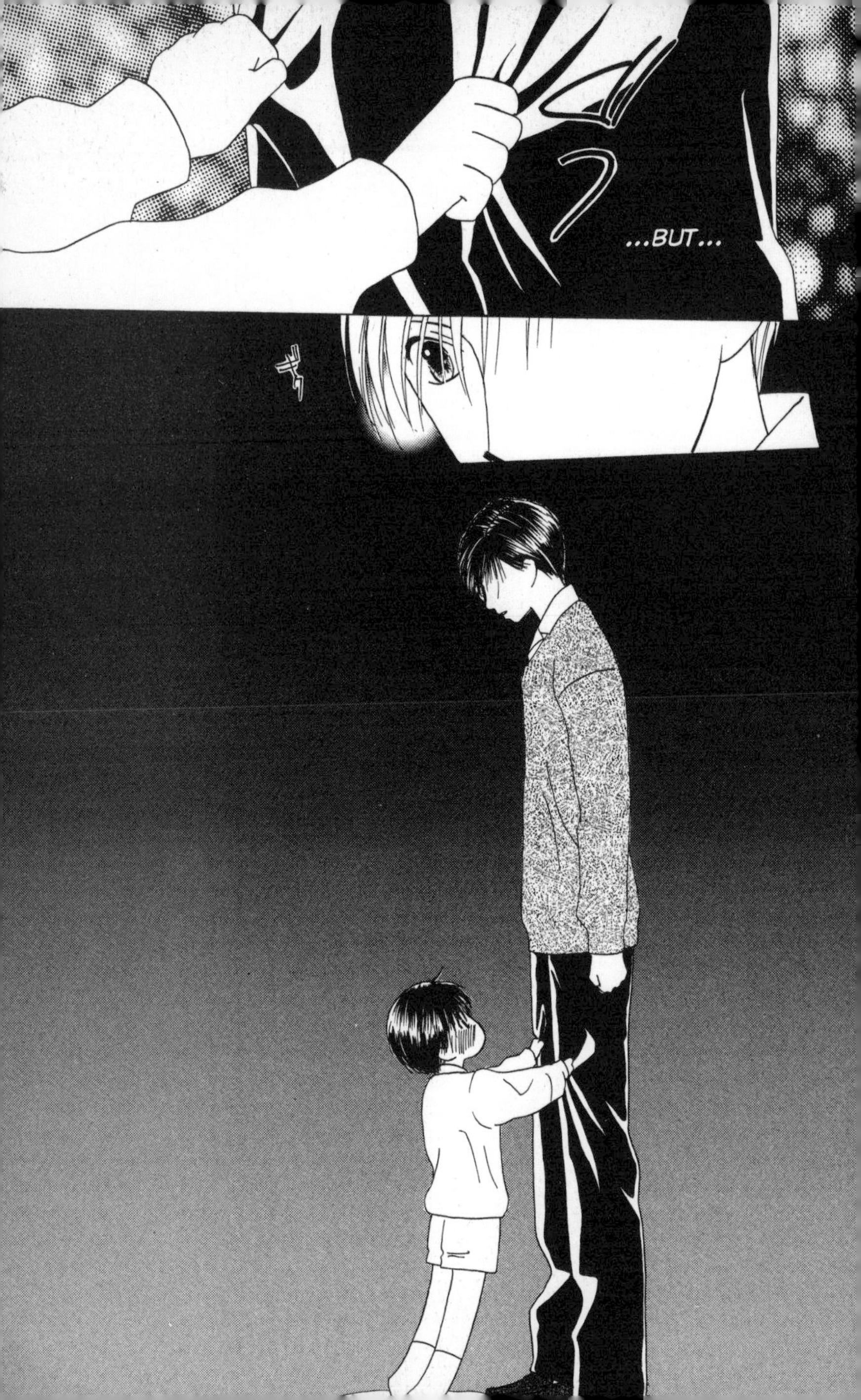
...BUT...

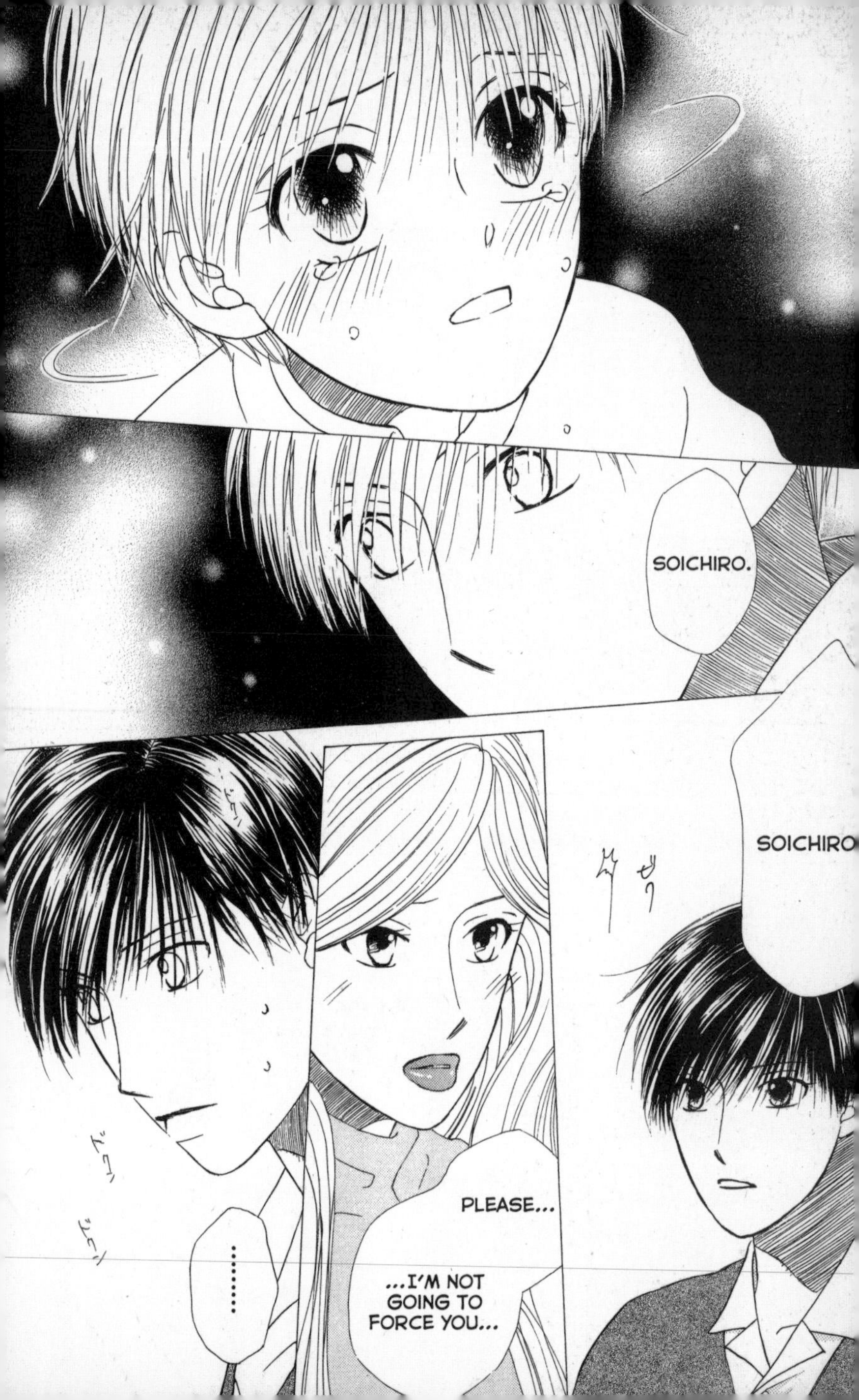
SOICHIRO.
SOICHIRO
PLEASE...
...I'M NOT GOING TO FORCE YOU...
......

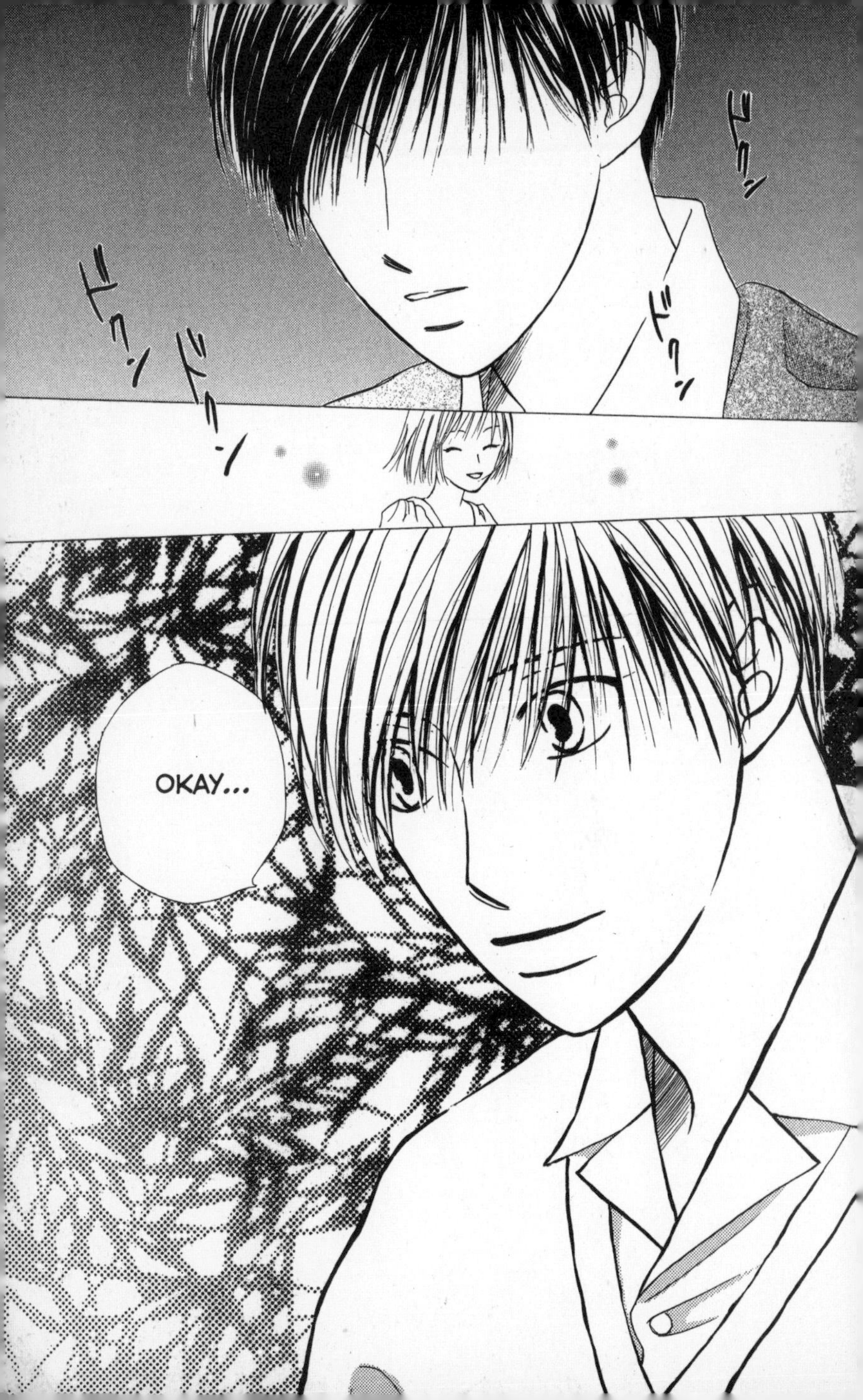
ドクン
ドクン
ドクン
ドクン
OKAY...

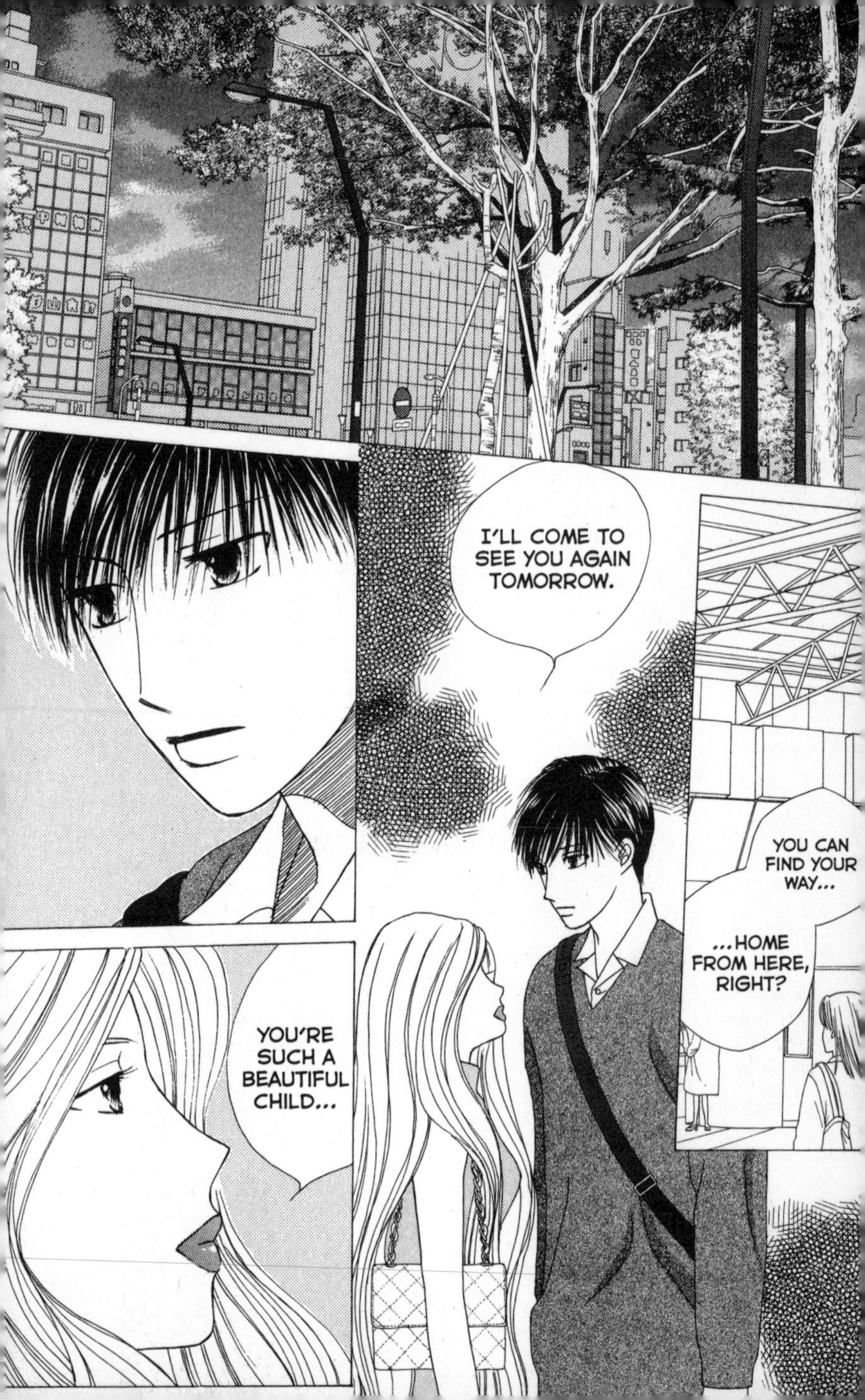
I'LL COME TO SEE YOU AGAIN TOMORROW.
YOU CAN FIND YOUR WAY...
...HOME FROM HERE, RIGHT?
YOU'RE SUCH A BEAUTIFUL CHILD...

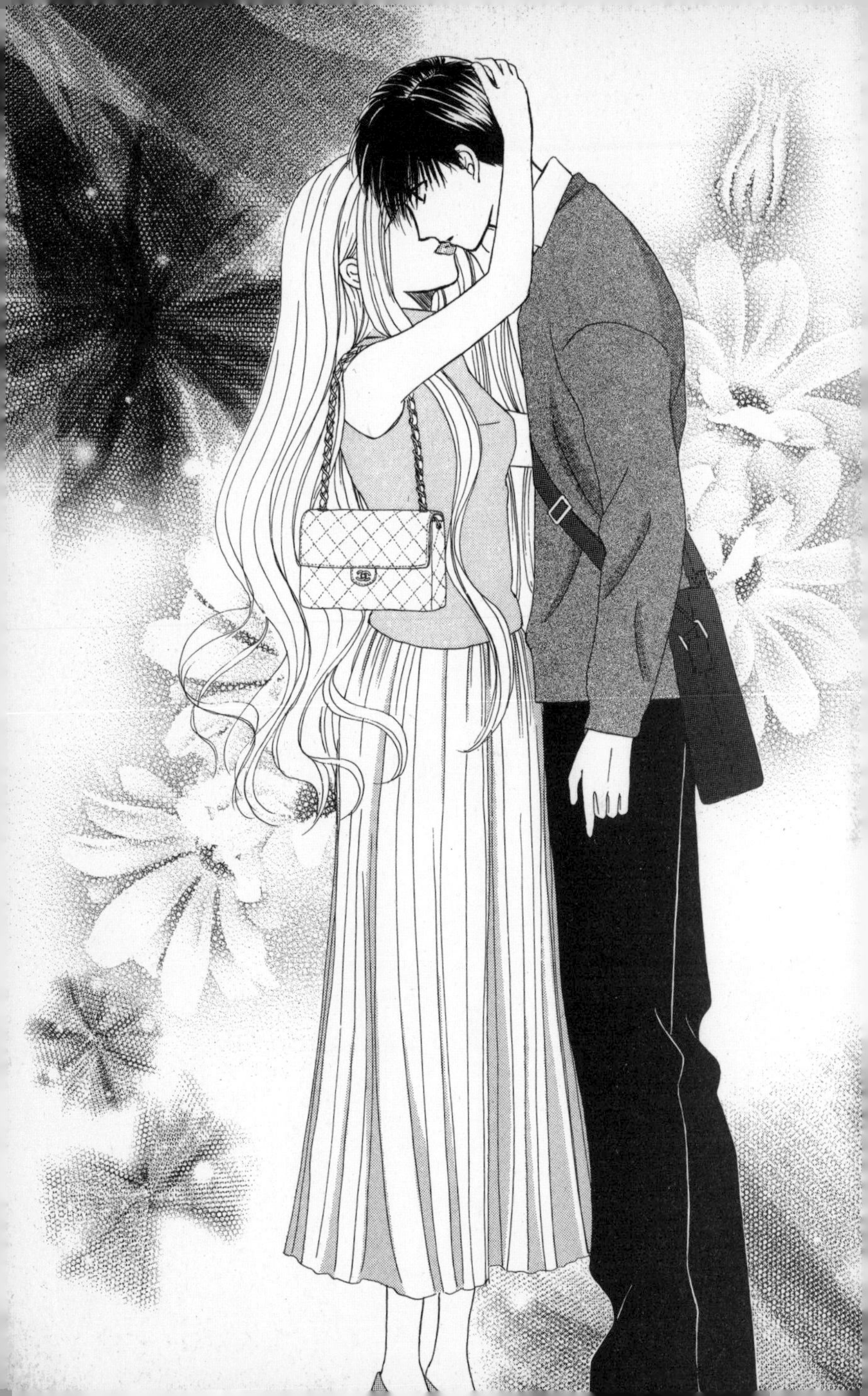

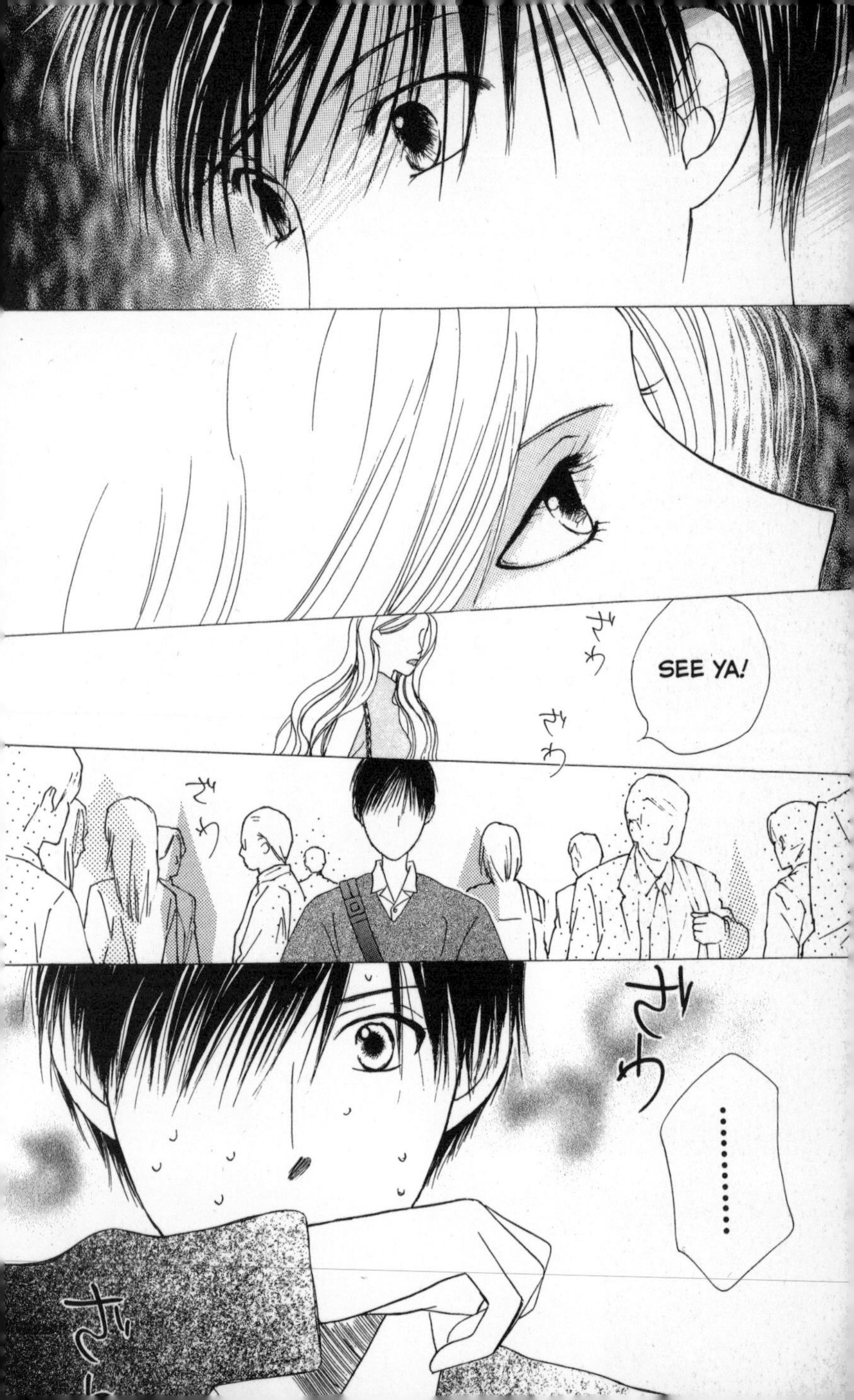
SEE YA!
ざわ
ざわ
ざわ
ざわ
…………

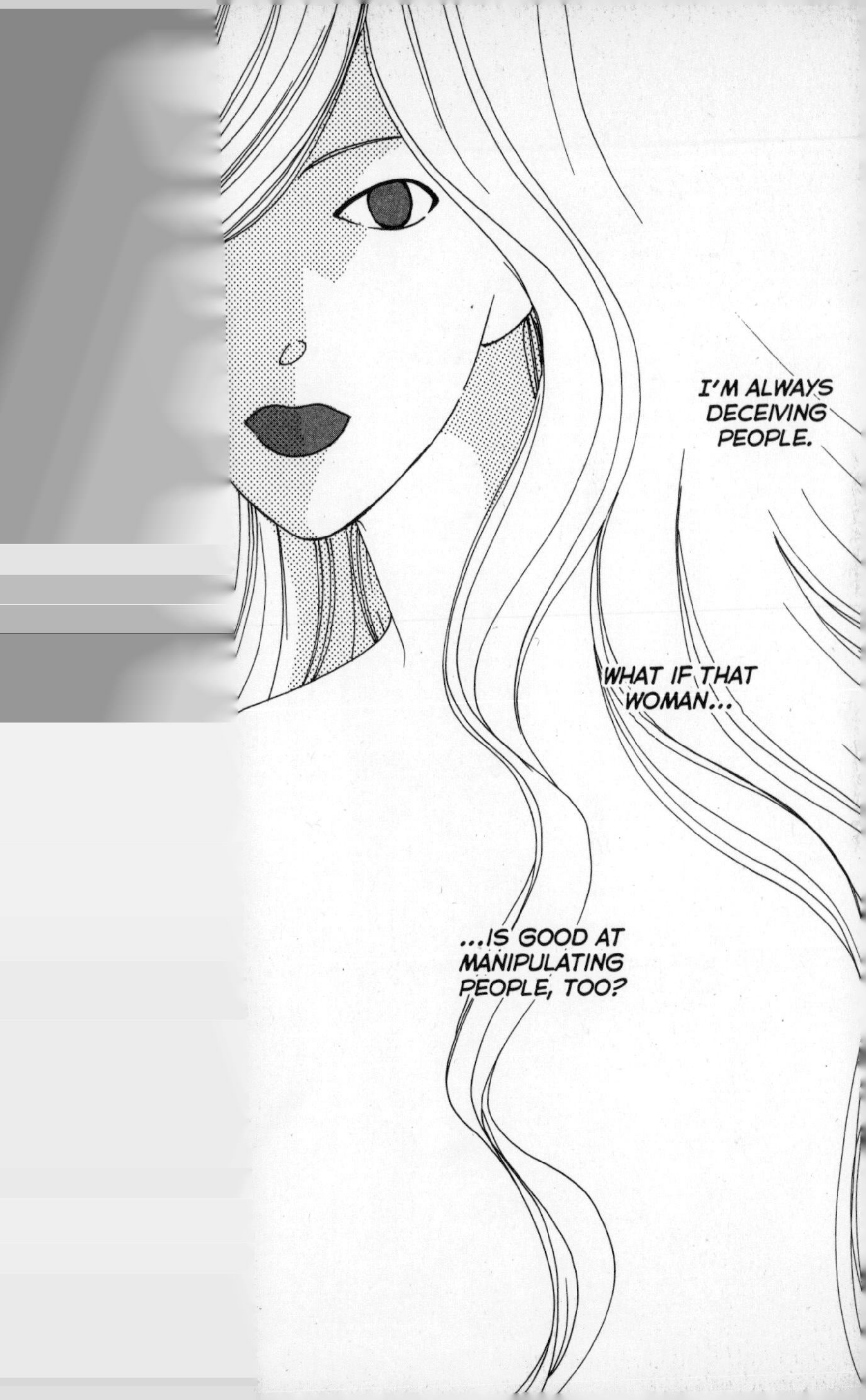
I'M ALWAYS DECEIVING PEOPLE.
WHAT IF THAT WOMAN...
...IS GOOD AT MANIPULATING PEOPLE, TOO?

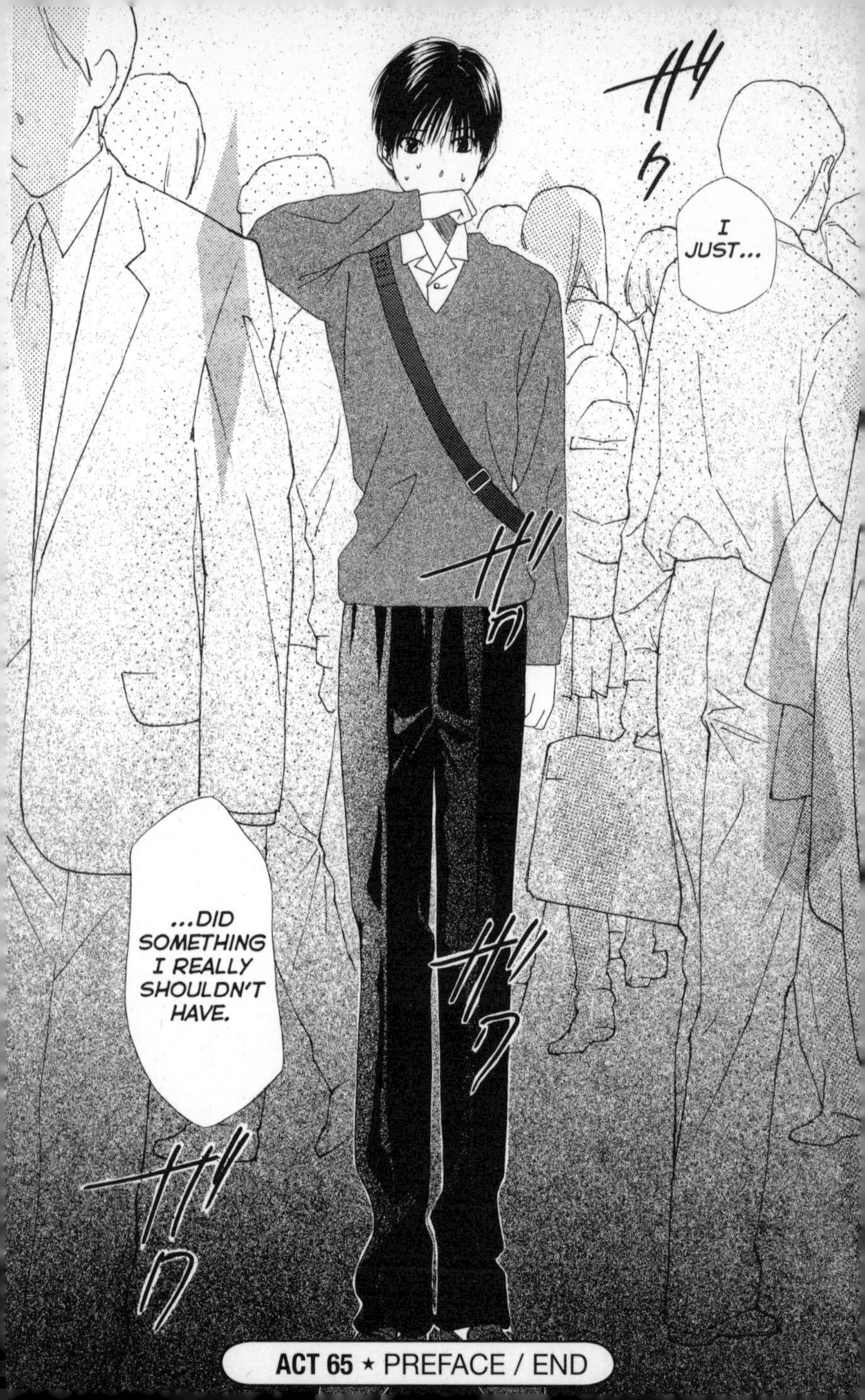
I JUST...
...DID SOMETHING I REALLY SHOULDN'T HAVE.
ACT 65 ★ PREFACE / END

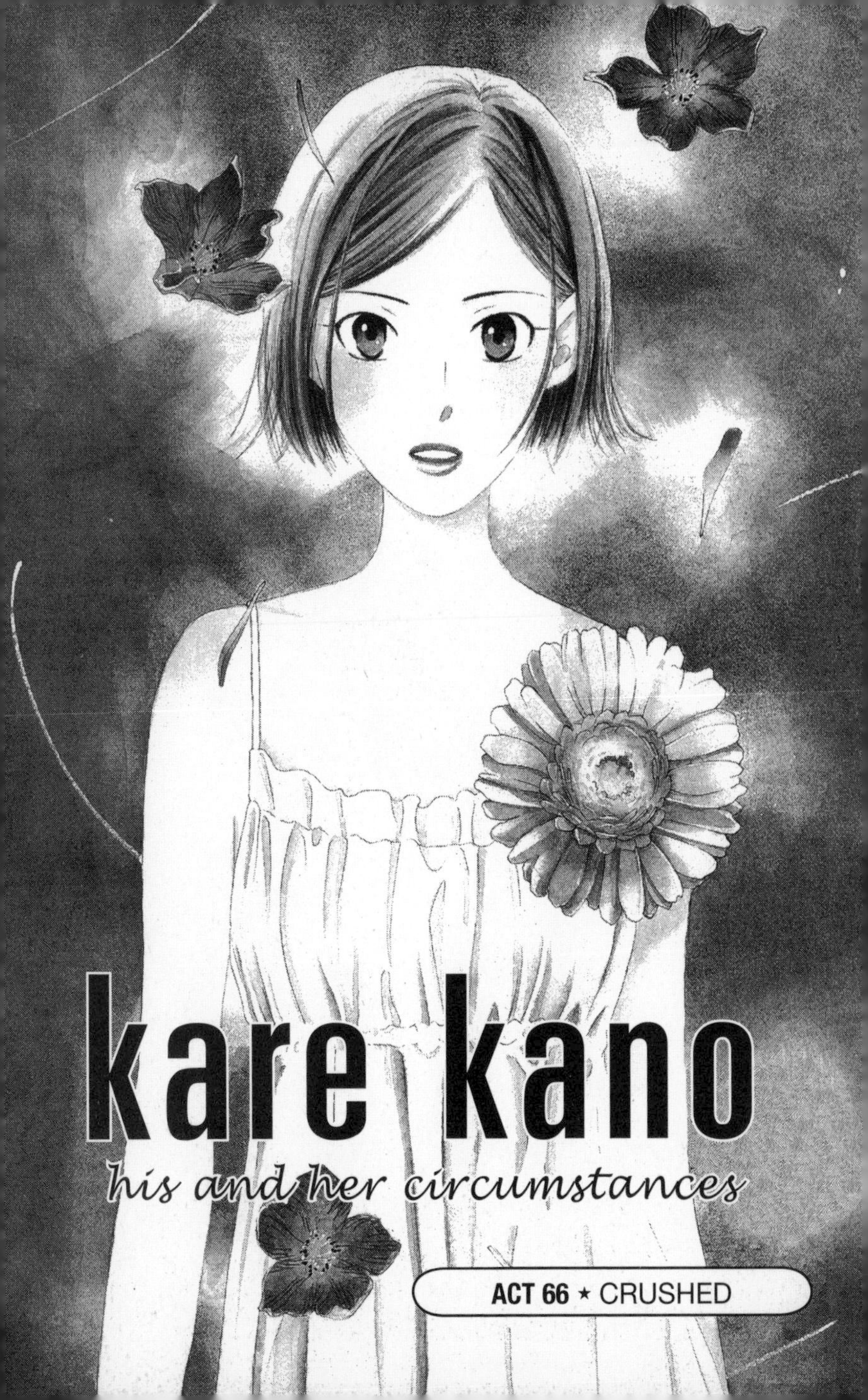
kare kano
his and her circumstances
ACT 66 ★ CRUSHED

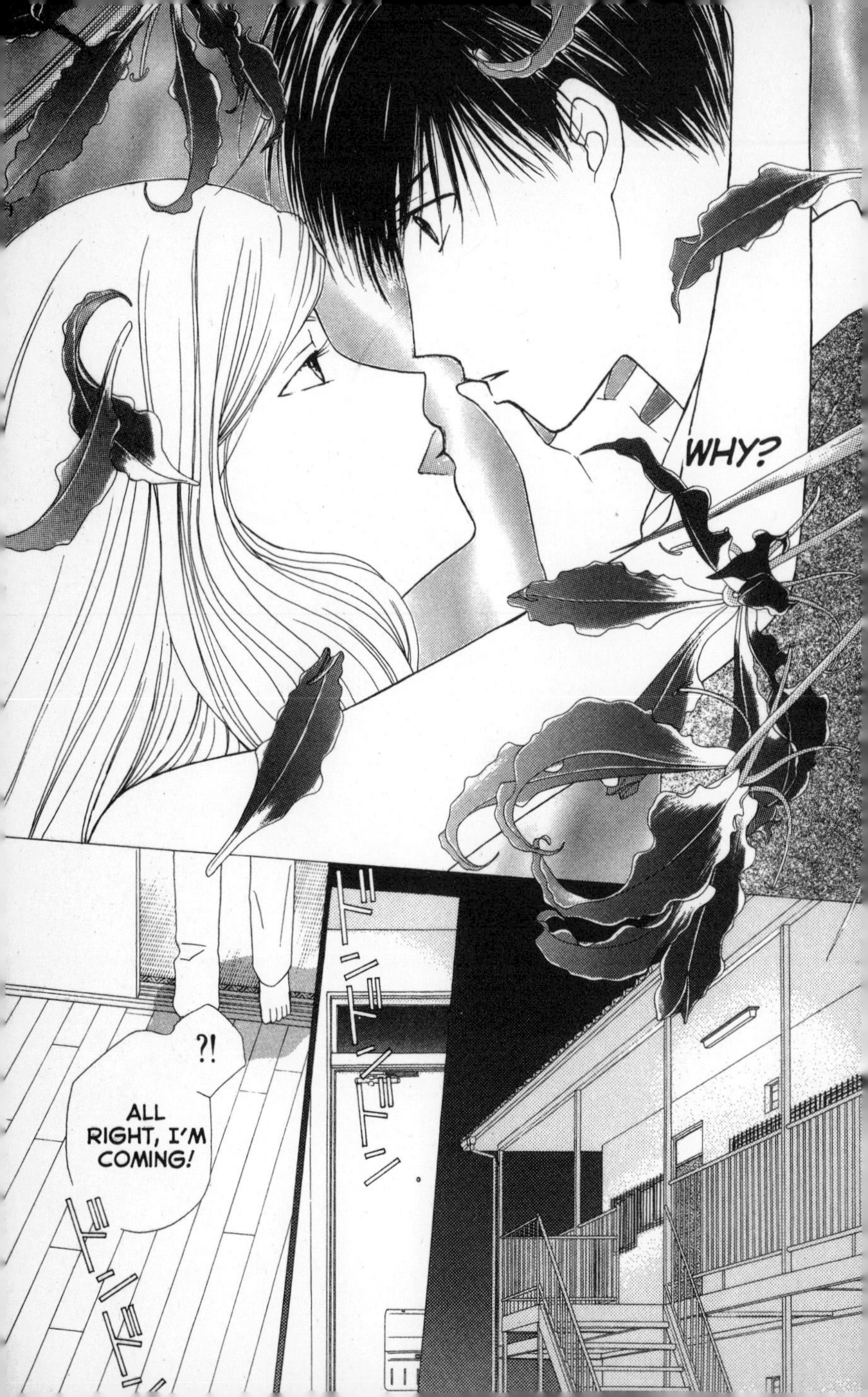
WHY?
?!
ALL RIGHT, I'M COMING!

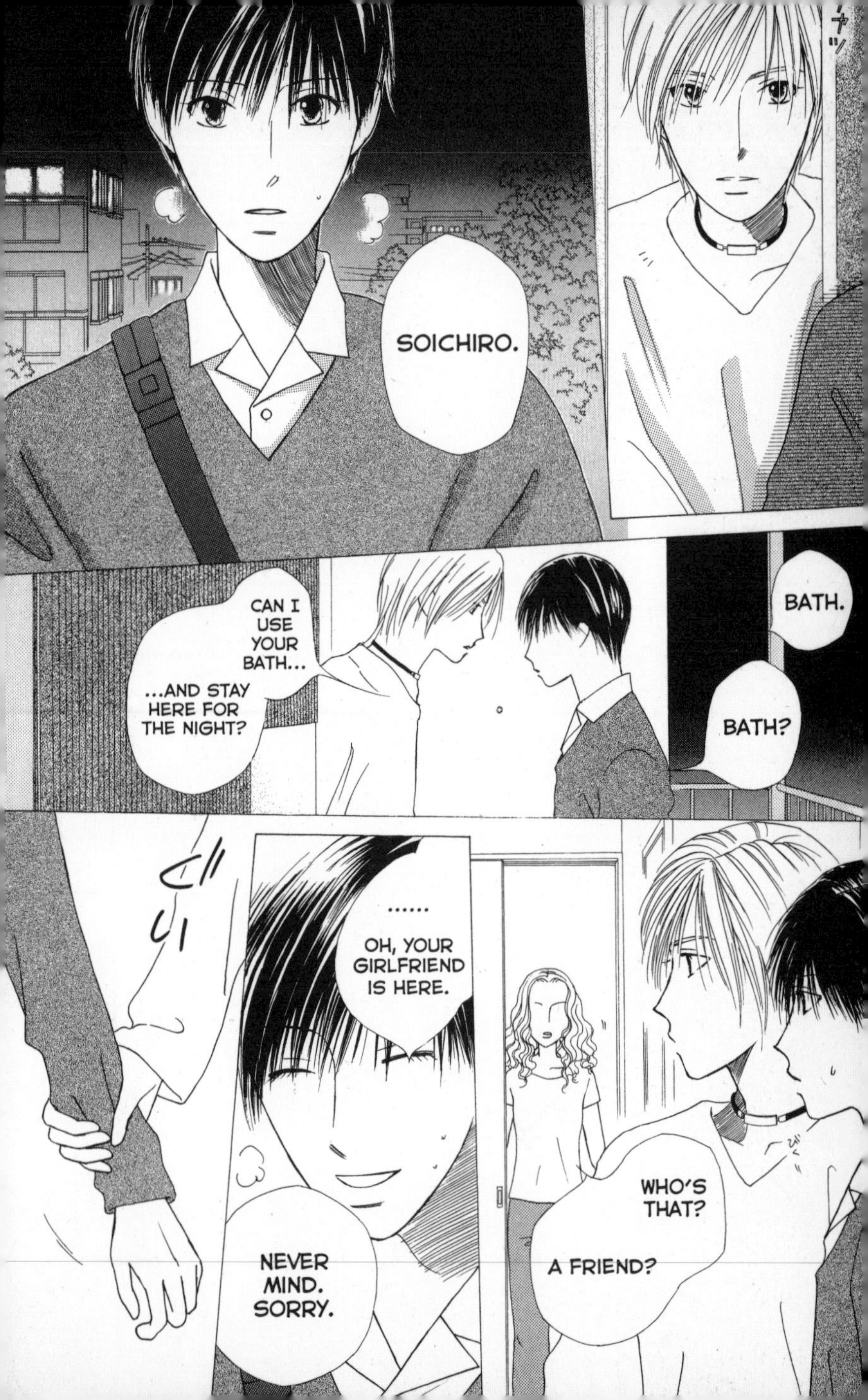
SOICHIRO.
BATH.
BATH?
CAN I USE YOUR BATH...
...AND STAY HERE FOR THE NIGHT?
WHO'S THAT?
A FRIEND?
......
OH, YOUR GIRLFRIEND IS HERE.
NEVER MIND. SORRY.

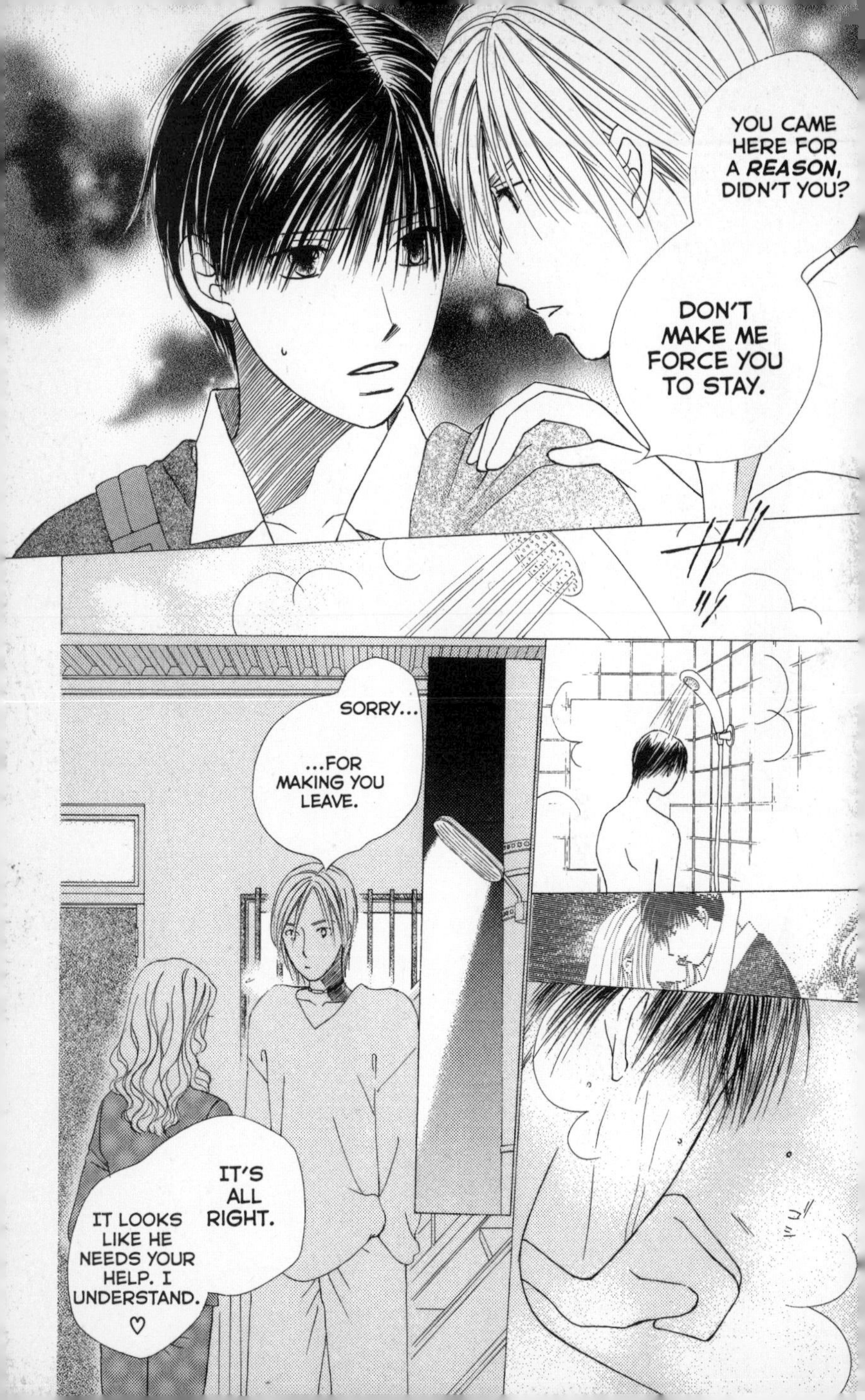
YOU CAME HERE FOR A *REASON*, DIDN'T YOU?
DON'T MAKE ME FORCE YOU TO STAY.
SORRY...
...FOR MAKING YOU LEAVE.
IT'S ALL RIGHT.
IT LOOKS LIKE HE NEEDS YOUR HELP. I UNDERSTAND. ♡

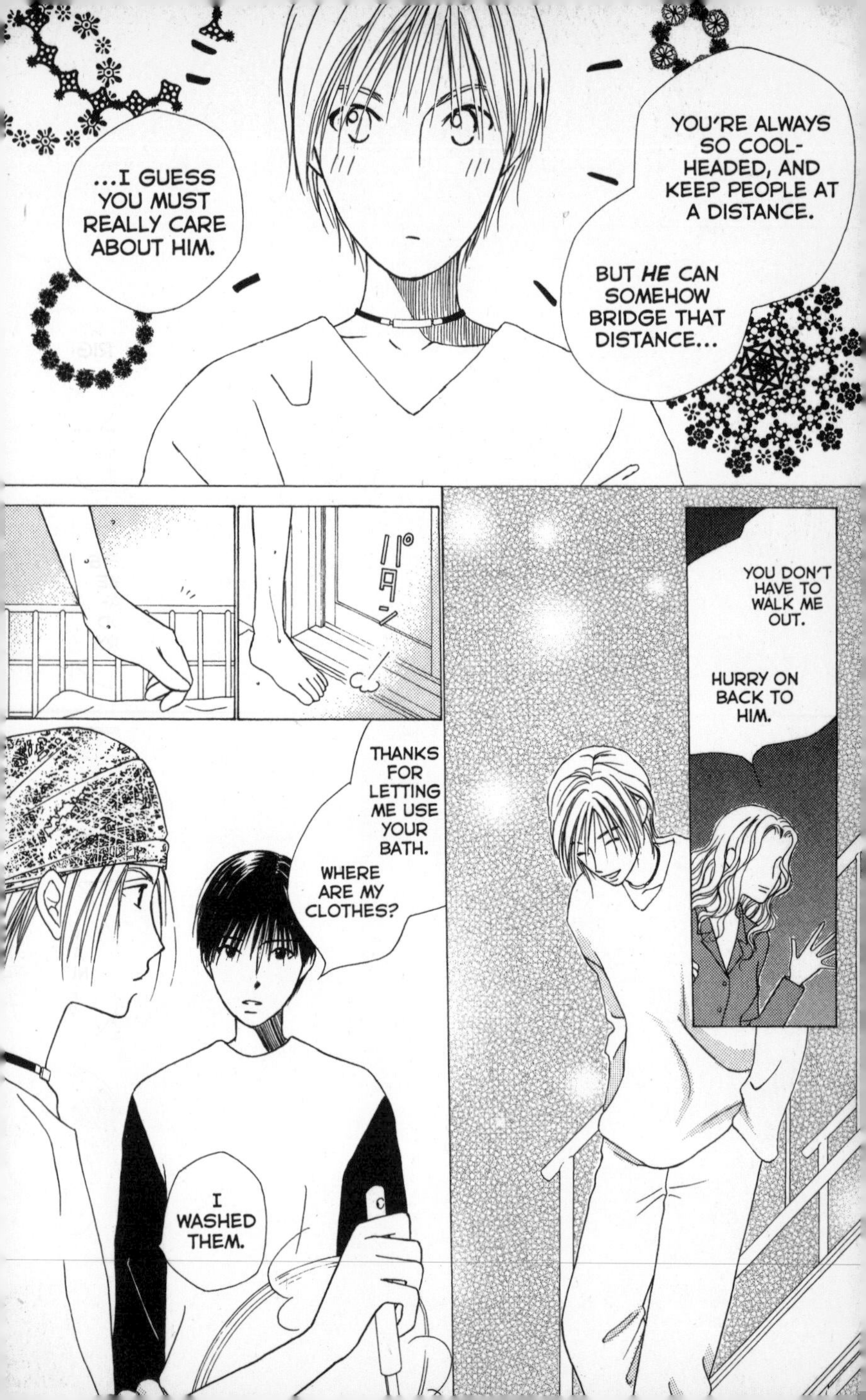
YOU'RE ALWAYS SO COOL-HEADED, AND KEEP PEOPLE AT A DISTANCE.
BUT *HE* CAN SOMEHOW BRIDGE THAT DISTANCE...
...I GUESS YOU MUST REALLY CARE ABOUT HIM.
YOU DON'T HAVE TO WALK ME OUT.
HURRY ON BACK TO HIM.
パタン
THANKS FOR LETTING ME USE YOUR BATH.
WHERE ARE MY CLOTHES?
I WASHED THEM.

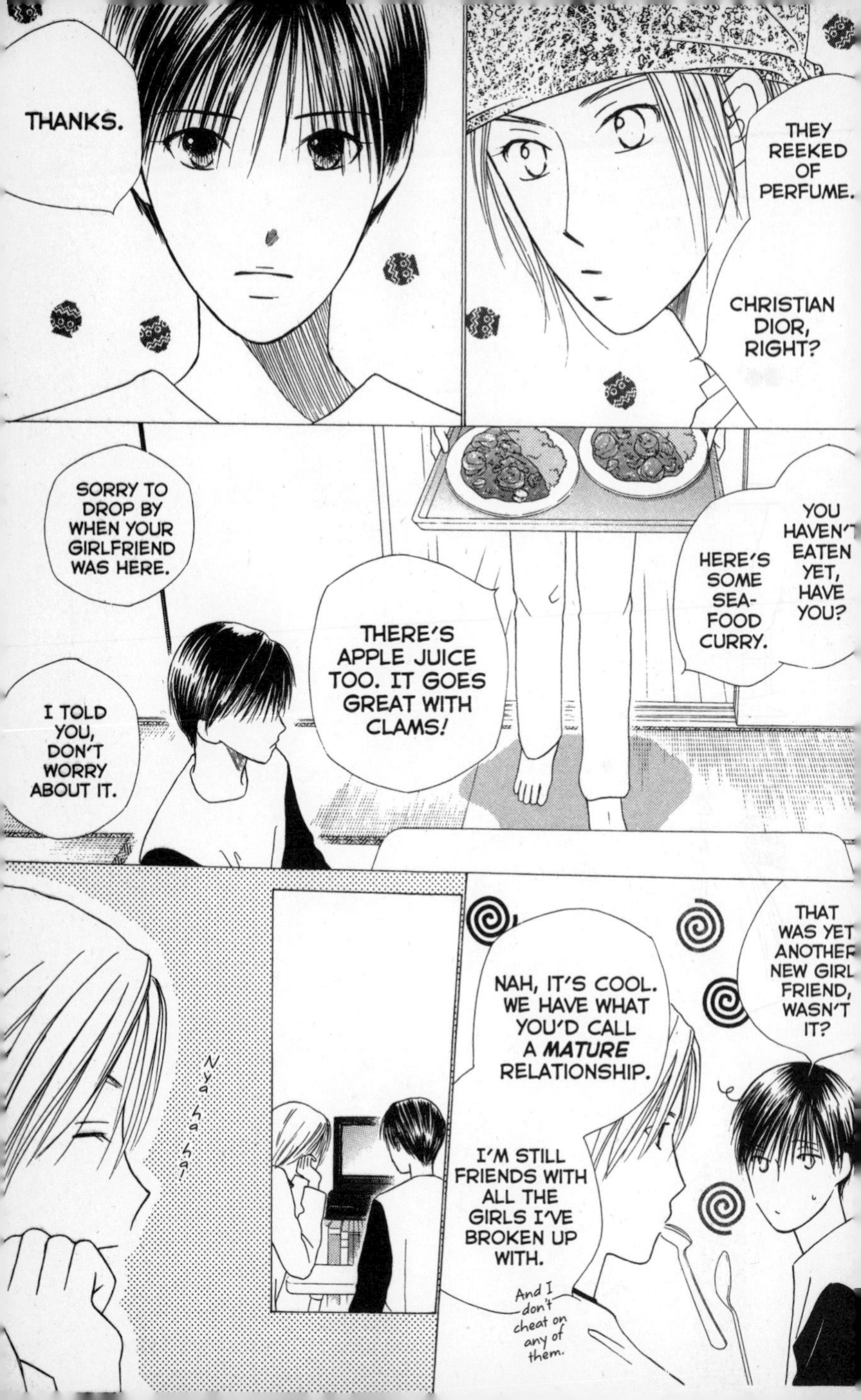
THEY REEKED OF PERFUME.
CHRISTIAN DIOR, RIGHT?
THANKS.
YOU HAVEN'T EATEN YET, HAVE YOU?
HERE'S SOME SEA-FOOD CURRY.
THERE'S APPLE JUICE TOO. IT GOES GREAT WITH CLAMS!
SORRY TO DROP BY WHEN YOUR GIRLFRIEND WAS HERE.
I TOLD YOU, DON'T WORRY ABOUT IT.
THAT WAS YET ANOTHER NEW GIRL FRIEND, WASN'T IT?
NAH, IT'S COOL. WE HAVE WHAT YOU'D CALL A *MATURE* RELATIONSHIP.
I'M STILL FRIENDS WITH ALL THE GIRLS I'VE BROKEN UP WITH.
And I don't cheat on any of them.
Nya ha ha ha

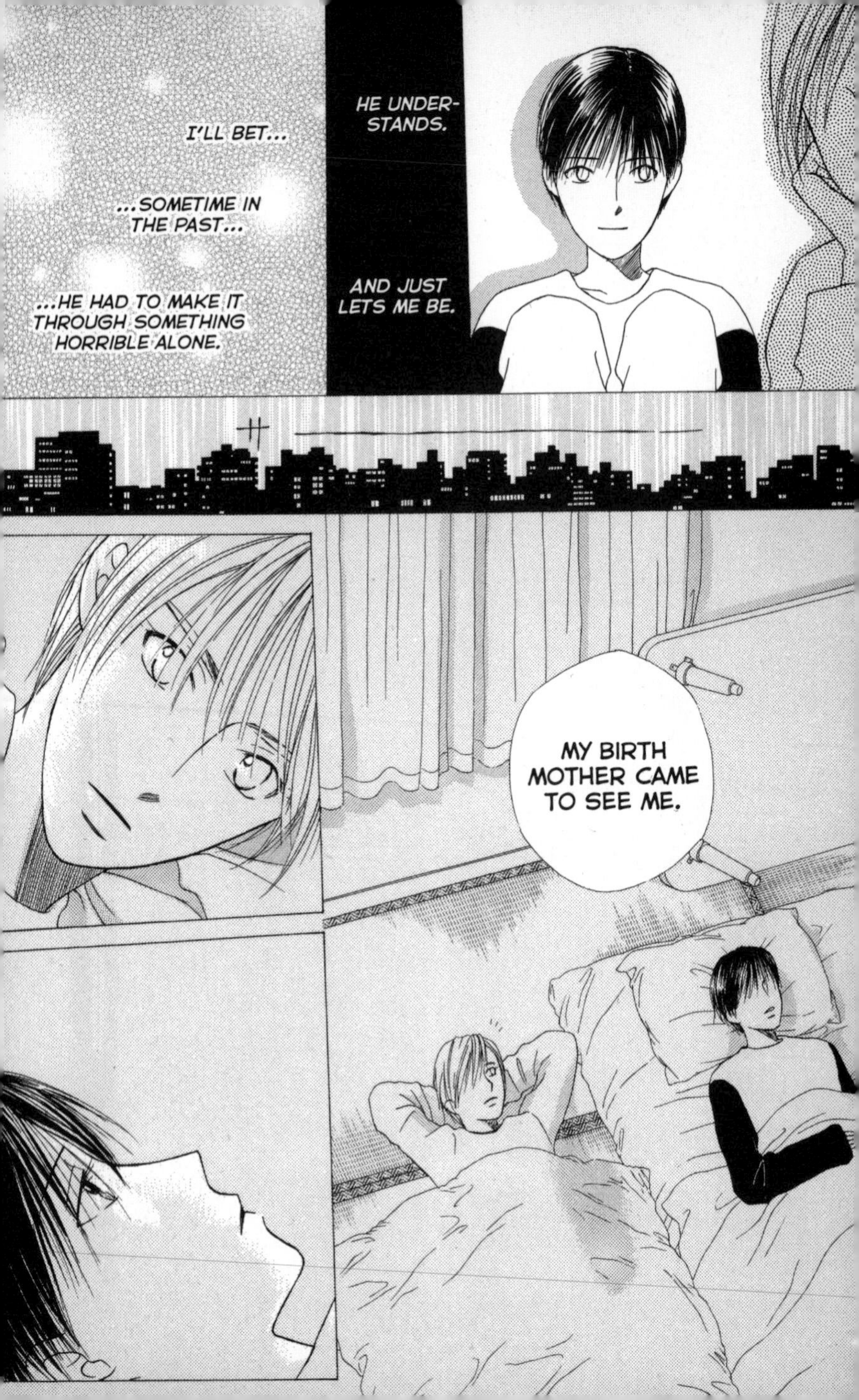
HE UNDER-STANDS.
AND JUST LETS ME BE.
I'LL BET...
...SOMETIME IN THE PAST...
...HE HAD TO MAKE IT THROUGH SOMETHING HORRIBLE ALONE.
MY BIRTH MOTHER CAME TO SEE ME.

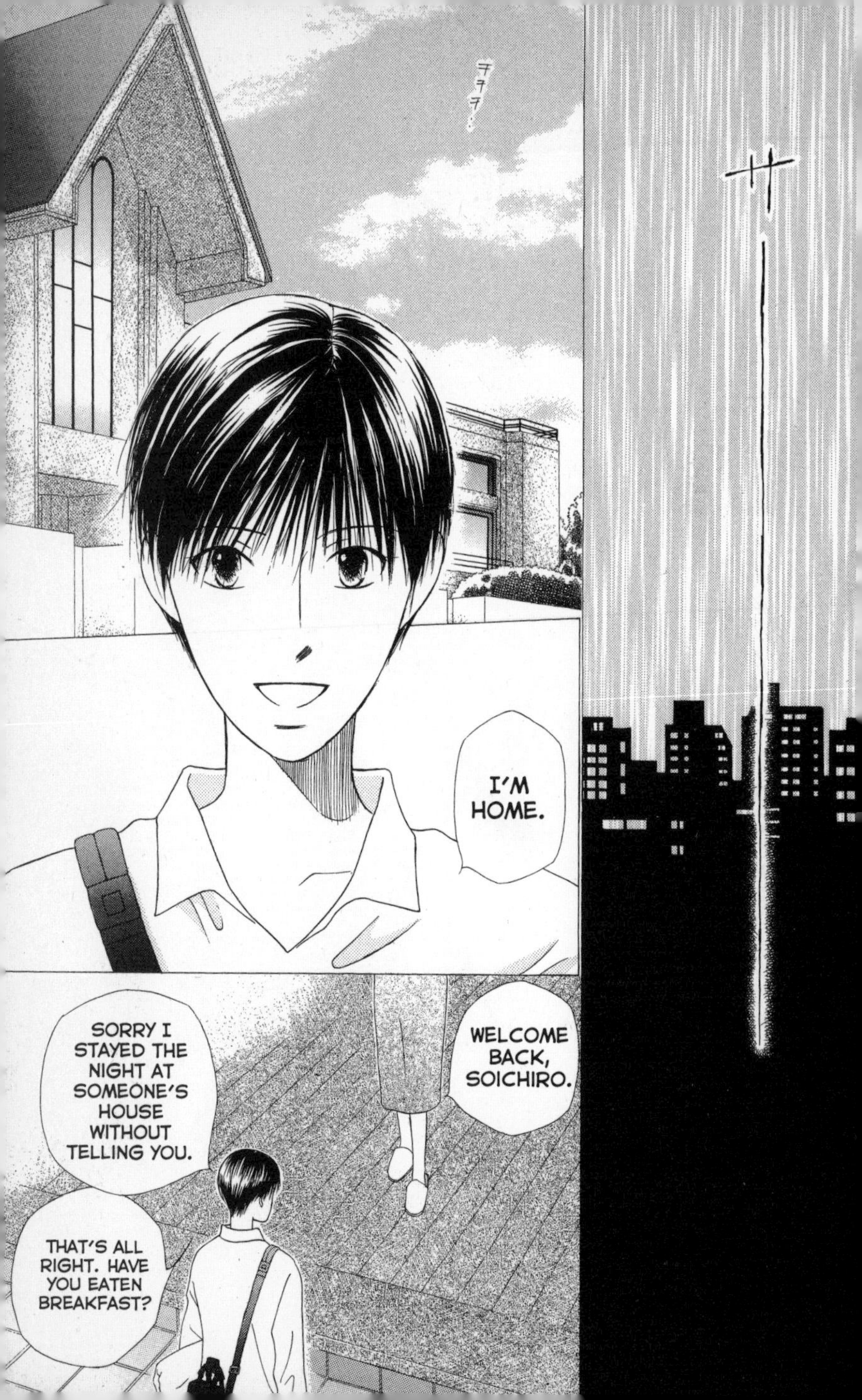
I'M HOME.
WELCOME BACK, SOICHIRO.
SORRY I STAYED THE NIGHT AT SOMEONE'S HOUSE WITHOUT TELLING YOU.
THAT'S ALL RIGHT. HAVE YOU EATEN BREAKFAST?

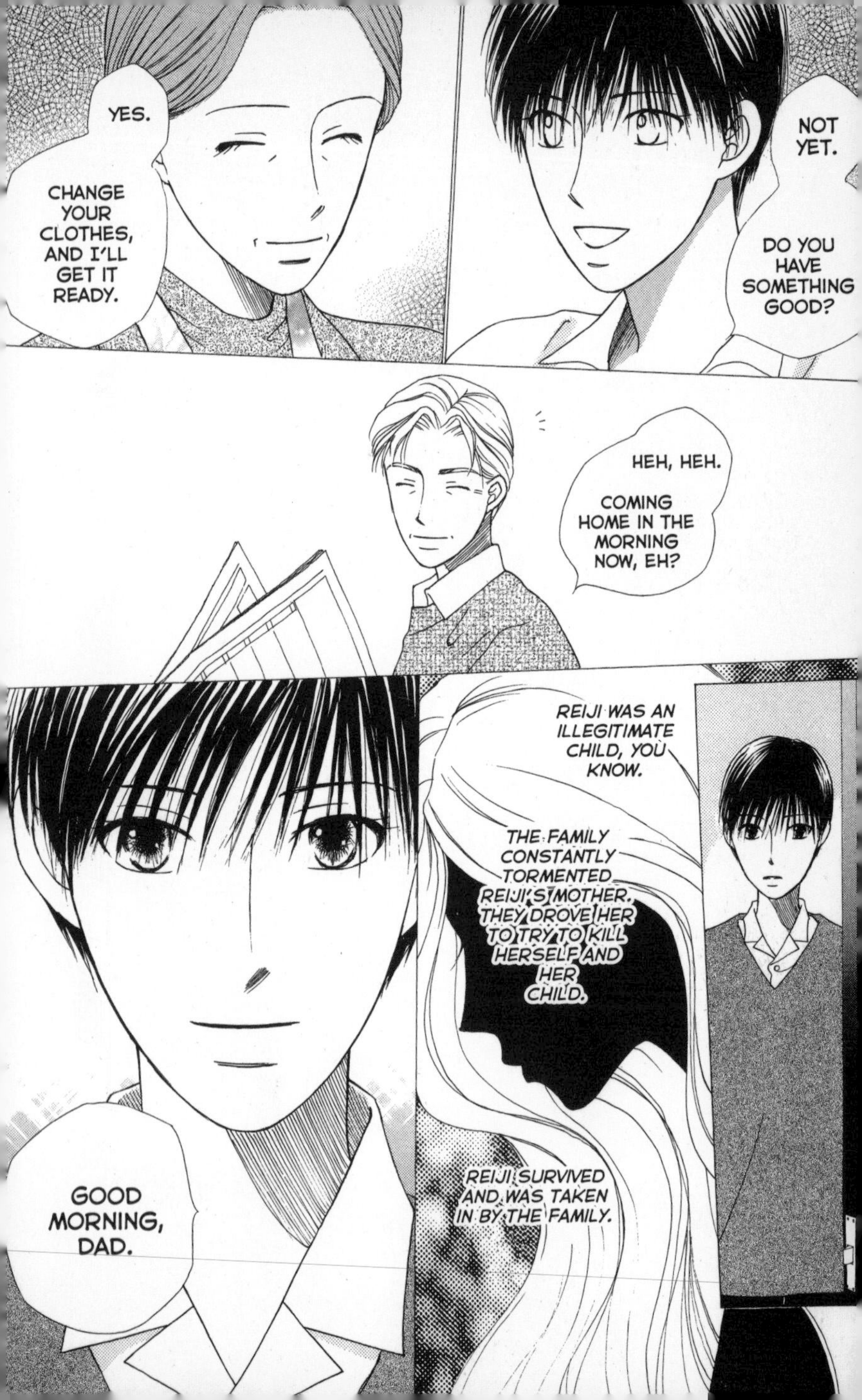
NOT YET.
DO YOU HAVE SOMETHING GOOD?
YES.
CHANGE YOUR CLOTHES, AND I'LL GET IT READY.
HEH, HEH.
COMING HOME IN THE MORNING NOW, EH?
REIJI WAS AN ILLEGITIMATE CHILD, YOU KNOW.
THE FAMILY CONSTANTLY TORMENTED REIJI'S MOTHER. THEY DROVE HER TO TRY TO KILL HERSELF AND HER CHILD.
REIJI SURVIVED AND WAS TAKEN IN BY THE FAMILY.
GOOD MORNING, DAD.

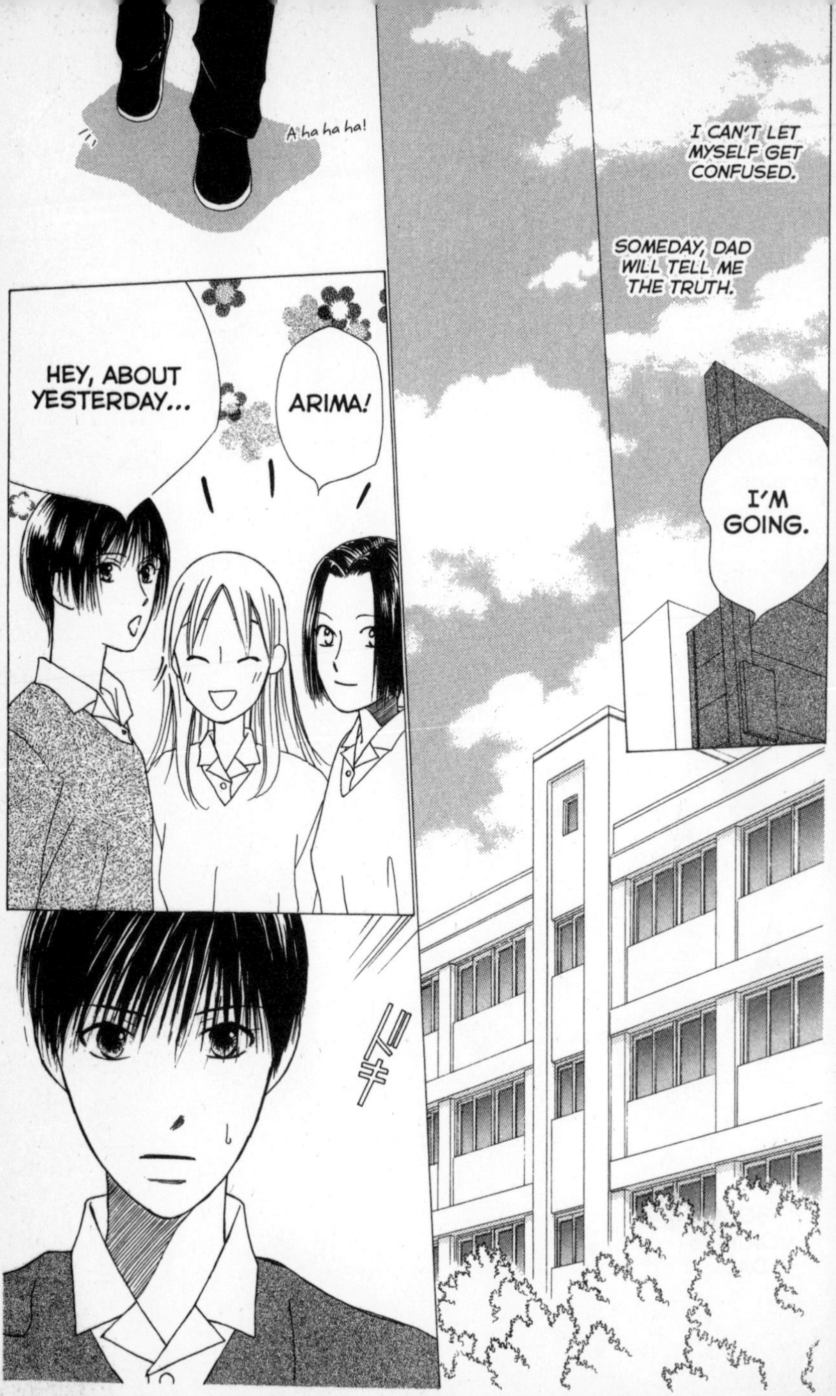
I CAN'T LET MYSELF GET CONFUSED.
SOMEDAY, DAD WILL TELL ME THE TRUTH.
I'M GOING.
A ha ha ha!
ARIMA!
HEY, ABOUT YESTERDAY...

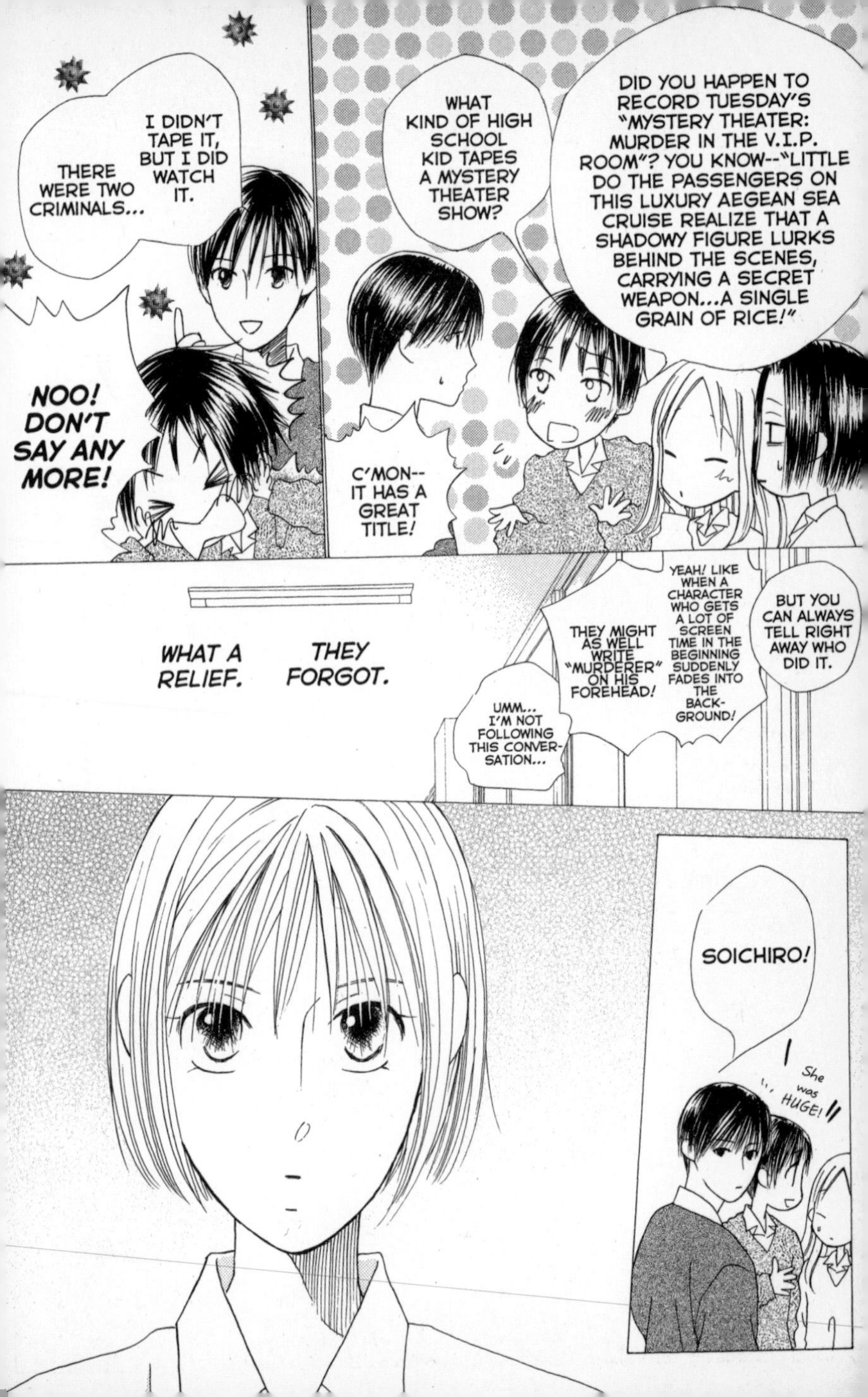
DID YOU HAPPEN TO RECORD TUESDAY'S "MYSTERY THEATER: MURDER IN THE V.I.P. ROOM"? YOU KNOW--"LITTLE DO THE PASSENGERS ON THIS LUXURY AEGEAN SEA CRUISE REALIZE THAT A SHADOWY FIGURE LURKS BEHIND THE SCENES, CARRYING A SECRET WEAPON...A SINGLE GRAIN OF RICE!"
WHAT KIND OF HIGH SCHOOL KID TAPES A MYSTERY THEATER SHOW?
C'MON-- IT HAS A GREAT TITLE!
I DIDN'T TAPE IT, BUT I DID WATCH IT.
THERE WERE TWO CRIMINALS...
NOO! DON'T SAY ANY MORE!
BUT YOU CAN ALWAYS TELL RIGHT AWAY WHO DID IT.
YEAH! LIKE WHEN A CHARACTER WHO GETS A LOT OF SCREEN TIME IN THE BEGINNING SUDDENLY FADES INTO THE BACK-GROUND!
THEY MIGHT AS WELL WRITE "MURDERER" ON HIS FOREHEAD!
UMM... I'M NOT FOLLOWING THIS CONVER-SATION...
THEY FORGOT.
WHAT A RELIEF.
SOICHIRO!
She was HUGE!

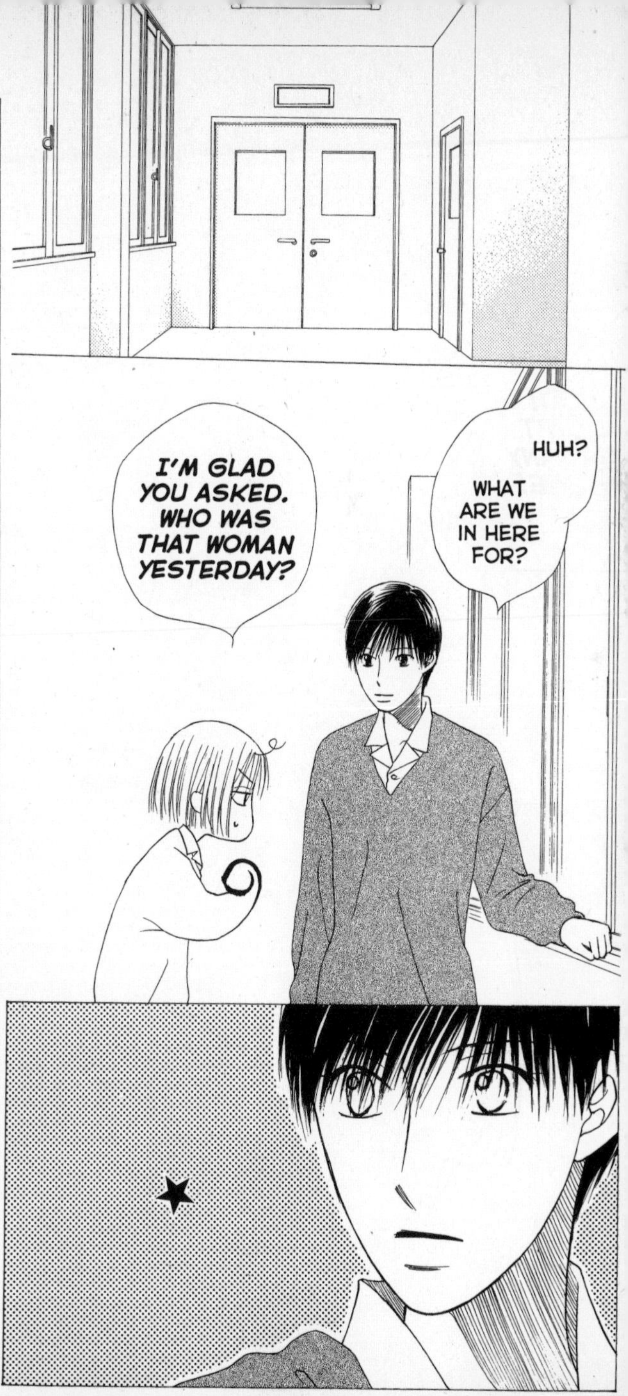
HUH?
WHAT ARE WE IN HERE FOR?
I'M GLAD YOU ASKED. WHO WAS THAT WOMAN YESTERDAY?

3

Kyoto.

I went there again. My eighth trip already! This time I went to the southern part.

I visited Fushimi Inari Taisha, Teradaya, and Uji.

I also stopped by Gekkeikan's Ogura Memorial Hall, which is close to Teradaya... but it was closed, so I couldn't get in. Aww...I wanted to taste some sake. But the river behind it was gorgeous! I almost wanted to live there!

Uji was great, too. I was eyeing the Uwaji tea-flavored soft ice cream and tea dumplings there...but I'm on a diet!

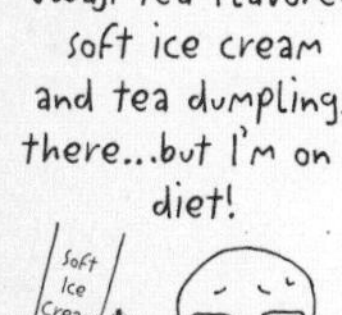
Soft Ice Cream

I also went to the museum of "The Tale of Genji." I might go to Kyoto again next year...but I think I'll focus on Nara.

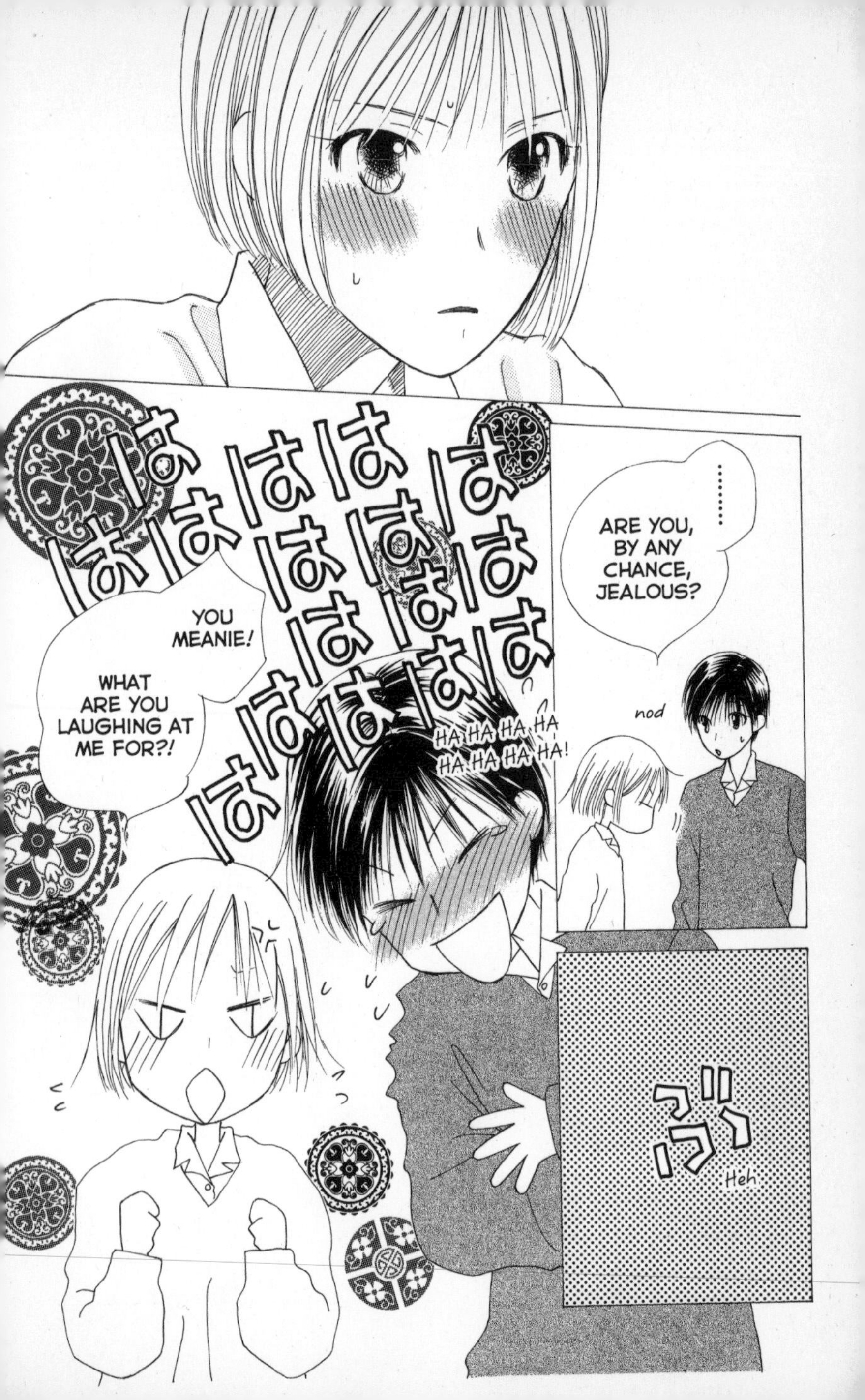

……
ARE YOU, BY ANY CHANCE, JEALOUS?
nod
Heh
HA HA HA HA HA HA HA HA!
YOU MEANIE!
WHAT ARE YOU LAUGHING AT ME FOR?!

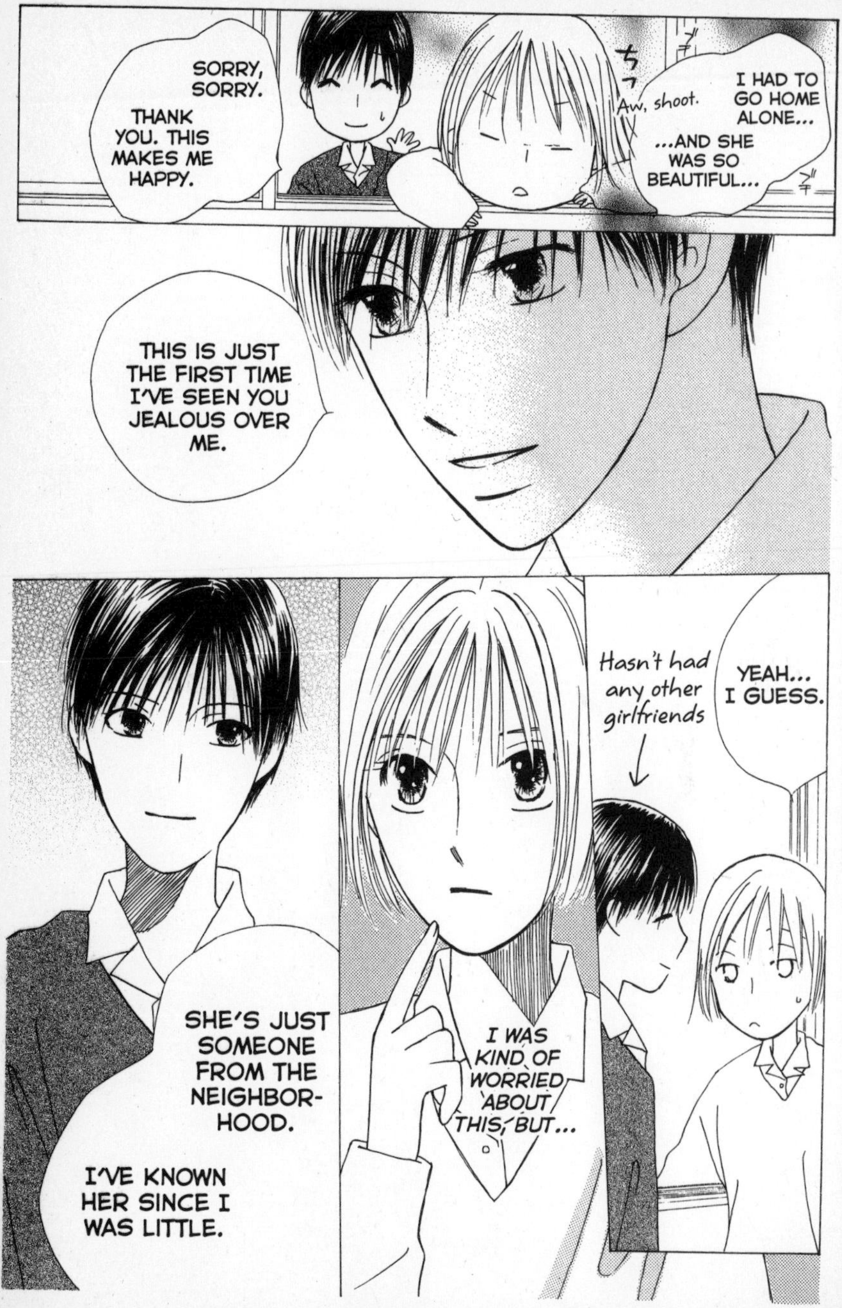
I HAD TO GO HOME ALONE...
...AND SHE WAS SO BEAUTIFUL...
Aw, shoot.
SORRY, SORRY.
THANK YOU. THIS MAKES ME HAPPY.
THIS IS JUST THE FIRST TIME I'VE SEEN YOU JEALOUS OVER ME.
YEAH... I GUESS.
Hasn't had any other girlfriends
I WAS KIND OF WORRIED ABOUT THIS, BUT...
SHE'S JUST SOMEONE FROM THE NEIGHBOR-HOOD.
I'VE KNOWN HER SINCE I WAS LITTLE.

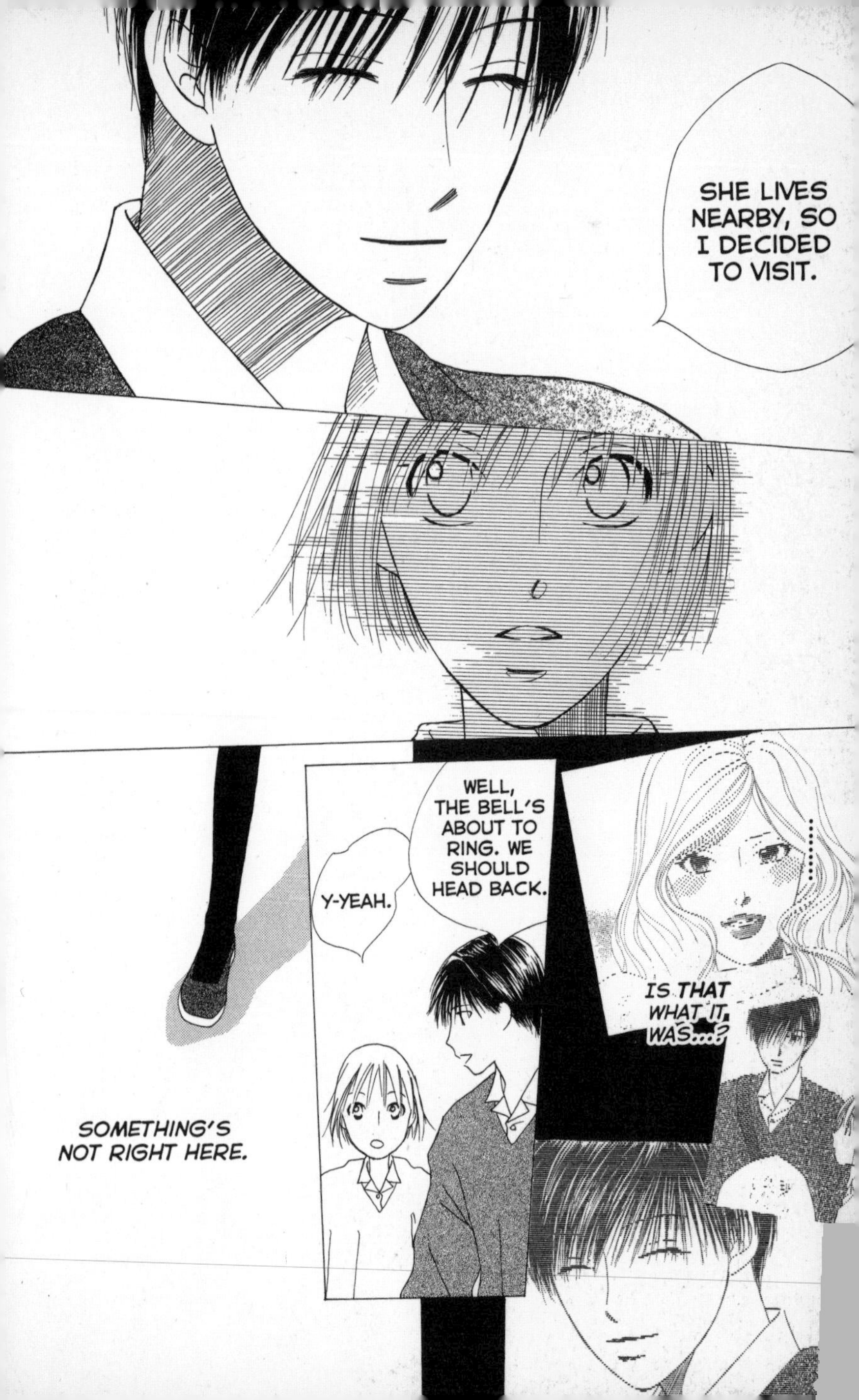
SHE LIVES NEARBY, SO I DECIDED TO VISIT.
......
IS THAT WHAT IT WAS...?
WELL, THE BELL'S ABOUT TO RING. WE SHOULD HEAD BACK.
Y-YEAH.
SOMETHING'S NOT RIGHT HERE.

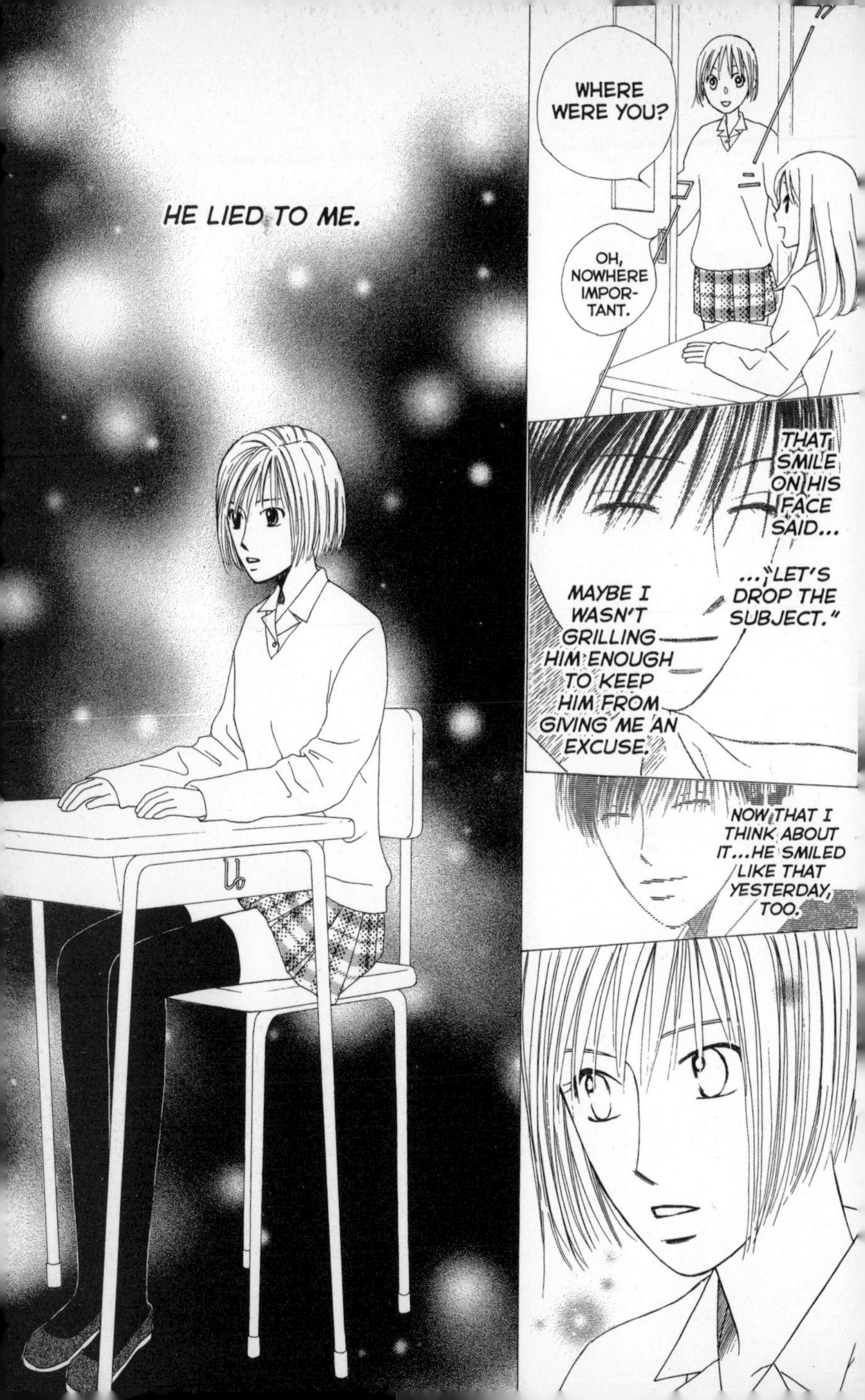
WHERE WERE YOU?
OH, NOWHERE IMPOR-TANT.
THAT SMILE ON HIS FACE SAID...
..."LET'S DROP THE SUBJECT."
MAYBE I WASN'T GRILLING HIM ENOUGH TO KEEP HIM FROM GIVING ME AN EXCUSE.
NOW THAT I THINK ABOUT IT...HE SMILED LIKE THAT YESTERDAY, TOO.
HE LIED TO ME.

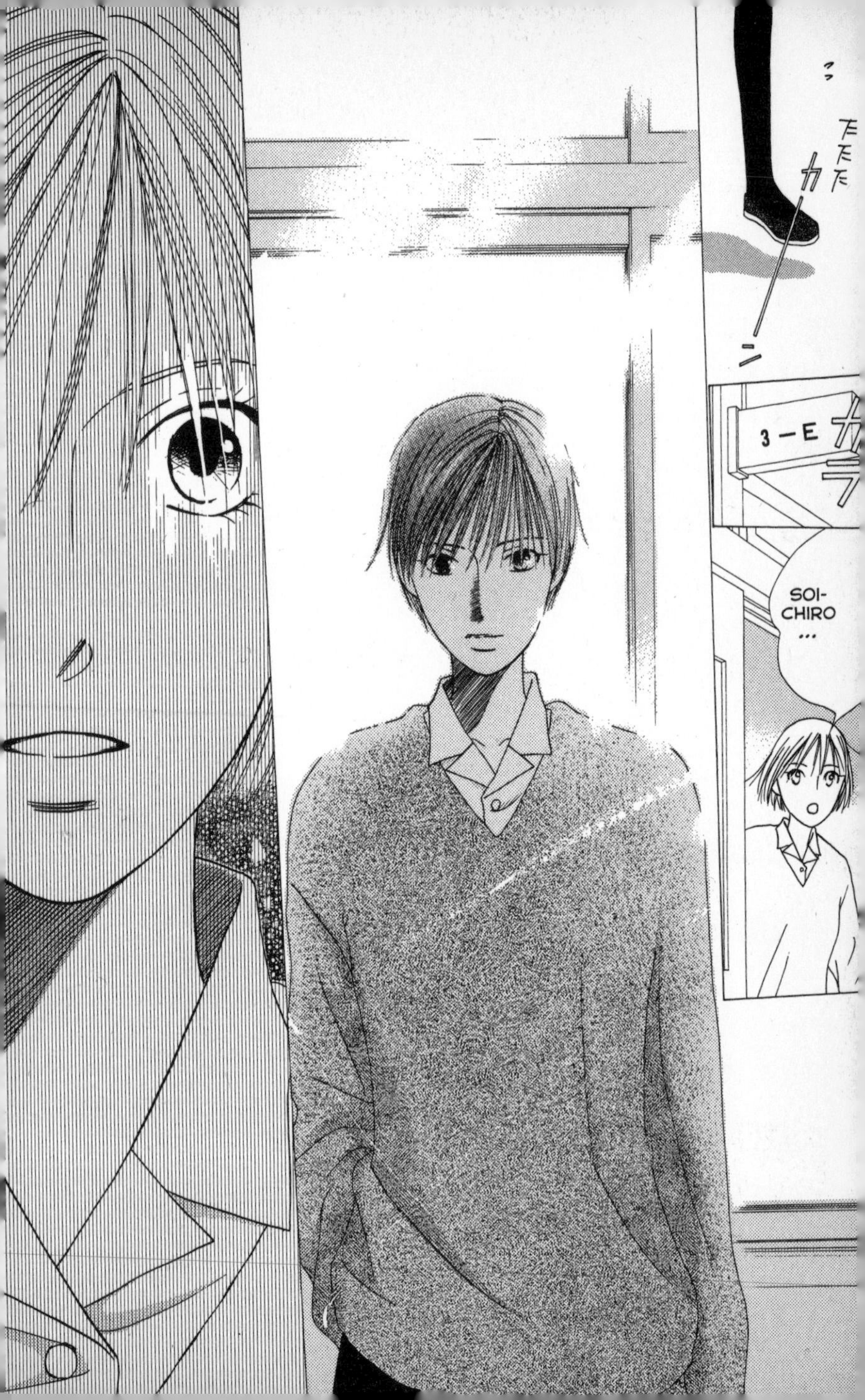
タタタ
カーン
3-E
ガラ
SOI-CHIRO ...

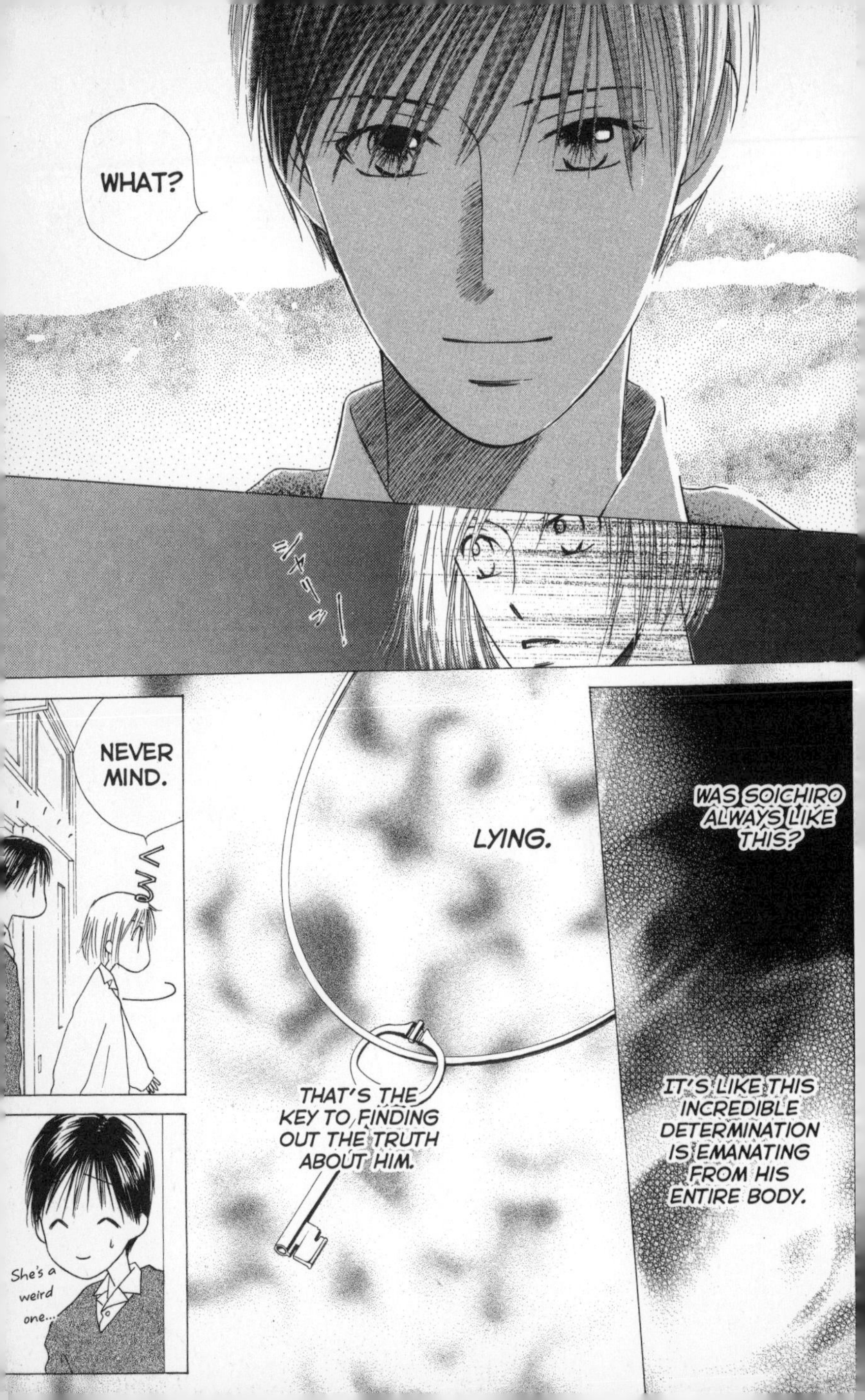
WHAT?
WAS SOICHIRO ALWAYS LIKE THIS?
IT'S LIKE THIS INCREDIBLE DETERMINATION IS EMANATING FROM HIS ENTIRE BODY.
LYING.
THAT'S THE KEY TO FINDING OUT THE TRUTH ABOUT HIM.
NEVER MIND.
She's a weird one...

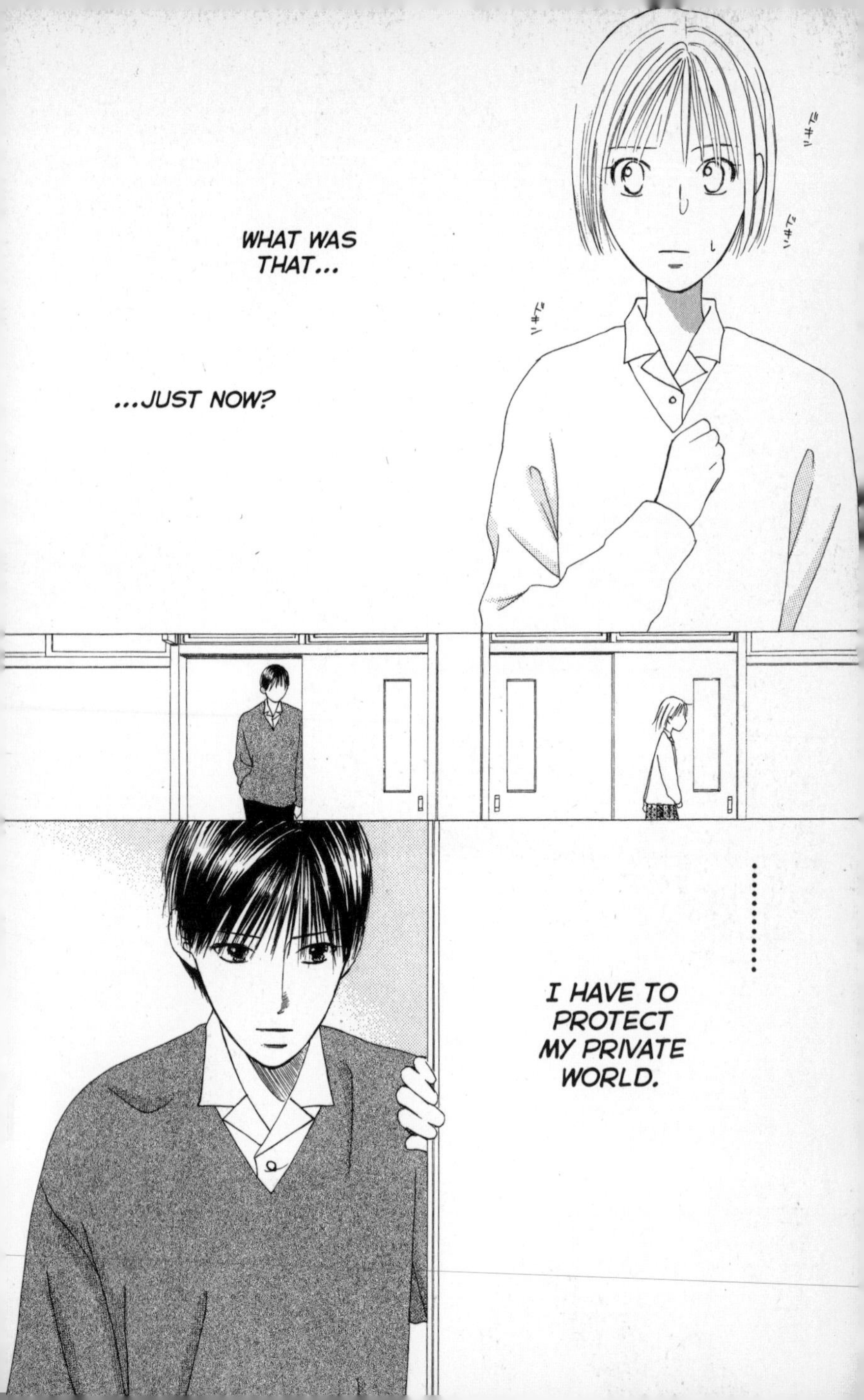
WHAT WAS THAT...
...JUST NOW?
....
I HAVE TO PROTECT MY PRIVATE WORLD.

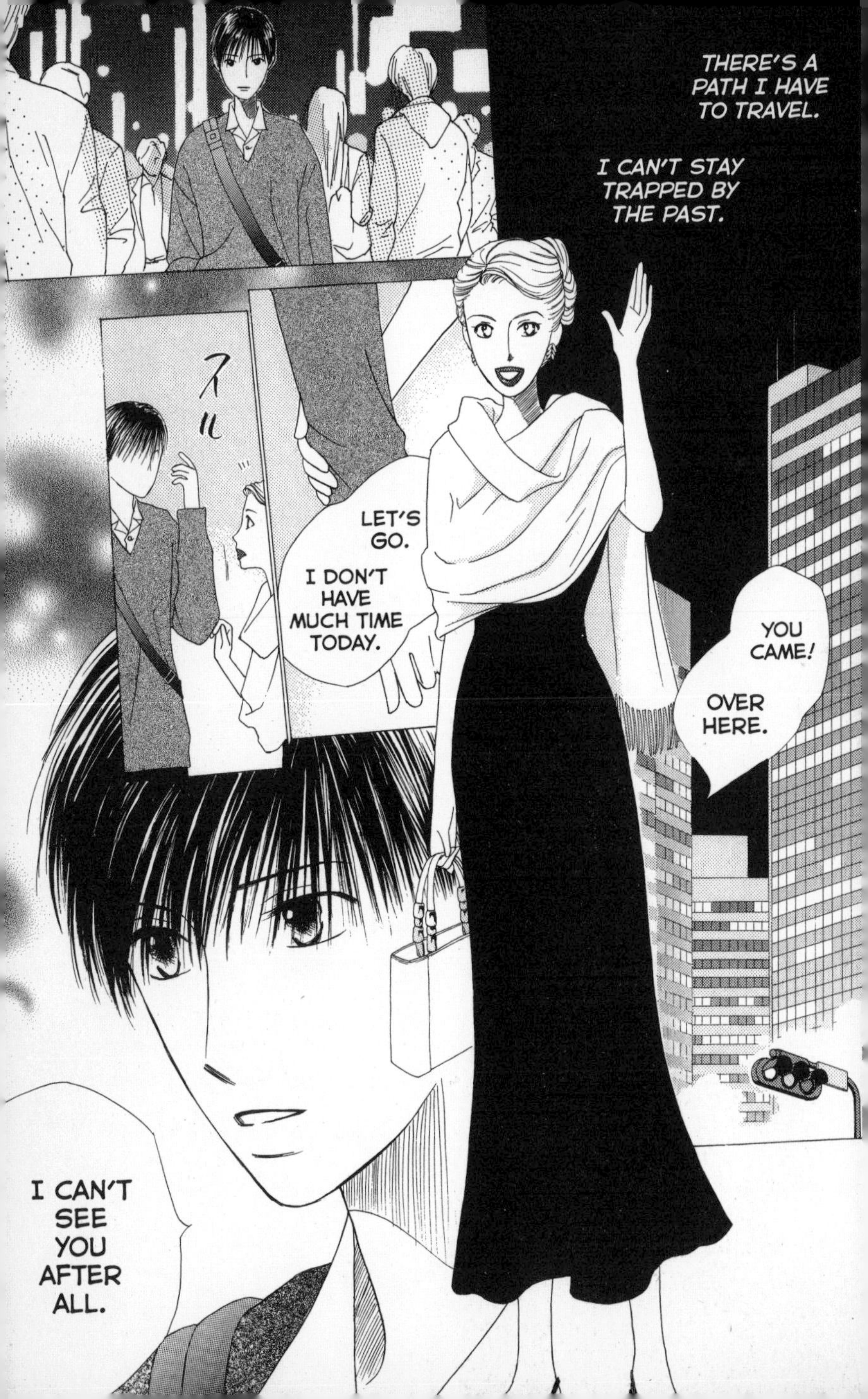
THERE'S A PATH I HAVE TO TRAVEL.
I CAN'T STAY TRAPPED BY THE PAST.
YOU CAME! OVER HERE.
LET'S GO. I DON'T HAVE MUCH TIME TODAY.
I CAN'T SEE YOU AFTER ALL.

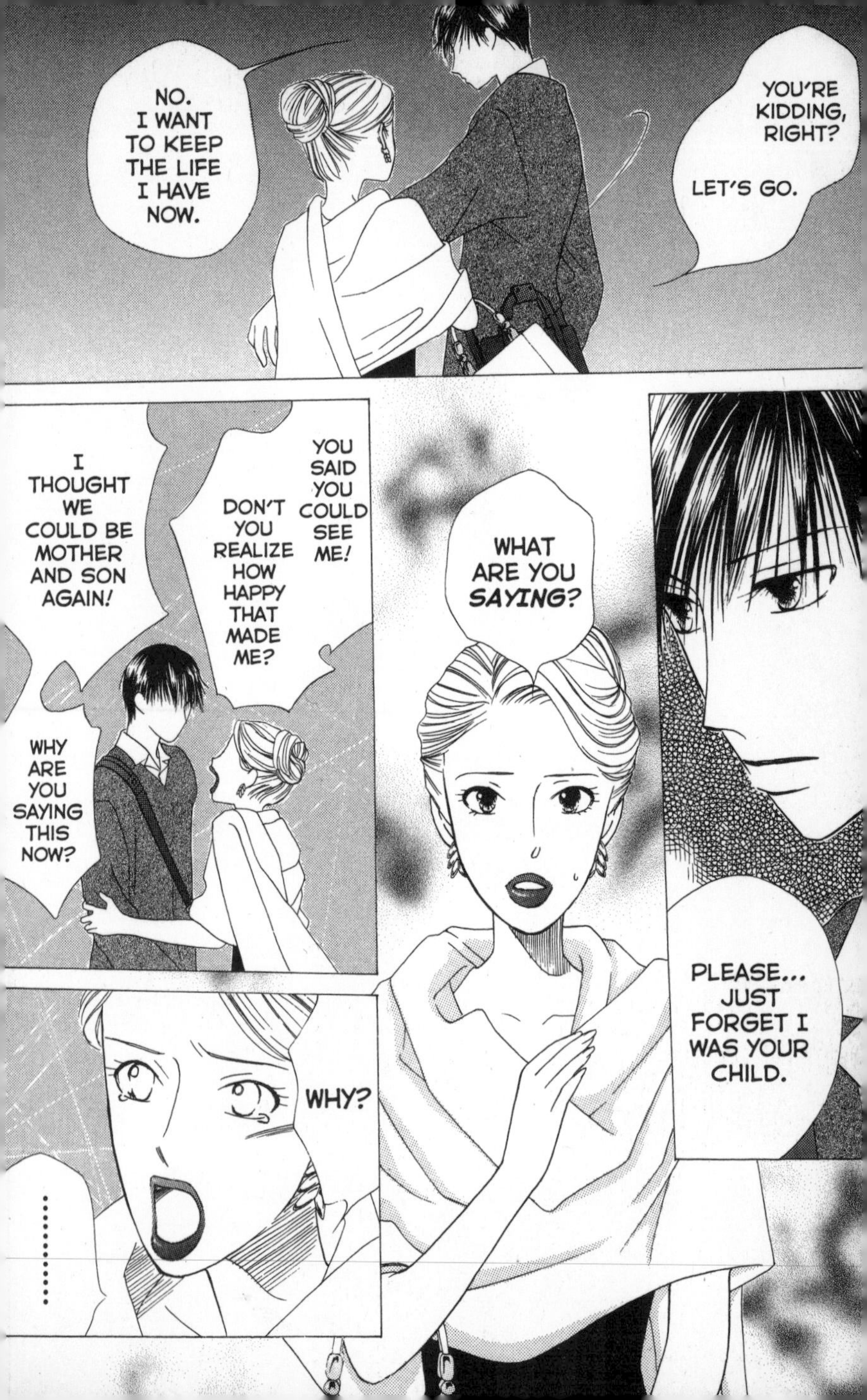
YOU'RE KIDDING, RIGHT?
LET'S GO.
NO. I WANT TO KEEP THE LIFE I HAVE NOW.
PLEASE... JUST FORGET I WAS YOUR CHILD.
WHAT ARE YOU *SAYING*?
YOU SAID YOU COULD SEE ME!
DON'T YOU REALIZE HOW HAPPY THAT MADE ME?
I THOUGHT WE COULD BE MOTHER AND SON AGAIN!
WHY ARE YOU SAYING THIS NOW?
WHY?
....

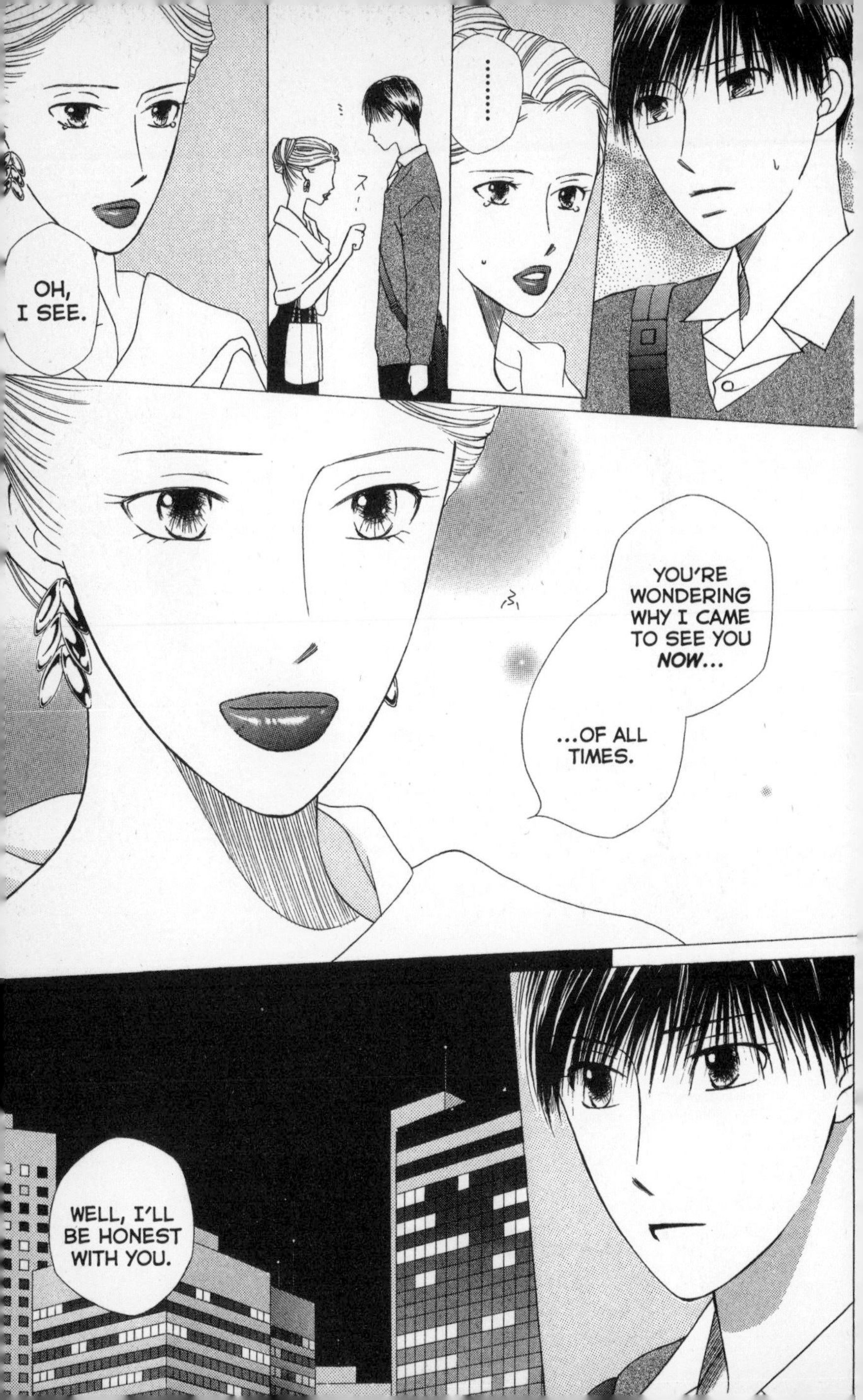
......
OH, I SEE.
YOU'RE WONDERING WHY I CAME TO SEE YOU *NOW*...
...OF ALL TIMES.
WELL, I'LL BE HONEST WITH YOU.

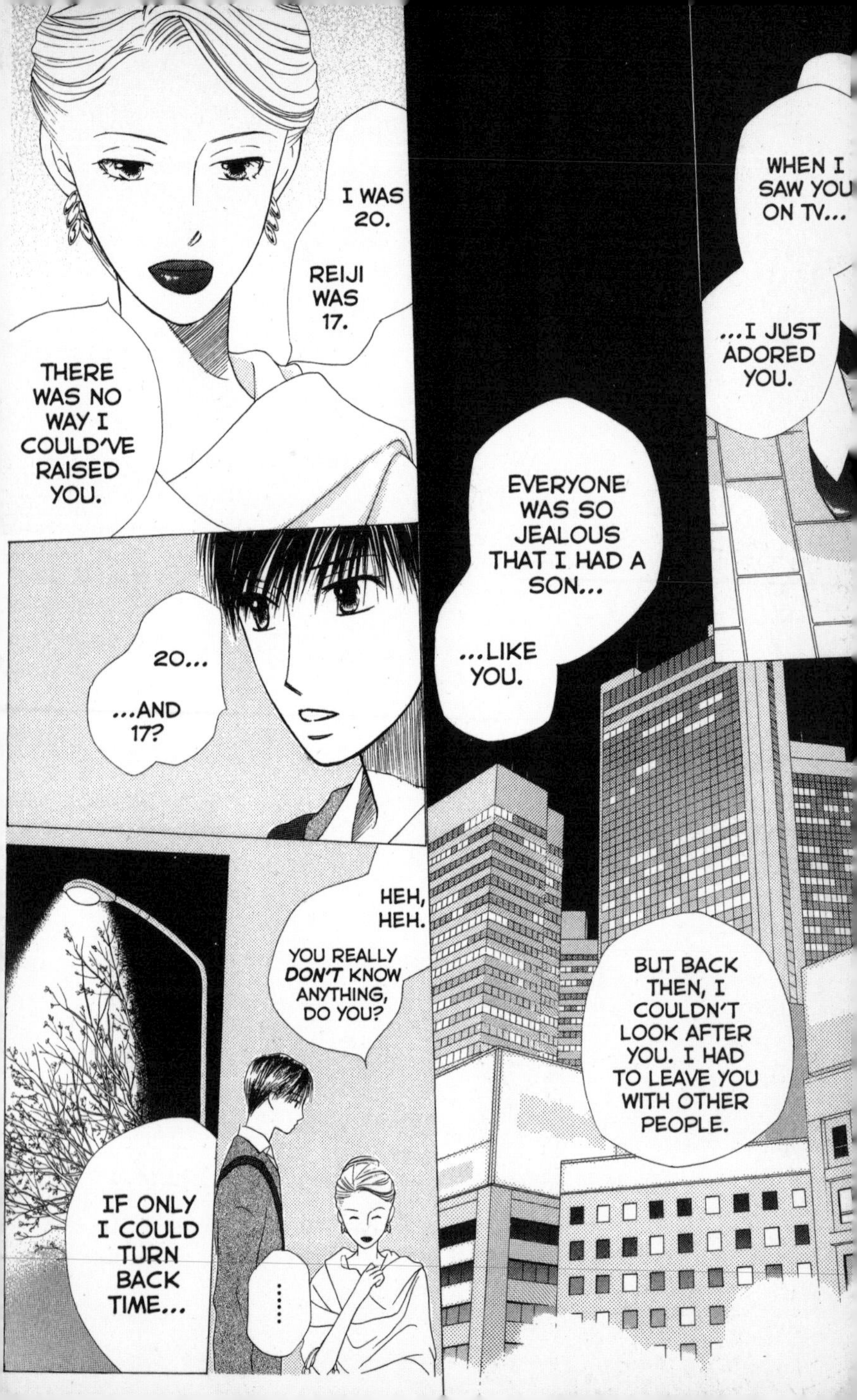

WHEN I SAW YOU ON TV...
...I JUST ADORED YOU.
EVERYONE WAS SO JEALOUS THAT I HAD A SON...
...LIKE YOU.
BUT BACK THEN, I COULDN'T LOOK AFTER YOU. I HAD TO LEAVE YOU WITH OTHER PEOPLE.
I WAS 20.
REIJI WAS 17.
THERE WAS NO WAY I COULD'VE RAISED YOU.
20...
...AND 17?
HEH, HEH.
YOU REALLY *DON'T* KNOW ANYTHING, DO YOU?
IF ONLY I COULD TURN BACK TIME...
......

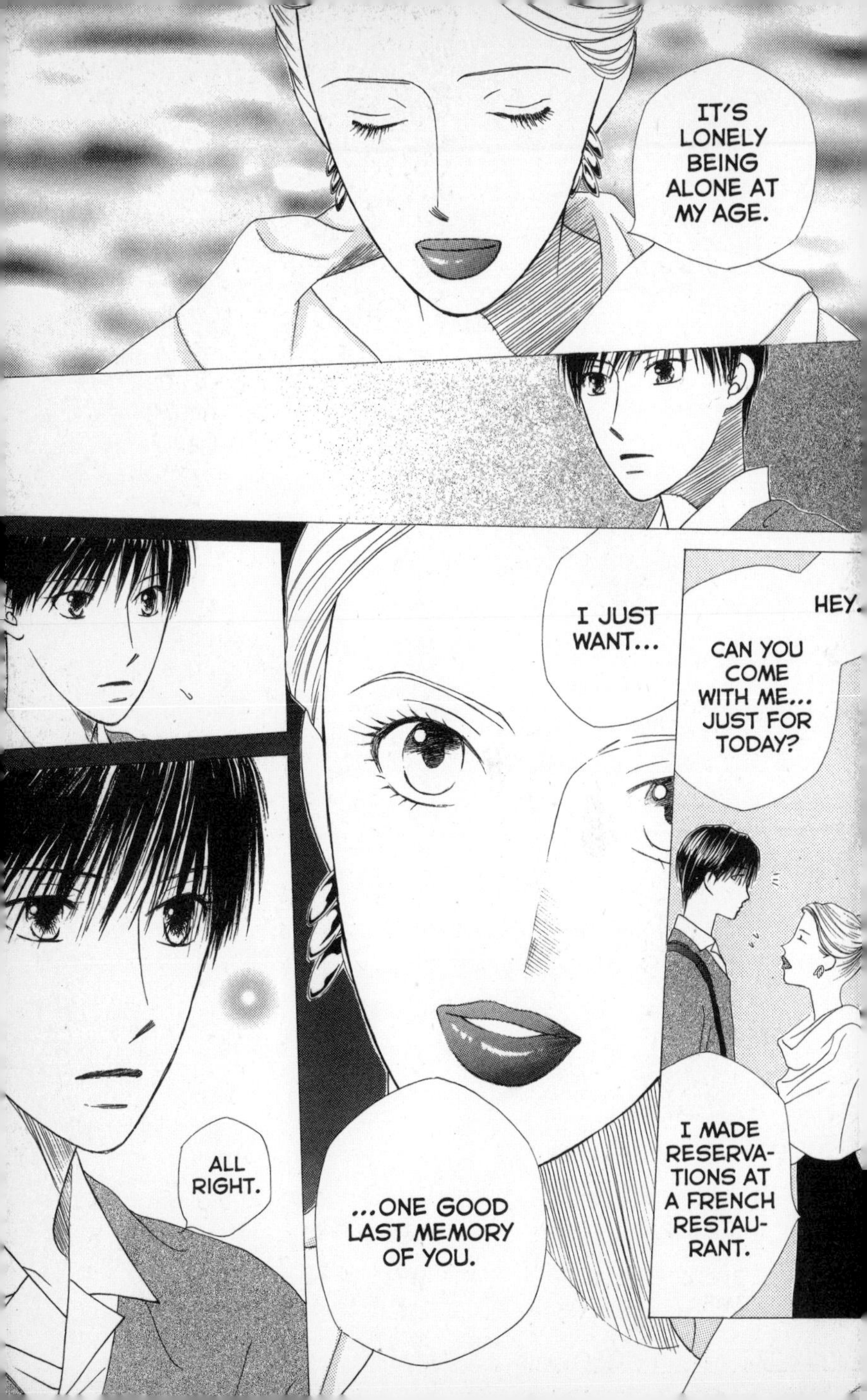
IT'S LONELY BEING ALONE AT MY AGE.
HEY.
CAN YOU COME WITH ME... JUST FOR TODAY?
I MADE RESERVATIONS AT A FRENCH RESTAURANT.
I JUST WANT...
...ONE GOOD LAST MEMORY OF YOU.
ALL RIGHT.

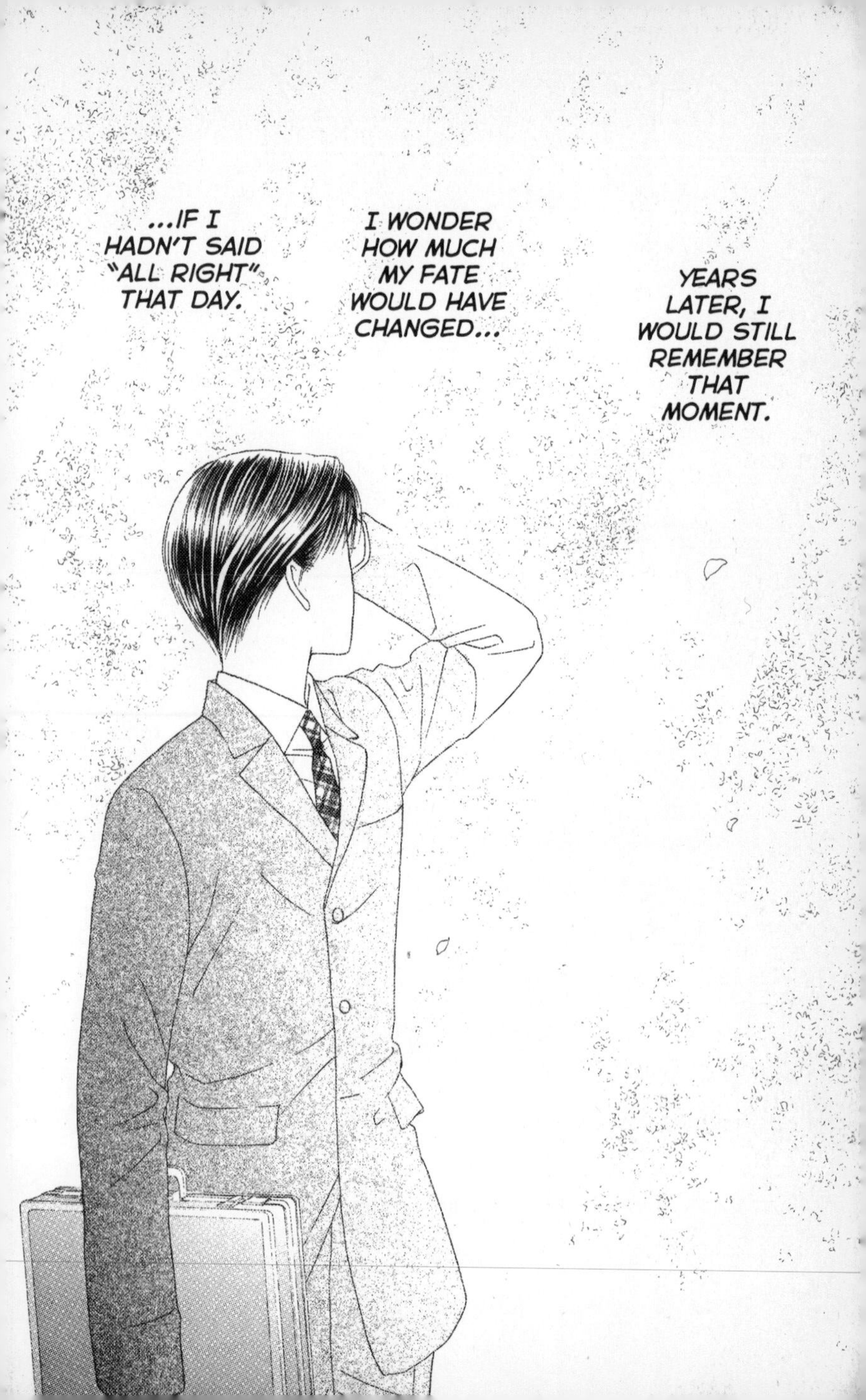
YEARS LATER, I WOULD STILL REMEMBER THAT MOMENT.
I WONDER HOW MUCH MY FATE WOULD HAVE CHANGED...
...IF I HADN'T SAID "ALL RIGHT" THAT DAY.

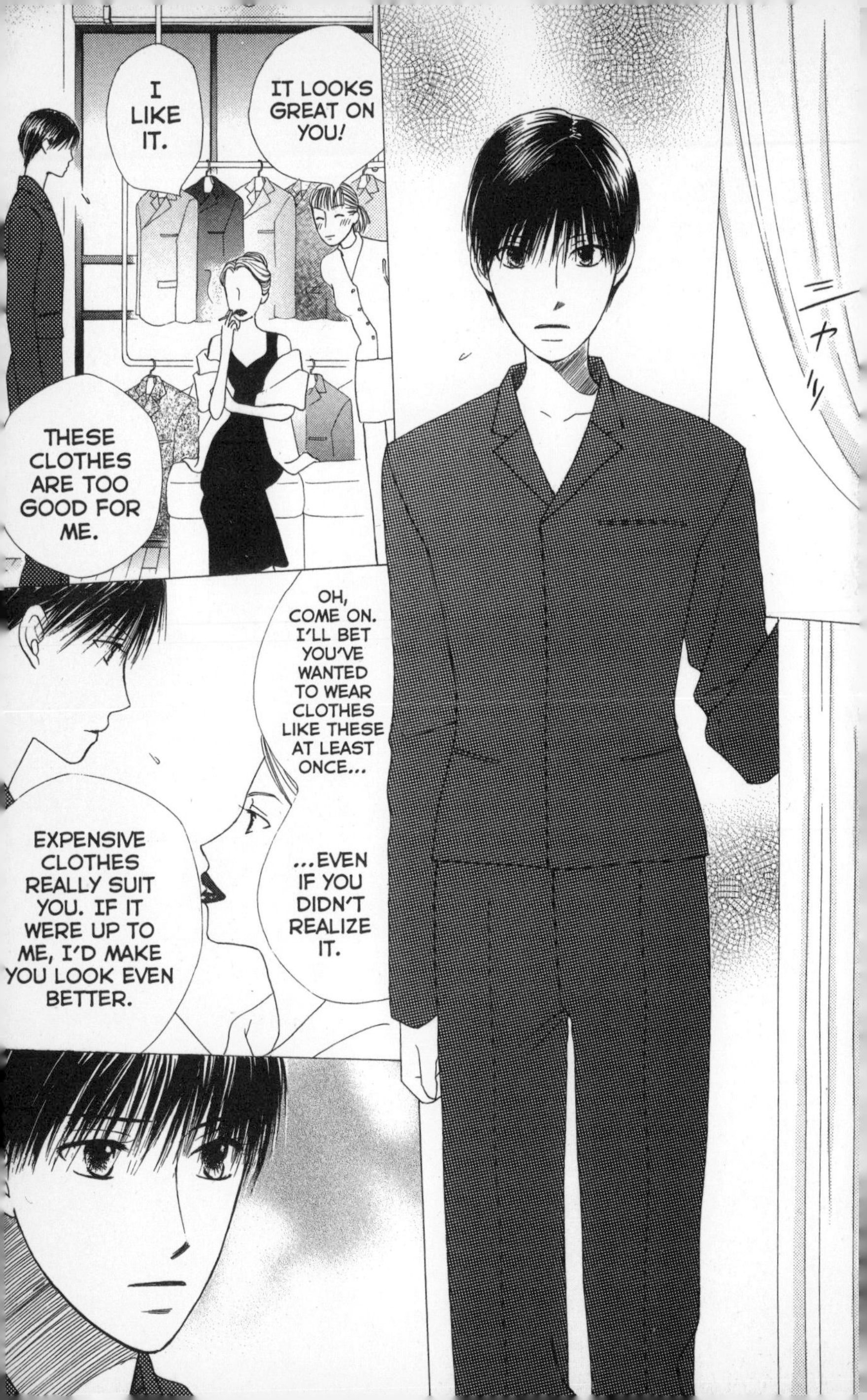
シャッ
IT LOOKS GREAT ON YOU!
I LIKE IT.
THESE CLOTHES ARE TOO GOOD FOR ME.
OH, COME ON. I'LL BET YOU'VE WANTED TO WEAR CLOTHES LIKE THESE AT LEAST ONCE...
...EVEN IF YOU DIDN'T REALIZE IT.
EXPENSIVE CLOTHES REALLY SUIT YOU. IF IT WERE UP TO ME, I'D MAKE YOU LOOK EVEN BETTER.

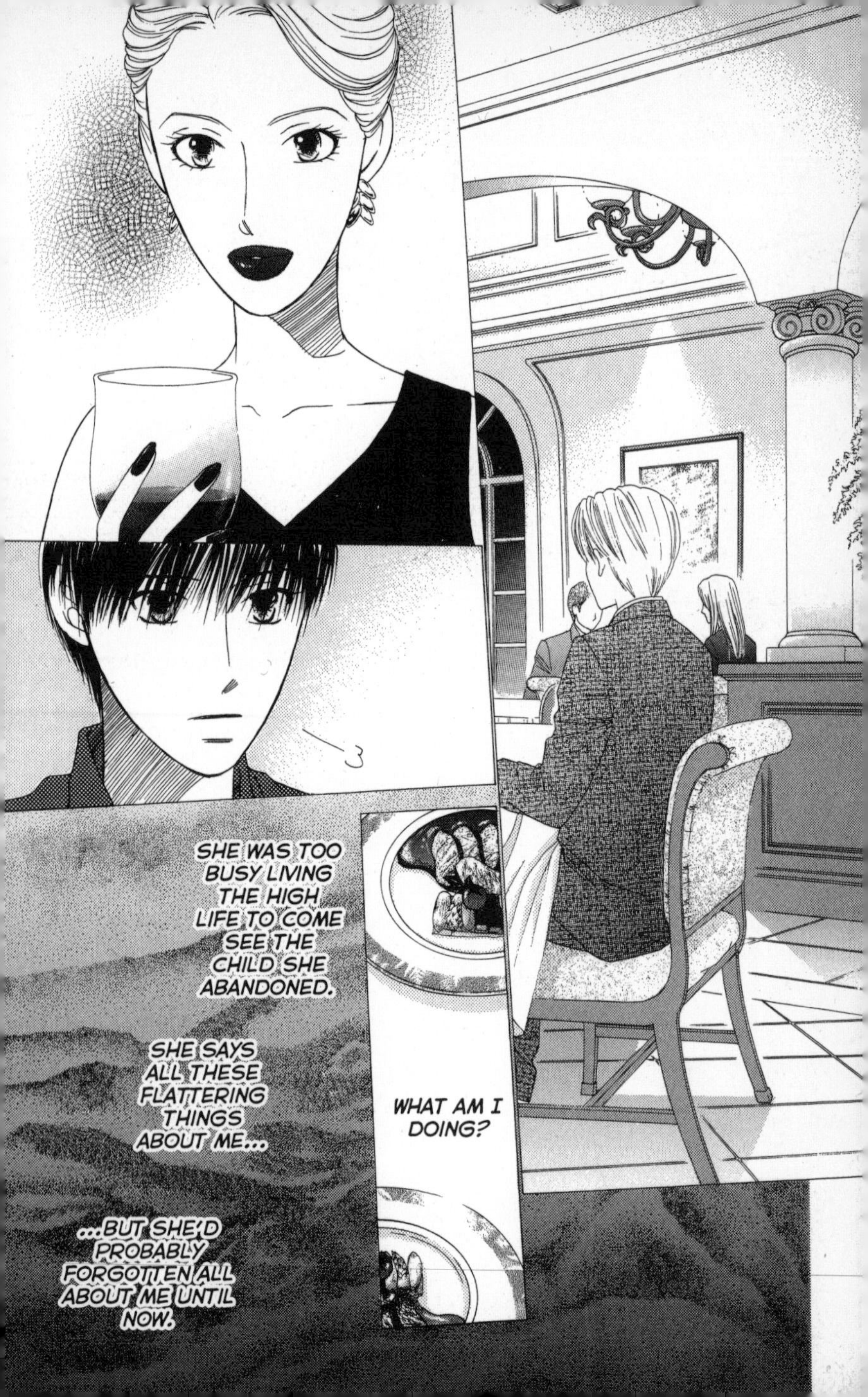
WHAT AM I DOING?
SHE WAS TOO BUSY LIVING THE HIGH LIFE TO COME SEE THE CHILD SHE ABANDONED.
SHE SAYS ALL THESE FLATTERING THINGS ABOUT ME...
...BUT SHE'D PROBABLY FORGOTTEN ALL ABOUT ME UNTIL NOW.

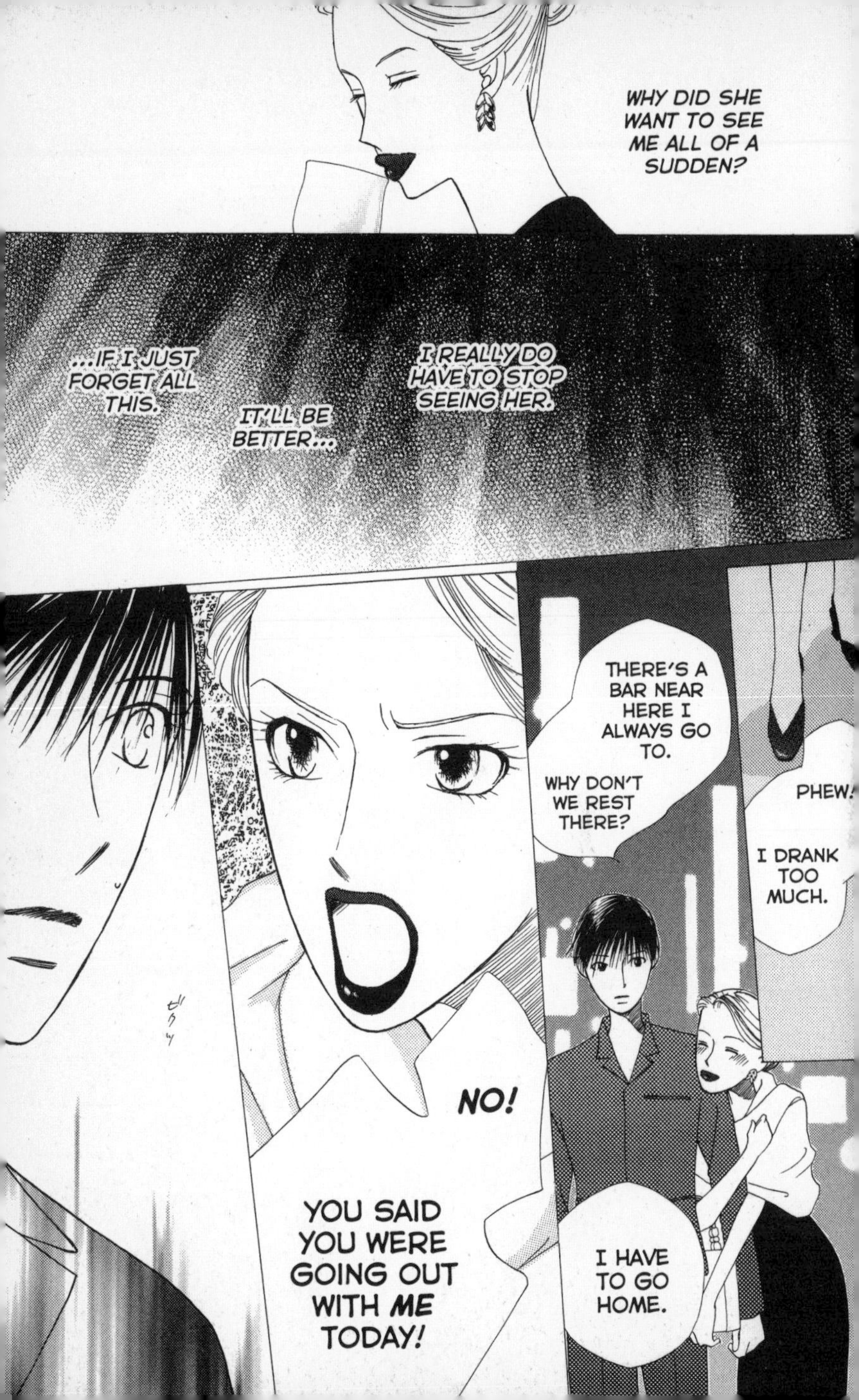
WHY DID SHE WANT TO SEE ME ALL OF A SUDDEN?
I REALLY DO HAVE TO STOP SEEING HER.
IT'LL BE BETTER...
...IF I JUST FORGET ALL THIS.
PHEW!
I DRANK TOO MUCH.
THERE'S A BAR NEAR HERE I ALWAYS GO TO.
WHY DON'T WE REST THERE?
I HAVE TO GO HOME.
NO!
YOU SAID YOU WERE GOING OUT WITH *ME* TODAY!

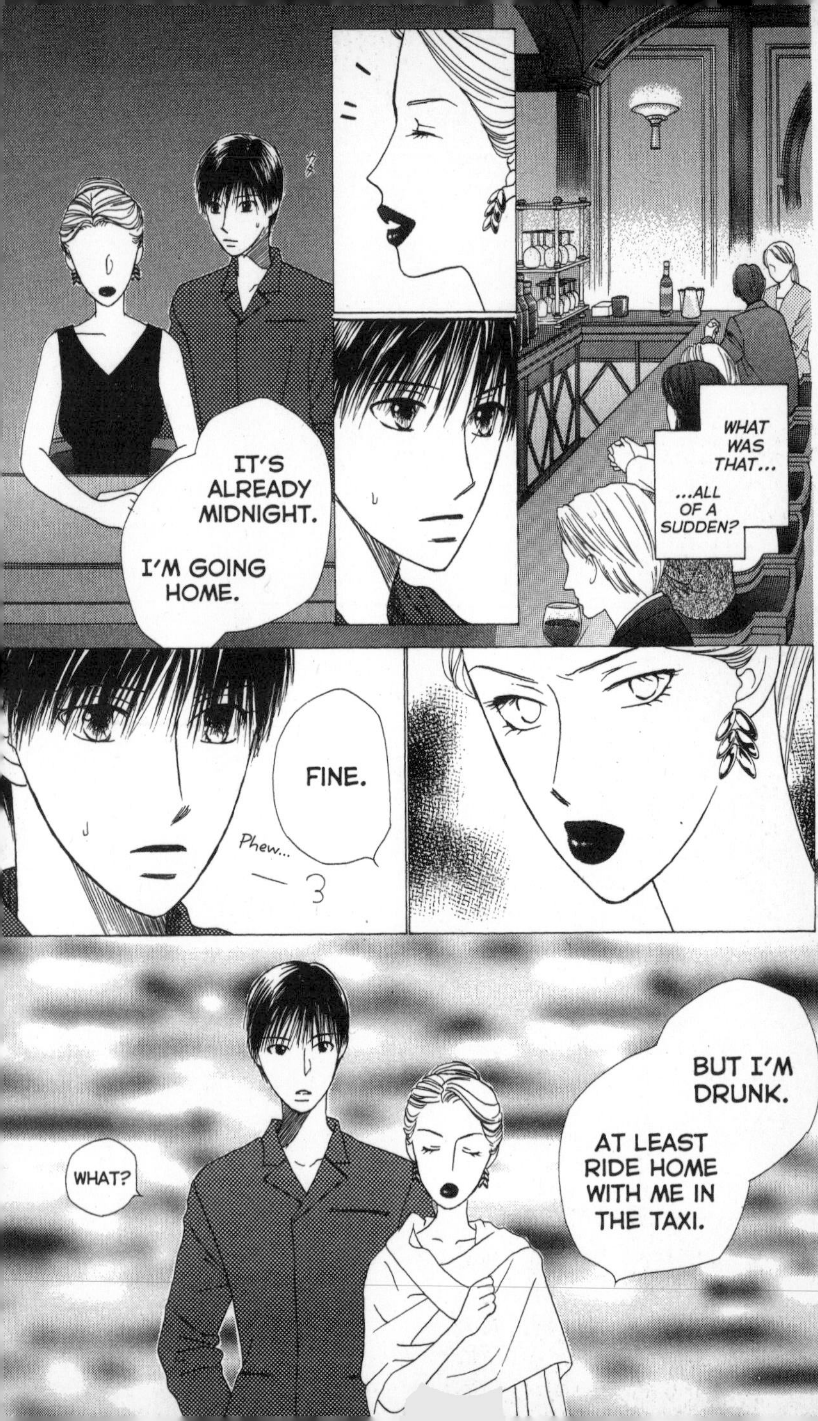
WHAT WAS THAT...
...ALL OF A SUDDEN?
IT'S ALREADY MIDNIGHT.
I'M GOING HOME.
FINE.
Phew...
BUT I'M DRUNK.
AT LEAST RIDE HOME WITH ME IN THE TAXI.
WHAT?

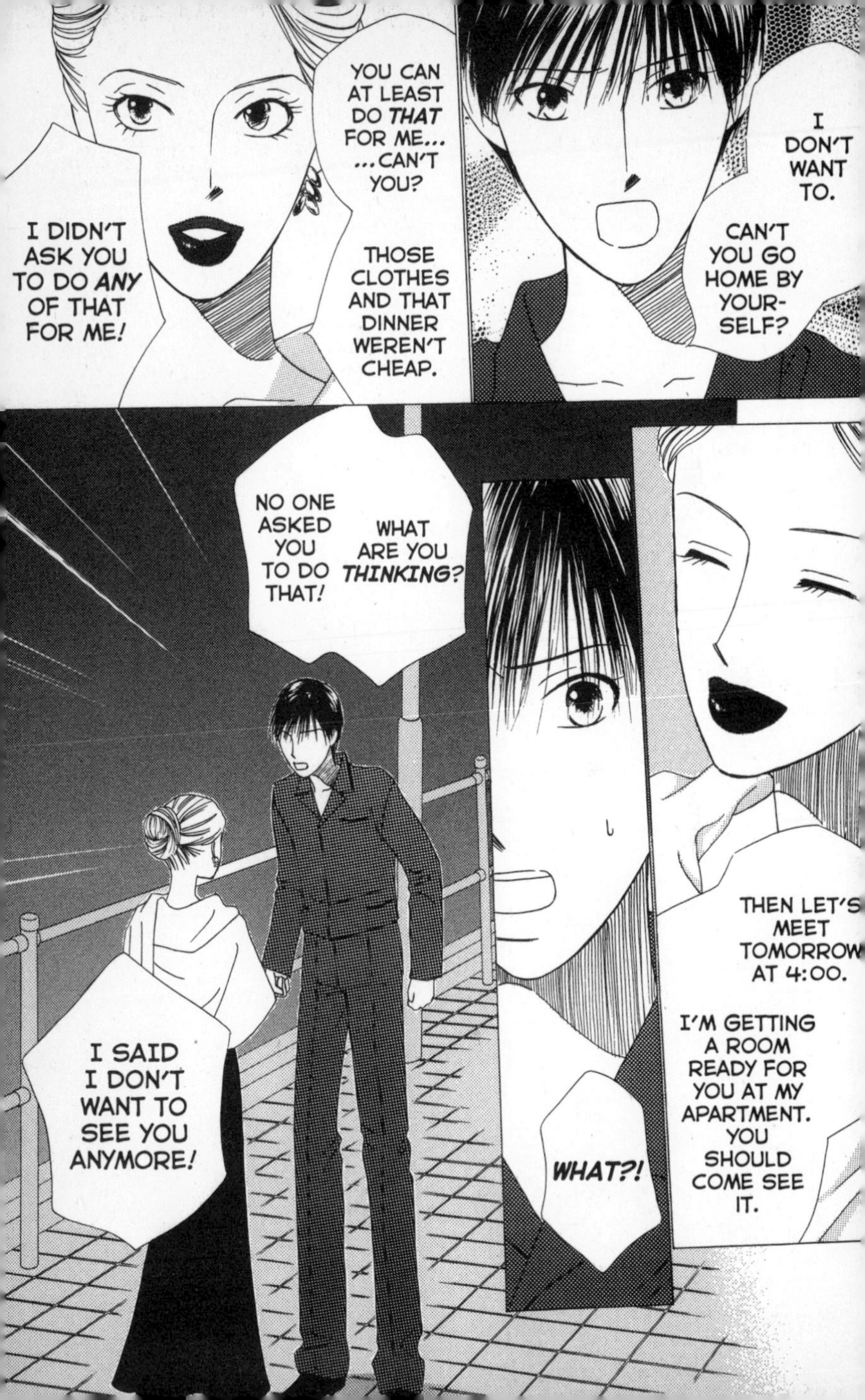
I DON'T WANT TO.
CAN'T YOU GO HOME BY YOURSELF?
YOU CAN AT LEAST DO *THAT* FOR ME... ...CAN'T YOU?
THOSE CLOTHES AND THAT DINNER WEREN'T CHEAP.
I DIDN'T ASK YOU TO DO *ANY* OF THAT FOR ME!
THEN LET'S MEET TOMORROW AT 4:00.
I'M GETTING A ROOM READY FOR YOU AT MY APARTMENT. YOU SHOULD COME SEE IT.
WHAT?!
WHAT ARE YOU *THINKING?*
NO ONE ASKED YOU TO DO THAT!
I SAID I DON'T WANT TO SEE YOU ANYMORE!

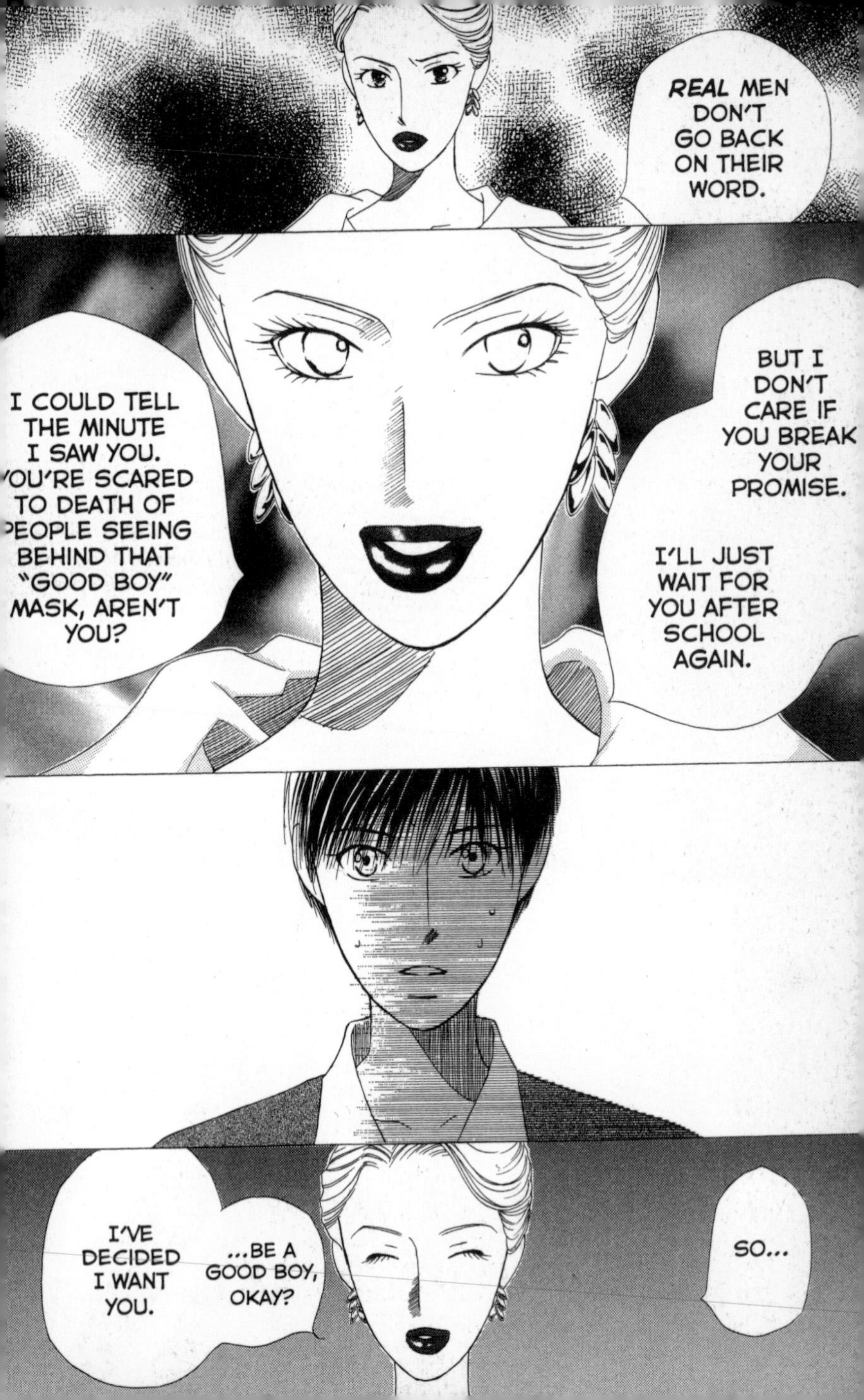

REAL MEN DON'T GO BACK ON THEIR WORD.
BUT I DON'T CARE IF YOU BREAK YOUR PROMISE.
I'LL JUST WAIT FOR YOU AFTER SCHOOL AGAIN.
I COULD TELL THE MINUTE I SAW YOU. 'OU'RE SCARED TO DEATH OF 'EOPLE SEEING BEHIND THAT "GOOD BOY" MASK, AREN'T YOU?
SO...
...BE A GOOD BOY, OKAY?
I'VE DECIDED I WANT YOU.

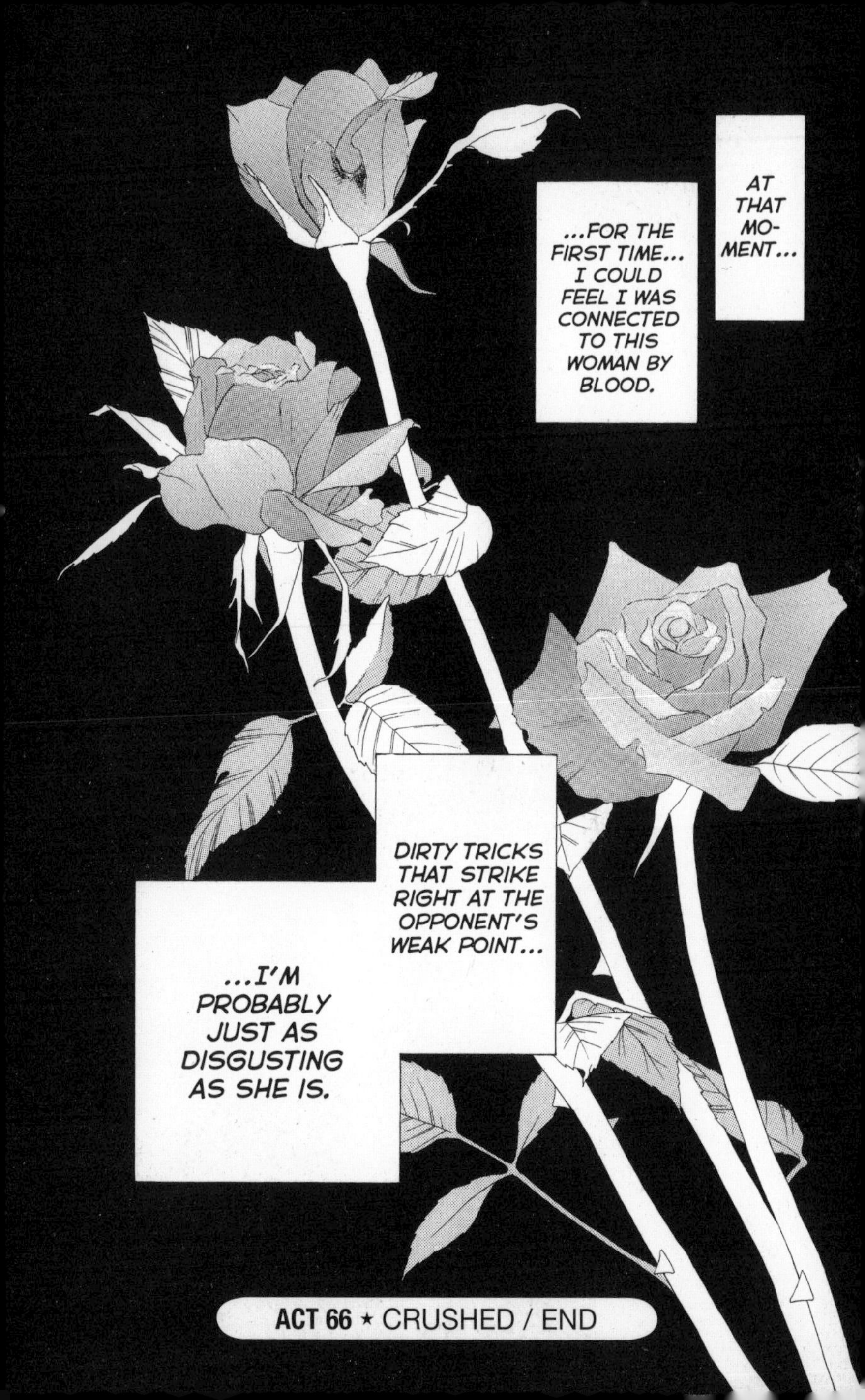
AT THAT MO- MENT...
...FOR THE FIRST TIME... I COULD FEEL I WAS CONNECTED TO THIS WOMAN BY BLOOD.
DIRTY TRICKS THAT STRIKE RIGHT AT THE OPPONENT'S WEAK POINT...
...I'M PROBABLY JUST AS DISGUSTING AS SHE IS.
ACT 66 ⋆ CRUSHED / END

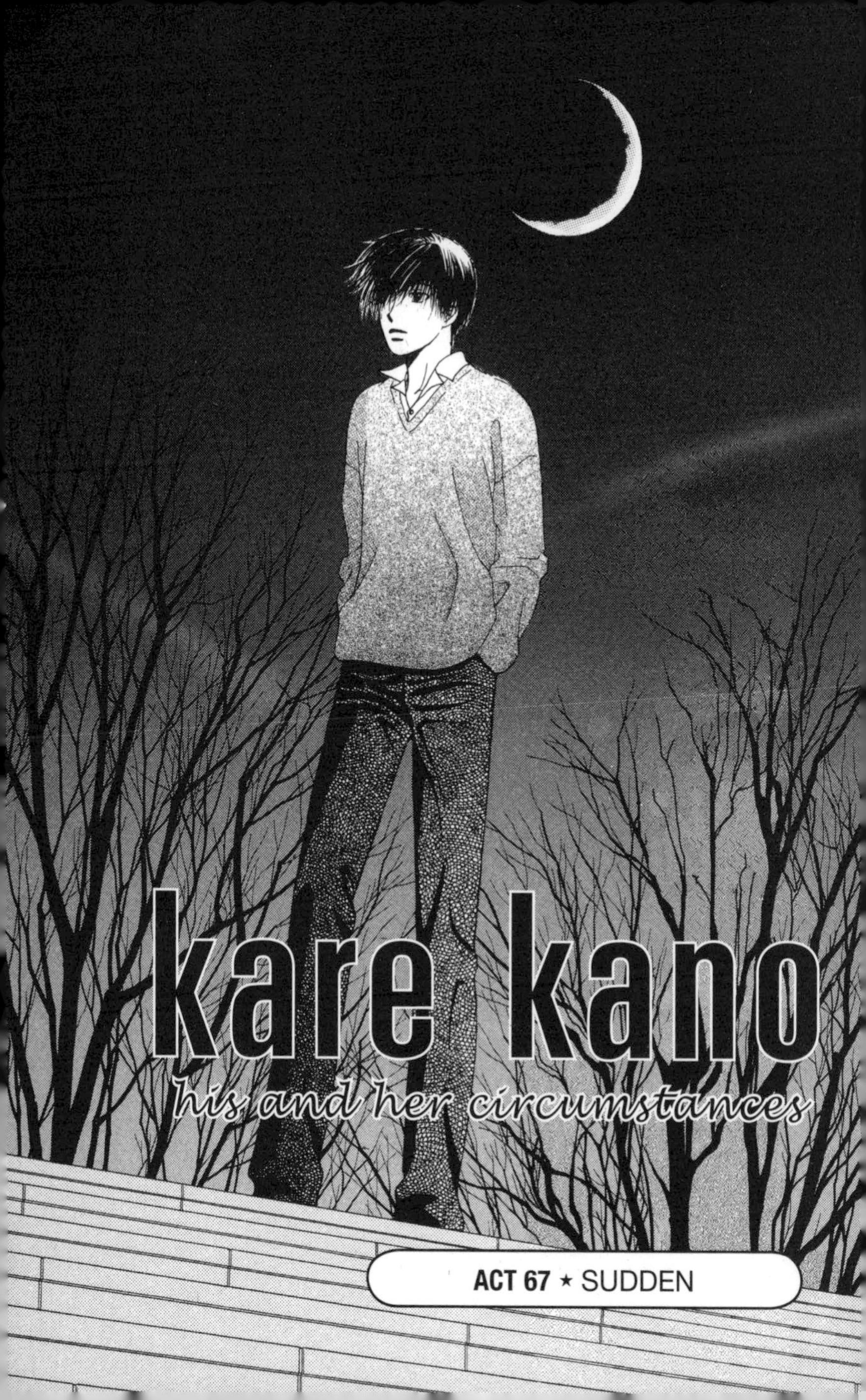
kare kano
his and her circumstances
ACT 67 ★ SUDDEN

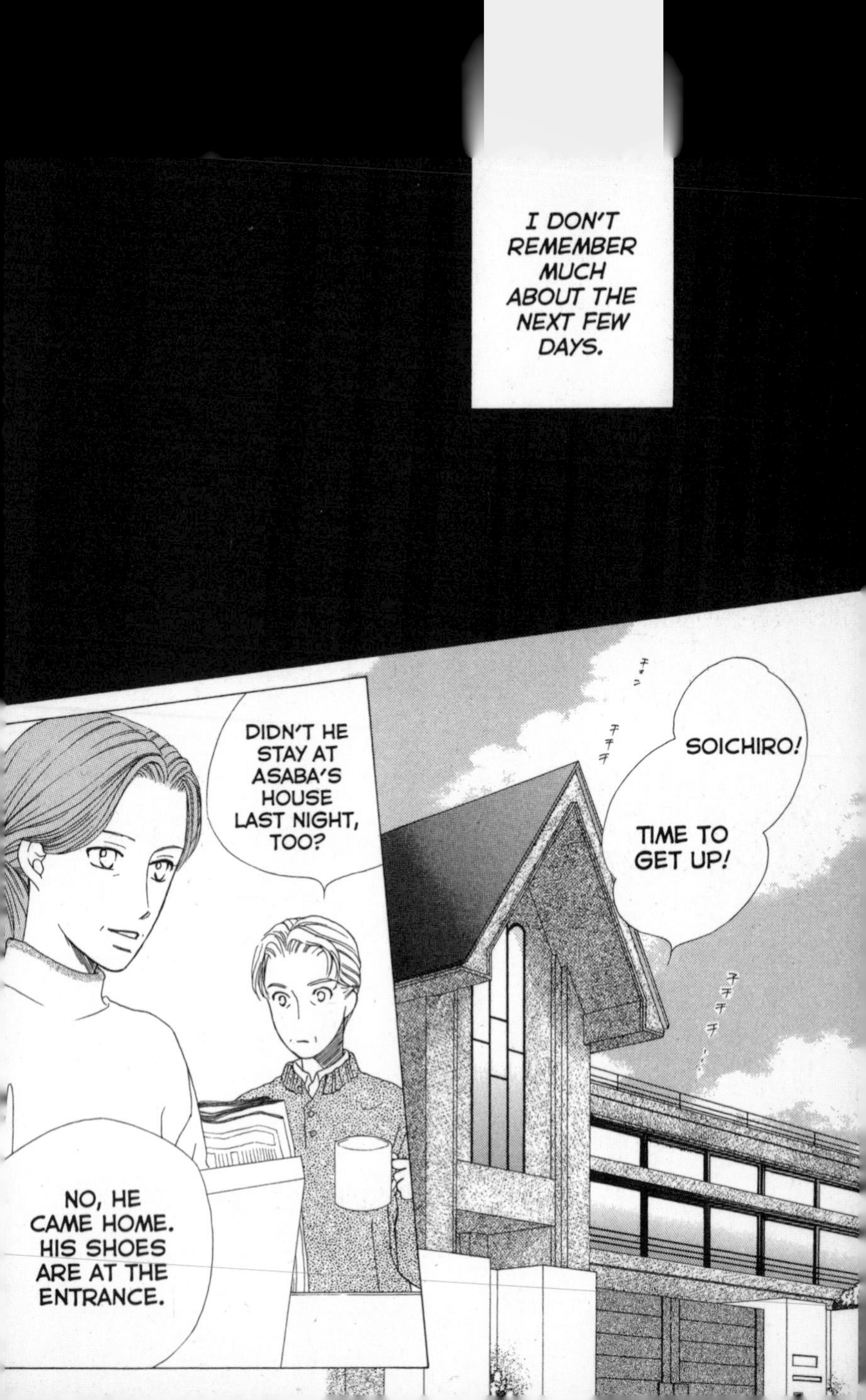
I DON'T REMEMBER MUCH ABOUT THE NEXT FEW DAYS.
SOICHIRO!
TIME TO GET UP!
DIDN'T HE STAY AT ASABA'S HOUSE LAST NIGHT, TOO?
NO, HE CAME HOME. HIS SHOES ARE AT THE ENTRANCE.

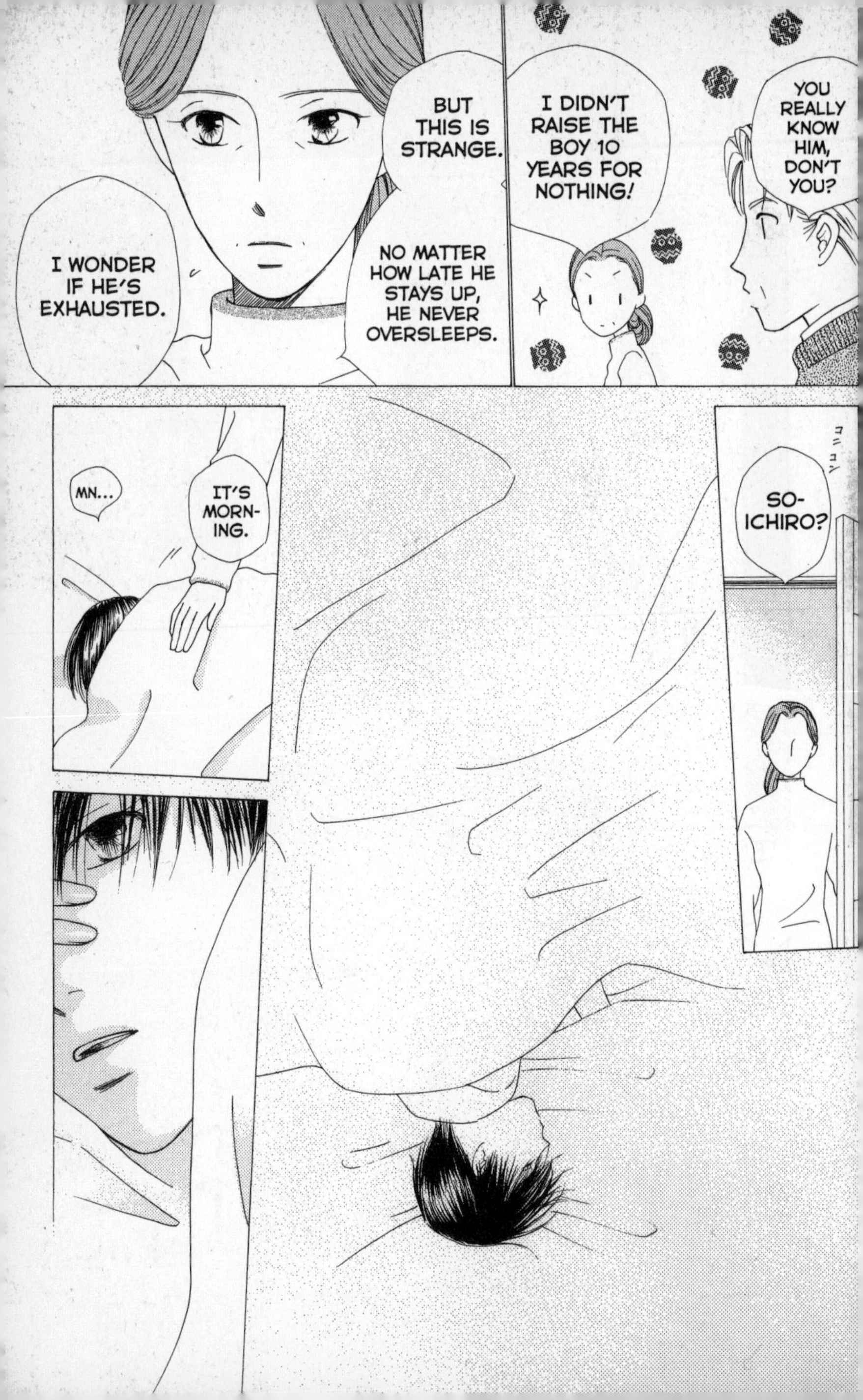
YOU REALLY KNOW HIM, DON'T YOU?
I DIDN'T RAISE THE BOY 10 YEARS FOR NOTHING!
BUT THIS IS STRANGE.
NO MATTER HOW LATE HE STAYS UP, HE NEVER OVERSLEEPS.
I WONDER IF HE'S EXHAUSTED.
SO-ICHIRO?
IT'S MORNING.
MN...

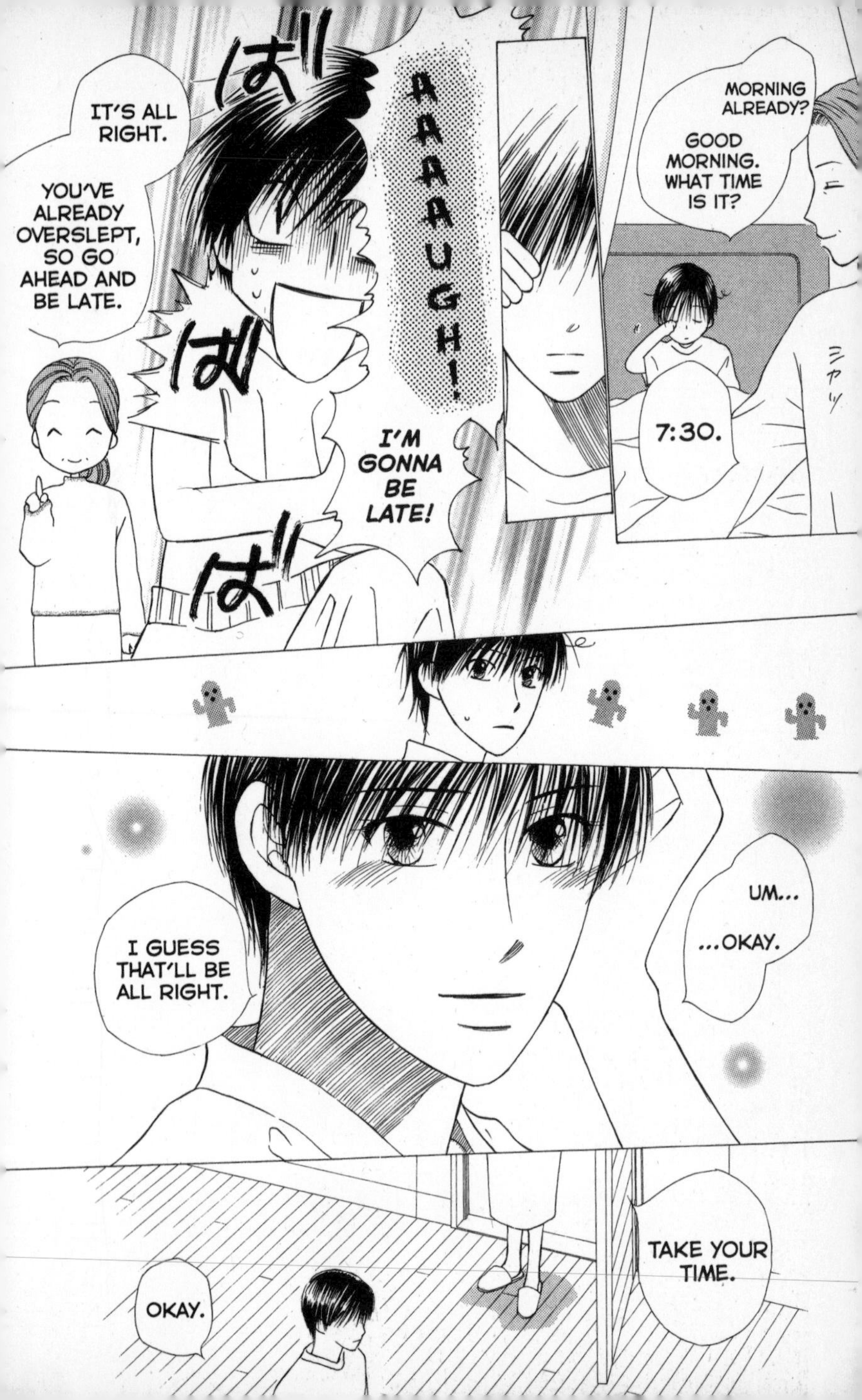
MORNING ALREADY?
GOOD MORNING. WHAT TIME IS IT?
シャッ
7:30.
AAAAUGH!
I'M GONNA BE LATE!
ば
ば
ば
IT'S ALL RIGHT.
YOU'VE ALREADY OVERSLEPT, SO GO AHEAD AND BE LATE.
UM... ...OKAY.
I GUESS THAT'LL BE ALL RIGHT.
TAKE YOUR TIME.
OKAY.

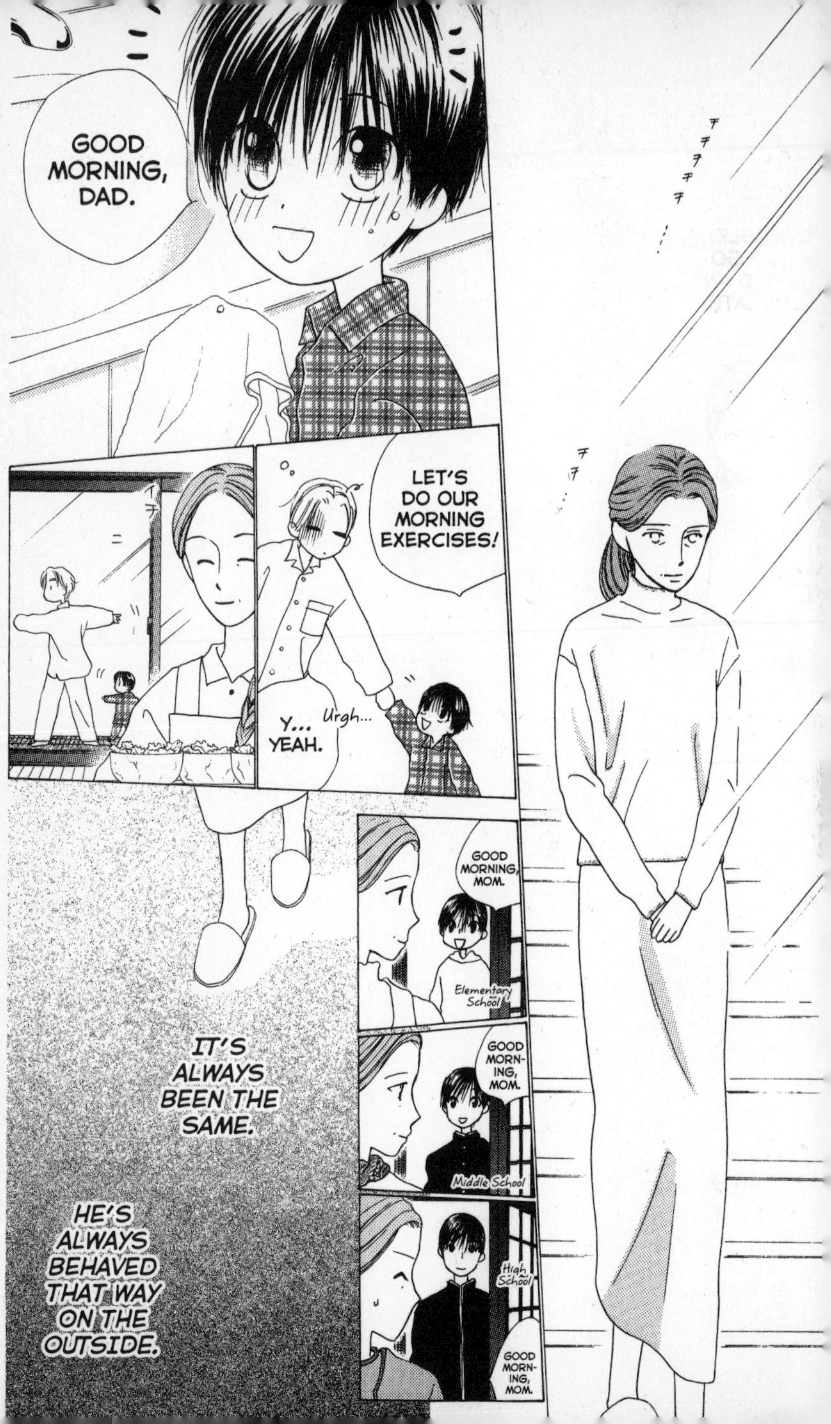
GOOD MORNING, DAD.
LET'S DO OUR MORNING EXERCISES!
Y... YEAH.
Urgh...
GOOD MORNING, MOM.
Elementary School
GOOD MORN-ING, MOM.
Middle School
High School
GOOD MORN-ING, MOM.
IT'S ALWAYS BEEN THE SAME.
HE'S ALWAYS BEHAVED THAT WAY ON THE OUTSIDE.

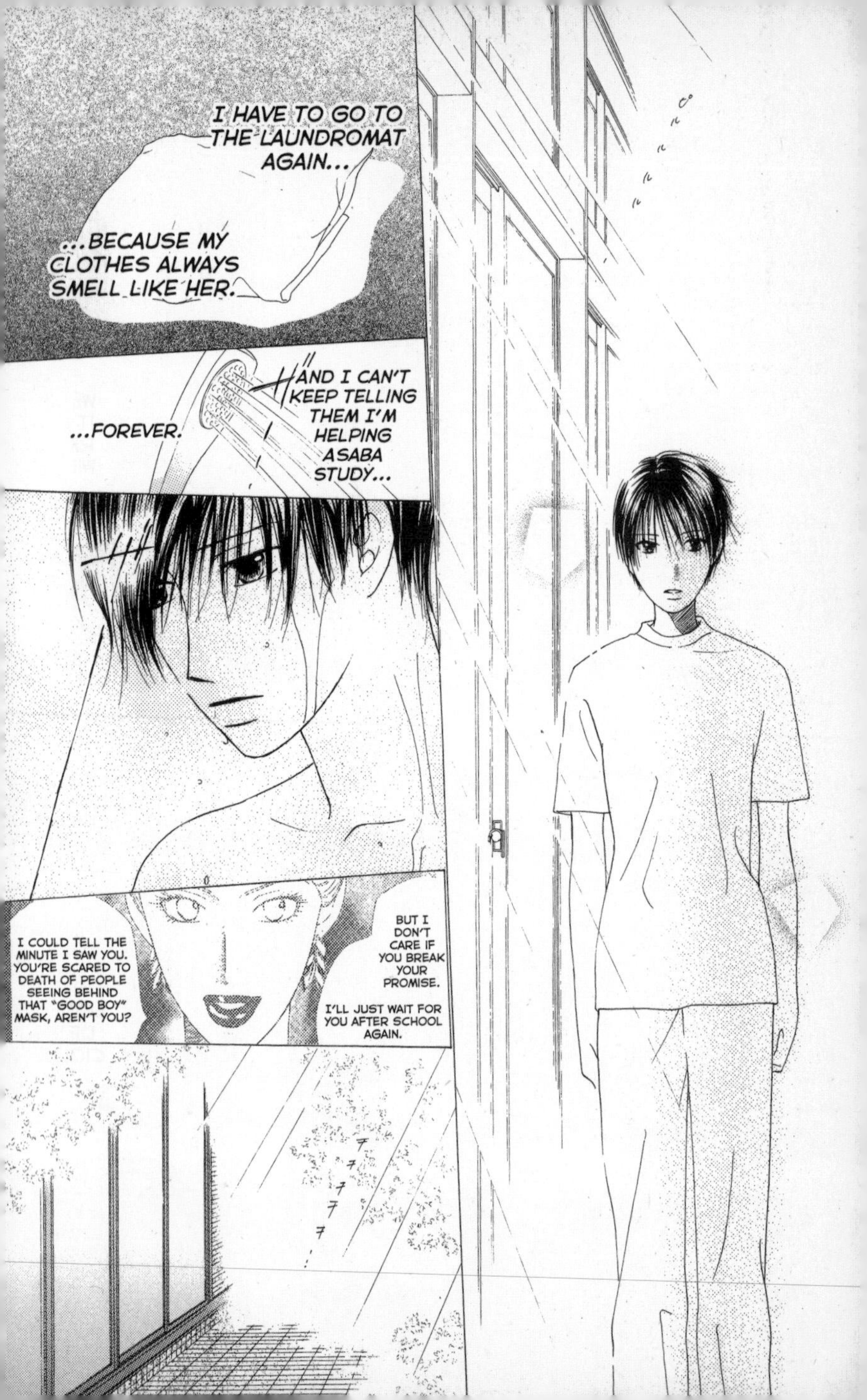
I HAVE TO GO TO THE LAUNDROMAT AGAIN...
...BECAUSE MY CLOTHES ALWAYS SMELL LIKE HER.
AND I CAN'T KEEP TELLING THEM I'M HELPING ASABA STUDY...
...FOREVER.
I COULD TELL THE MINUTE I SAW YOU. YOU'RE SCARED TO DEATH OF PEOPLE SEEING BEHIND THAT "GOOD BOY" MASK, AREN'T YOU?
BUT I DON'T CARE IF YOU BREAK YOUR PROMISE.
I'LL JUST WAIT FOR YOU AFTER SCHOOL AGAIN.

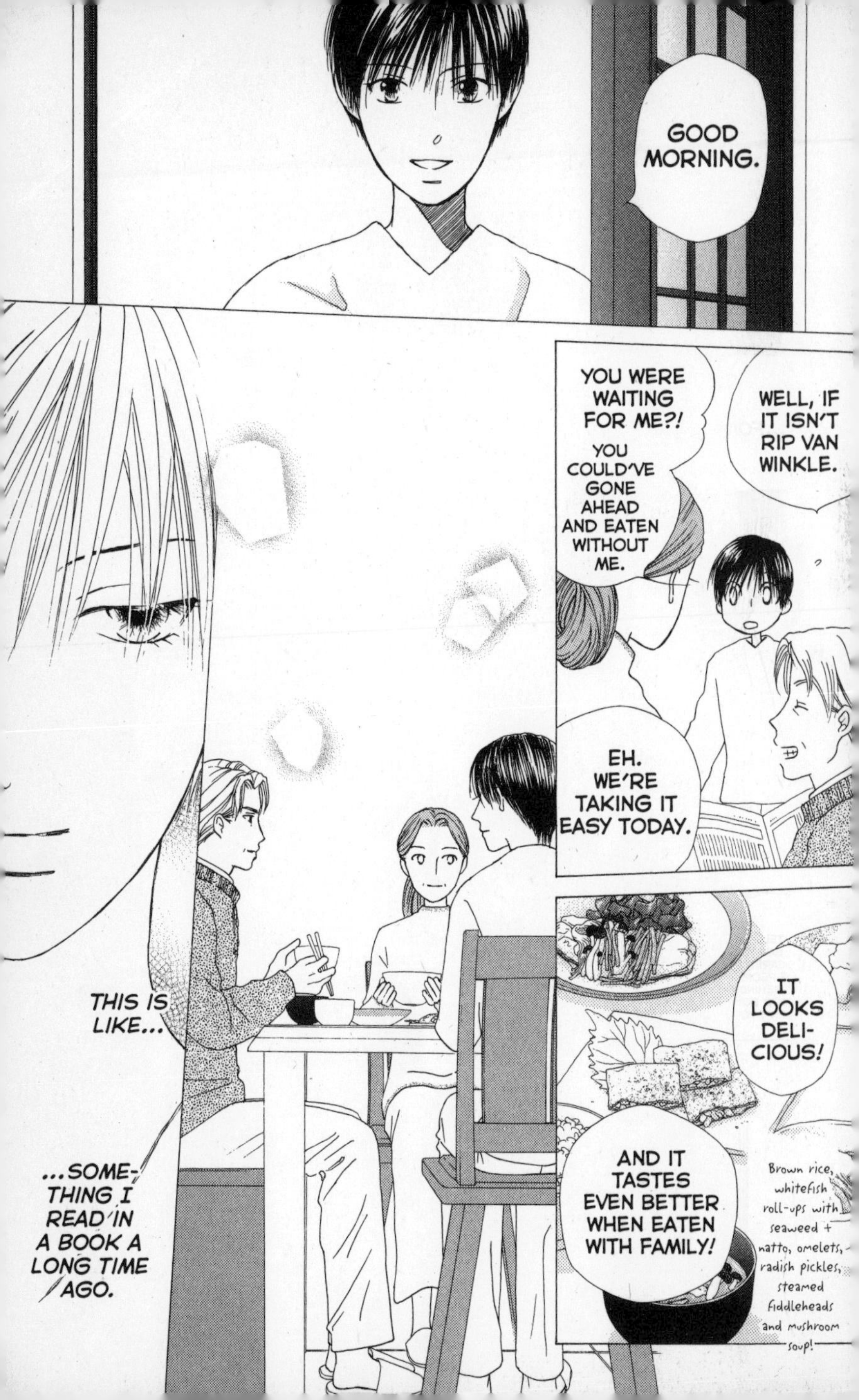
GOOD MORNING.
WELL, IF IT ISN'T RIP VAN WINKLE.
YOU WERE WAITING FOR ME?!
YOU COULD'VE GONE AHEAD AND EATEN WITHOUT ME.
EH. WE'RE TAKING IT EASY TODAY.
IT LOOKS DELI- CIOUS!
AND IT TASTES EVEN BETTER WHEN EATEN WITH FAMILY!
Brown rice, whitefish roll-ups with seaweed + natto, omelets, radish pickles, steamed fiddleheads and mushroom soup!
THIS IS LIKE...
...SOME- THING I READ IN A BOOK A LONG TIME AGO.

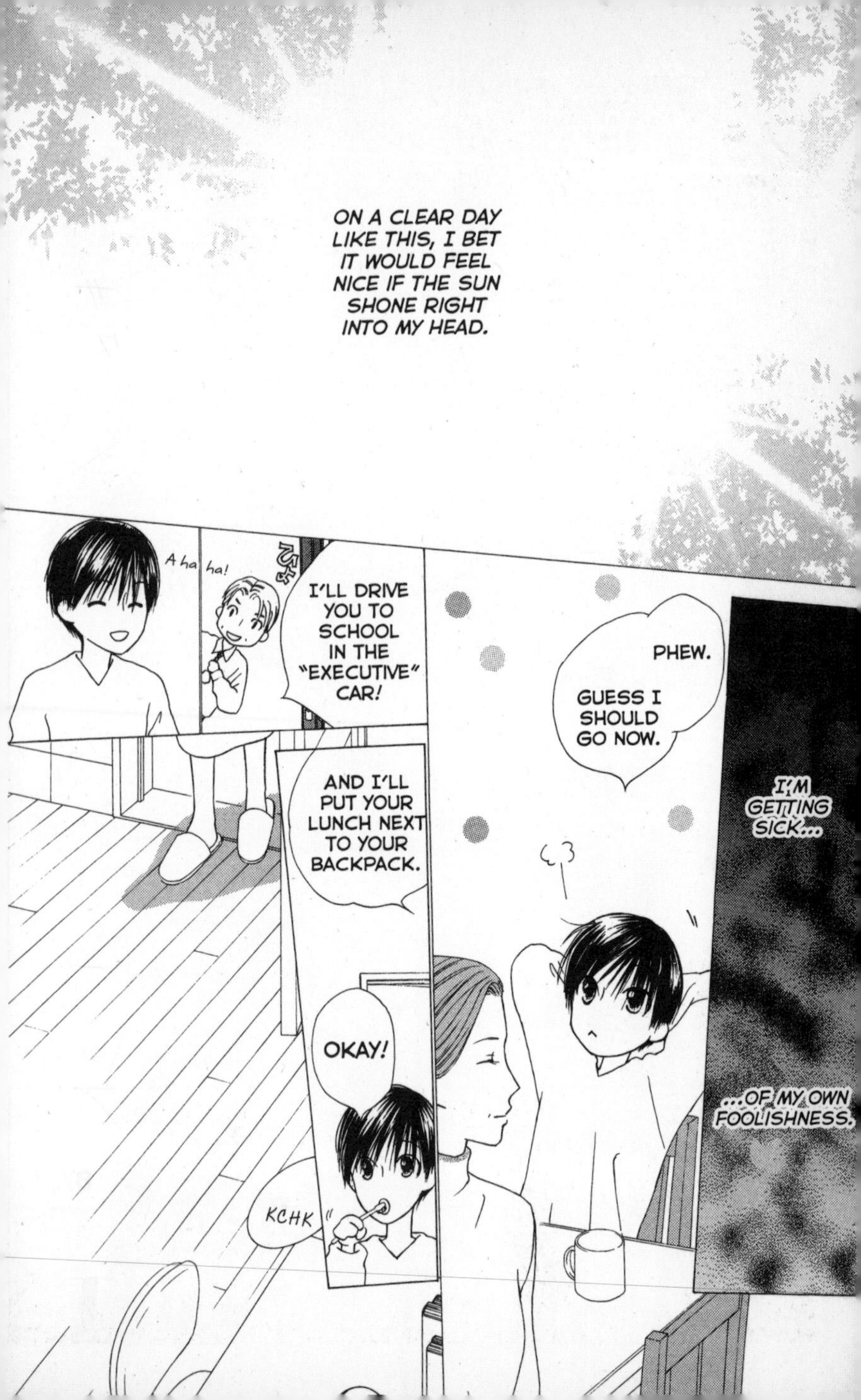
ON A CLEAR DAY LIKE THIS, I BET IT WOULD FEEL NICE IF THE SUN SHONE RIGHT INTO MY HEAD.
I'M GETTING SICK...
...OF MY OWN FOOLISHNESS.
PHEW.
GUESS I SHOULD GO NOW.
I'LL DRIVE YOU TO SCHOOL IN THE "EXECUTIVE" CAR!
A ha ha!
AND I'LL PUT YOUR LUNCH NEXT TO YOUR BACKPACK.
OKAY!
KCHK

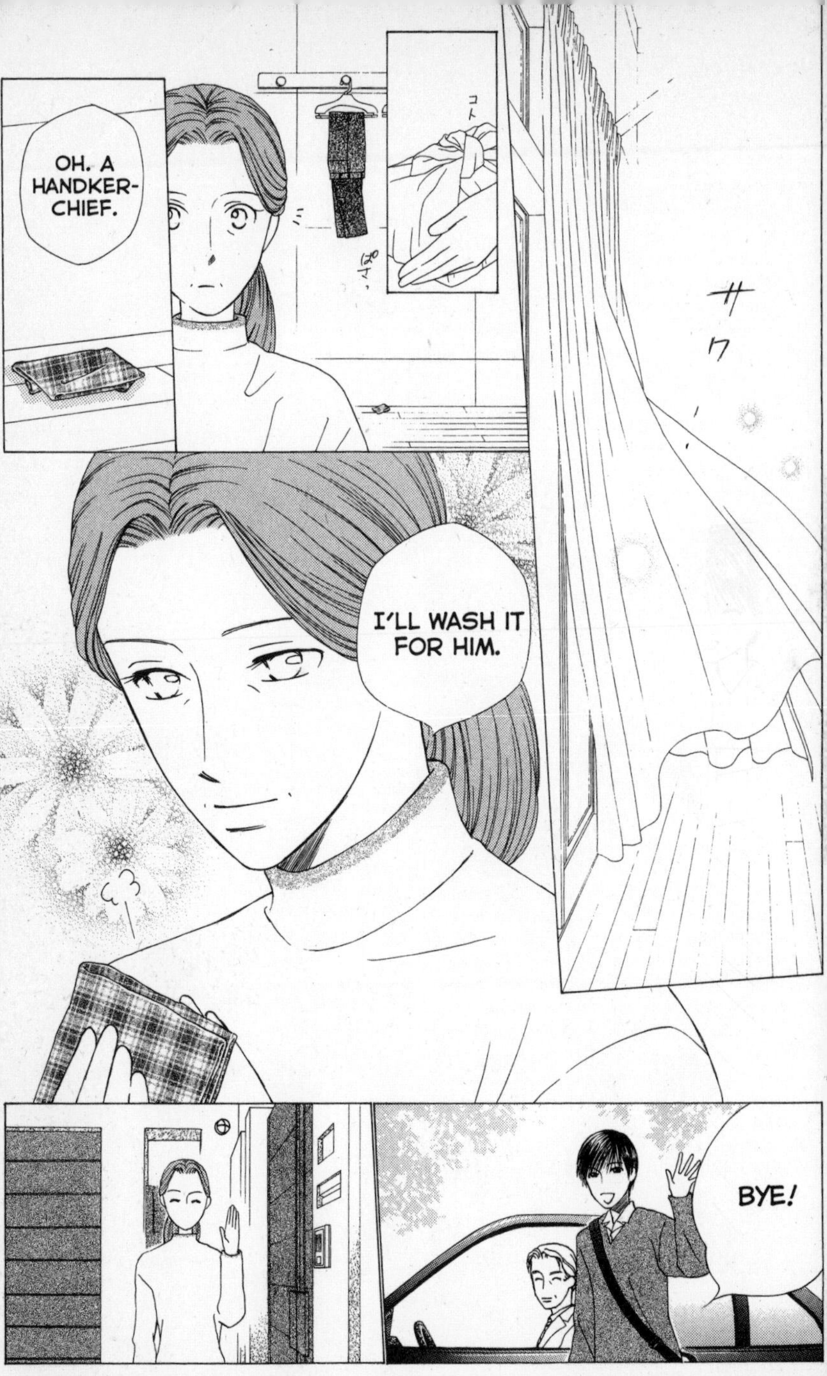
サワ
コト
ぱさ
OH. A HANDKER-CHIEF.
I'LL WASH IT FOR HIM.
BYE!

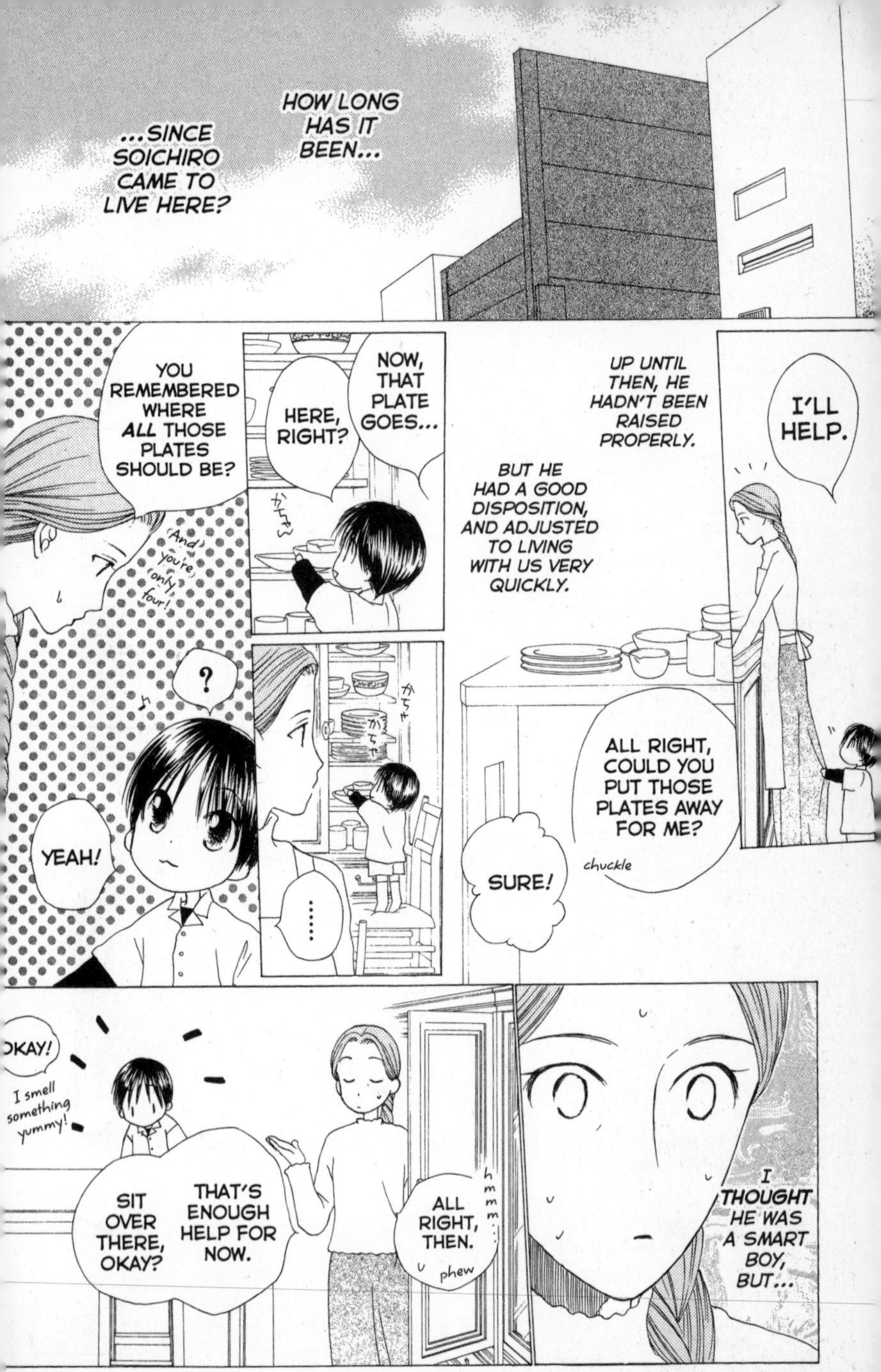
HOW LONG HAS IT BEEN...
...SINCE SOICHIRO CAME TO LIVE HERE?
I'LL HELP.
UP UNTIL THEN, HE HADN'T BEEN RAISED PROPERLY.
BUT HE HAD A GOOD DISPOSITION, AND ADJUSTED TO LIVING WITH US VERY QUICKLY.
ALL RIGHT, COULD YOU PUT THOSE PLATES AWAY FOR ME?
chuckle
SURE!
NOW, THAT PLATE GOES...
HERE, RIGHT?
かちゃん
かちゃ
かちゃ
......
YOU REMEMBERED WHERE ALL THOSE PLATES SHOULD BE?
(And you're only four!)
?
YEAH!
I THOUGHT HE WAS A SMART BOY, BUT...
hmmm...
ALL RIGHT, THEN.
phew
THAT'S ENOUGH HELP FOR NOW.
SIT OVER THERE, OKAY?
OKAY!
I smell something yummy!

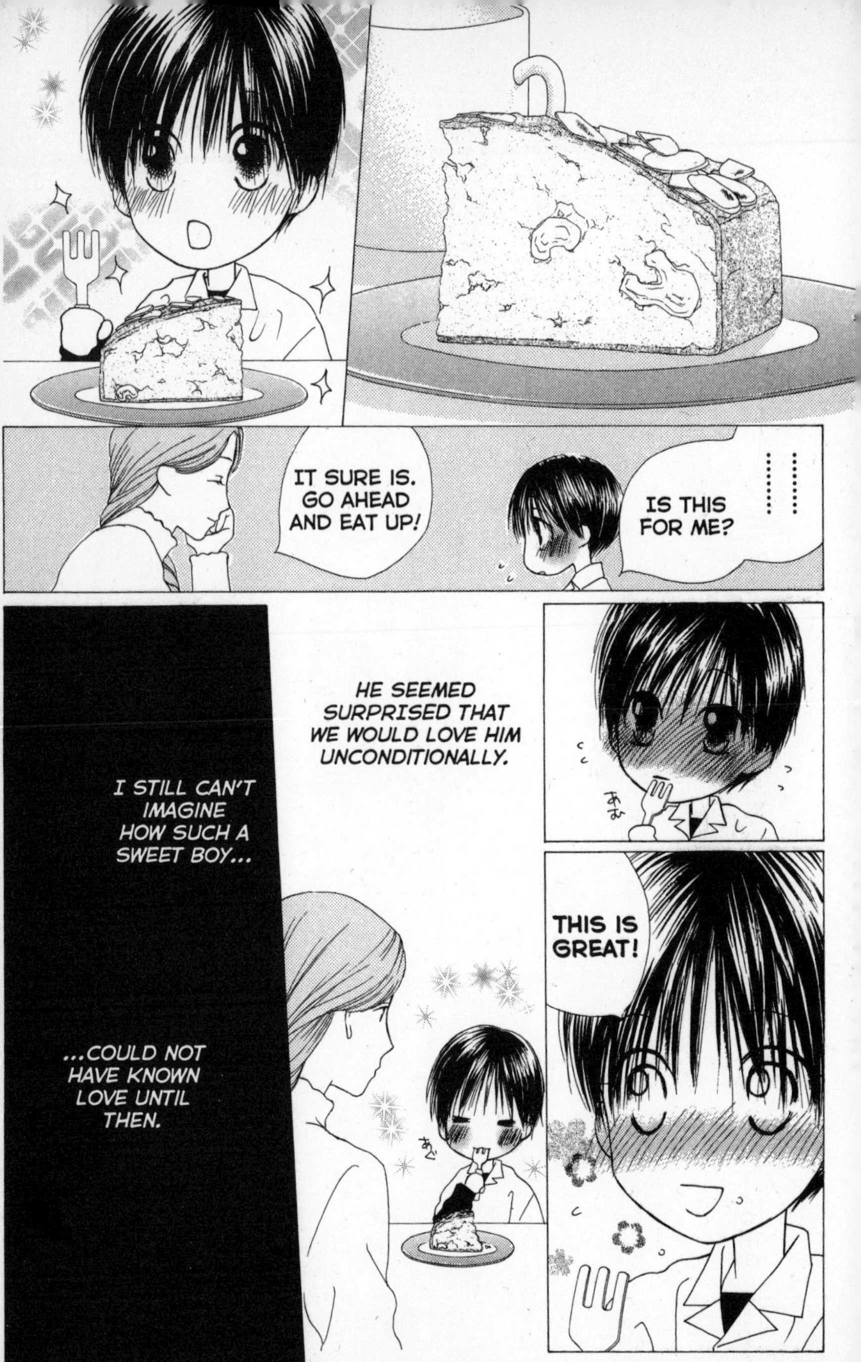
......
IS THIS FOR ME?
IT SURE IS. GO AHEAD AND EAT UP!
あむ
THIS IS GREAT!
HE SEEMED SURPRISED THAT WE WOULD LOVE HIM UNCONDITIONALLY.
I STILL CAN'T IMAGINE HOW SUCH A SWEET BOY...
あぐ
...COULD NOT HAVE KNOWN LOVE UNTIL THEN.

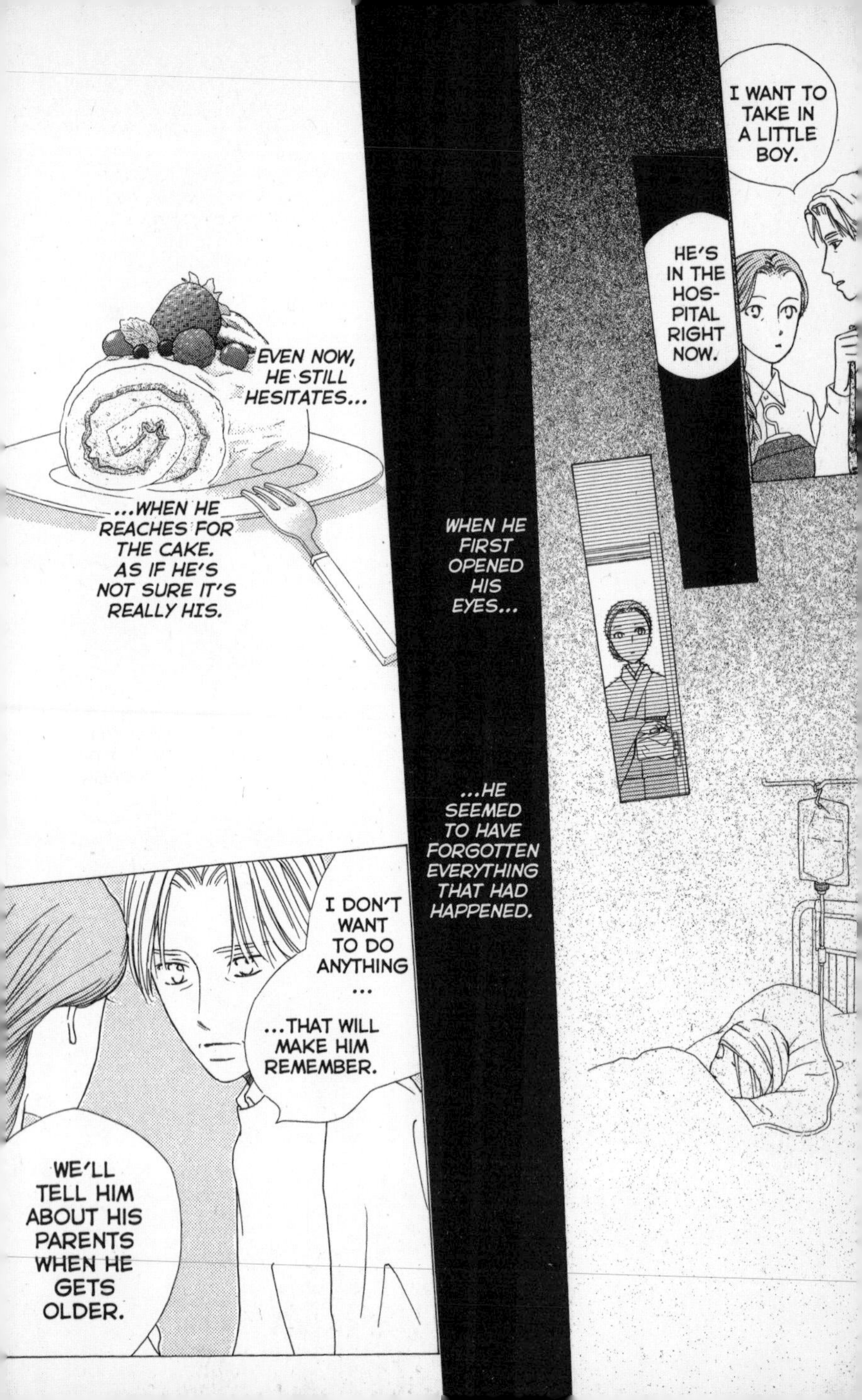
I WANT TO TAKE IN A LITTLE BOY.
HE'S IN THE HOS-PITAL RIGHT NOW.
WHEN HE FIRST OPENED HIS EYES...
...HE SEEMED TO HAVE FORGOTTEN EVERYTHING THAT HAD HAPPENED.
EVEN NOW, HE STILL HESITATES...
...WHEN HE REACHES FOR THE CAKE. AS IF HE'S NOT SURE IT'S REALLY HIS.
I DON'T WANT TO DO ANYTHING...
...THAT WILL MAKE HIM REMEMBER.
WE'LL TELL HIM ABOUT HIS PARENTS WHEN HE GETS OLDER.

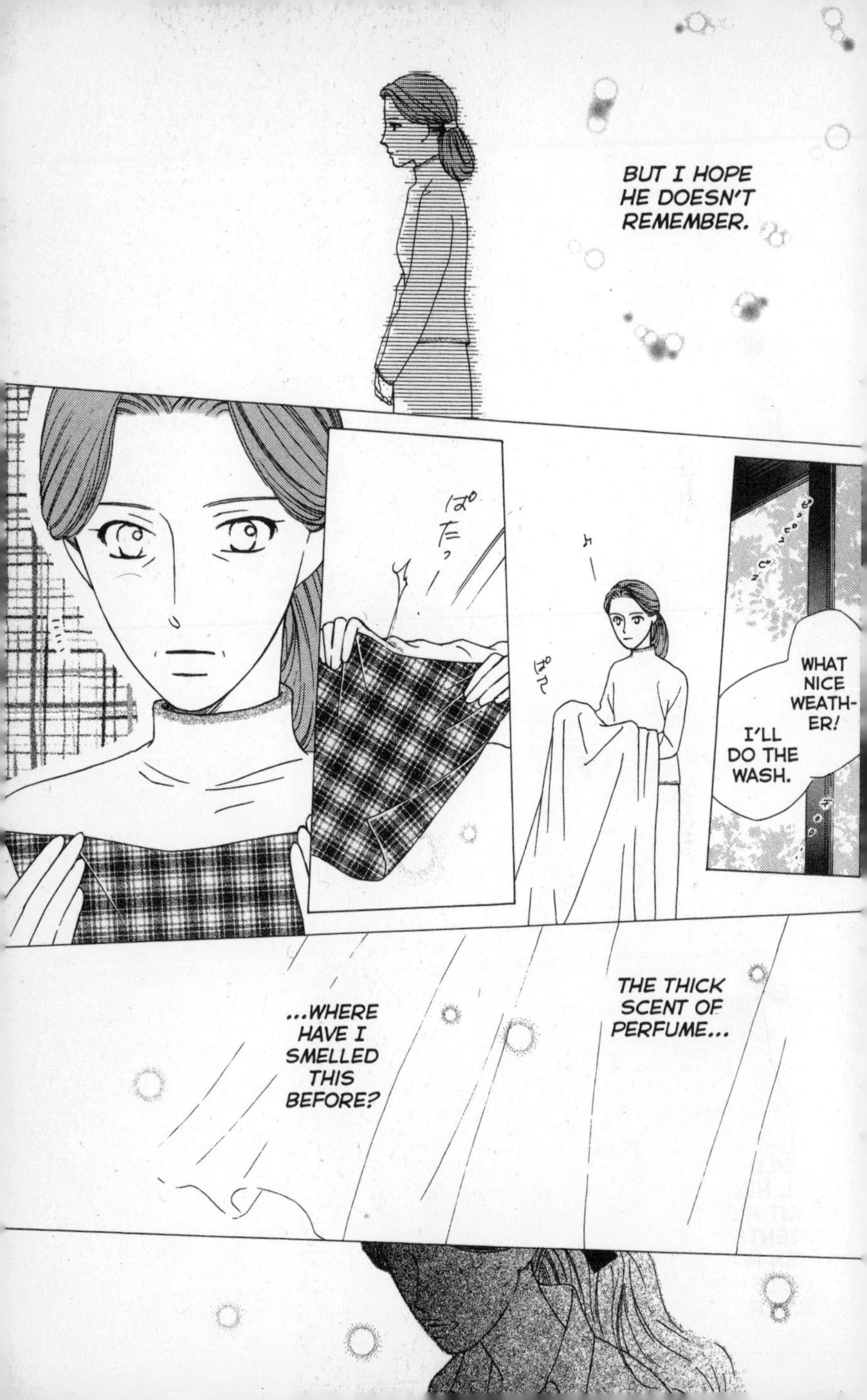
BUT I HOPE HE DOESN'T REMEMBER.
WHAT NICE WEATHER!
I'LL DO THE WASH.
THE THICK SCENT OF PERFUME...
...WHERE HAVE I SMELLED THIS BEFORE?

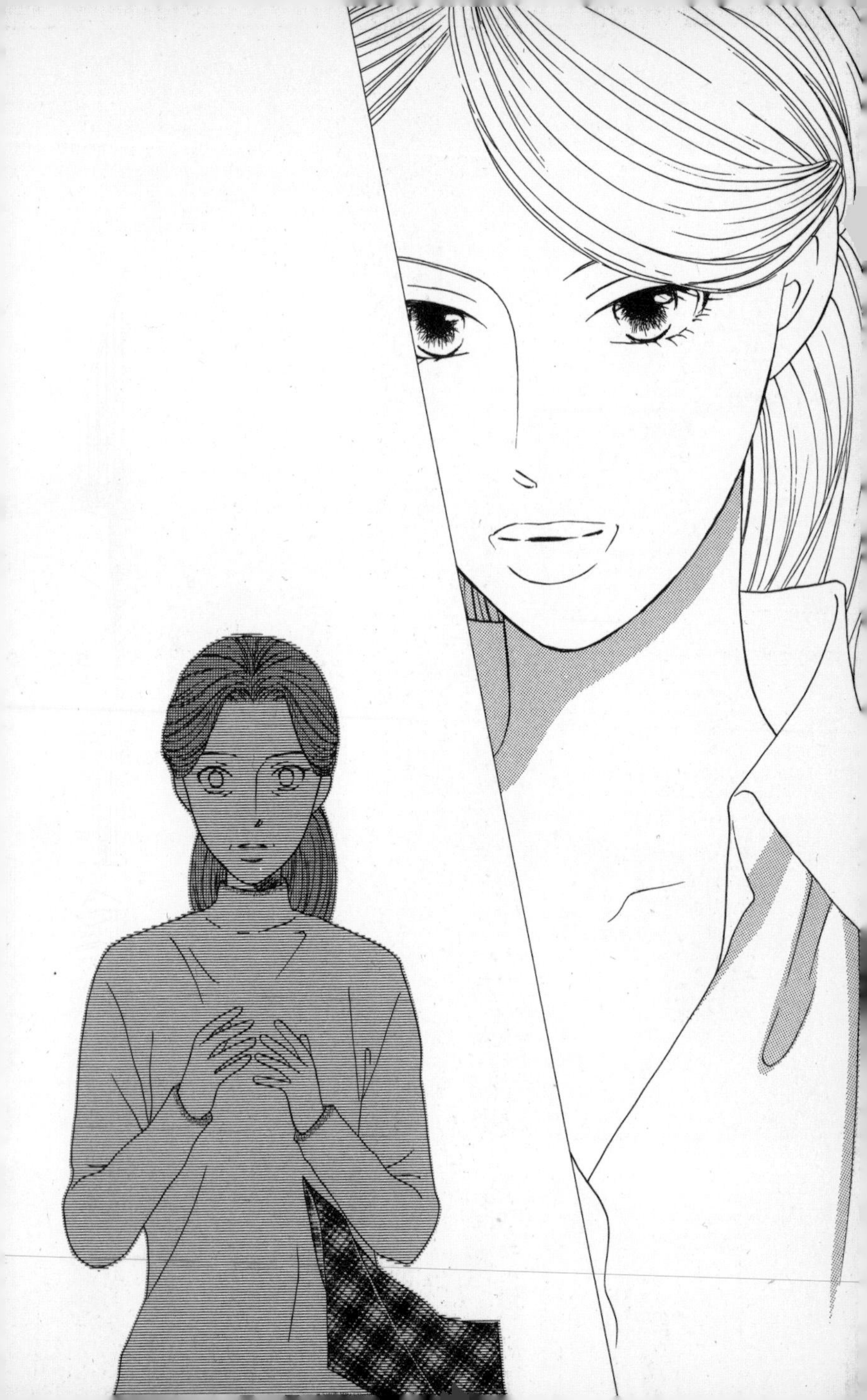

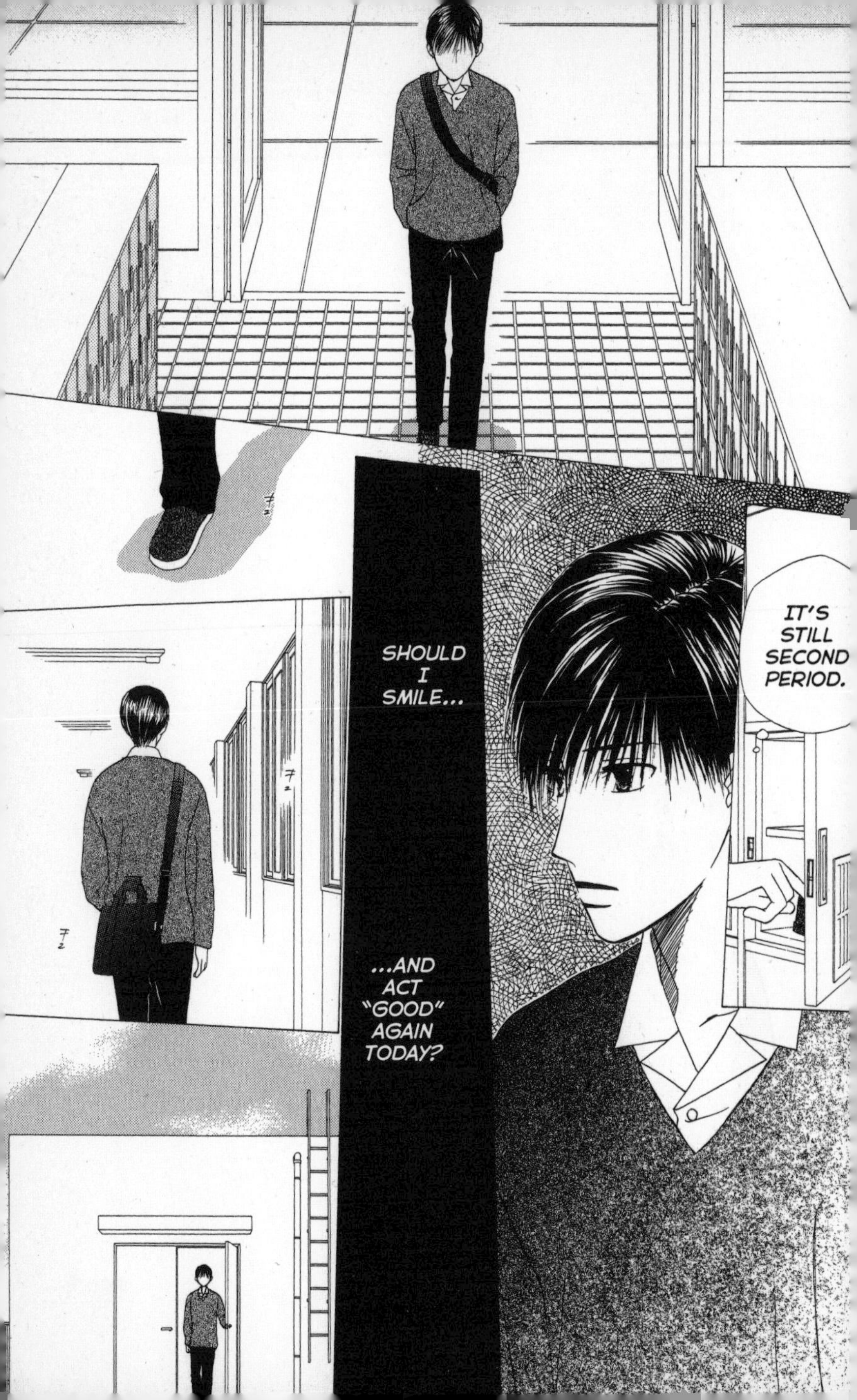
IT'S STILL SECOND PERIOD.
SHOULD I SMILE...
...AND ACT "GOOD" AGAIN TODAY?

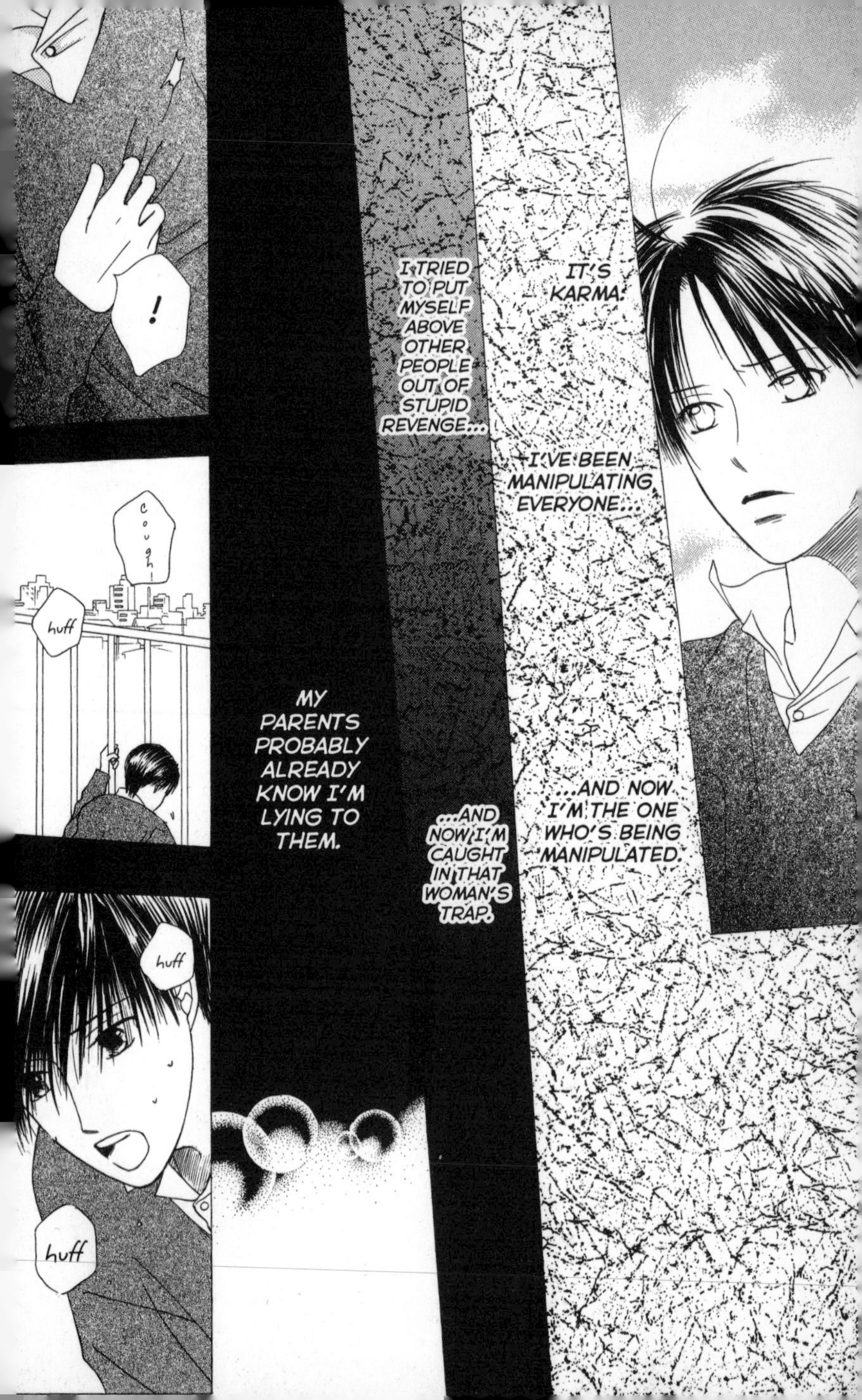
IT'S KARMA.
I'VE BEEN MANIPULATING EVERYONE...
...AND NOW I'M THE ONE WHO'S BEING MANIPULATED.
I TRIED TO PUT MYSELF ABOVE OTHER PEOPLE OUT OF STUPID REVENGE...
...AND NOW I'M CAUGHT IN THAT WOMAN'S TRAP.
MY PARENTS PROBABLY ALREADY KNOW I'M LYING TO THEM.
!
cough!
huff
huff
huff

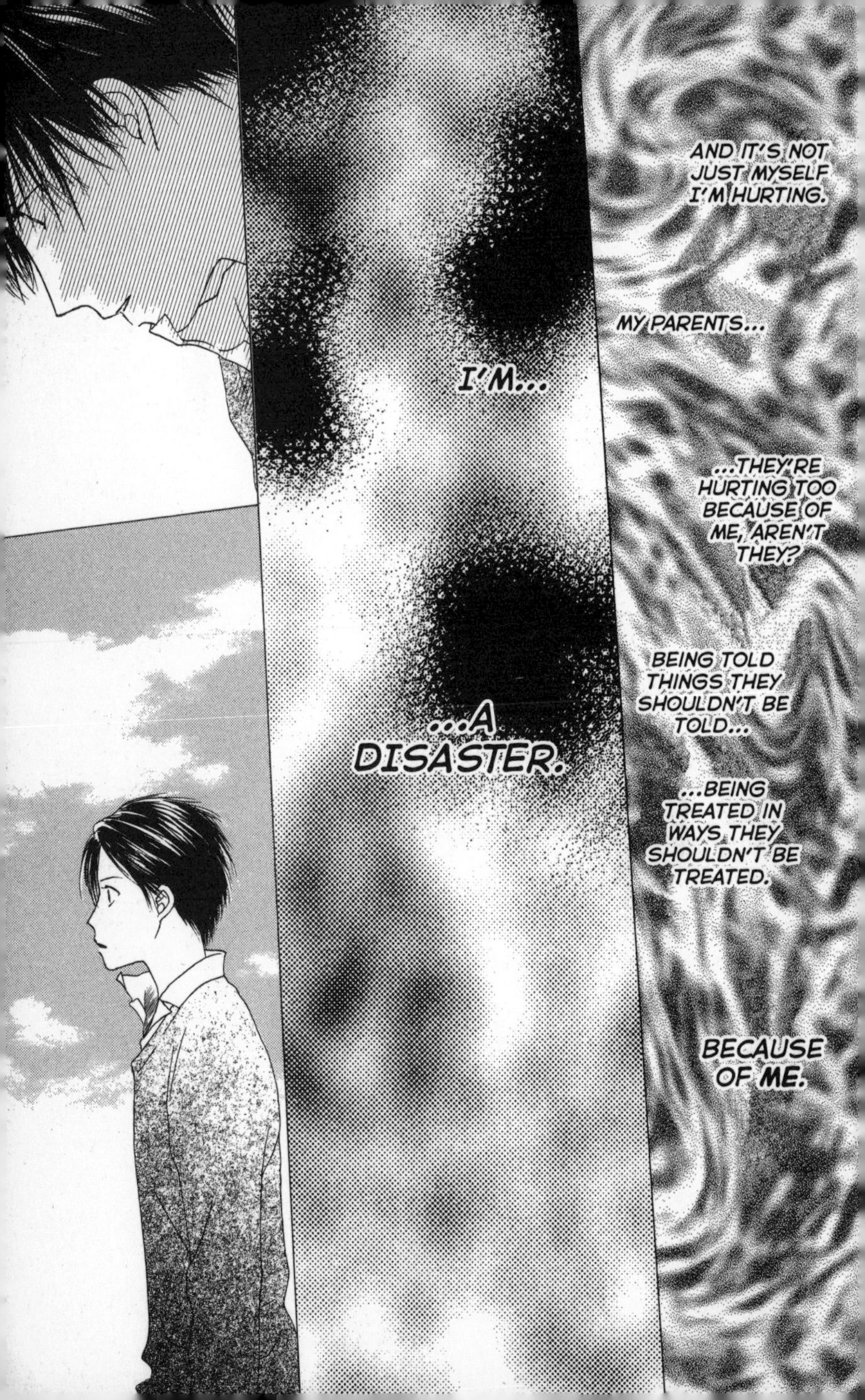
AND IT'S NOT JUST MYSELF I'M HURTING.
MY PARENTS...
...THEY'RE HURTING TOO BECAUSE OF ME, AREN'T THEY?
BEING TOLD THINGS THEY SHOULDN'T BE TOLD...
...BEING TREATED IN WAYS THEY SHOULDN'T BE TREATED.
BECAUSE OF ME.
I'M...
...A DISASTER.

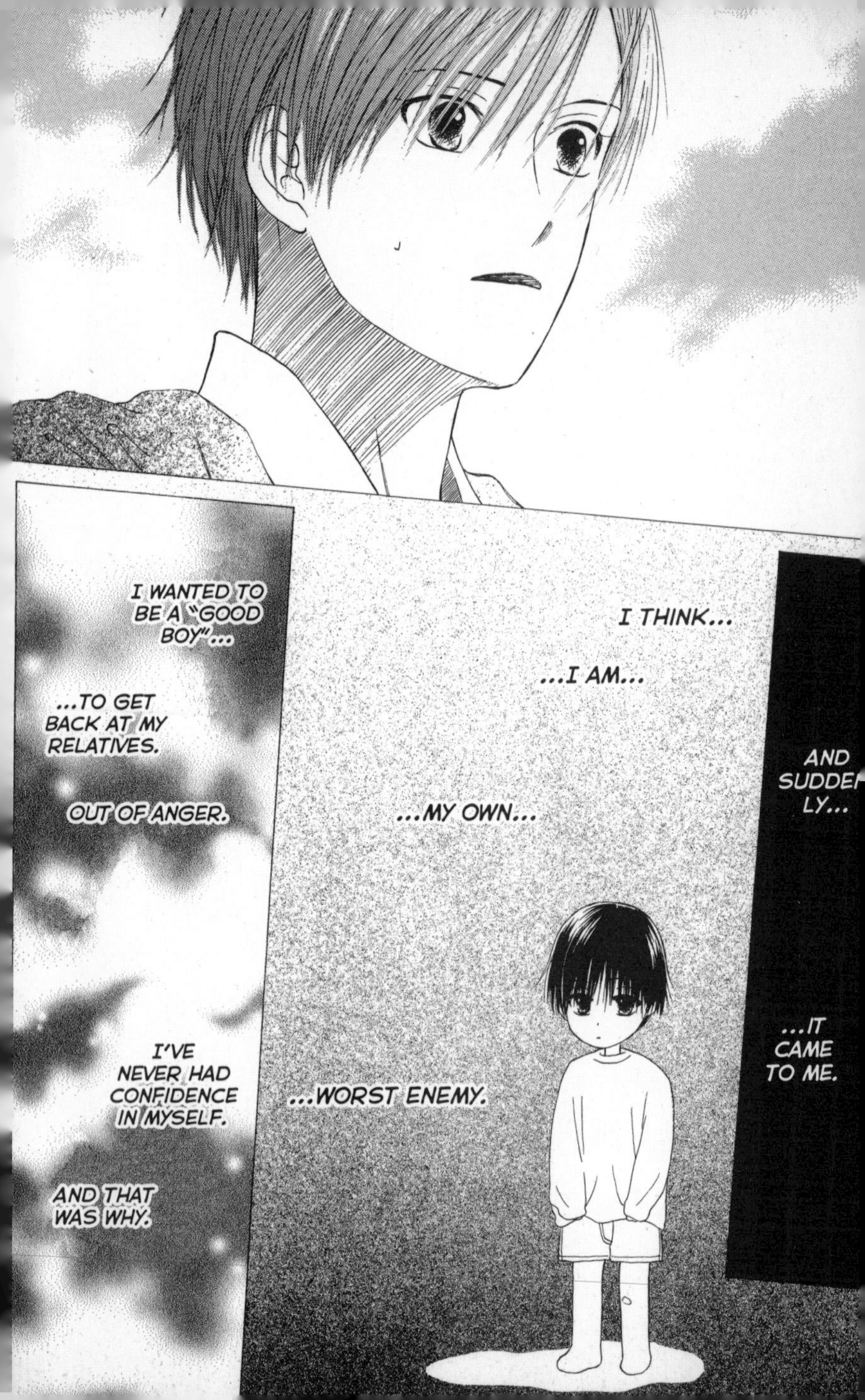
AND SUDDE LY...
...IT CAME TO ME.
I THINK...
...I AM...
...MY OWN...
...WORST ENEMY.
I WANTED TO BE A "GOOD BOY"...
...TO GET BACK AT MY RELATIVES.
OUT OF ANGER.
I'VE NEVER HAD CONFIDENCE IN MYSELF.
AND THAT WAS WHY.

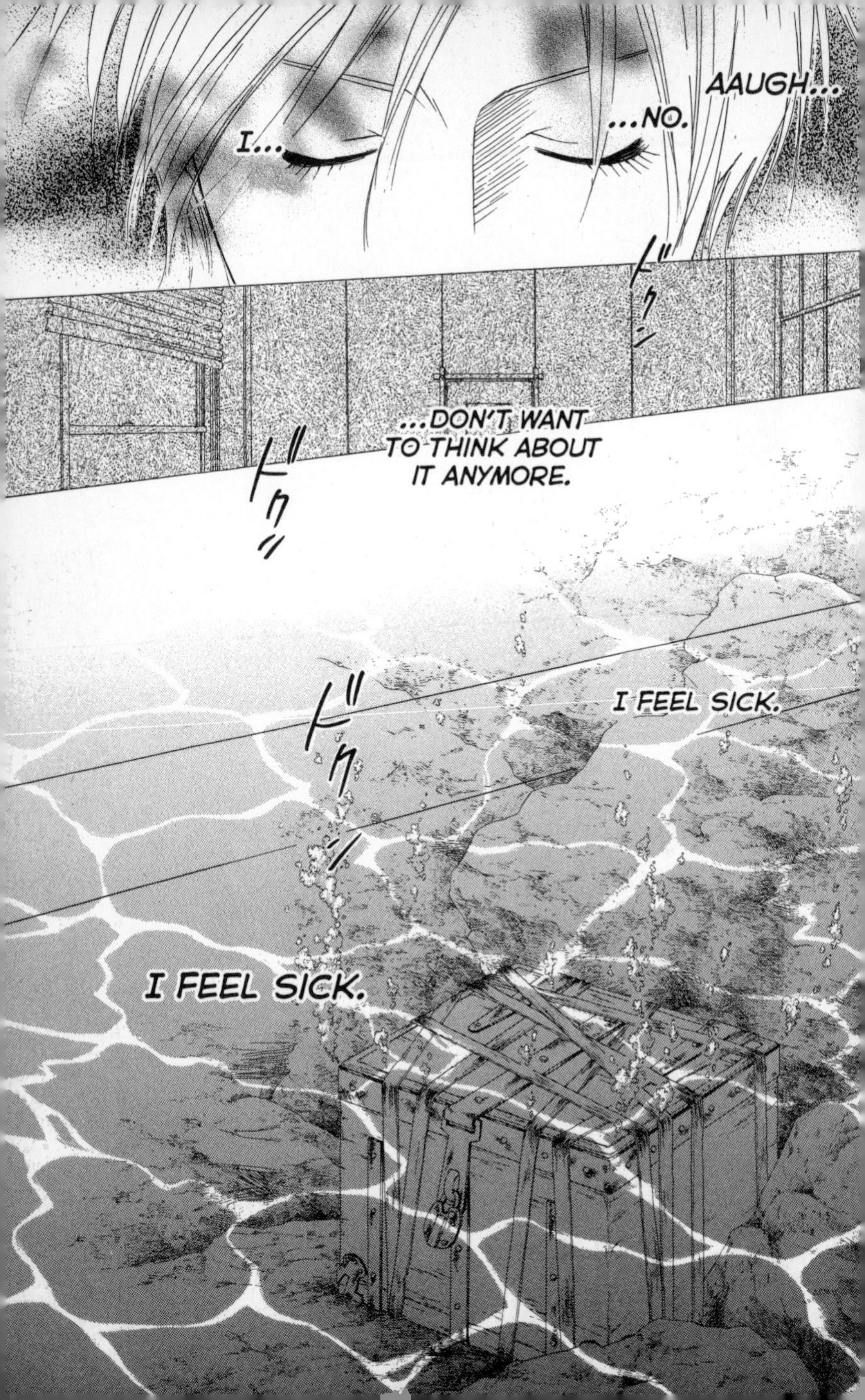
AAUGH...
...NO.
I...
ドクン
...DON'T WANT TO THINK ABOUT IT ANYMORE.
ドクン
I FEEL SICK.
ドクン
I FEEL SICK.

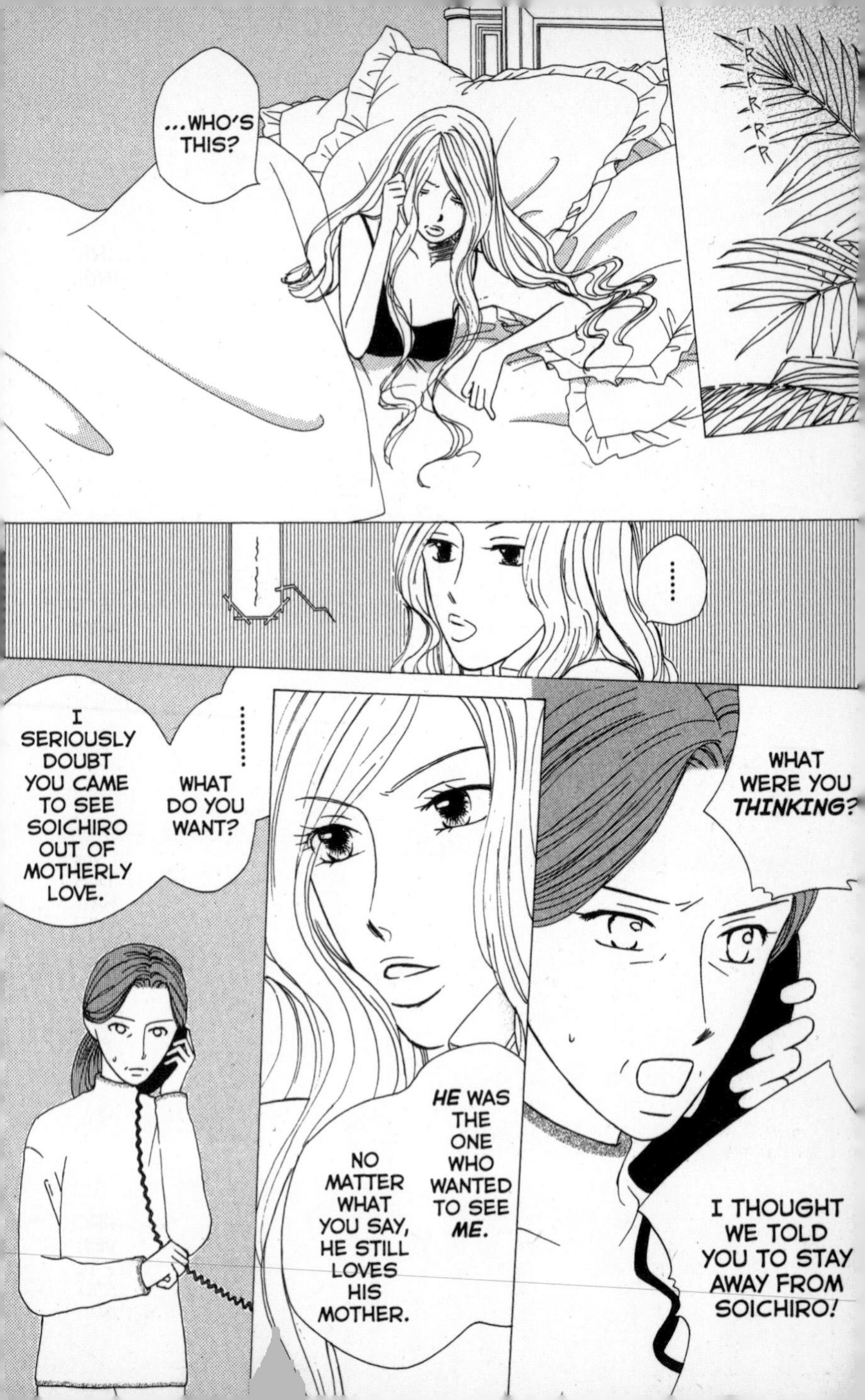
TRRRRR
...WHO'S THIS?
......
WHAT WERE YOU *THINKING?*
I THOUGHT WE TOLD YOU TO STAY AWAY FROM SOICHIRO!
HE WAS THE ONE WHO WANTED TO SEE *ME.*
NO MATTER WHAT YOU SAY, HE STILL LOVES HIS MOTHER.
......
WHAT DO YOU WANT?
I SERIOUSLY DOUBT YOU CAME TO SEE SOICHIRO OUT OF MOTHERLY LOVE.

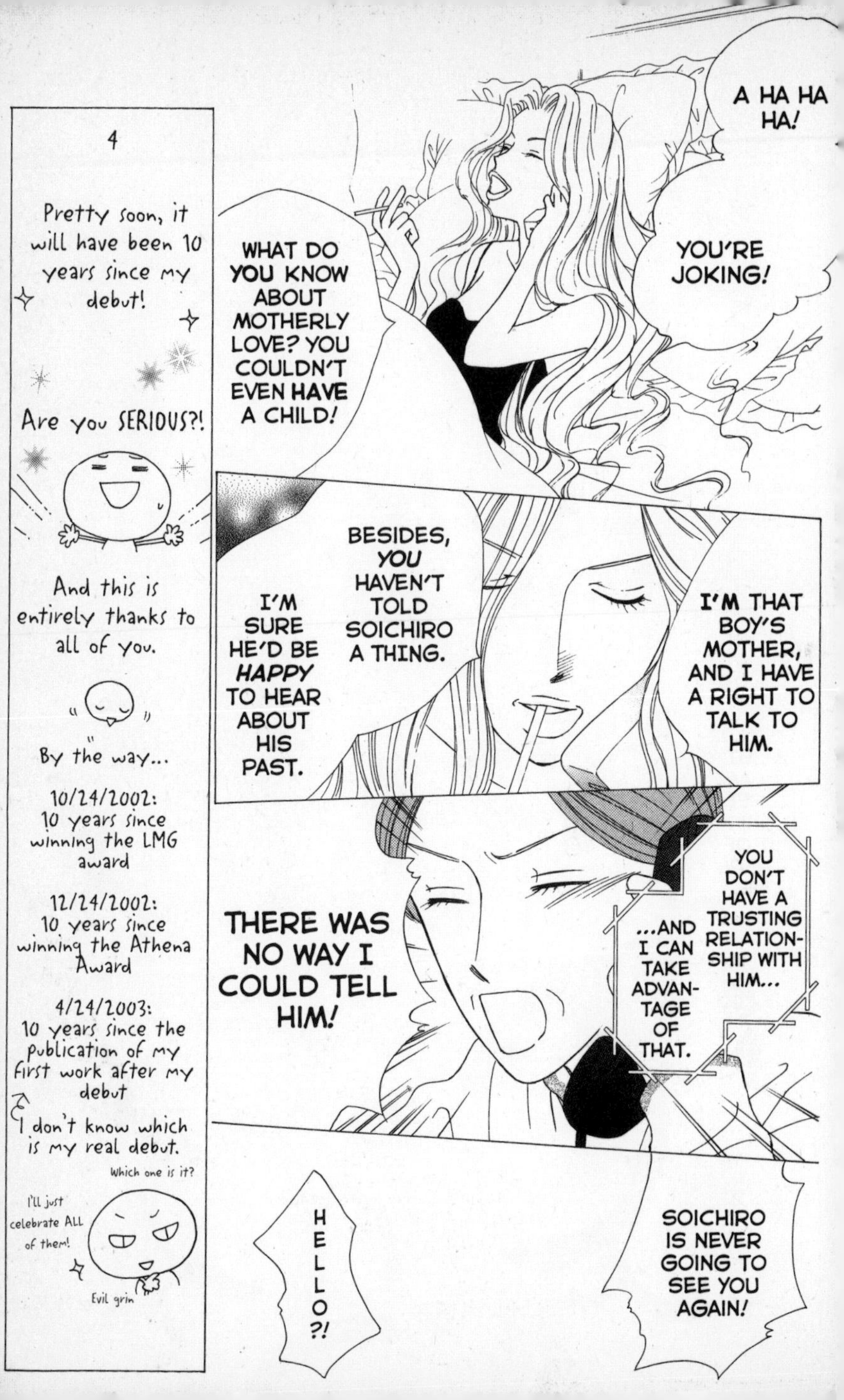
A HA HA HA!
YOU'RE JOKING!
WHAT DO YOU KNOW ABOUT MOTHERLY LOVE? YOU COULDN'T EVEN HAVE A CHILD!
I'M THAT BOY'S MOTHER, AND I HAVE A RIGHT TO TALK TO HIM.
BESIDES, *YOU* HAVEN'T TOLD SOICHIRO A THING.
I'M SURE HE'D BE *HAPPY* TO HEAR ABOUT HIS PAST.
YOU DON'T HAVE A TRUSTING RELATIONSHIP WITH HIM...
...AND I CAN TAKE ADVANTAGE OF THAT.
THERE WAS NO WAY I COULD TELL HIM!
SOICHIRO IS NEVER GOING TO SEE YOU AGAIN!
HELLO?!

4

Pretty soon, it will have been 10 years since my debut!

Are you SERIOUS?!

And this is entirely thanks to all of you.

By the way...

10/24/2002:
10 years since winning the LMG award

12/24/2002:
10 years since winning the Athena Award

4/24/2003:
10 years since the publication of my first work after my debut

I don't know which is my real debut.

Which one is it?

I'll just celebrate ALL of them!

Evil grin

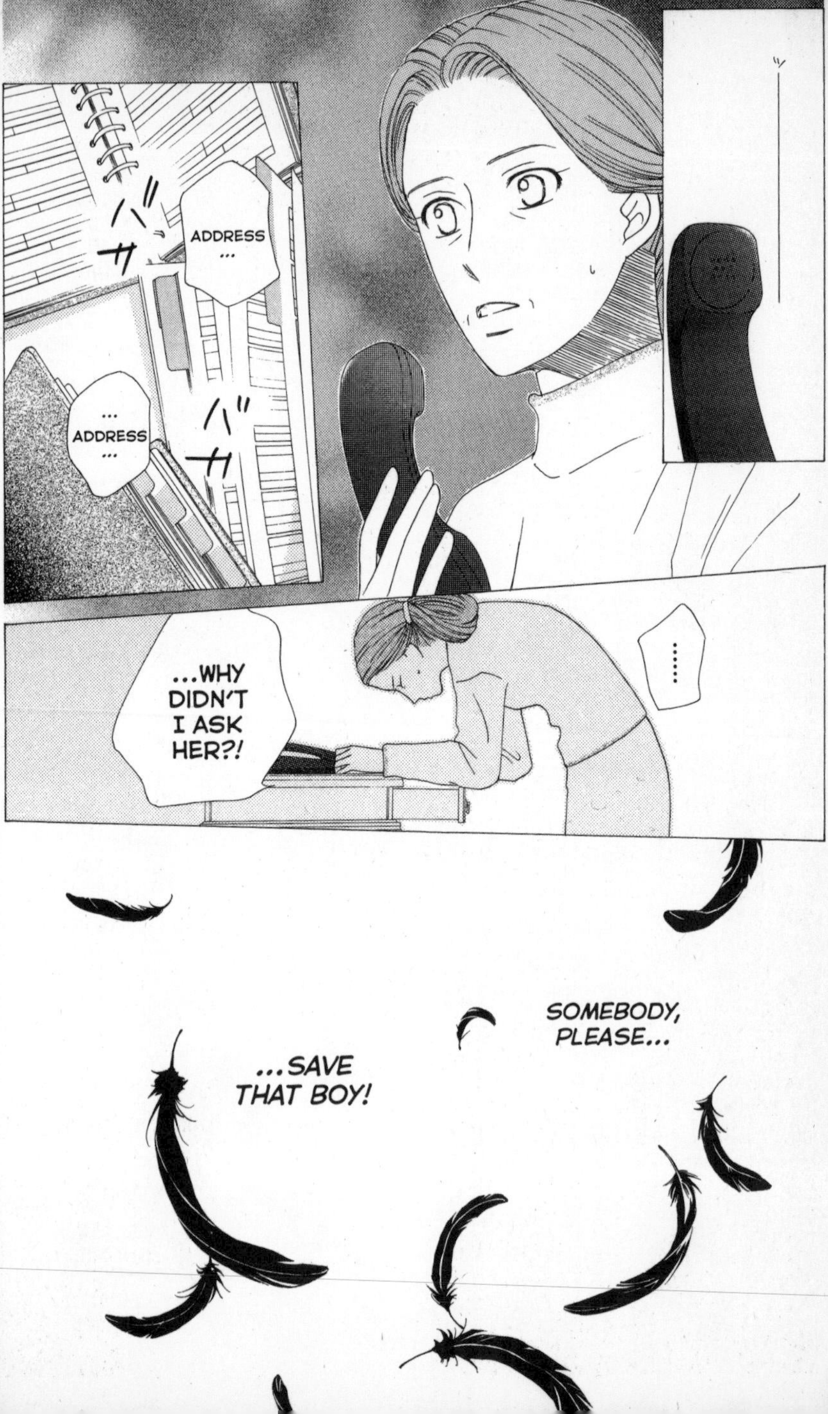

バサ
ADDRESS ...
... ADDRESS ...
バサ
......
...WHY DIDN'T I ASK HER?!
SOMEBODY, PLEASE...
...SAVE THAT BOY!

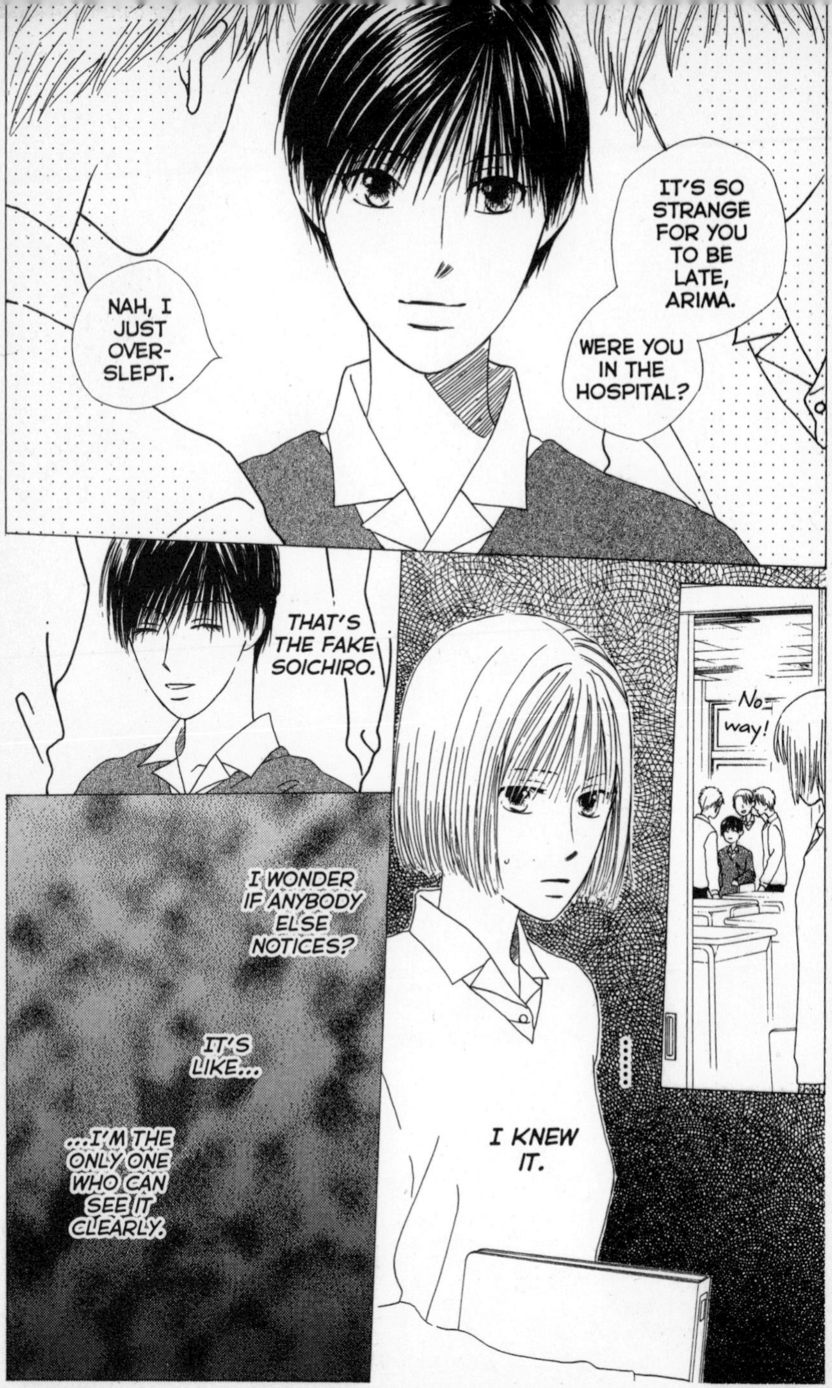
IT'S SO STRANGE FOR YOU TO BE LATE, ARIMA.
WERE YOU IN THE HOSPITAL?
NAH, I JUST OVER-SLEPT.
No way!
......
I KNEW IT.
THAT'S THE FAKE SOICHIRO.
I WONDER IF ANYBODY ELSE NOTICES?
IT'S LIKE...
...I'M THE ONLY ONE WHO CAN SEE IT CLEARLY.

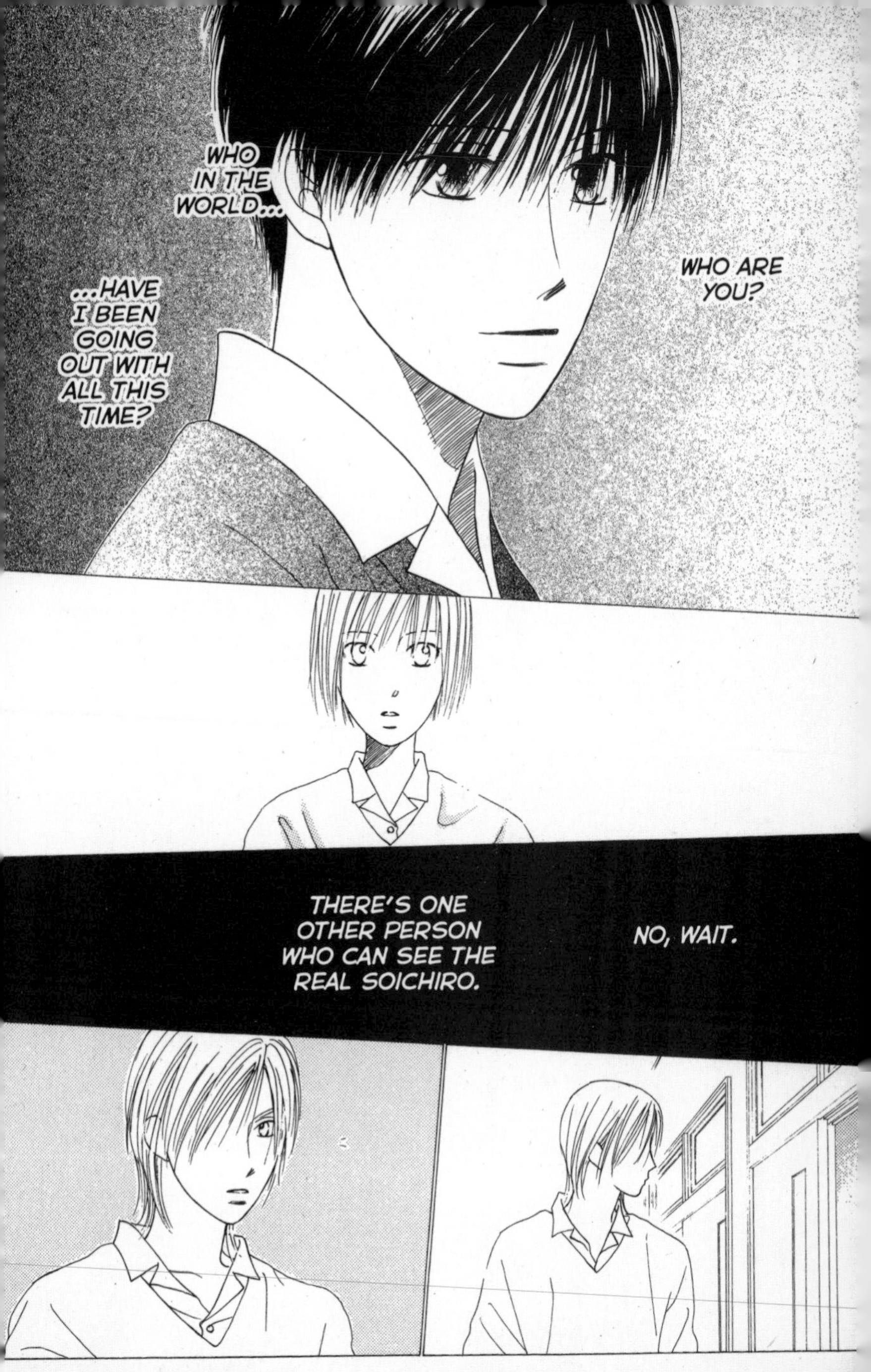
WHO ARE YOU?
WHO IN THE WORLD...
...HAVE I BEEN GOING OUT WITH ALL THIS TIME?
NO, WAIT.
THERE'S ONE OTHER PERSON WHO CAN SEE THE REAL SOICHIRO.

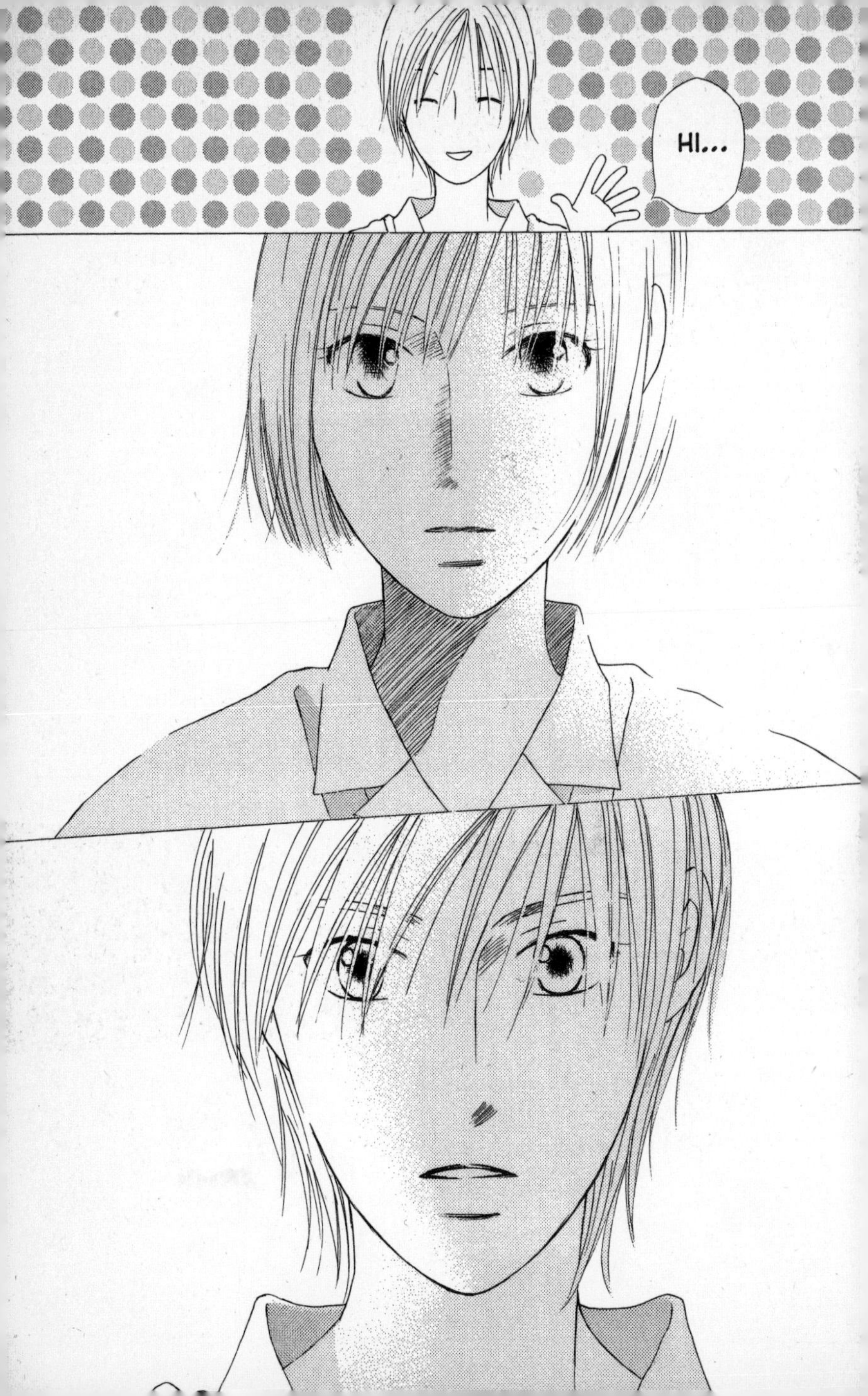
HI...

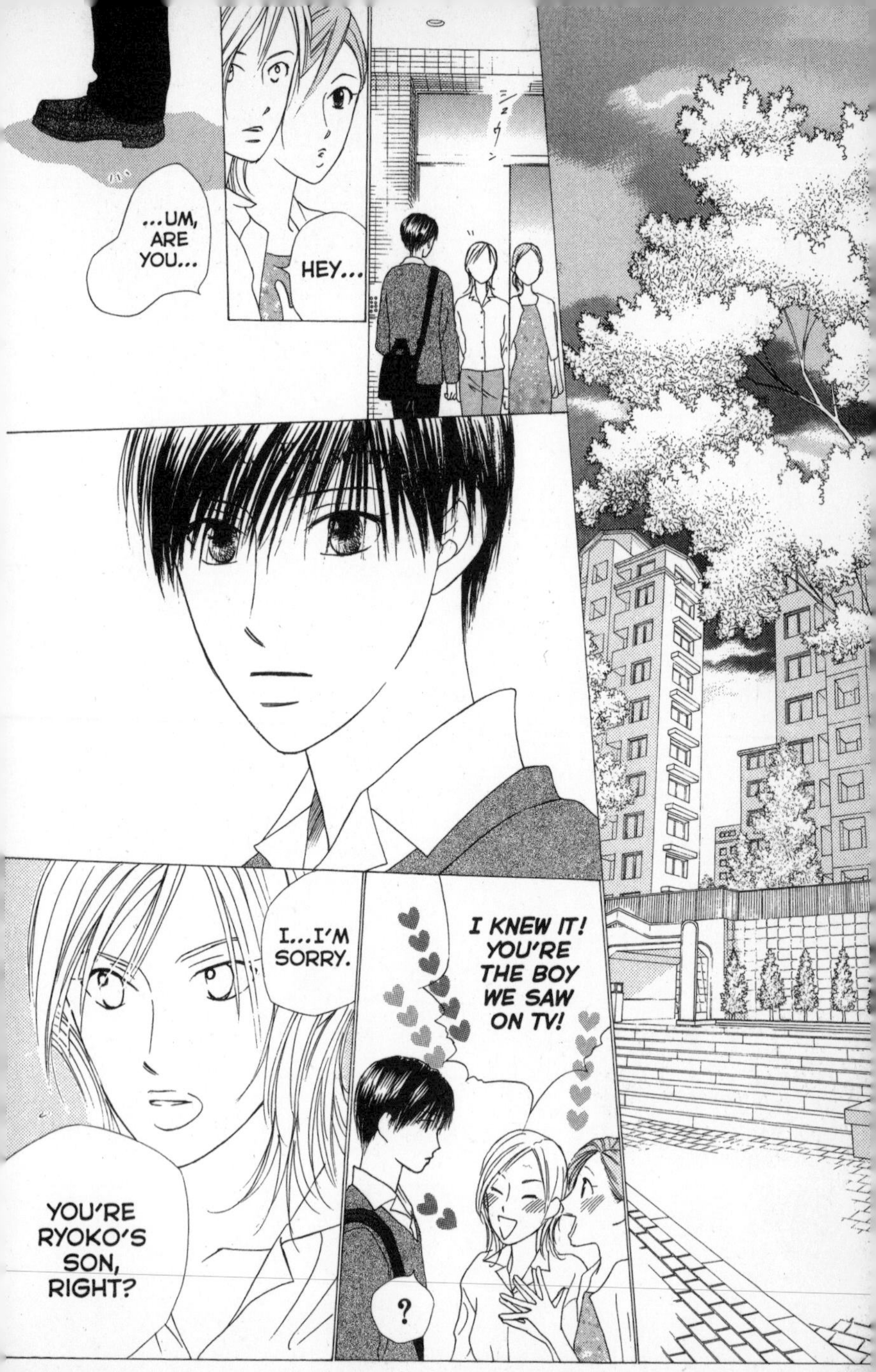
HEY...
...UM, ARE YOU...
I KNEW IT! YOU'RE THE BOY WE SAW ON TV!
?
I...I'M SORRY.
YOU'RE RYOKO'S SON, RIGHT?

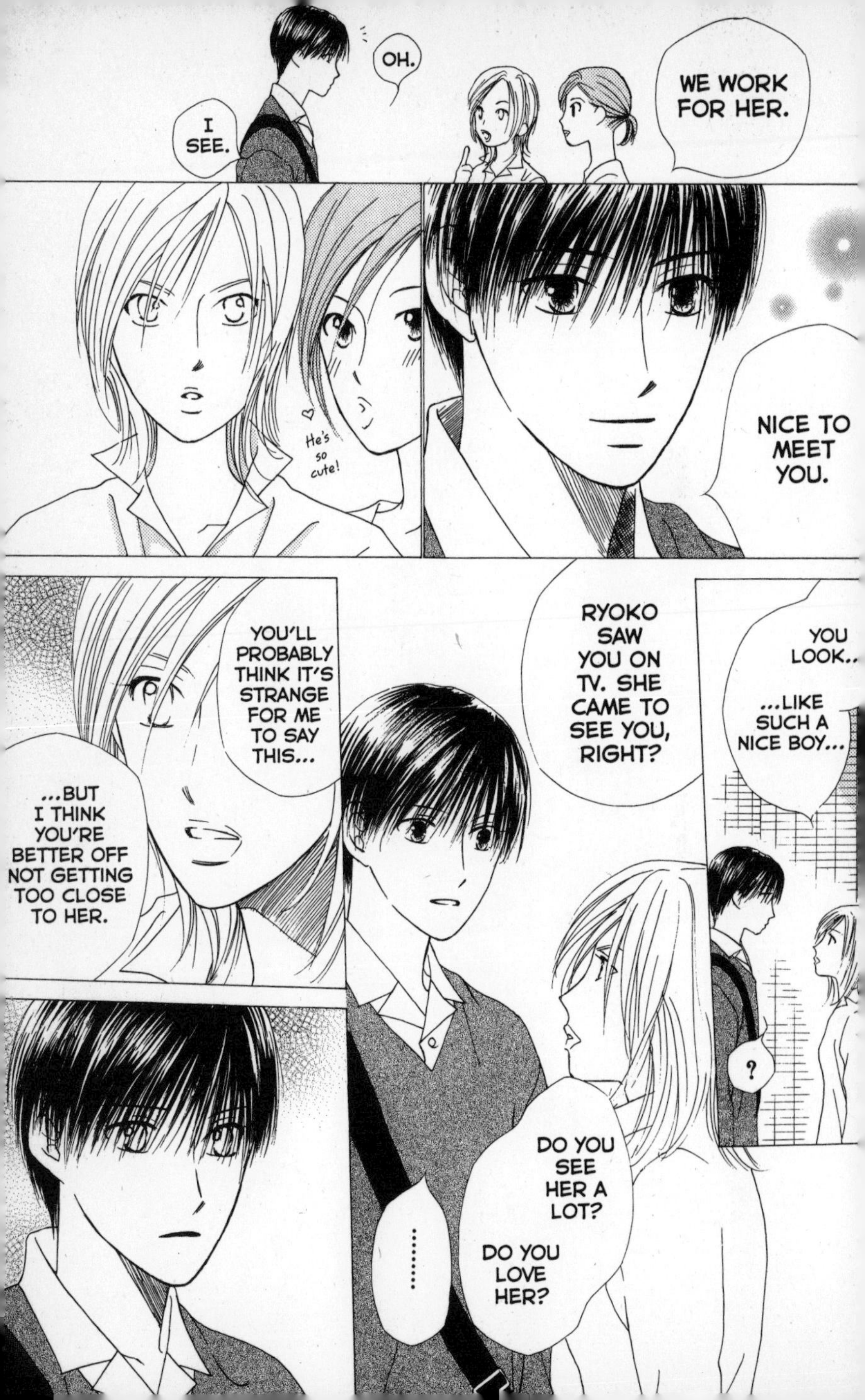
WE WORK FOR HER.
OH.
I SEE.
NICE TO MEET YOU.
He's so cute!
YOU LOOK...
...LIKE SUCH A NICE BOY...
?
RYOKO SAW YOU ON TV. SHE CAME TO SEE YOU, RIGHT?
DO YOU SEE HER A LOT?
DO YOU LOVE HER?
......
YOU'LL PROBABLY THINK IT'S STRANGE FOR ME TO SAY THIS...
...BUT I THINK YOU'RE BETTER OFF NOT GETTING TOO CLOSE TO HER.

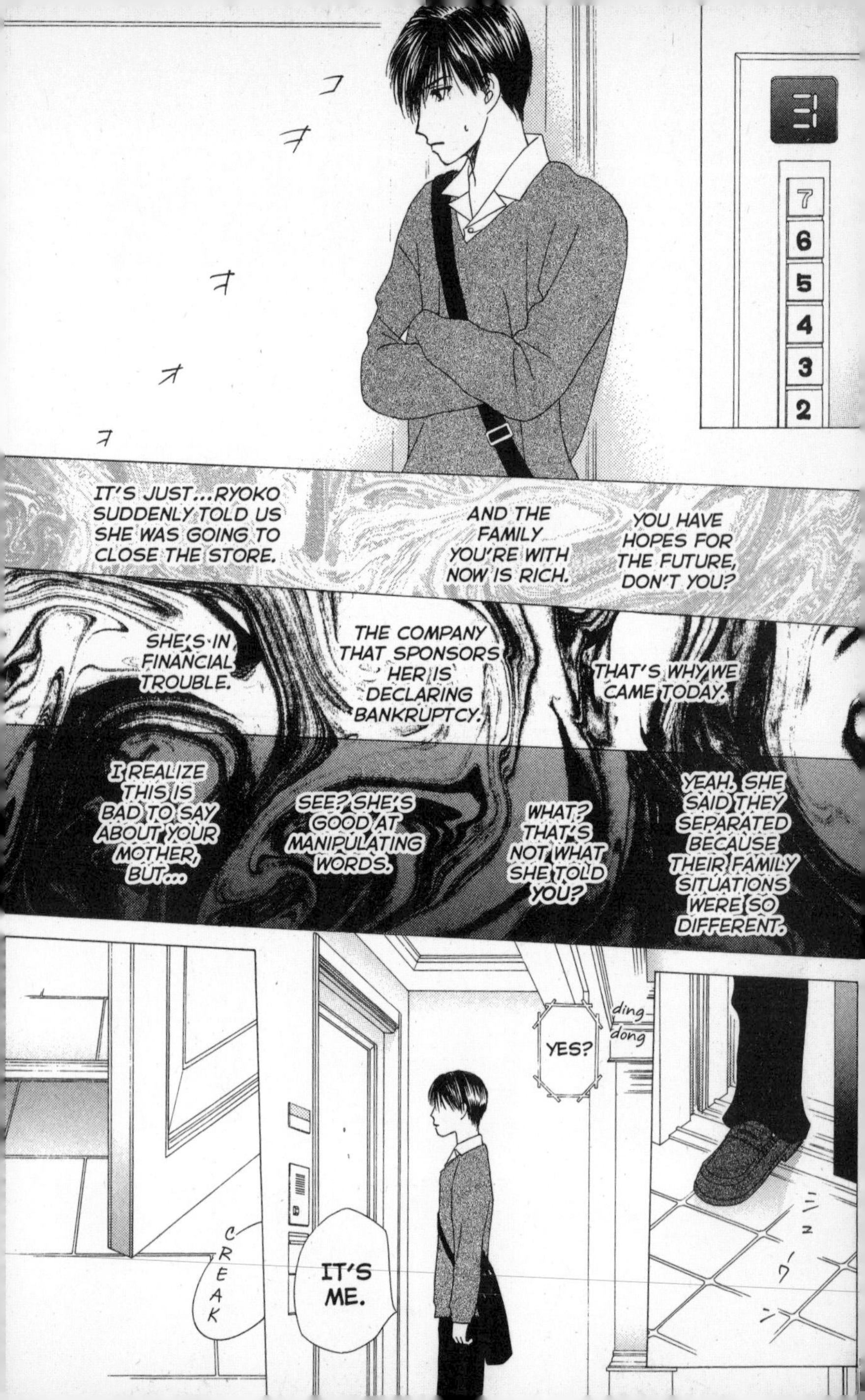

YOU HAVE HOPES FOR THE FUTURE, DON'T YOU?
AND THE FAMILY YOU'RE WITH NOW IS RICH.
IT'S JUST...RYOKO SUDDENLY TOLD US SHE WAS GOING TO CLOSE THE STORE.
THAT'S WHY WE CAME TODAY.
THE COMPANY THAT SPONSORS HER IS DECLARING BANKRUPTCY.
SHE'S IN FINANCIAL TROUBLE.
YEAH. SHE SAID THEY SEPARATED BECAUSE THEIR FAMILY SITUATIONS WERE SO DIFFERENT.
WHAT? THAT'S NOT WHAT SHE TOLD YOU?
SEE? SHE'S GOOD AT MANIPULATING WORDS.
I REALIZE THIS IS BAD TO SAY ABOUT YOUR MOTHER, BUT...
ding-dong
YES?
IT'S ME.
CREAK

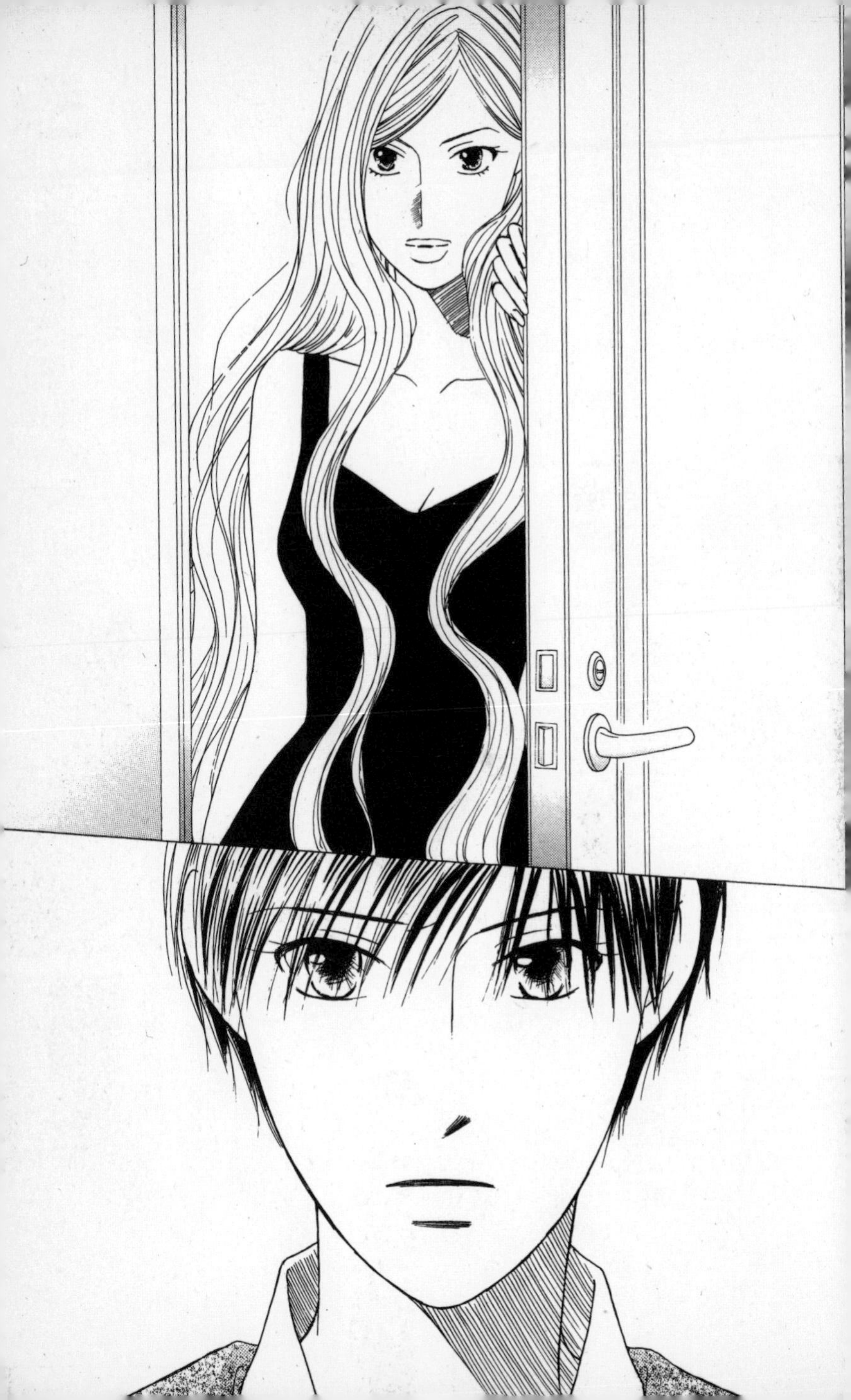

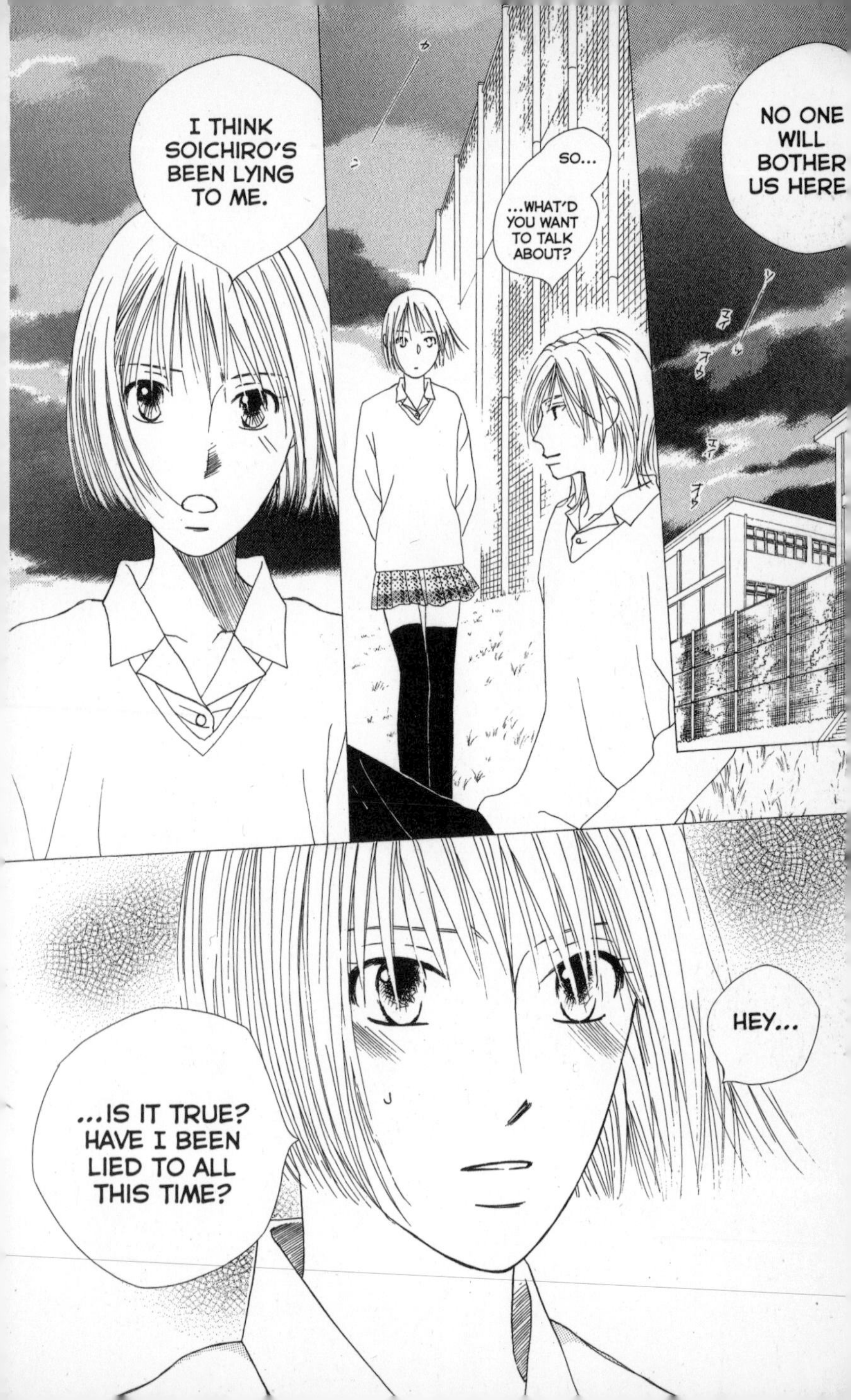
NO ONE WILL BOTHER US HERE
SO...
...WHAT'D YOU WANT TO TALK ABOUT?
I THINK SOICHIRO'S BEEN LYING TO ME.
HEY...
...IS IT TRUE? HAVE I BEEN LIED TO ALL THIS TIME?

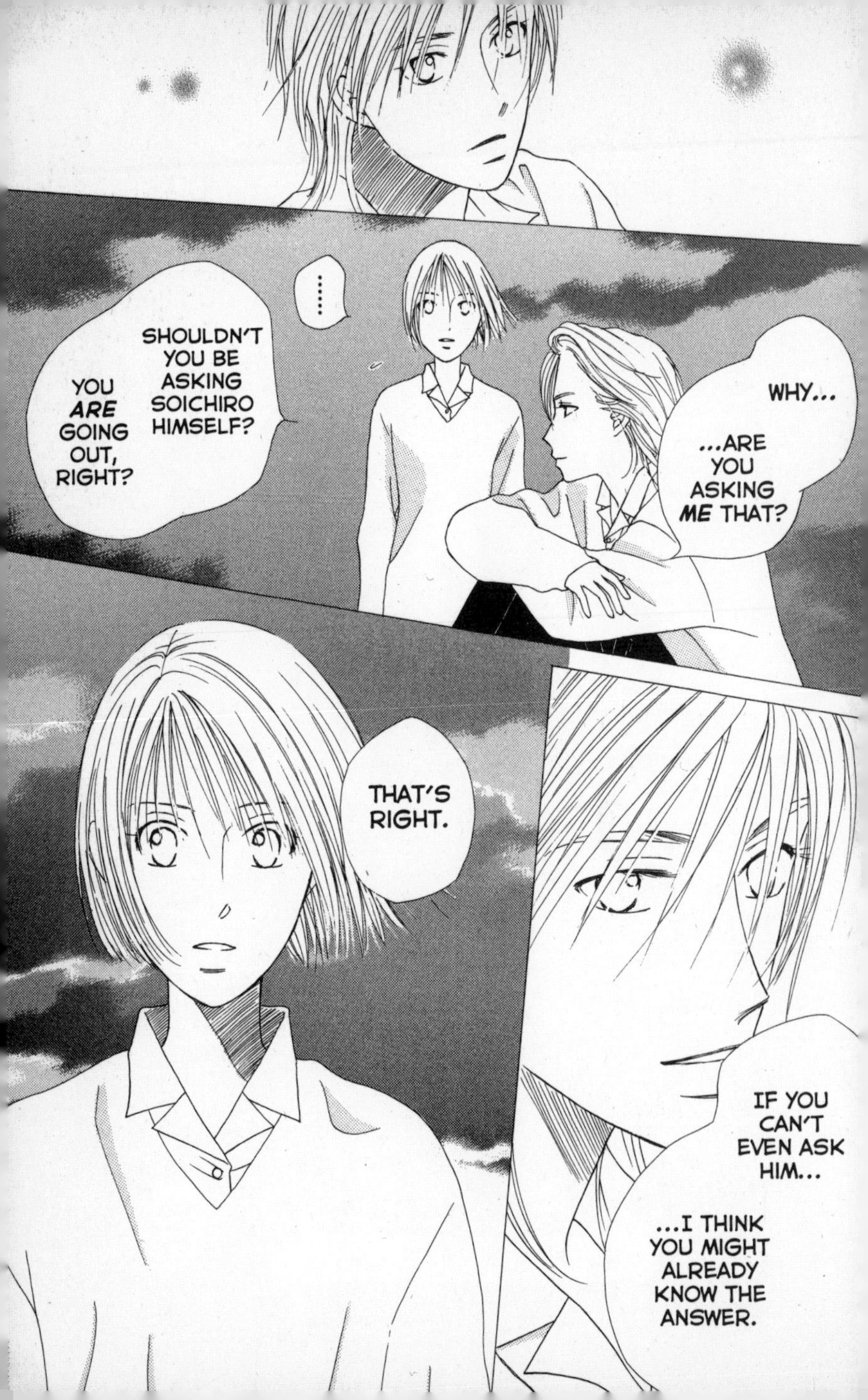
WHY...
...ARE YOU ASKING *ME* THAT?
......
SHOULDN'T YOU BE ASKING SOICHIRO HIMSELF?
YOU *ARE* GOING OUT, RIGHT?
IF YOU CAN'T EVEN ASK HIM...
...I THINK YOU MIGHT ALREADY KNOW THE ANSWER.
THAT'S RIGHT.

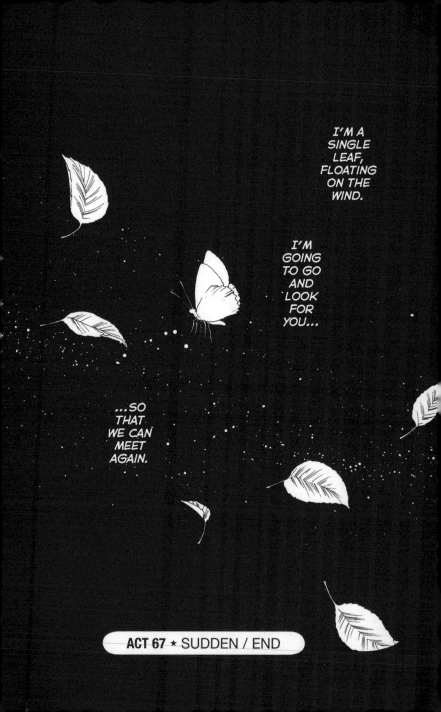

I'M A
SINGLE
LEAF,
FLOATING
ON THE
WIND.

I'M
GOING
TO GO
AND
LOOK
FOR
YOU...

...SO
THAT
WE CAN
MEET
AGAIN.

ACT 67 ★ SUDDEN / END

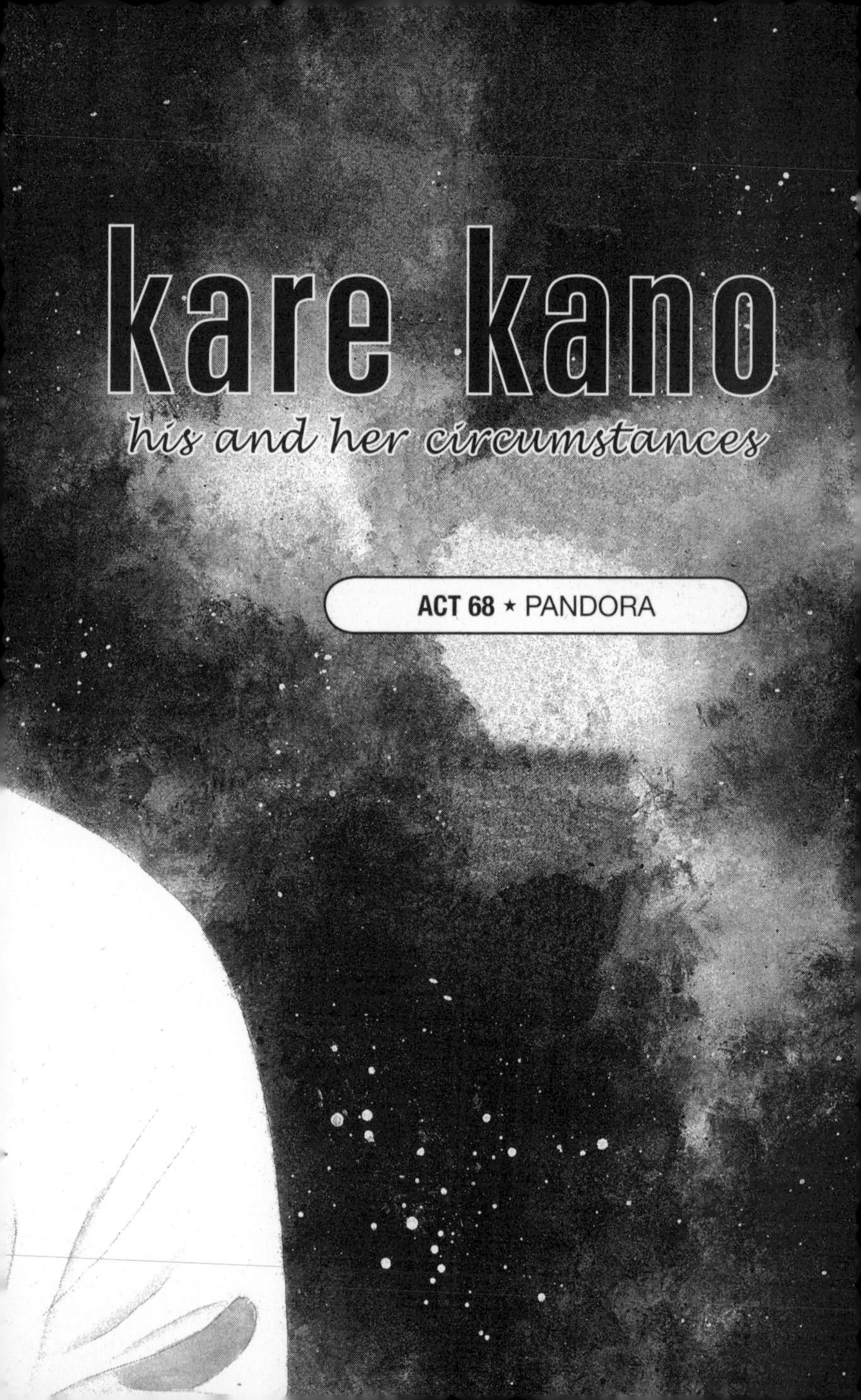
kare kano
his and her circumstances
ACT 68 ★ PANDORA

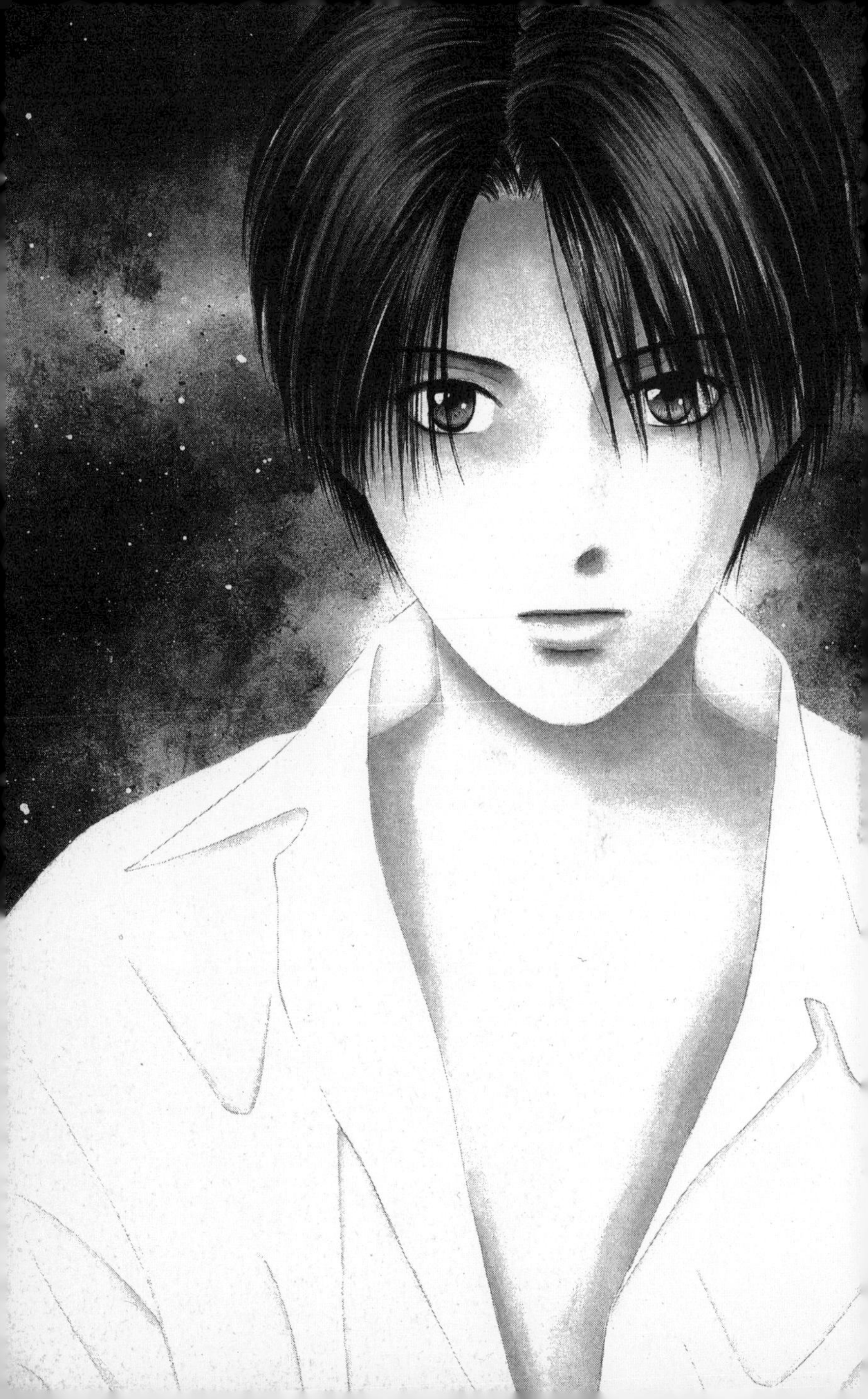

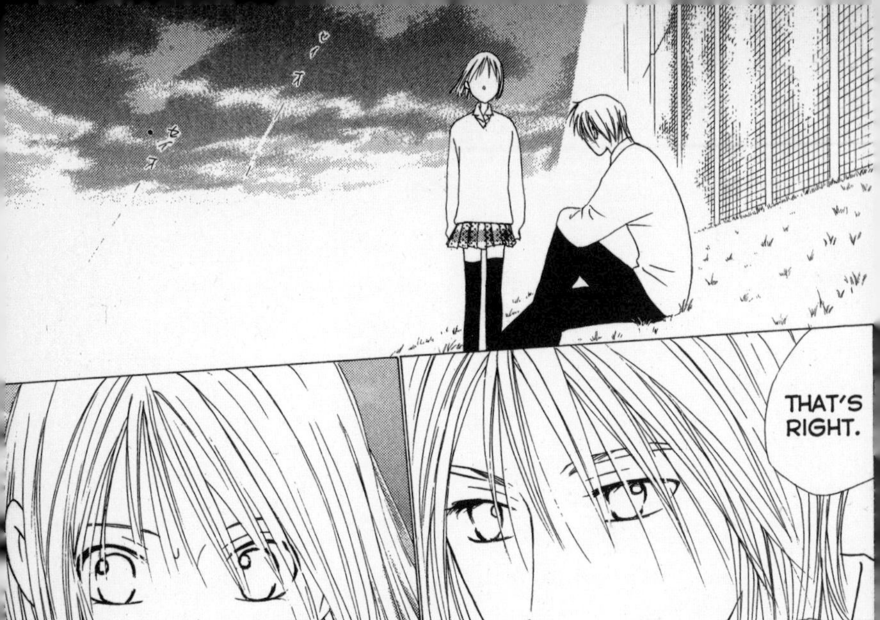
THAT'S RIGHT.
SOICHIRO ISN'T TELLING YOU WHAT HE REALLY FEELS.
EVEN I DON'T KNOW WHY.
....

I love hemp.

Summer fun! ♡

I have a hemp skirt, hemp socks, and a sweater woven with hemp.

My skin is sensitive, though, so they tickle a little.

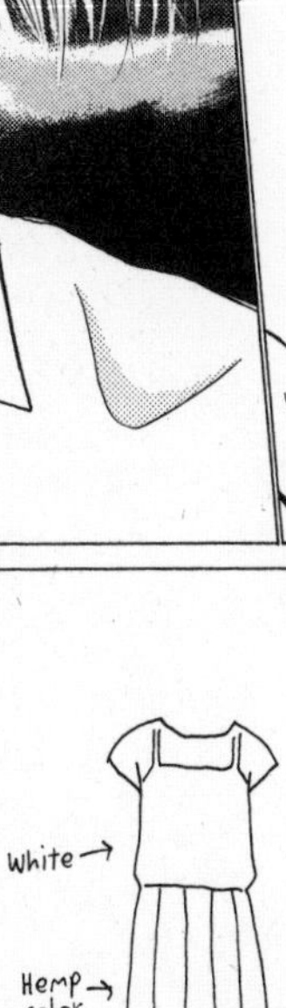
White
Hemp color

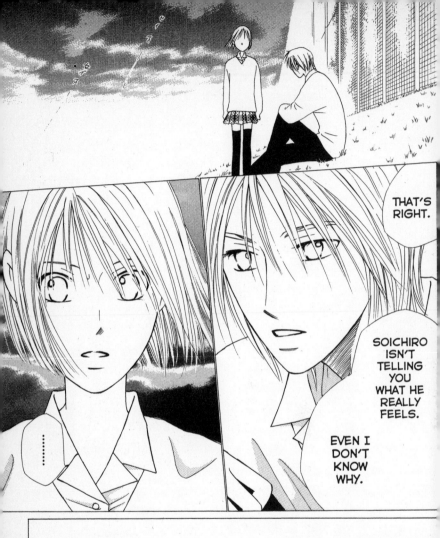

Next I want hemp sheets and curtains!

I'm just really into natural things like cotton right now.

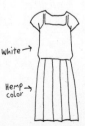

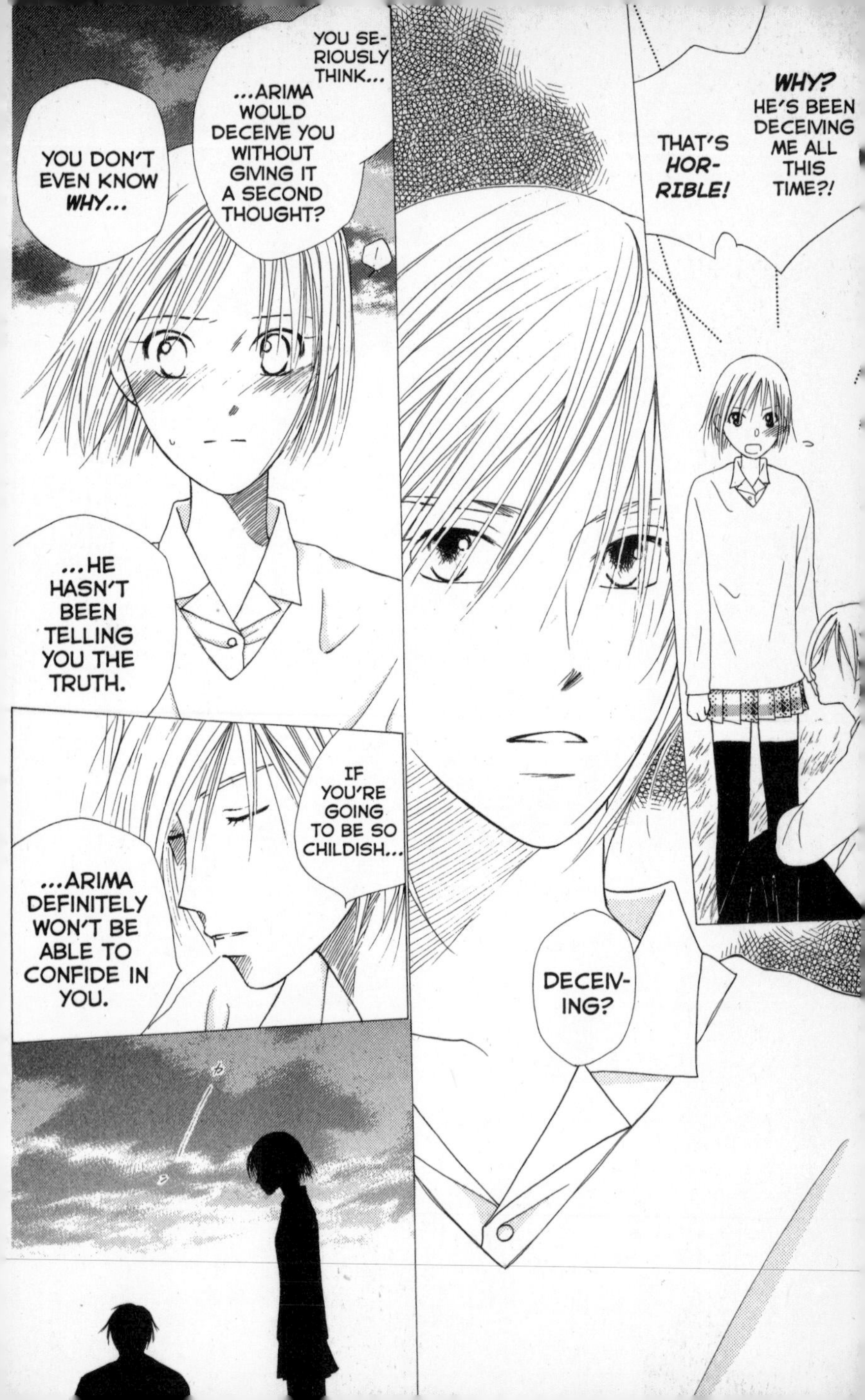
WHY? HE'S BEEN DECEIVING ME ALL THIS TIME?!
THAT'S HOR-RIBLE!
DECEIV-ING?
YOU SE-RIOUSLY THINK...
...ARIMA WOULD DECEIVE YOU WITHOUT GIVING IT A SECOND THOUGHT?
YOU DON'T EVEN KNOW WHY...
...HE HASN'T BEEN TELLING YOU THE TRUTH.
IF YOU'RE GOING TO BE SO CHILDISH...
...ARIMA DEFINITELY WON'T BE ABLE TO CONFIDE IN YOU.

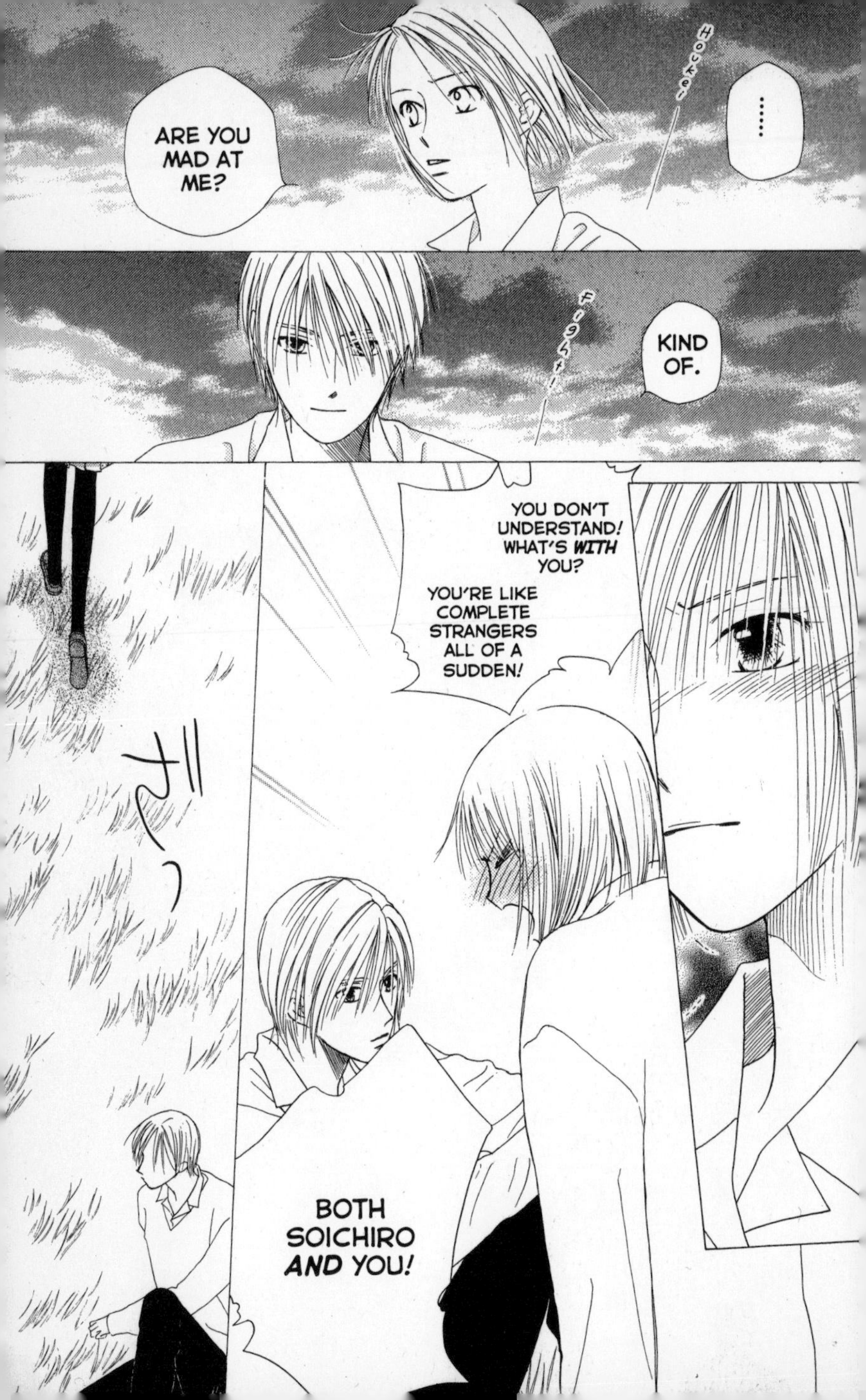
……
Houkei
ARE YOU MAD AT ME?
KIND OF.
Fight!
YOU DON'T UNDERSTAND! WHAT'S *WITH* YOU?
YOU'RE LIKE COMPLETE STRANGERS ALL OF A SUDDEN!
BOTH SOICHIRO *AND* YOU!

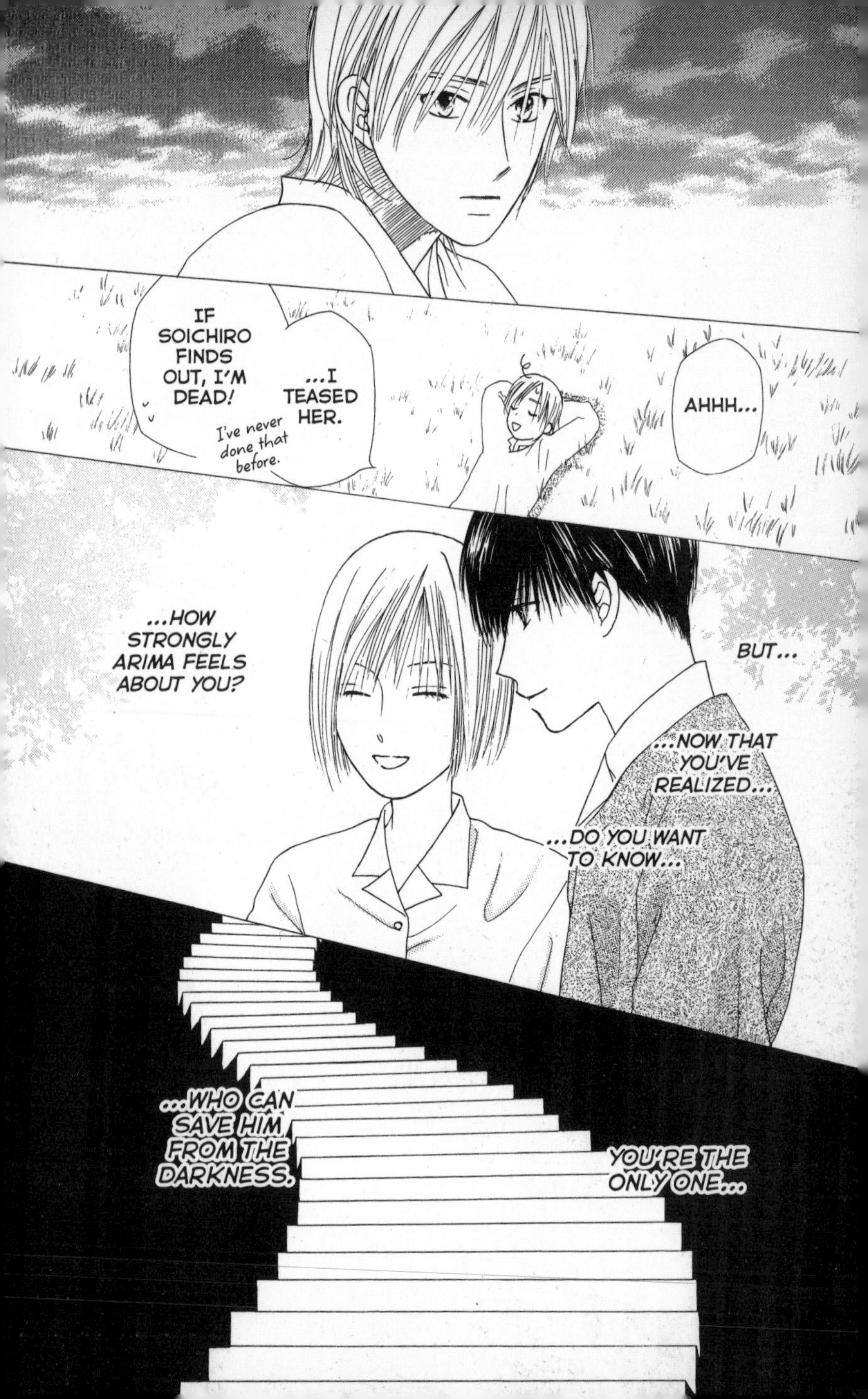
AHHH...
...I TEASED HER.
I've never done that before.
IF SOICHIRO FINDS OUT, I'M DEAD!
BUT...
...NOW THAT YOU'VE REALIZED...
...DO YOU WANT TO KNOW...
...HOW STRONGLY ARIMA FEELS ABOUT YOU?
YOU'RE THE ONLY ONE...
...WHO CAN SAVE HIM FROM THE DARKNESS.

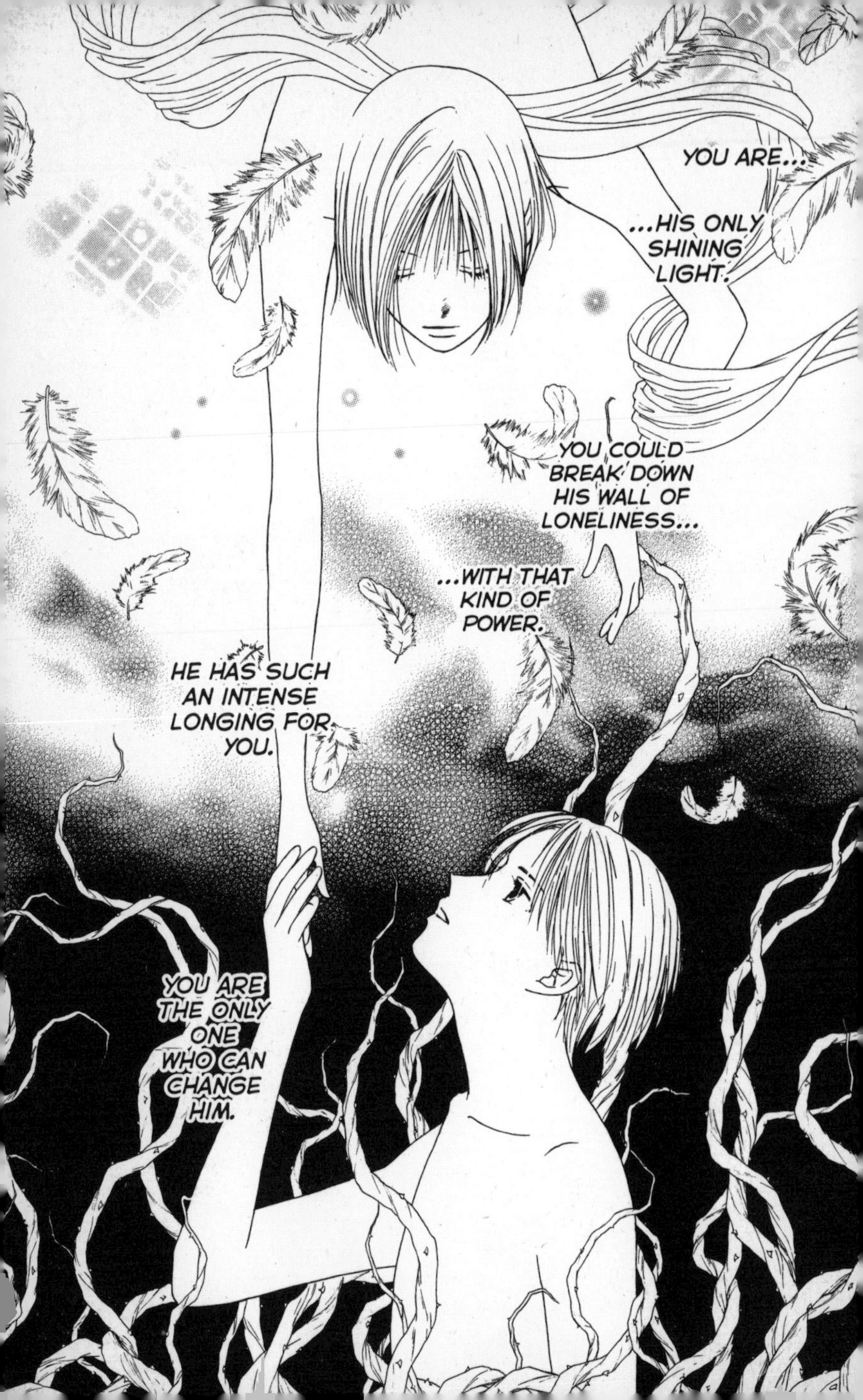
YOU ARE...
...HIS ONLY SHINING LIGHT.
YOU COULD BREAK DOWN HIS WALL OF LONELINESS...
...WITH THAT KIND OF POWER.
HE HAS SUCH AN INTENSE LONGING FOR YOU.
YOU ARE THE ONLY ONE WHO CAN CHANGE HIM.

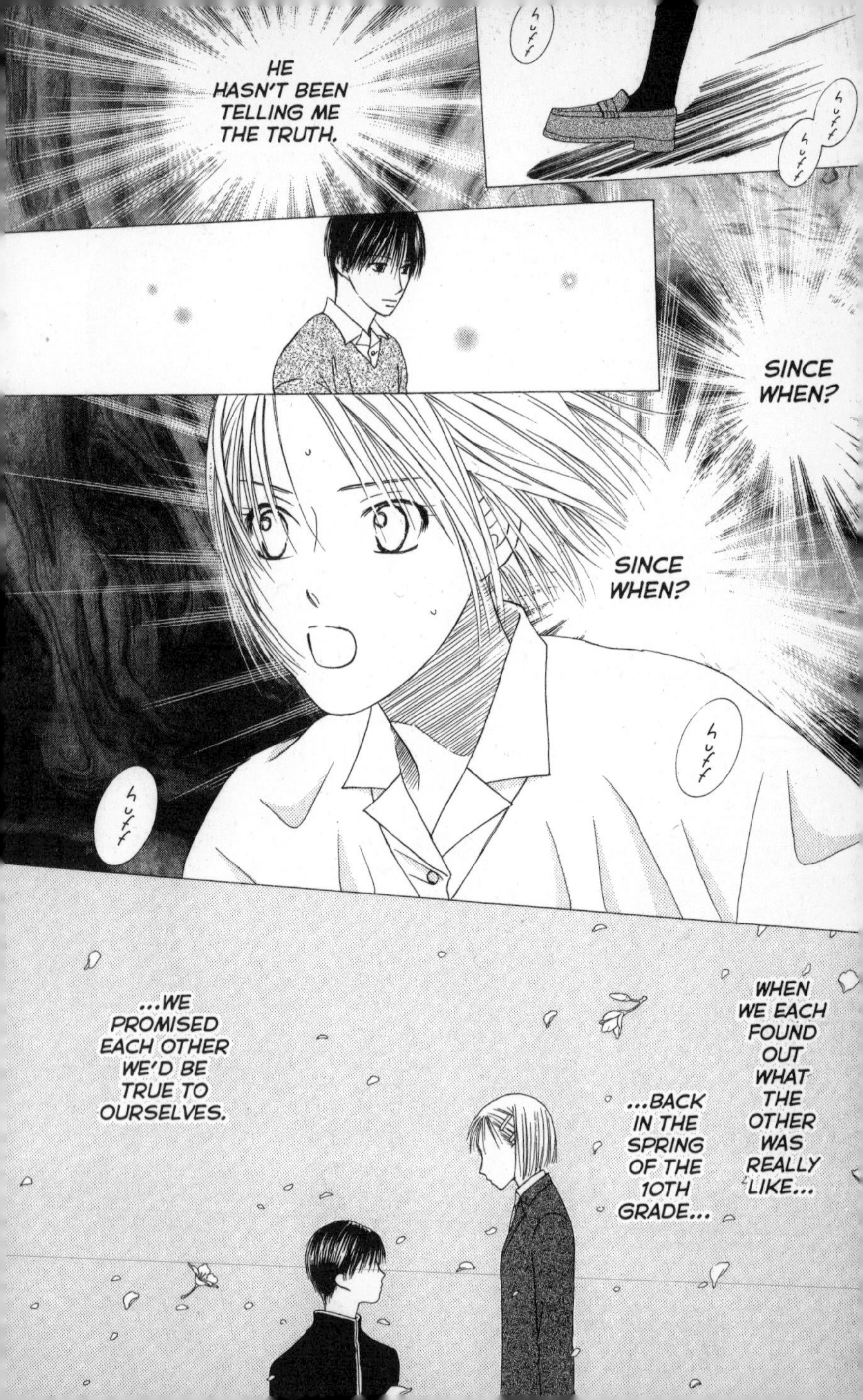
huff
huff
huff
HE HASN'T BEEN TELLING ME THE TRUTH.
SINCE WHEN?
SINCE WHEN?
huff
huff
WHEN WE EACH FOUND OUT WHAT THE OTHER WAS REALLY LIKE...
...BACK IN THE SPRING OF THE 10TH GRADE...
...WE PROMISED EACH OTHER WE'D BE TRUE TO OURSELVES.

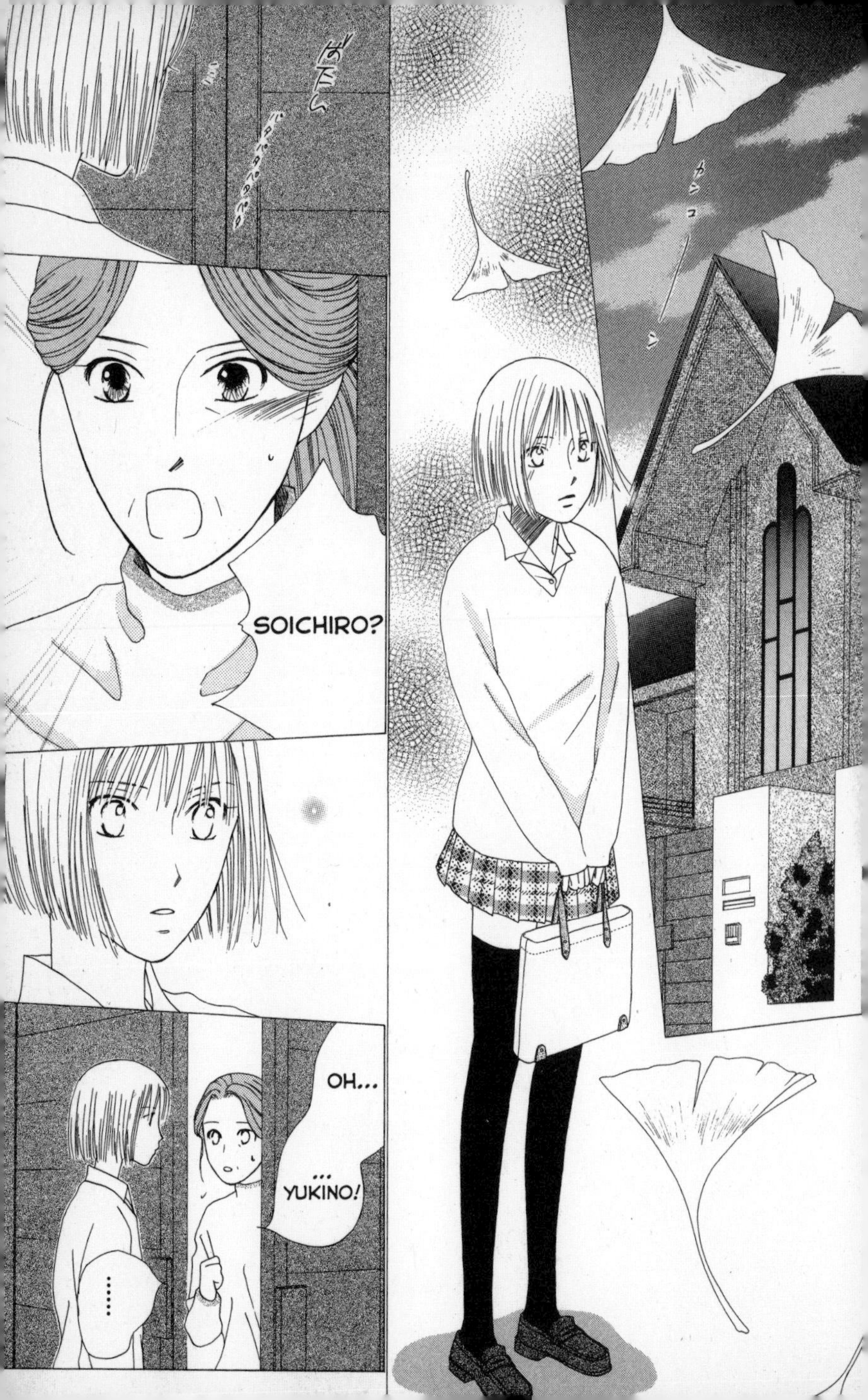
SOICHIRO?
OH...
...YUKINO!
......

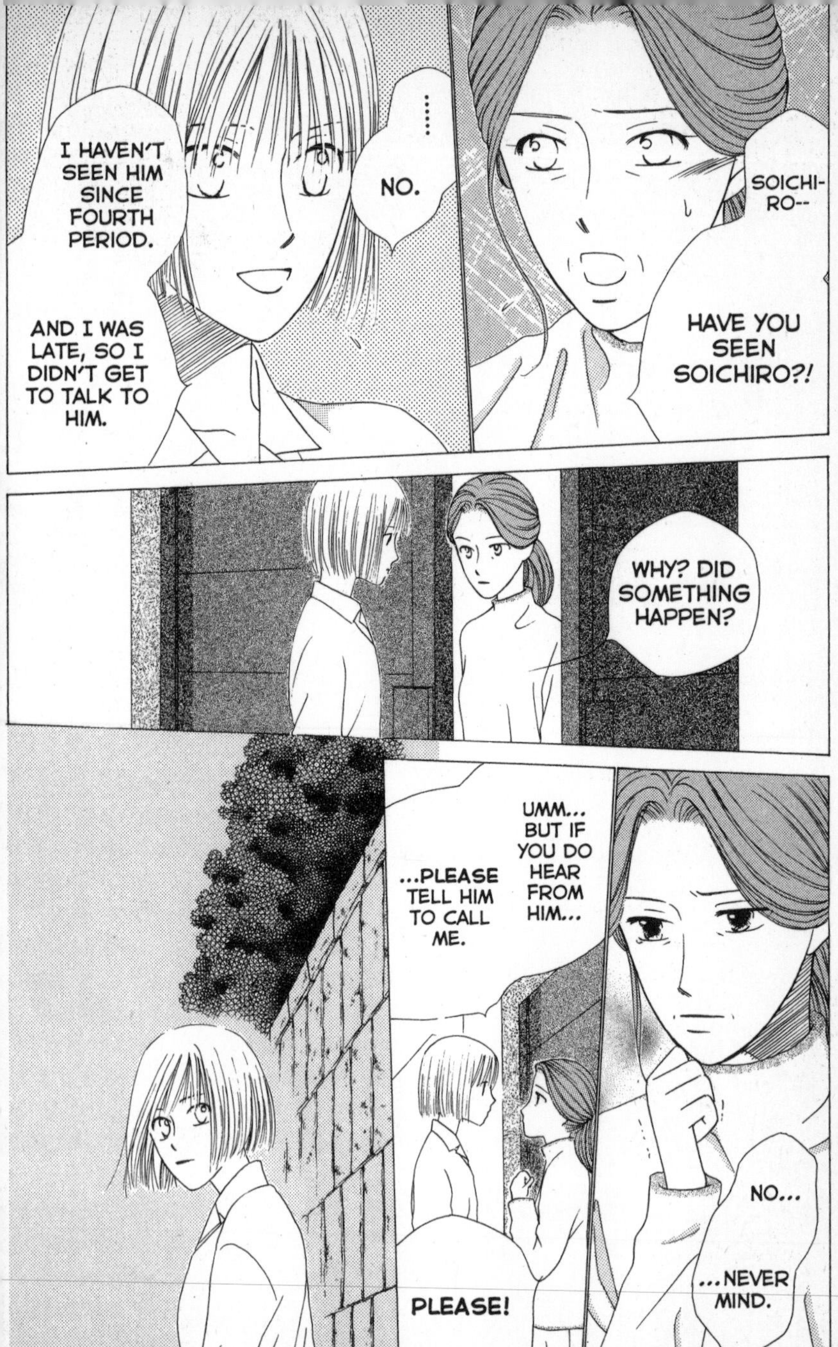
SOICHI-RO--
HAVE YOU SEEN SOICHIRO?!
......
NO.
I HAVEN'T SEEN HIM SINCE FOURTH PERIOD.
AND I WAS LATE, SO I DIDN'T GET TO TALK TO HIM.
WHY? DID SOMETHING HAPPEN?
NO...
...NEVER MIND.
UMM... BUT IF YOU DO HEAR FROM HIM...
...PLEASE TELL HIM TO CALL ME.
PLEASE!

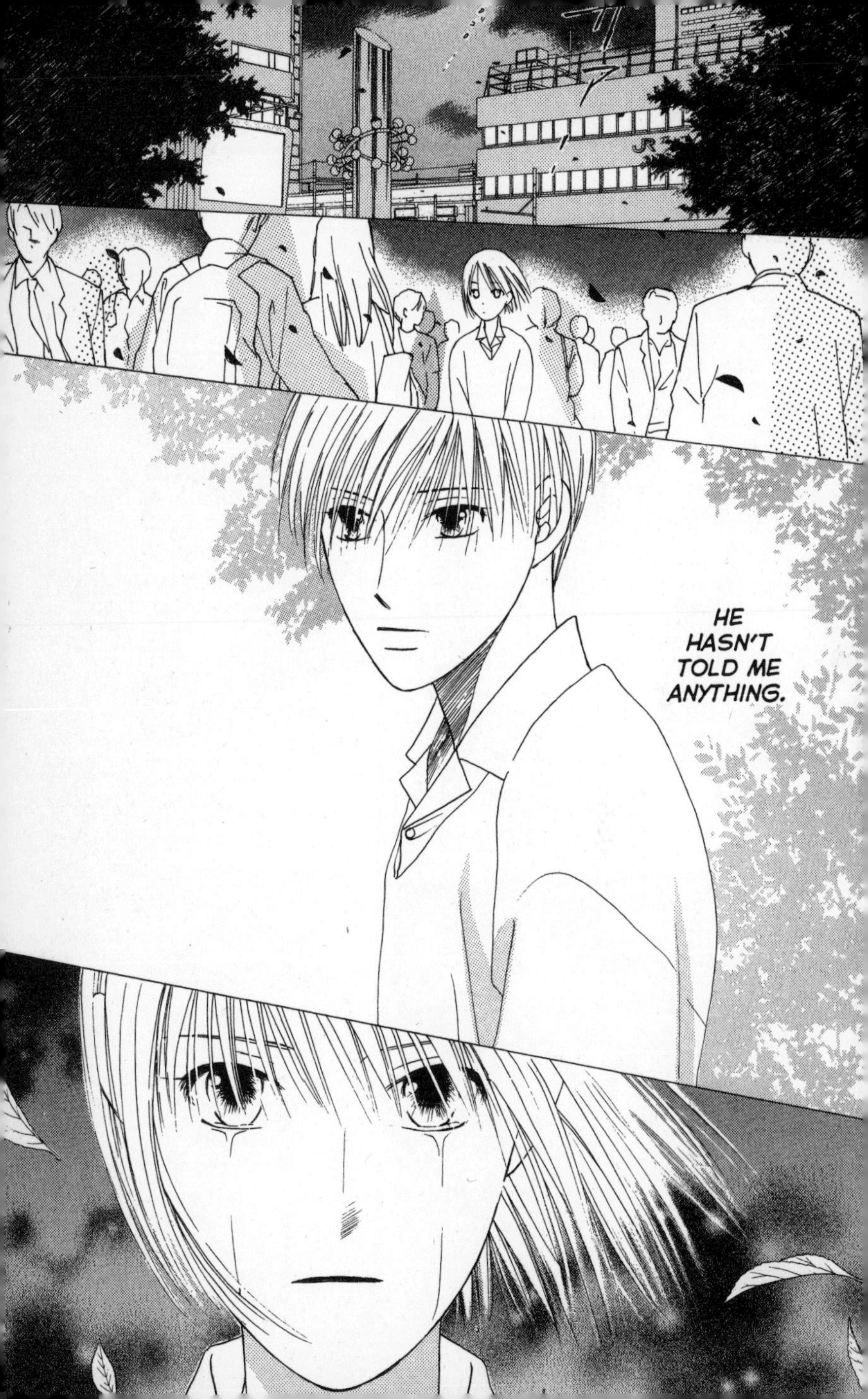
HE HASN'T TOLD ME ANYTHING.

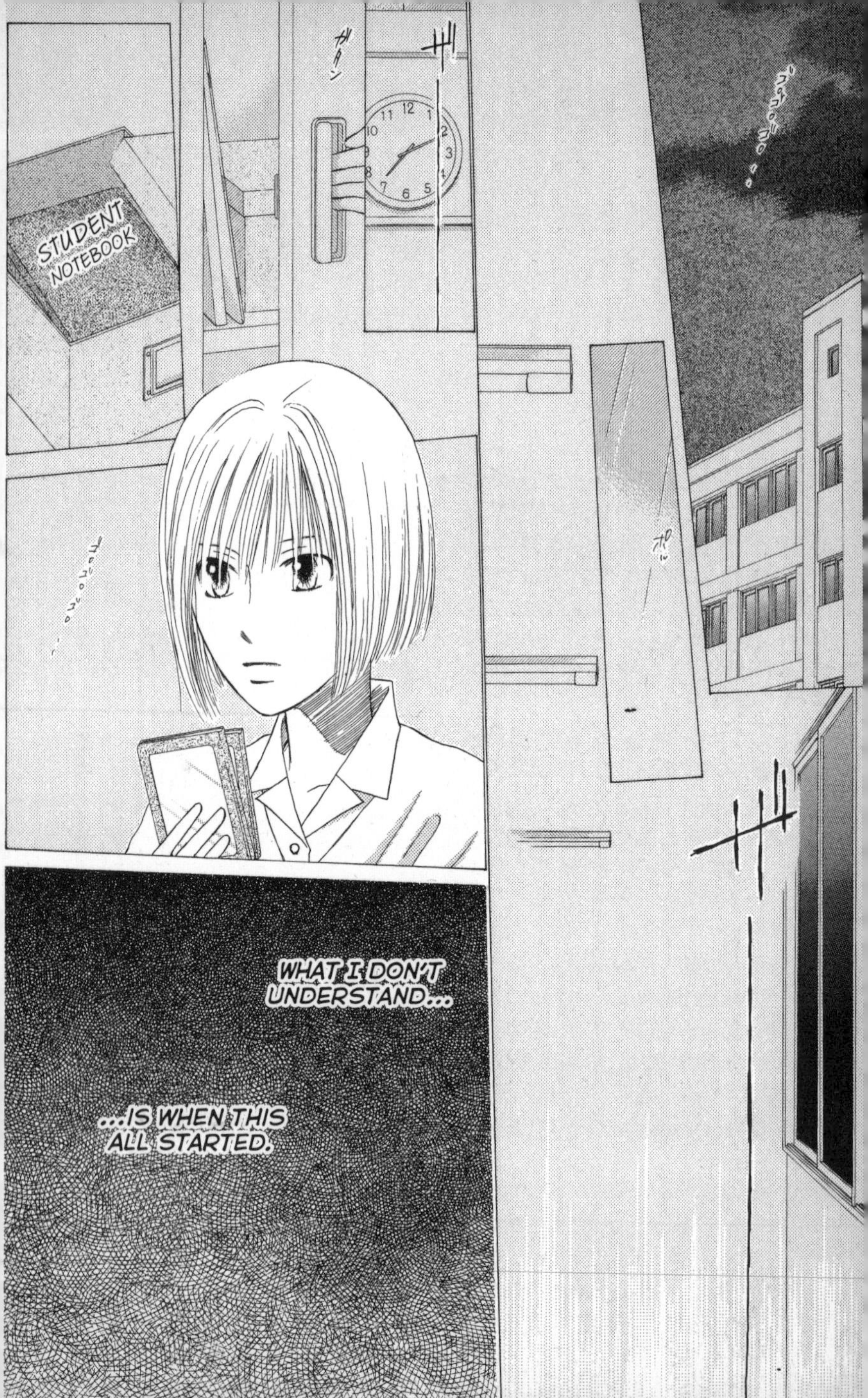
STUDENT NOTEBOOK
WHAT I DON'T UNDERSTAND...
...IS WHEN THIS ALL STARTED.

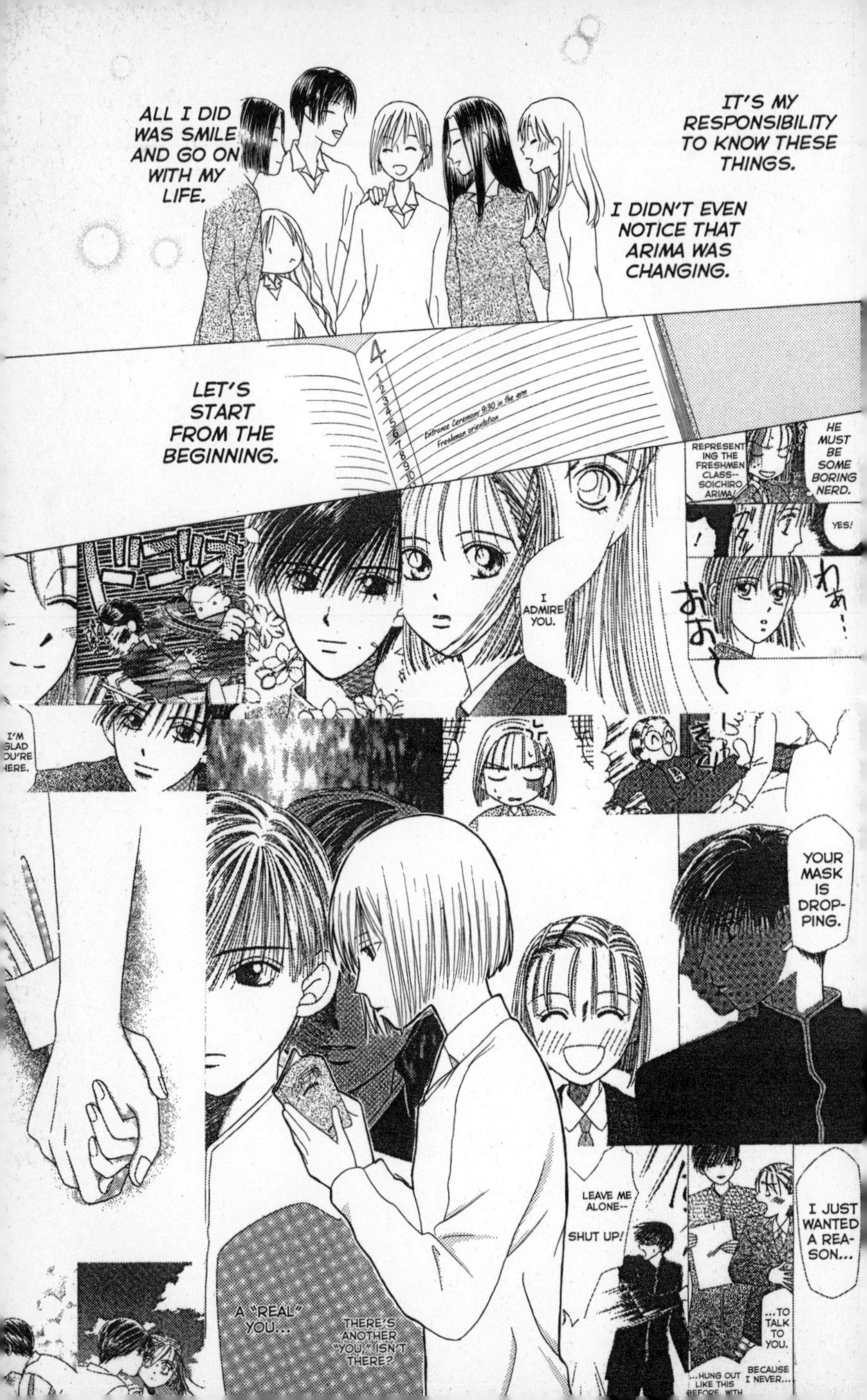
IT'S MY RESPONSIBILITY TO KNOW THESE THINGS.
I DIDN'T EVEN NOTICE THAT ARIMA WAS CHANGING.
ALL I DID WAS SMILE AND GO ON WITH MY LIFE.
4
Entrance Ceremony 9:30 in the gym
Freshman orientation
LET'S START FROM THE BEGINNING.
HE MUST BE SOME BORING NERD.
REPRESENTING THE FRESHMEN CLASS-- SOICHIRO ARIMA!
YES!
わぁ!
おお〜
I ADMIRE YOU.
I'M GLAD YOU'RE HERE.
YOUR MASK IS DROPPING.
I JUST WANTED A REASON...
...TO TALK TO YOU.
BECAUSE I NEVER...
...HUNG OUT LIKE THIS BEFORE, WITH
LEAVE ME ALONE--
SHUT UP!
THERE'S ANOTHER YOU, ISN'T THERE?
A "REAL" YOU...

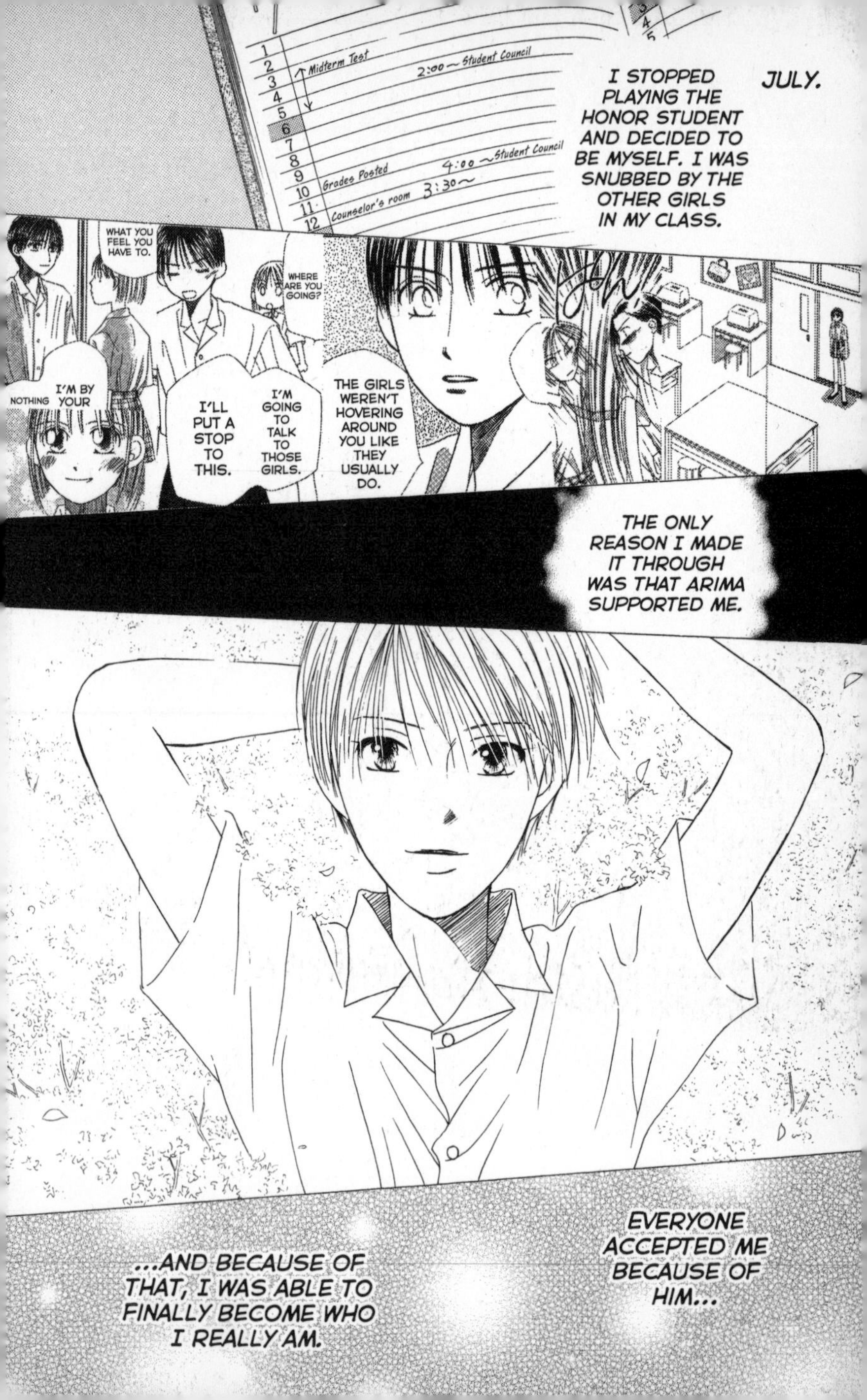
JULY.
I STOPPED PLAYING THE HONOR STUDENT AND DECIDED TO BE MYSELF. I WAS SNUBBED BY THE OTHER GIRLS IN MY CLASS.
1
2 Midterm Test
3 2:00 ~ Student Council
4
5
6
7
8
9 Grades Posted 4:00 ~ Student Council
10 Counselor's room 3:30 ~
11
12
THE GIRLS WEREN'T HOVERING AROUND YOU LIKE THEY USUALLY DO.
WHERE ARE YOU GOING?
I'M GOING TO TALK TO THOSE GIRLS.
I'LL PUT A STOP TO THIS.
WHAT YOU FEEL YOU HAVE TO.
I'M BY YOUR
NOTHING
THE ONLY REASON I MADE IT THROUGH WAS THAT ARIMA SUPPORTED ME.
EVERYONE ACCEPTED ME BECAUSE OF HIM...
...AND BECAUSE OF THAT, I WAS ABLE TO FINALLY BECOME WHO I REALLY AM.

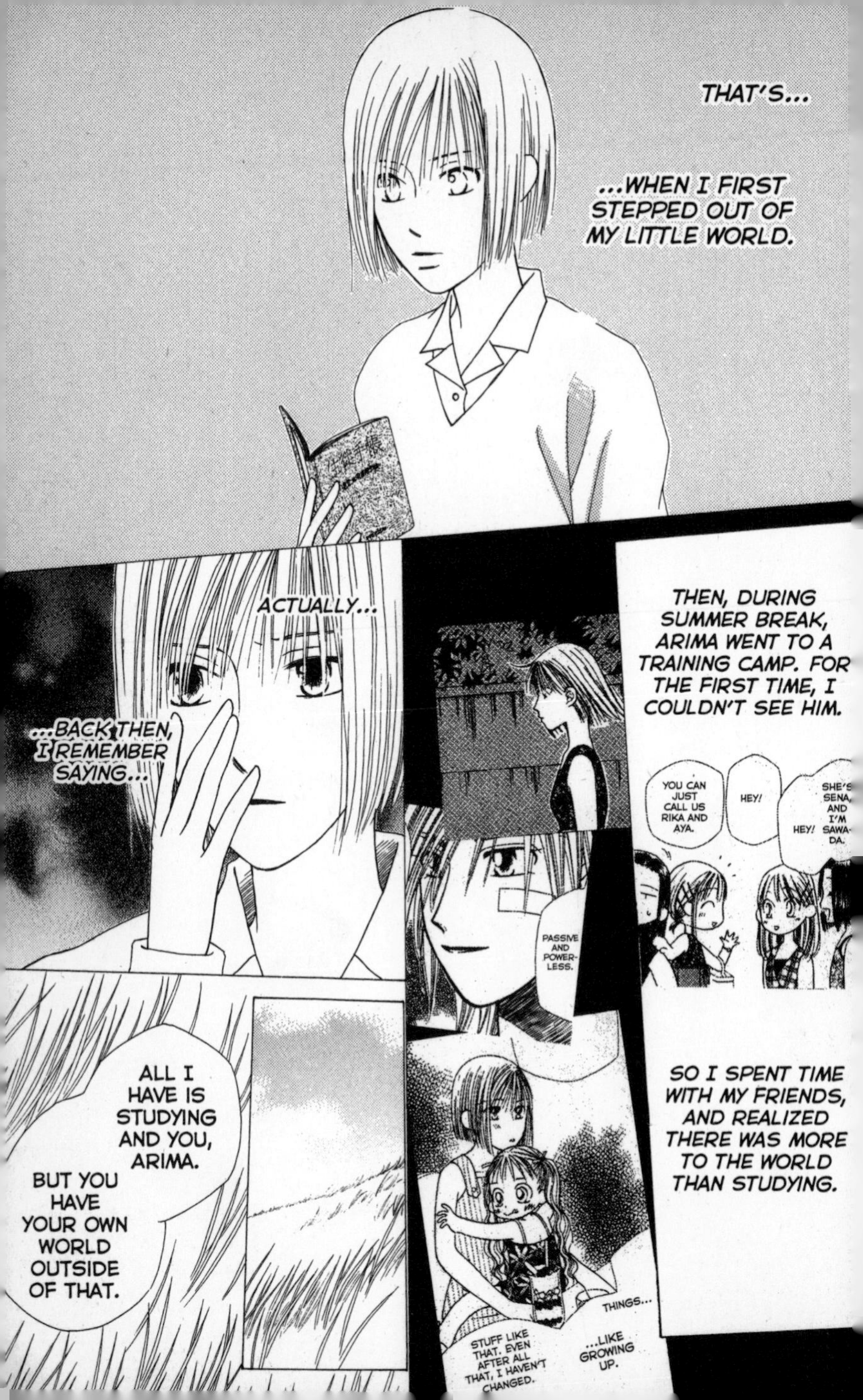
THAT'S...
...WHEN I FIRST STEPPED OUT OF MY LITTLE WORLD.
THEN, DURING SUMMER BREAK, ARIMA WENT TO A TRAINING CAMP. FOR THE FIRST TIME, I COULDN'T SEE HIM.
SHE'S SENA, AND I'M SAWADA.
HEY!
HEY!
YOU CAN JUST CALL US RIKA AND AYA.
PASSIVE AND POWERLESS.
ACTUALLY...
...BACK THEN, I REMEMBER SAYING...
SO I SPENT TIME WITH MY FRIENDS, AND REALIZED THERE WAS MORE TO THE WORLD THAN STUDYING.
THINGS...
...LIKE GROWING UP.
STUFF LIKE THAT. EVEN AFTER ALL THAT, I HAVEN'T CHANGED.
ALL I HAVE IS STUDYING AND YOU, ARIMA.
BUT YOU HAVE YOUR OWN WORLD OUTSIDE OF THAT.

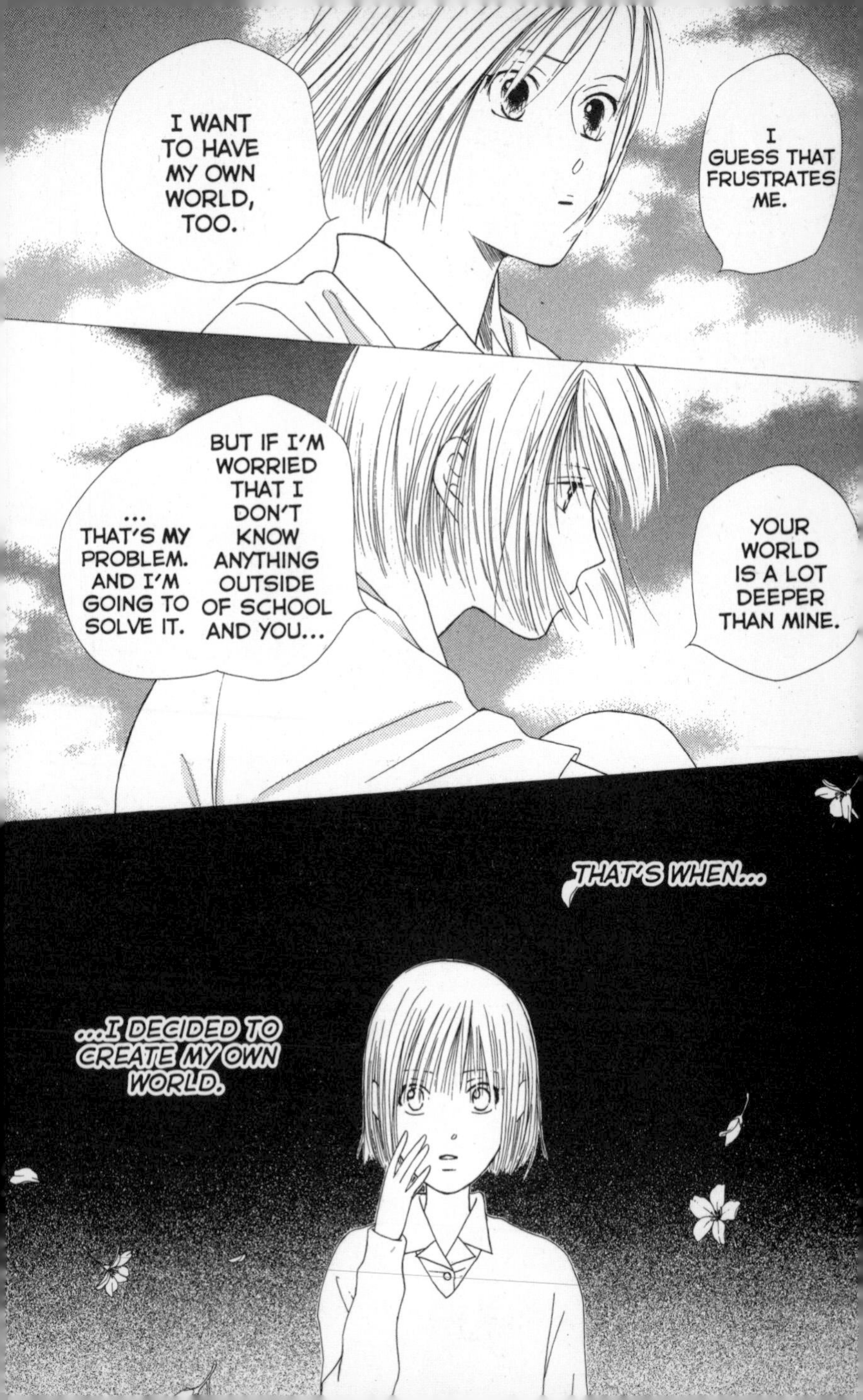
I GUESS THAT FRUSTRATES ME.
I WANT TO HAVE MY OWN WORLD, TOO.
YOUR WORLD IS A LOT DEEPER THAN MINE.
BUT IF I'M WORRIED THAT I DON'T KNOW ANYTHING OUTSIDE OF SCHOOL AND YOU...
... THAT'S MY PROBLEM. AND I'M GOING TO SOLVE IT.
THAT'S WHEN...
...I DECIDED TO CREATE MY OWN WORLD.

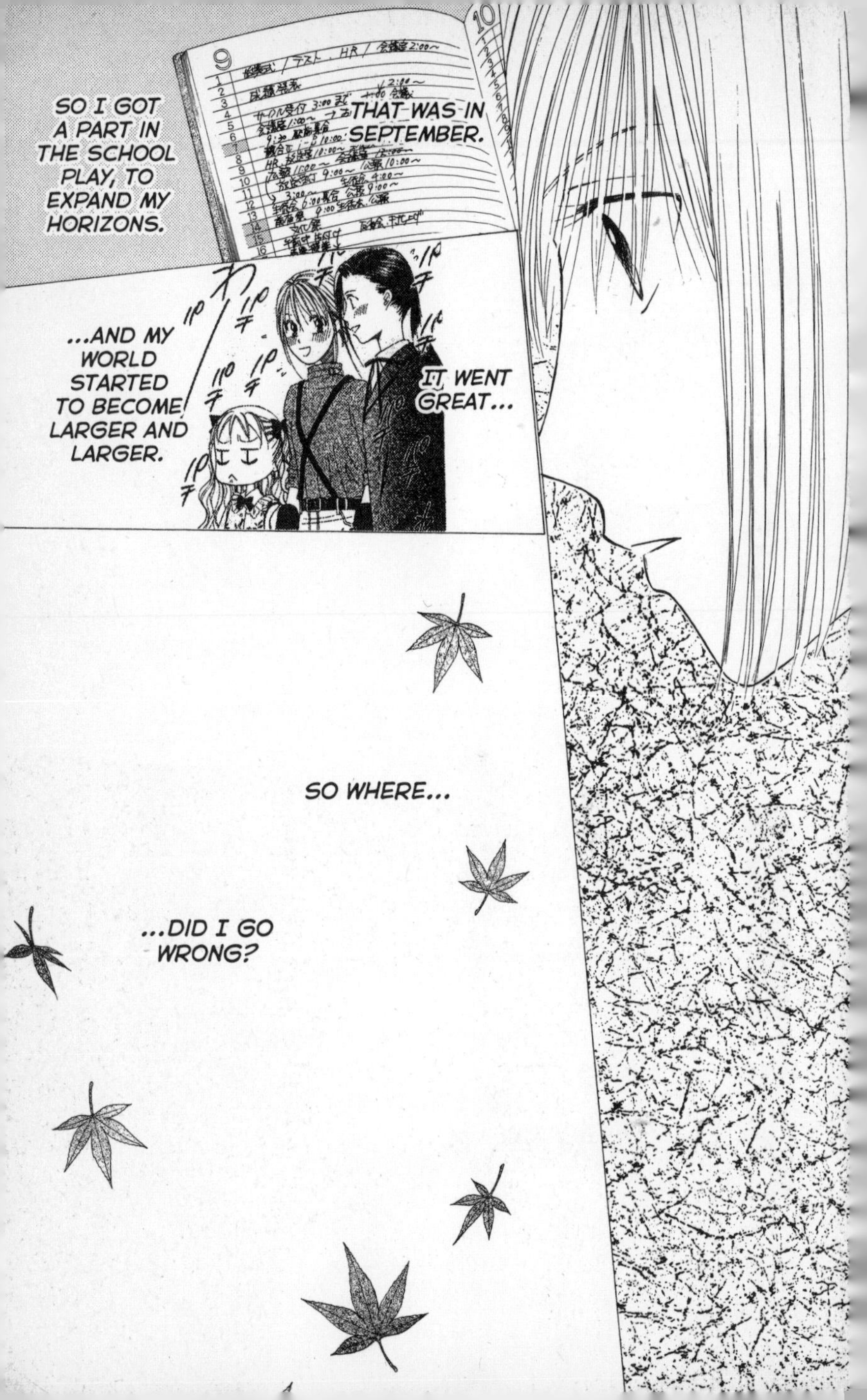
THAT WAS IN SEPTEMBER.
SO I GOT A PART IN THE SCHOOL PLAY, TO EXPAND MY HORIZONS.
IT WENT GREAT...
...AND MY WORLD STARTED TO BECOME LARGER AND LARGER.
SO WHERE...
...DID I GO WRONG?

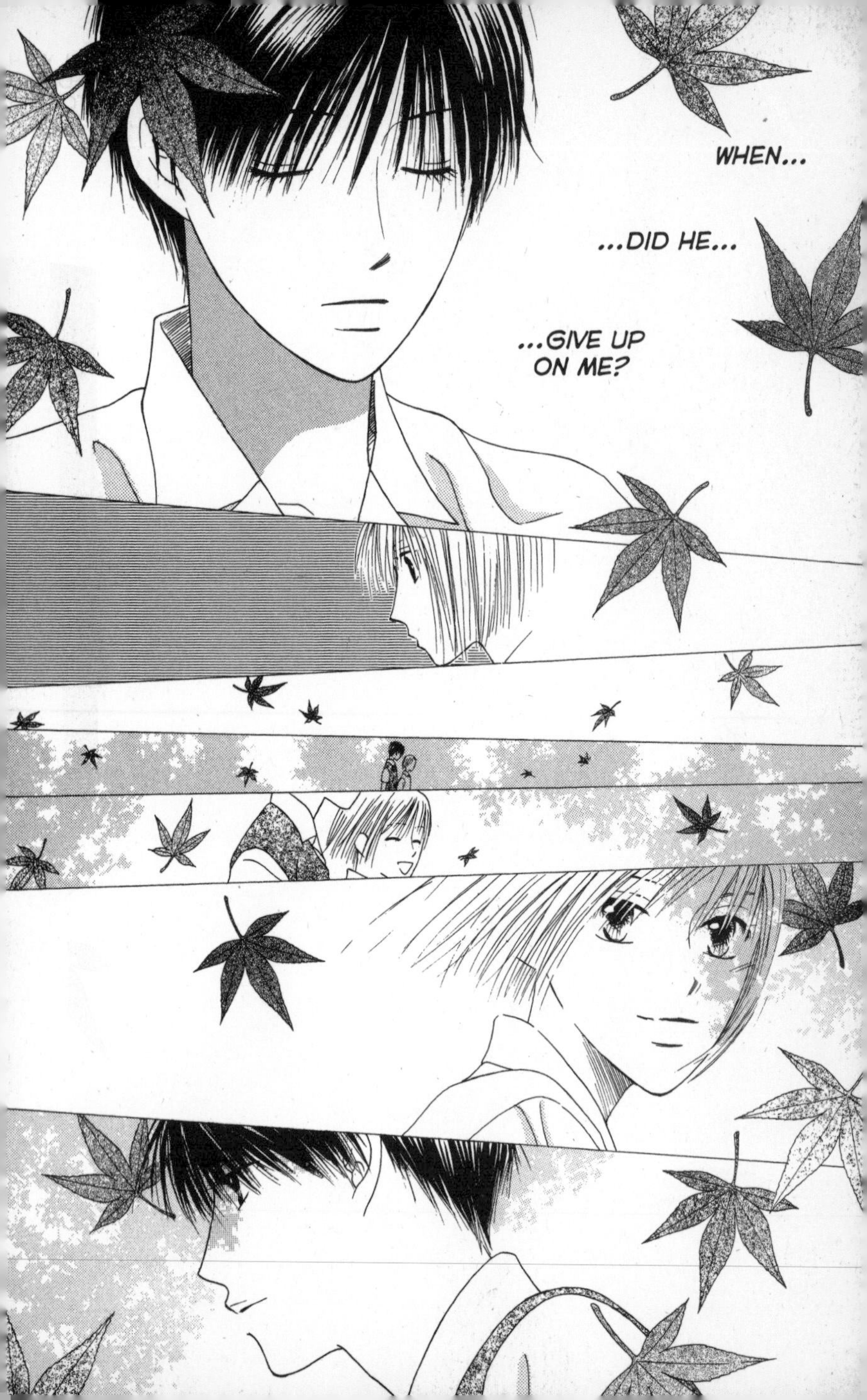
WHEN...
...DID HE...
...GIVE UP ON ME?

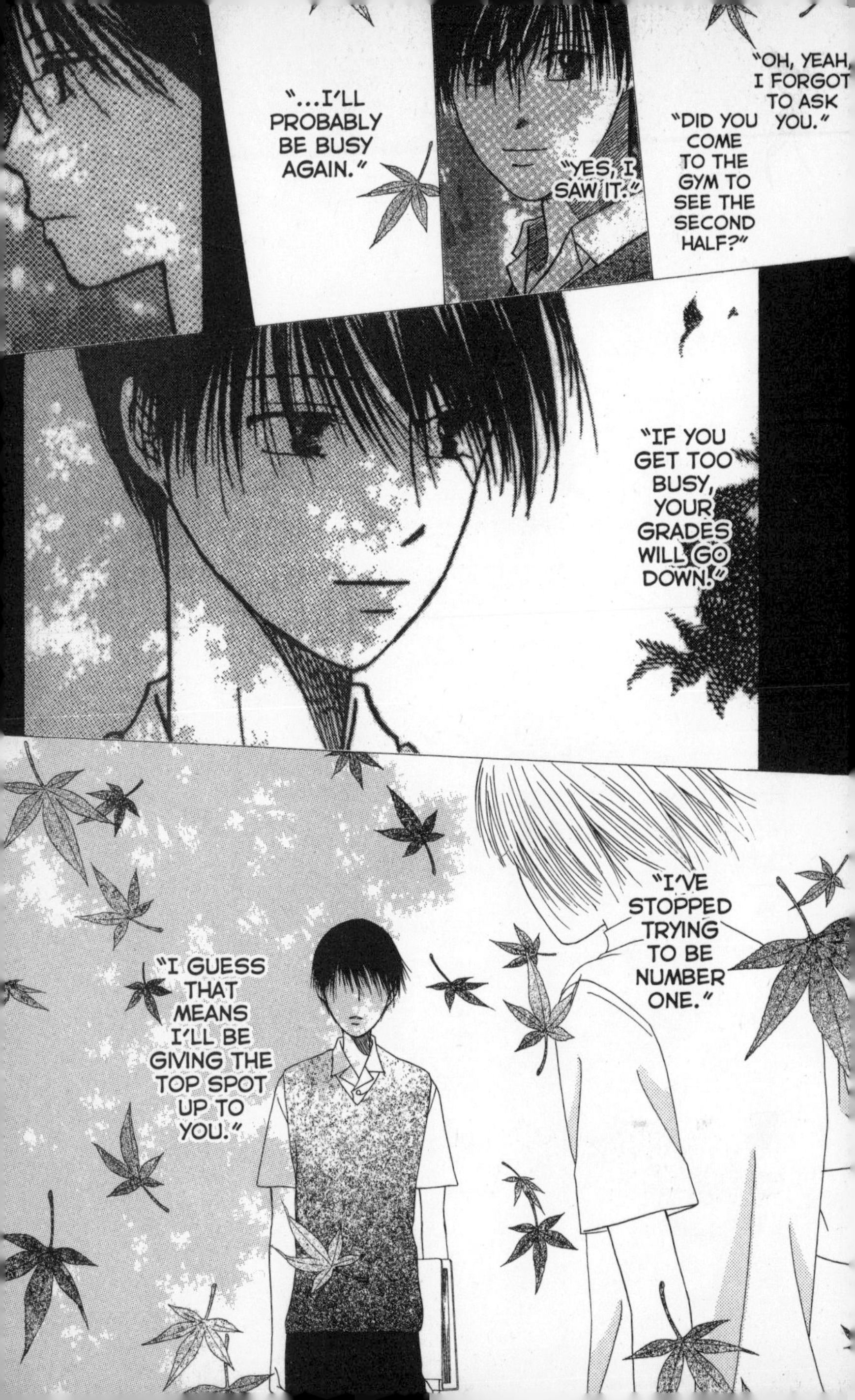
"OH, YEAH, I FORGOT TO ASK YOU."
"DID YOU COME TO THE GYM TO SEE THE SECOND HALF?"
"YES, I SAW IT."
"...I'LL PROBABLY BE BUSY AGAIN."
"IF YOU GET TOO BUSY, YOUR GRADES WILL GO DOWN."
"I'VE STOPPED TRYING TO BE NUMBER ONE."
"I GUESS THAT MEANS I'LL BE GIVING THE TOP SPOT UP TO YOU."

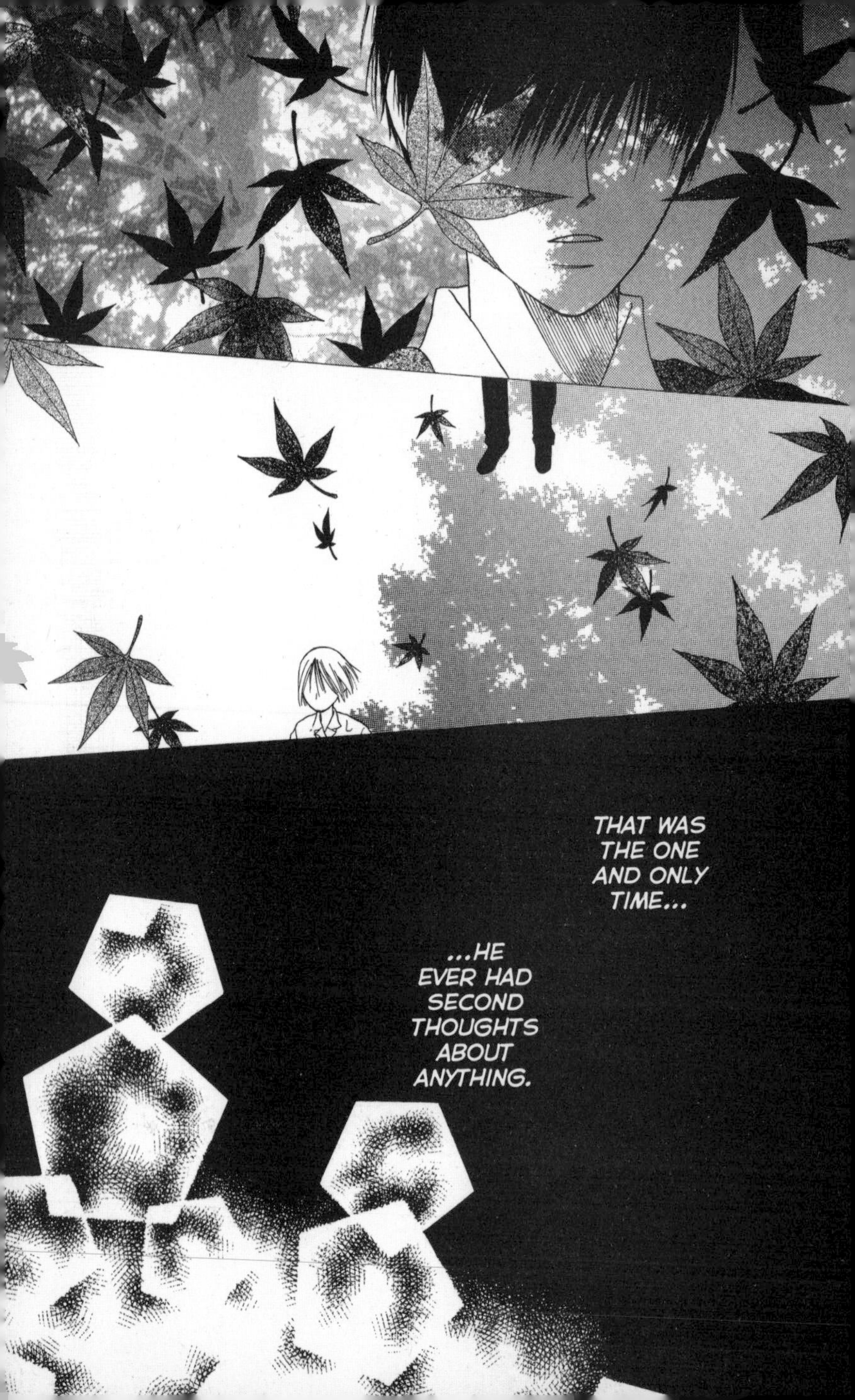
THAT WAS THE ONE AND ONLY TIME...
...HE EVER HAD SECOND THOUGHTS ABOUT ANYTHING.

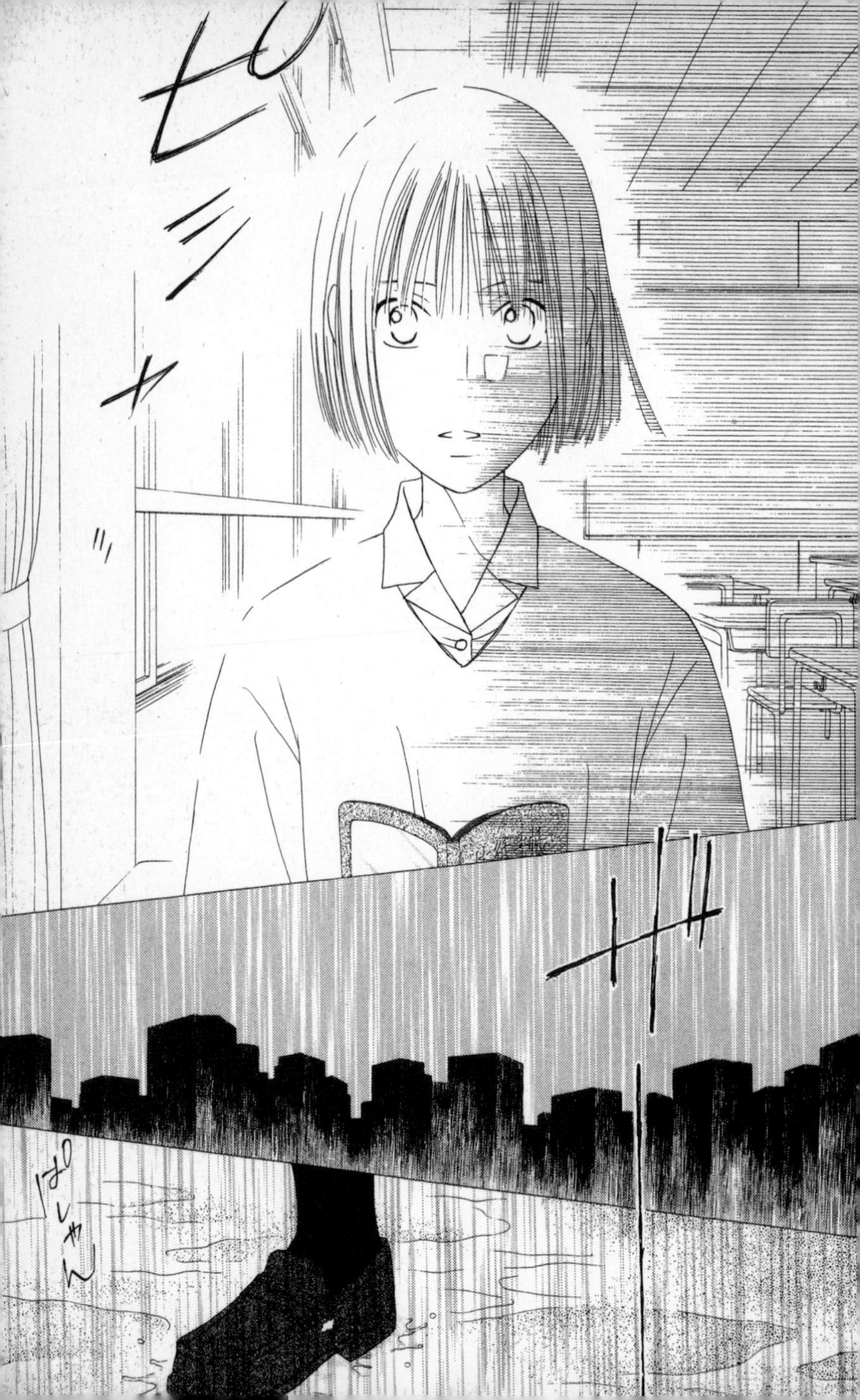
ピシャッ
ザー
ぱしゃん

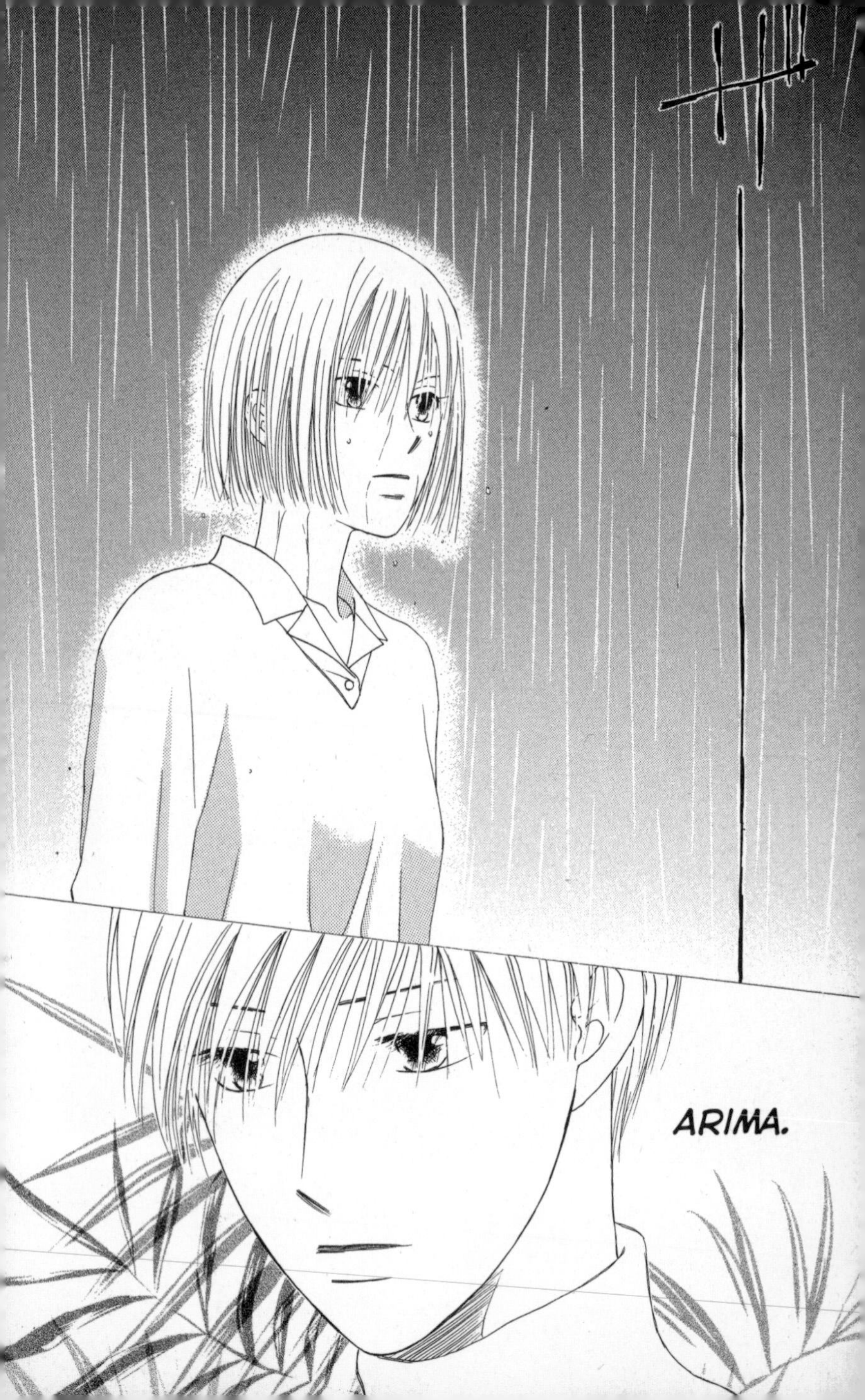
ARIMA.

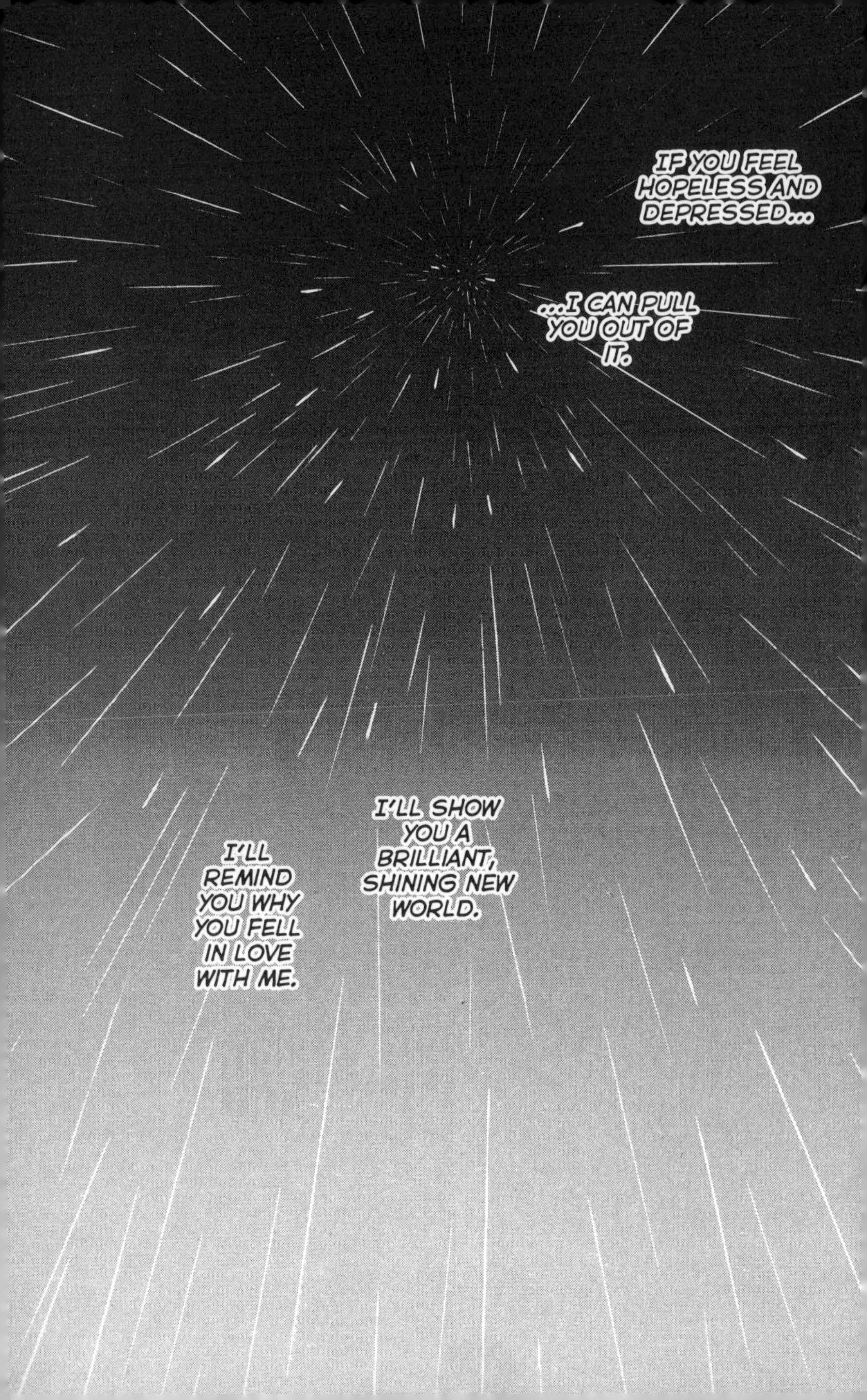
IF YOU FEEL HOPELESS AND DEPRESSED...
...I CAN PULL YOU OUT OF IT.
I'LL SHOW YOU A BRILLIANT, SHINING NEW WORLD.
I'LL REMIND YOU WHY YOU FELL IN LOVE WITH ME.

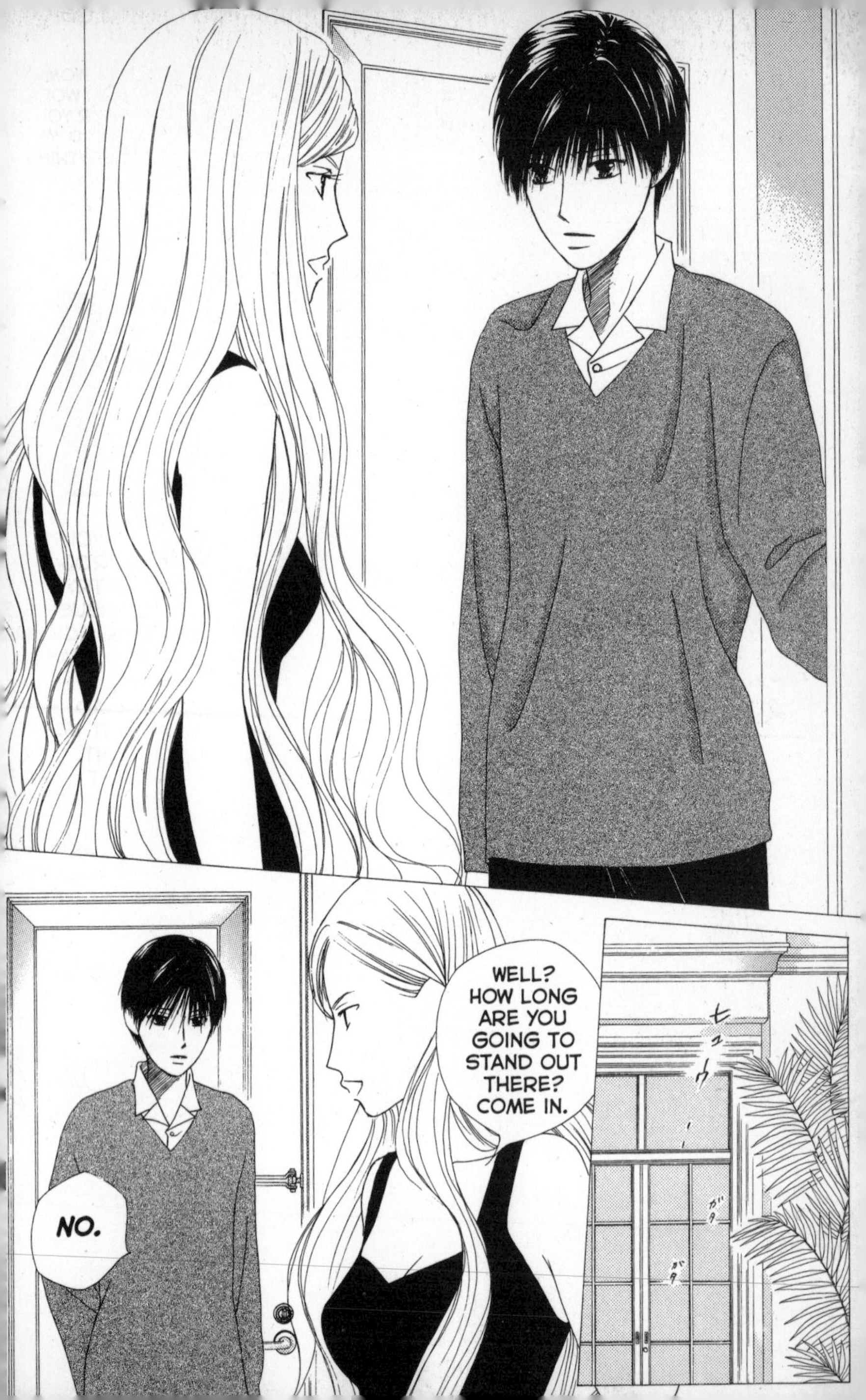
WELL? HOW LONG ARE YOU GOING TO STAND OUT THERE? COME IN.
NO.

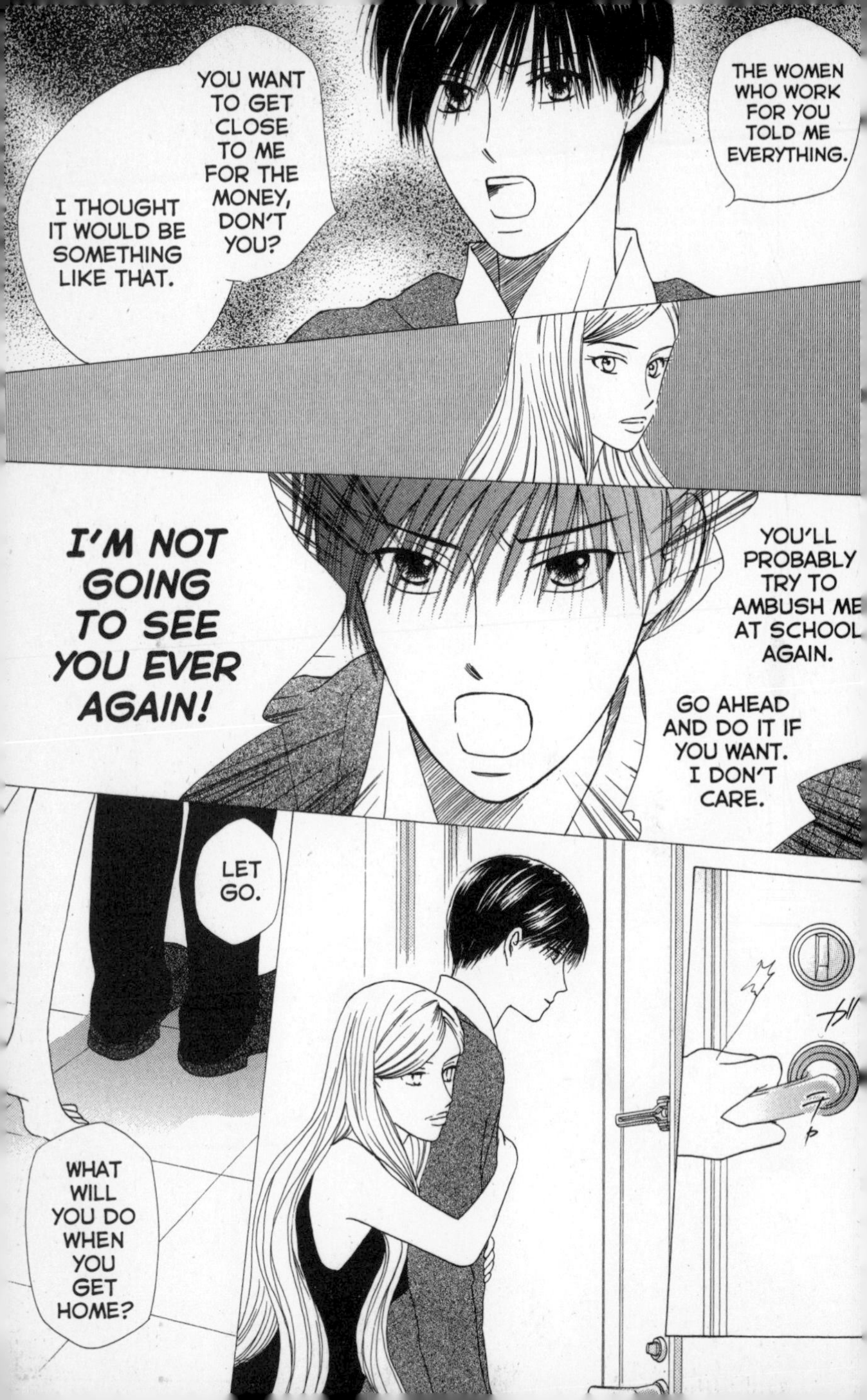
THE WOMEN WHO WORK FOR YOU TOLD ME EVERYTHING.
YOU WANT TO GET CLOSE TO ME FOR THE MONEY, DON'T YOU?
I THOUGHT IT WOULD BE SOMETHING LIKE THAT.
YOU'LL PROBABLY TRY TO AMBUSH ME AT SCHOOL AGAIN.
GO AHEAD AND DO IT IF YOU WANT. I DON'T CARE.
I'M NOT GOING TO SEE YOU EVER AGAIN!
LET GO.
WHAT WILL YOU DO WHEN YOU GET HOME?

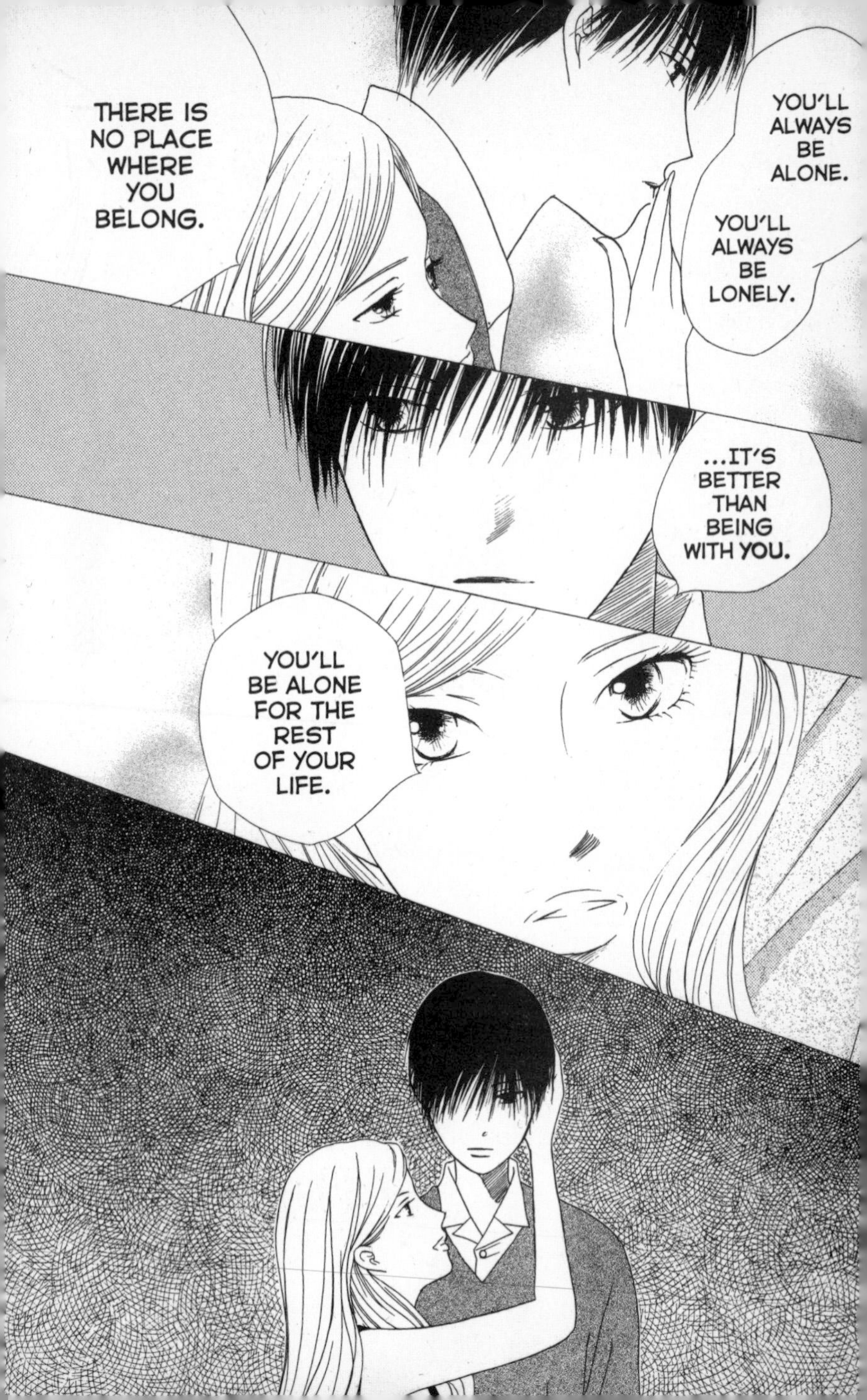
YOU'LL ALWAYS BE ALONE.
YOU'LL ALWAYS BE LONELY.
THERE IS NO PLACE WHERE YOU BELONG.
...IT'S BETTER THAN BEING WITH YOU.
YOU'LL BE ALONE FOR THE REST OF YOUR LIFE.

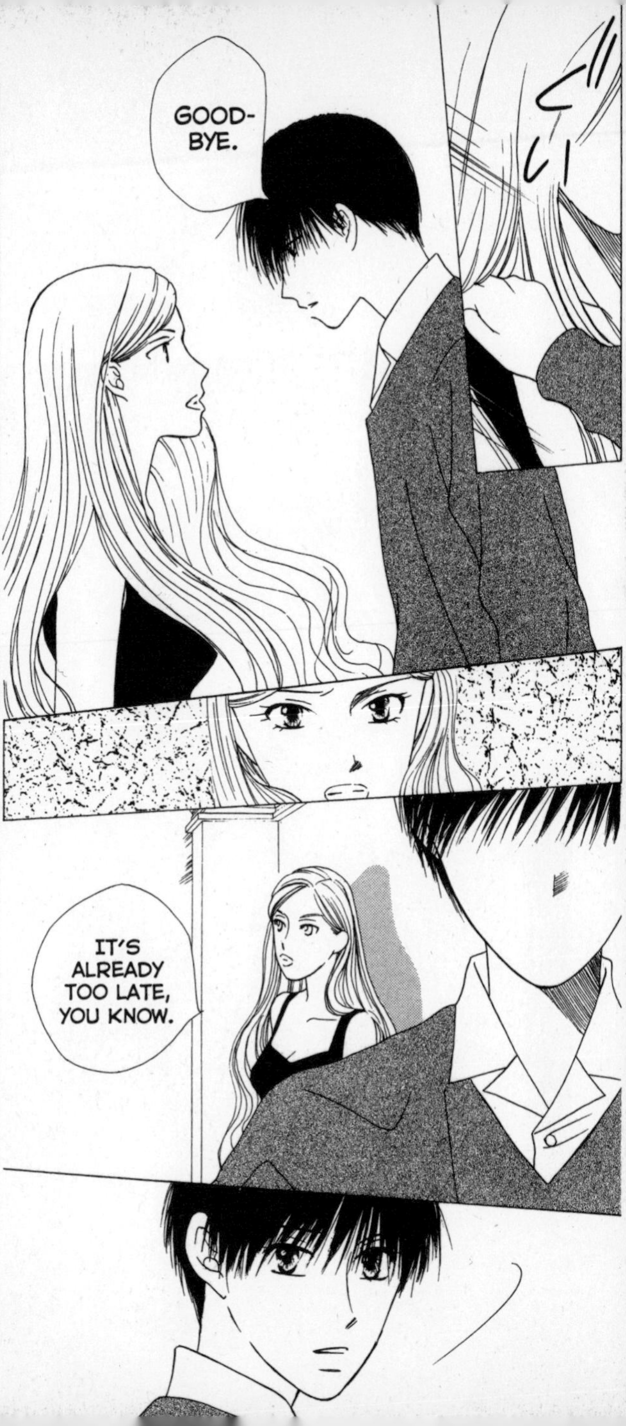
GOOD-BYE.
IT'S ALREADY TOO LATE, YOU KNOW.

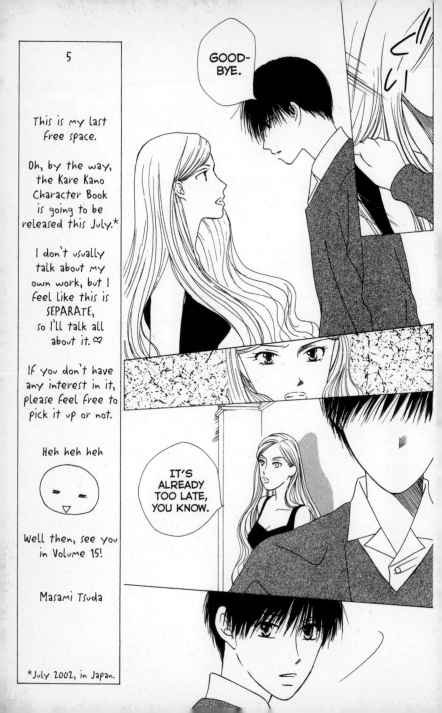

5

This is my last free space.

Oh, by the way, the Kare Kano Character Book is going to be released this July.*

I don't usually talk about my own work, but I feel like this is SEPARATE, so I'll talk all about it. ♡

If you don't have any interest in it, please feel free to pick it up or not.

Heh heh heh

Well then, see you in Volume 15!

Masami Tsuda

*July 2002, in Japan.

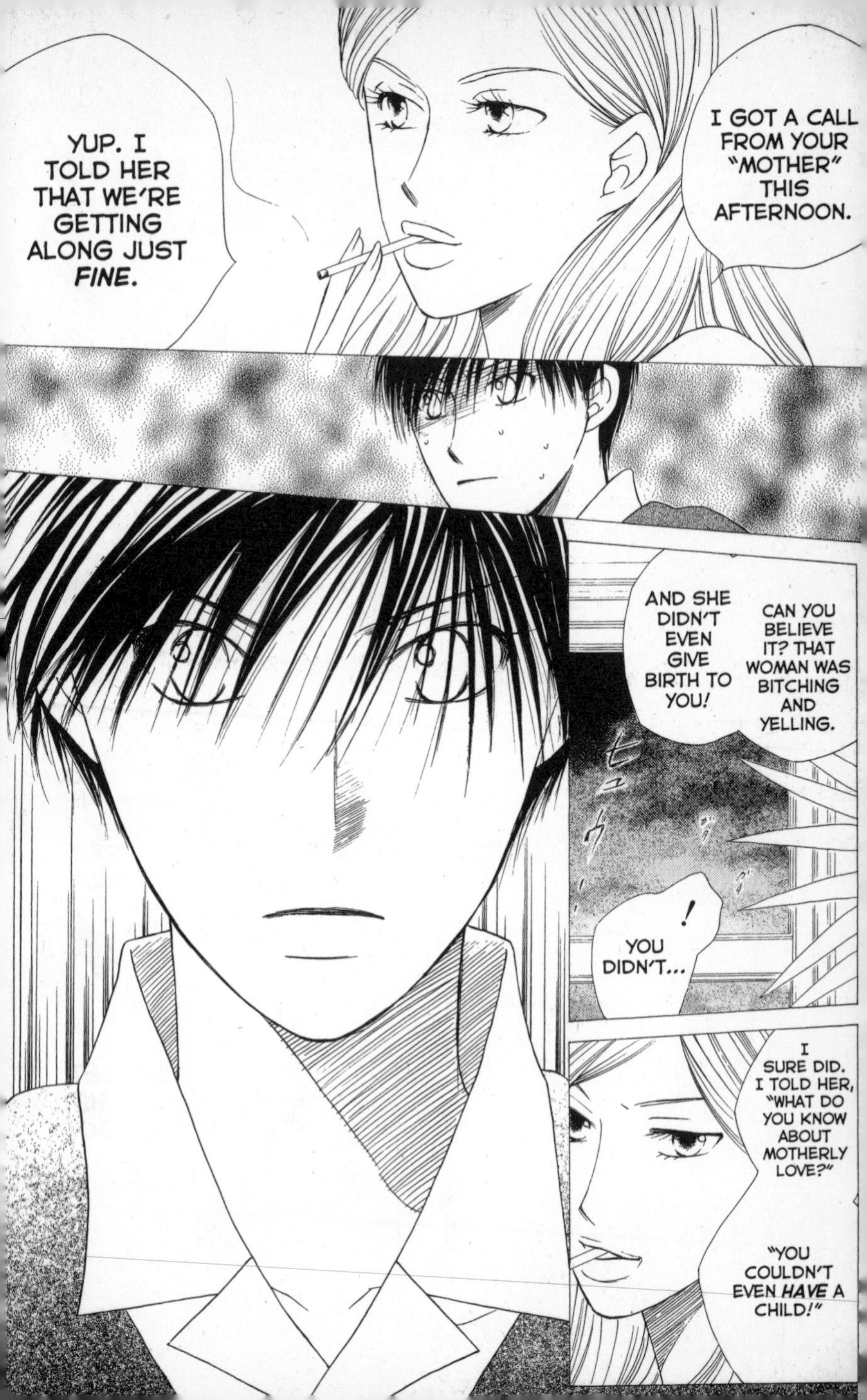
I GOT A CALL FROM YOUR "MOTHER" THIS AFTERNOON.
YUP. I TOLD HER THAT WE'RE GETTING ALONG JUST *FINE*.
CAN YOU BELIEVE IT? THAT WOMAN WAS BITCHING AND YELLING.
AND SHE DIDN'T EVEN GIVE BIRTH TO YOU!
!
YOU DIDN'T...
I SURE DID. I TOLD HER, "WHAT DO YOU KNOW ABOUT MOTHERLY LOVE?"
"YOU COULDN'T EVEN *HAVE* A CHILD!"

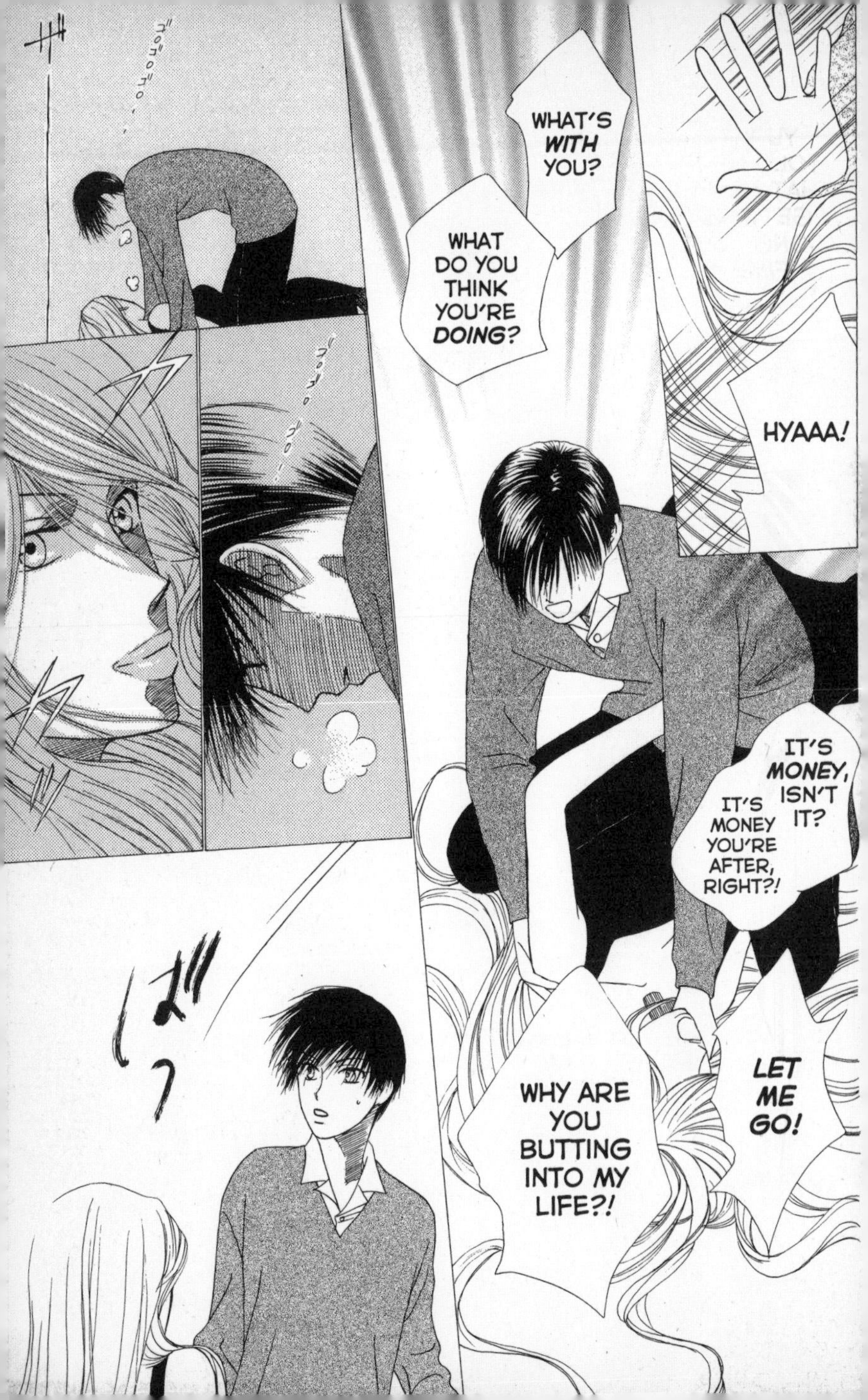
HYAAA!
WHAT'S WITH YOU?
WHAT DO YOU THINK YOU'RE DOING?
IT'S MONEY, ISN'T IT?
IT'S MONEY YOU'RE AFTER, RIGHT?!
LET ME GO!
WHY ARE YOU BUTTING INTO MY LIFE?!

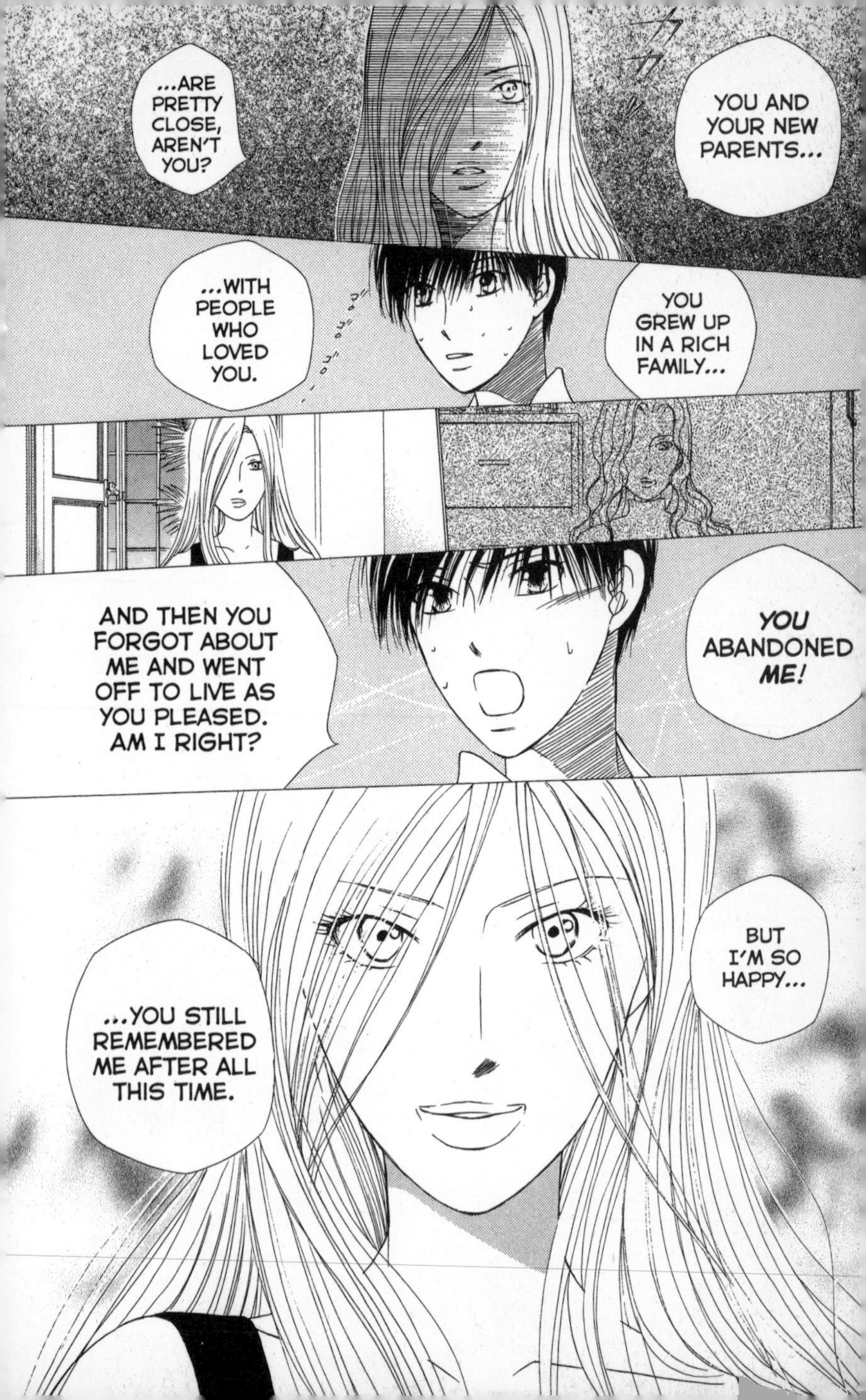
YOU AND YOUR NEW PARENTS...
...ARE PRETTY CLOSE, AREN'T YOU?
YOU GREW UP IN A RICH FAMILY...
...WITH PEOPLE WHO LOVED YOU.
YOU ABANDONED *ME!*
AND THEN YOU FORGOT ABOUT ME AND WENT OFF TO LIVE AS YOU PLEASED. AM I RIGHT?
BUT I'M SO HAPPY...
...YOU STILL REMEMBERED ME AFTER ALL THIS TIME.

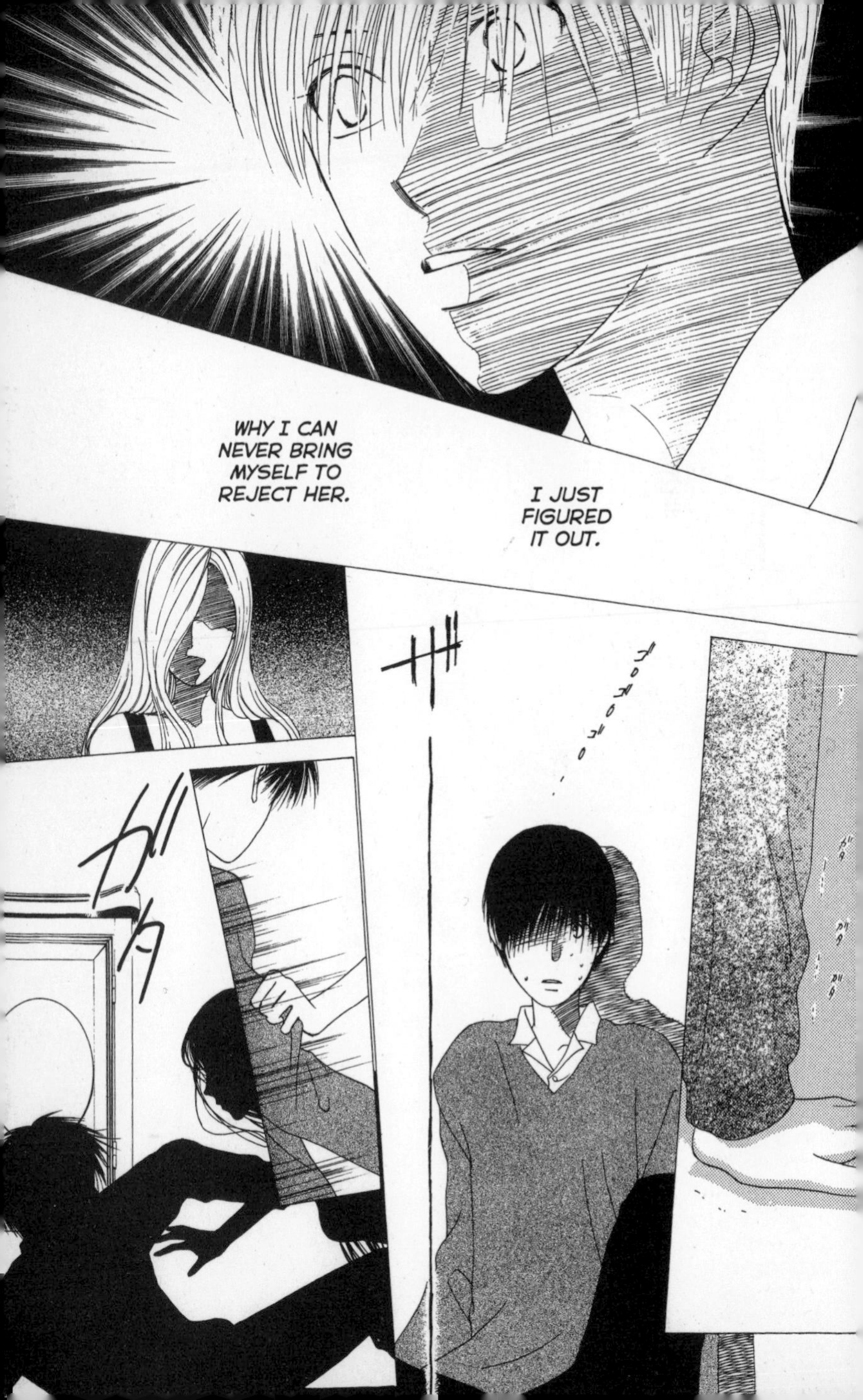
I JUST FIGURED IT OUT.
WHY I CAN NEVER BRING MYSELF TO REJECT HER.

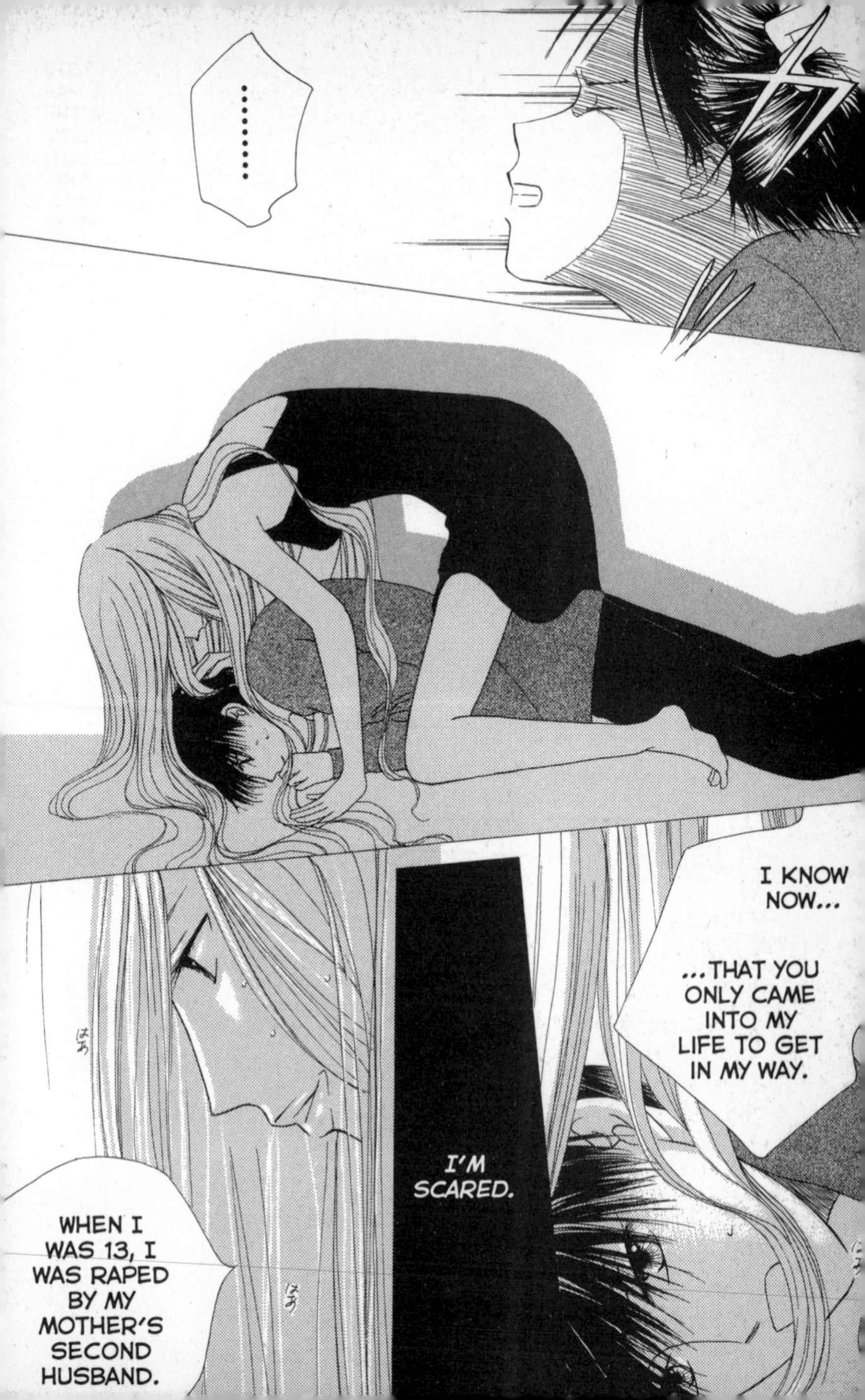

....
I KNOW NOW...
...THAT YOU ONLY CAME INTO MY LIFE TO GET IN MY WAY.
I'M SCARED.
はあ
はあ
WHEN I WAS 13, I WAS RAPED BY MY MOTHER'S SECOND HUSBAND.

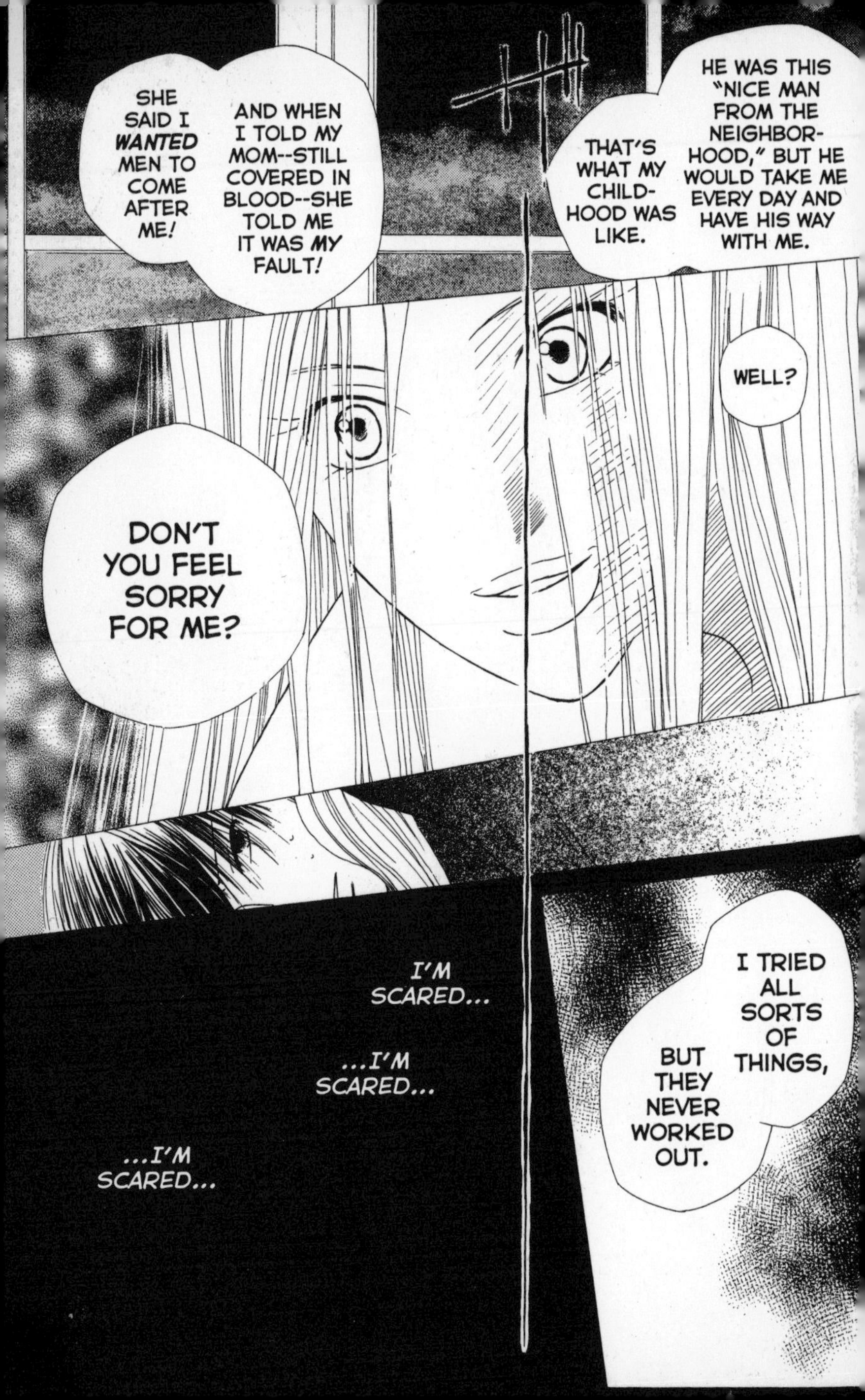
HE WAS THIS "NICE MAN FROM THE NEIGHBORHOOD," BUT HE WOULD TAKE ME EVERY DAY AND HAVE HIS WAY WITH ME.
THAT'S WHAT MY CHILDHOOD WAS LIKE.
AND WHEN I TOLD MY MOM--STILL COVERED IN BLOOD--SHE TOLD ME IT WAS *MY* FAULT!
SHE SAID I *WANTED* MEN TO COME AFTER ME!
WELL?
DON'T YOU FEEL SORRY FOR ME?
I TRIED ALL SORTS OF THINGS,
BUT THEY NEVER WORKED OUT.
I'M SCARED...
...I'M SCARED...
...I'M SCARED...

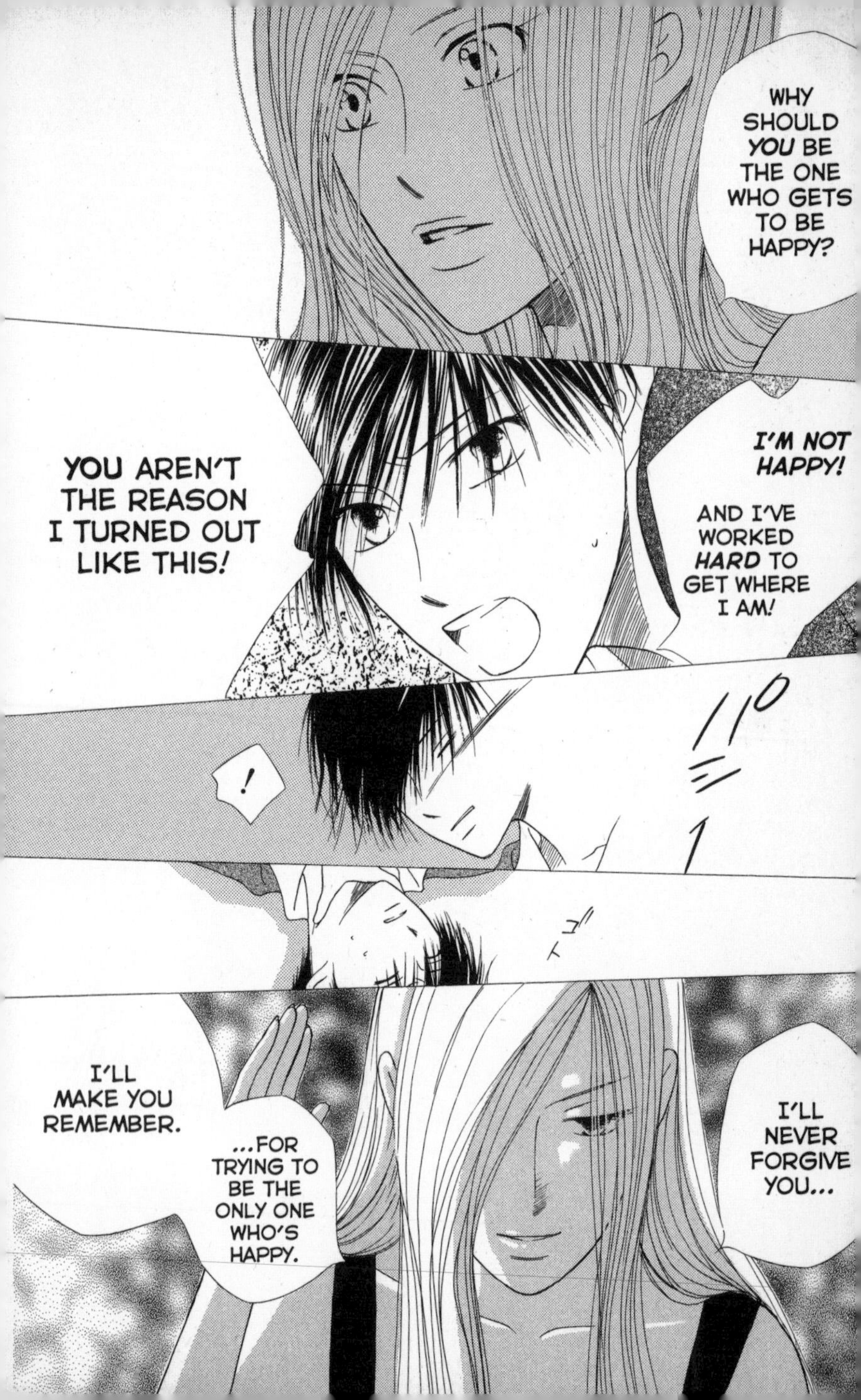
WHY SHOULD *YOU* BE THE ONE WHO GETS TO BE HAPPY?
I'M NOT HAPPY!
AND I'VE WORKED *HARD* TO GET WHERE I AM!
YOU AREN'T THE REASON I TURNED OUT LIKE THIS!
!
I'LL NEVER FORGIVE YOU...
...FOR TRYING TO BE THE ONLY ONE WHO'S HAPPY.
I'LL MAKE YOU REMEMBER.

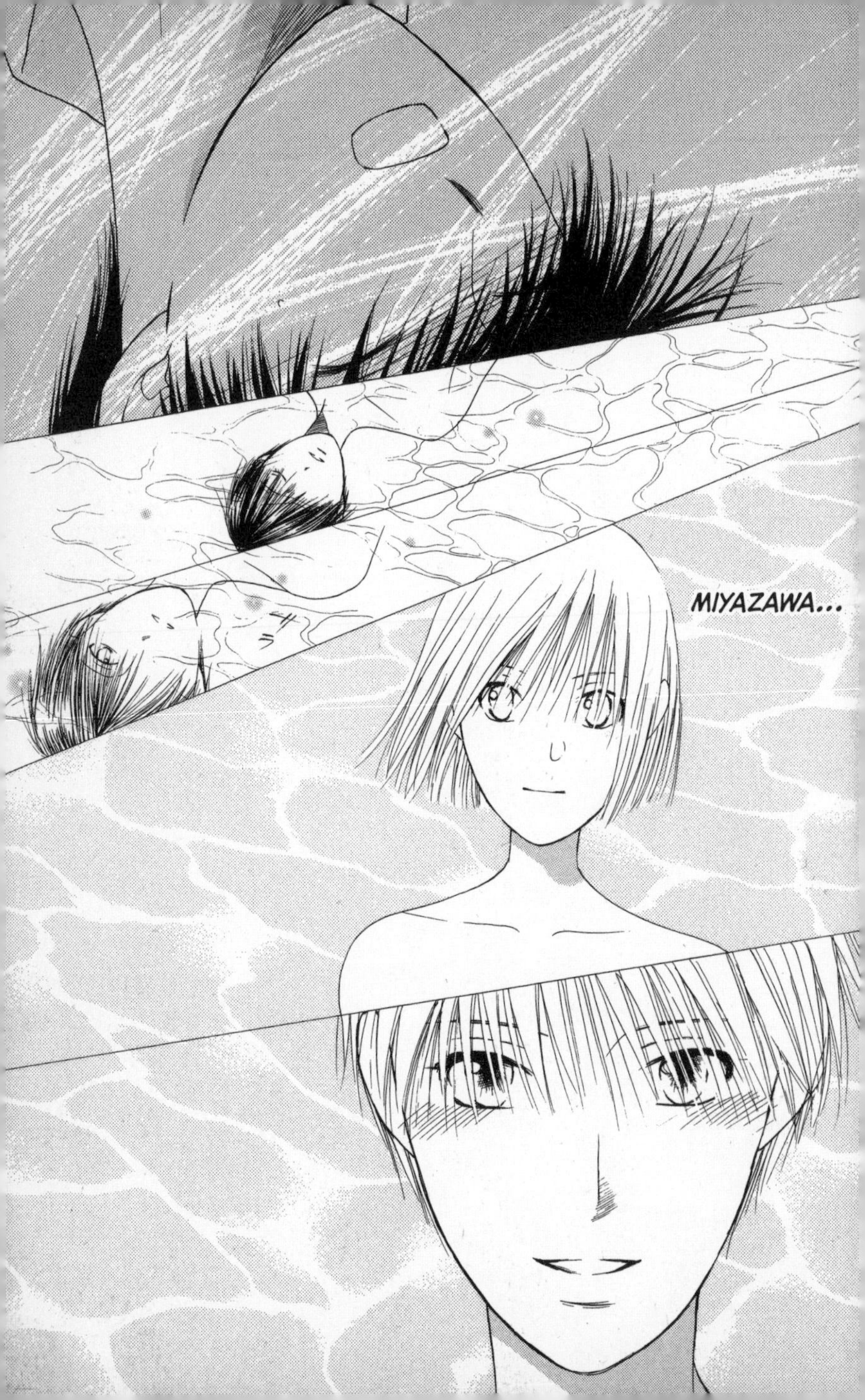
MIYAZAWA...

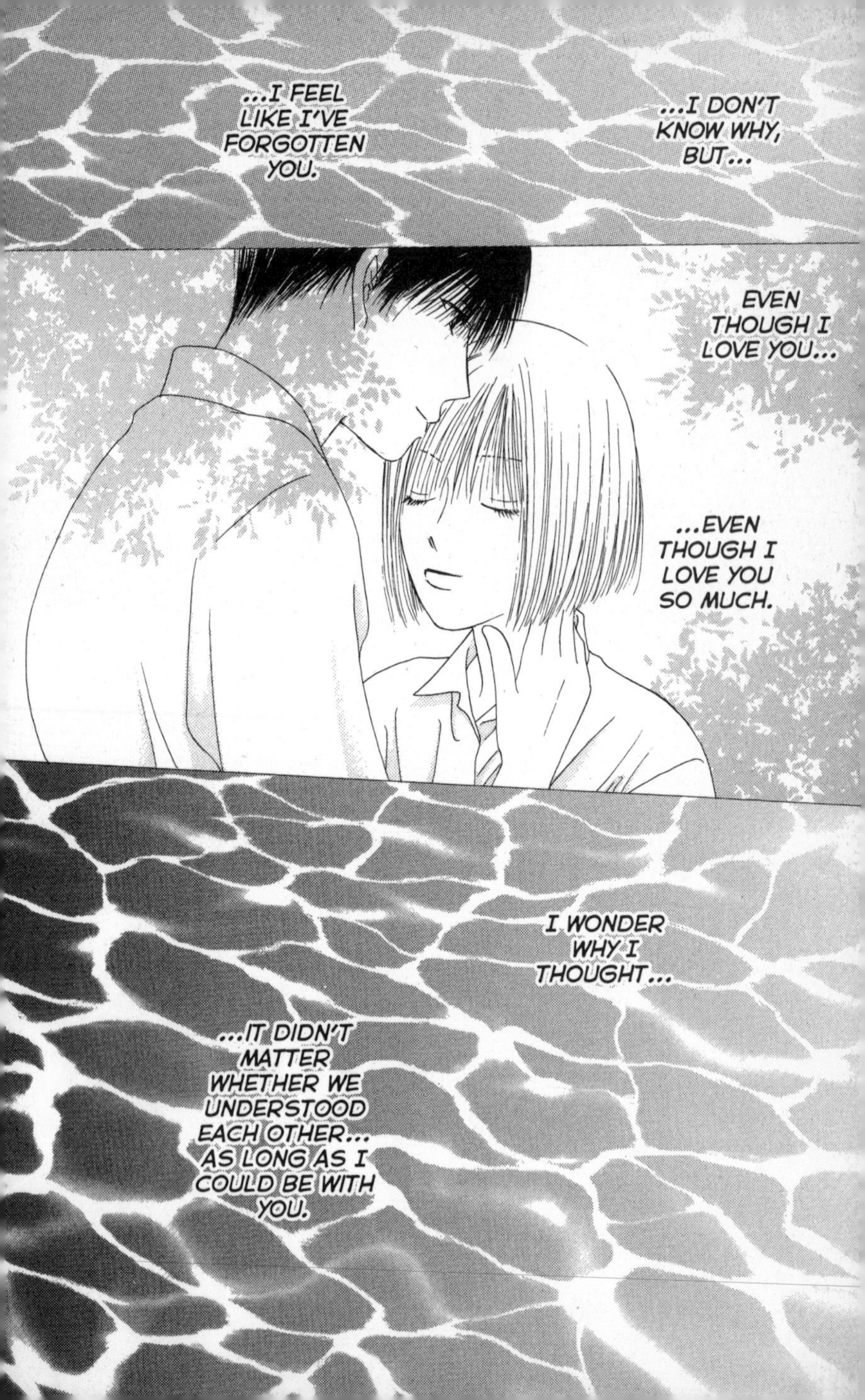
...I DON'T KNOW WHY, BUT...
...I FEEL LIKE I'VE FORGOTTEN YOU.
EVEN THOUGH I LOVE YOU...
...EVEN THOUGH I LOVE YOU SO MUCH.
I WONDER WHY I THOUGHT...
...IT DIDN'T MATTER WHETHER WE UNDERSTOOD EACH OTHER... AS LONG AS I COULD BE WITH YOU.

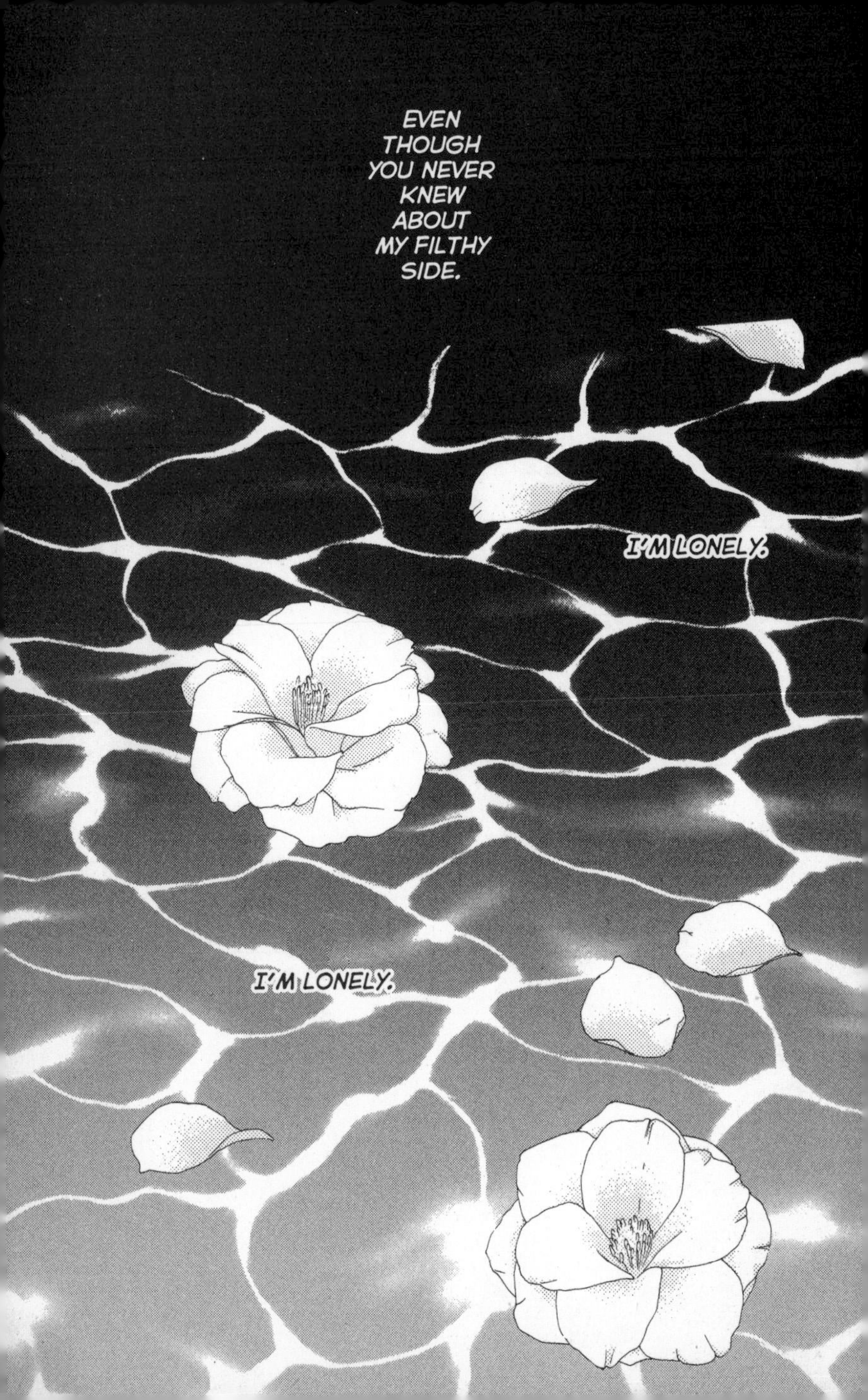
EVEN THOUGH YOU NEVER KNEW ABOUT MY FILTHY SIDE.
I'M LONELY.
I'M LONELY.

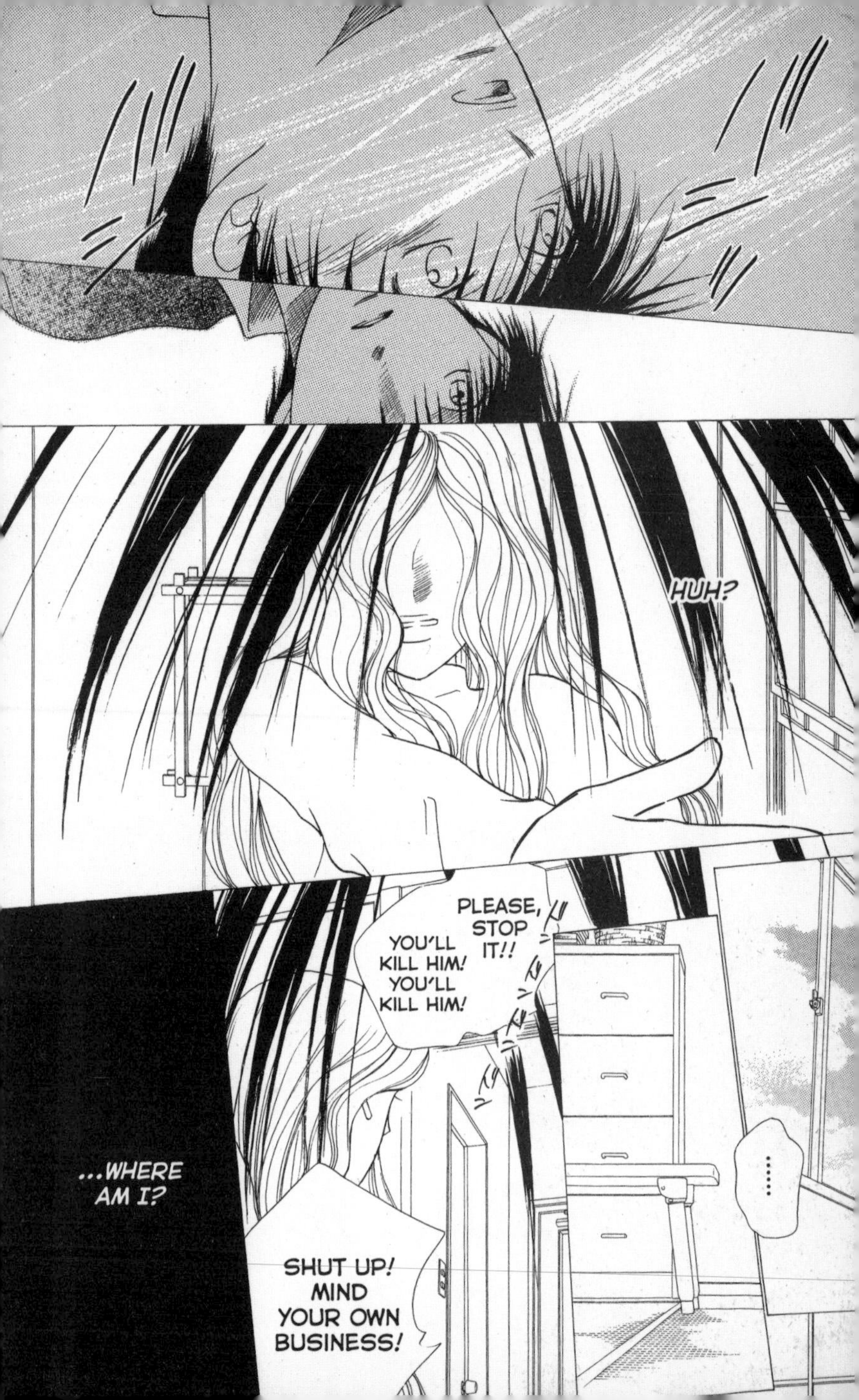
HUH?
PLEASE, STOP IT!!
YOU'LL KILL HIM! YOU'LL KILL HIM!
......
...WHERE AM I?
SHUT UP! MIND YOUR OWN BUSINESS!

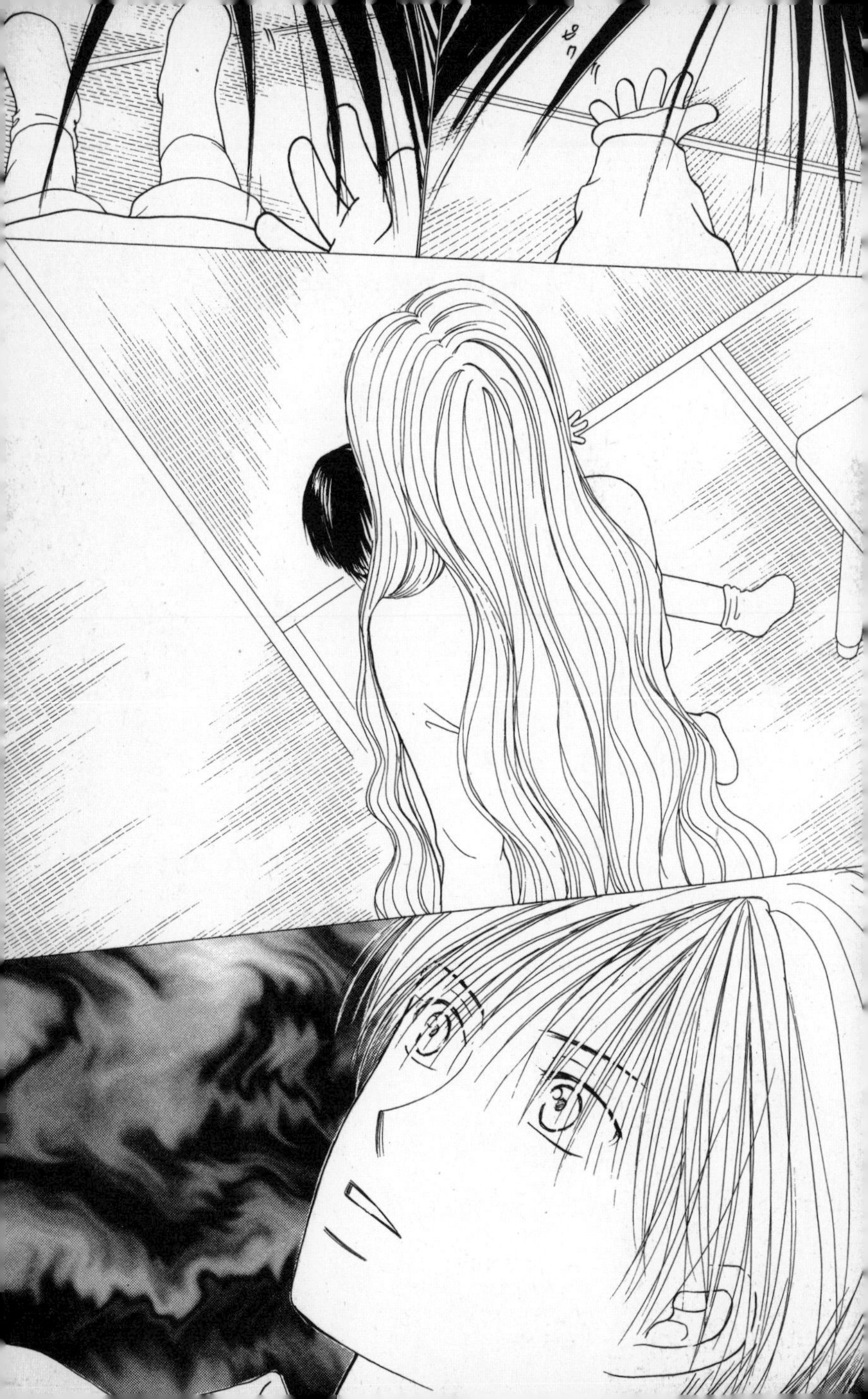
ピク

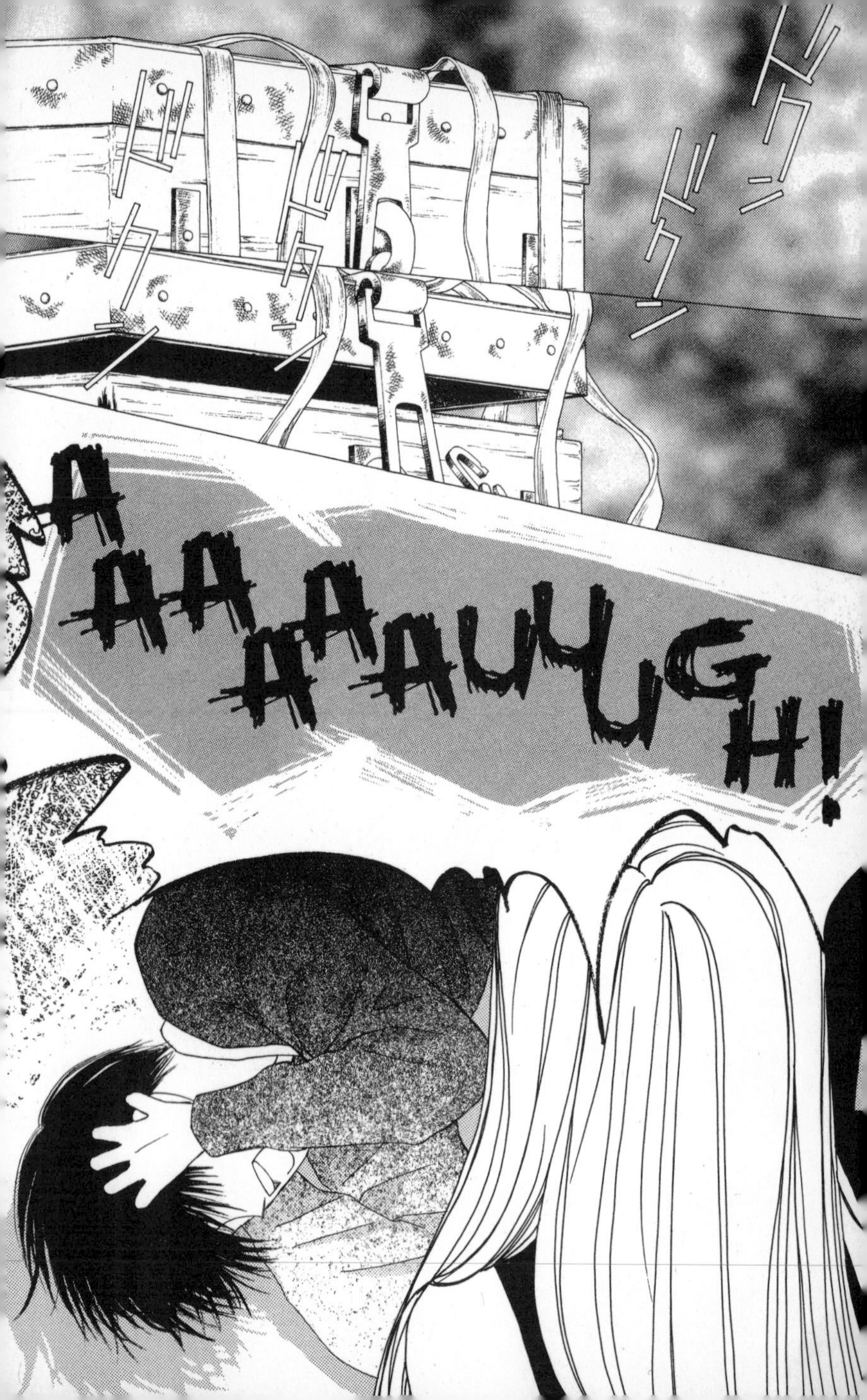
AAAAAAUUGH!

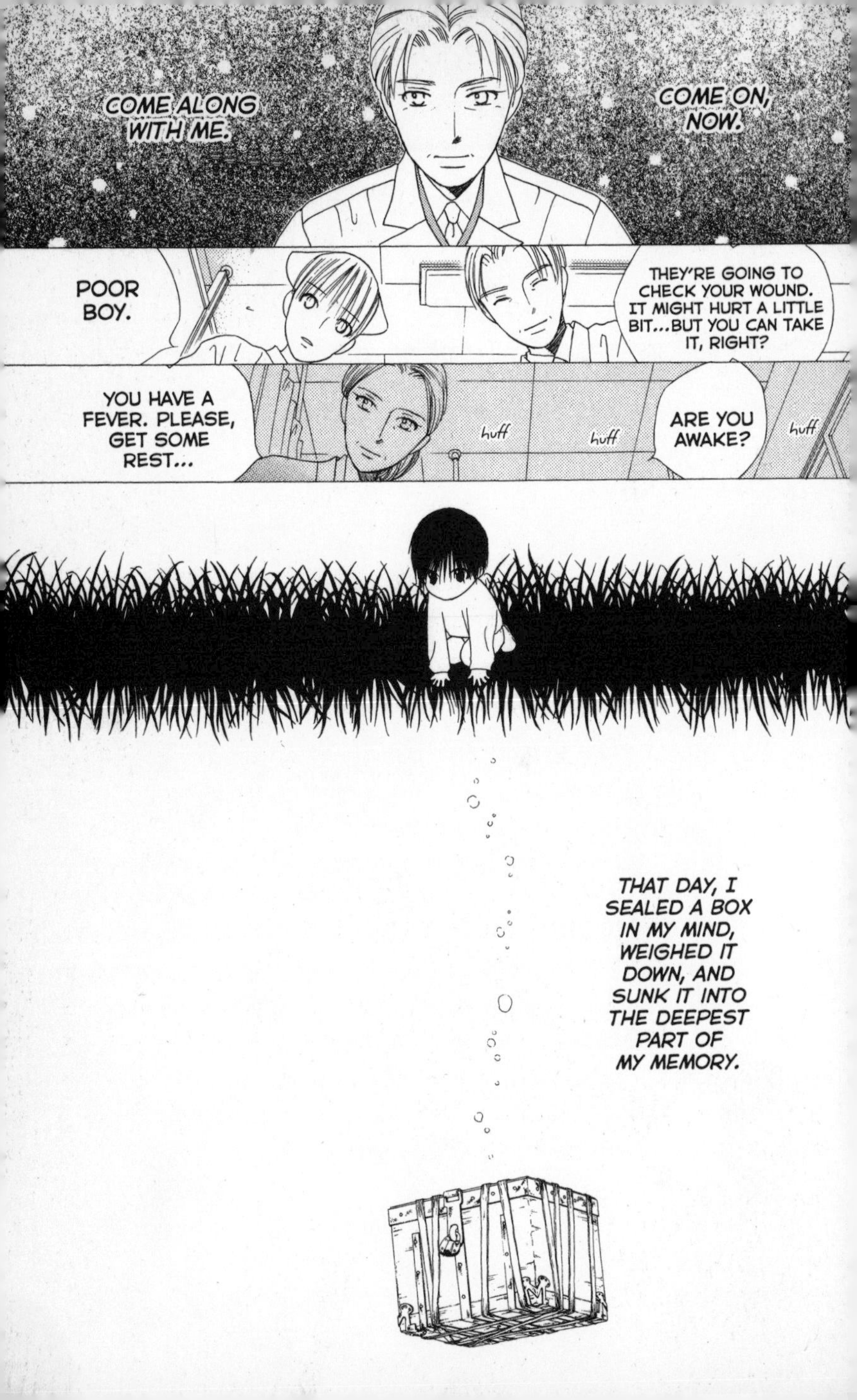
COME ON, NOW.
COME ALONG WITH ME.
THEY'RE GOING TO CHECK YOUR WOUND. IT MIGHT HURT A LITTLE BIT...BUT YOU CAN TAKE IT, RIGHT?
POOR BOY.
huff
ARE YOU AWAKE?
huff
huff
YOU HAVE A FEVER. PLEASE, GET SOME REST...
THAT DAY, I SEALED A BOX IN MY MIND, WEIGHED IT DOWN, AND SUNK IT INTO THE DEEPEST PART OF MY MEMORY.

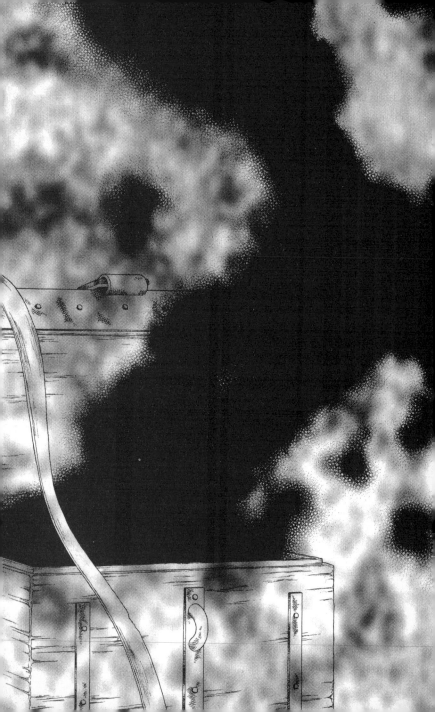

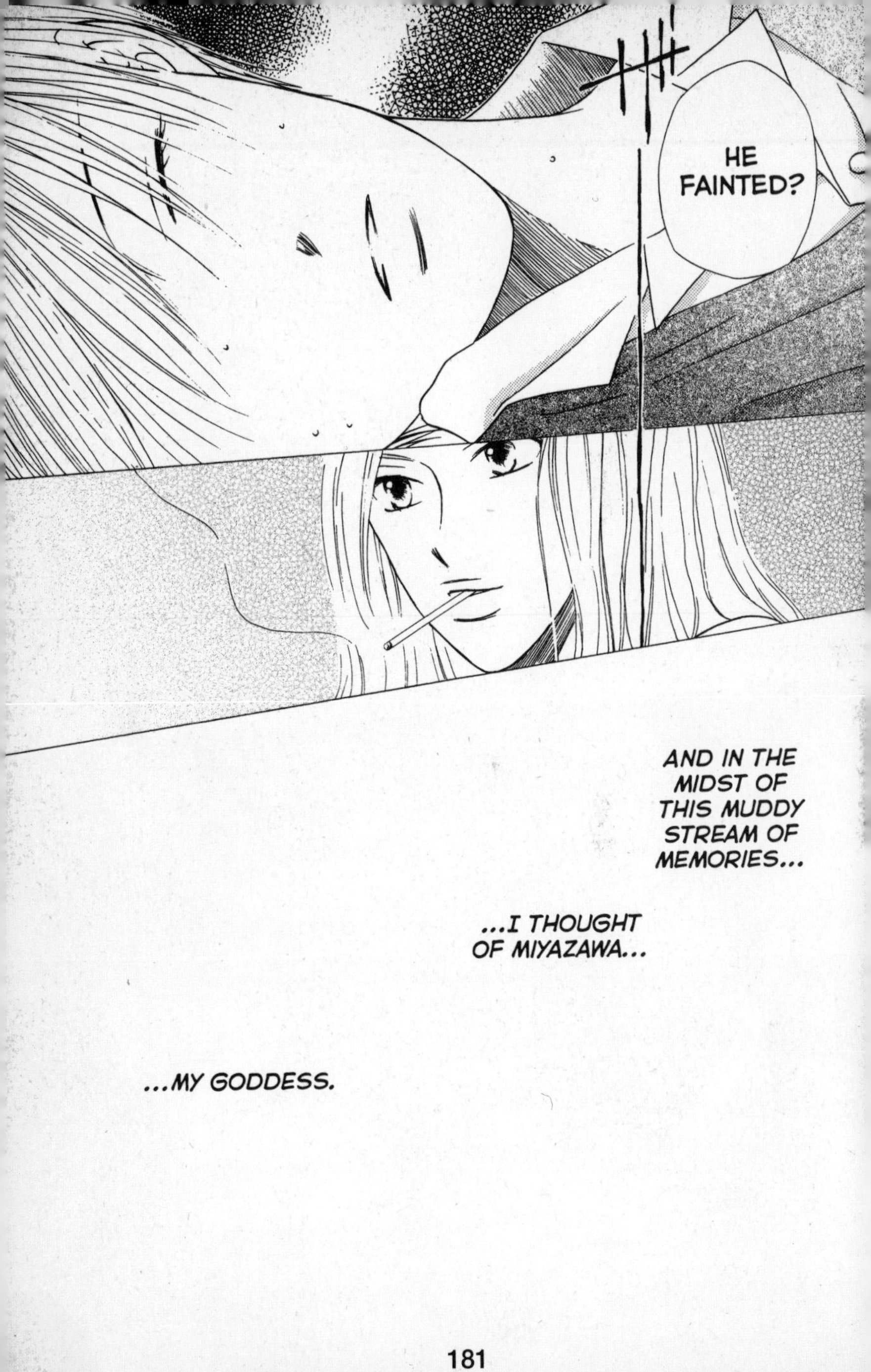
HE FAINTED?
AND IN THE MIDST OF THIS MUDDY STREAM OF MEMORIES...
...I THOUGHT OF MIYAZAWA...
...MY GODDESS.

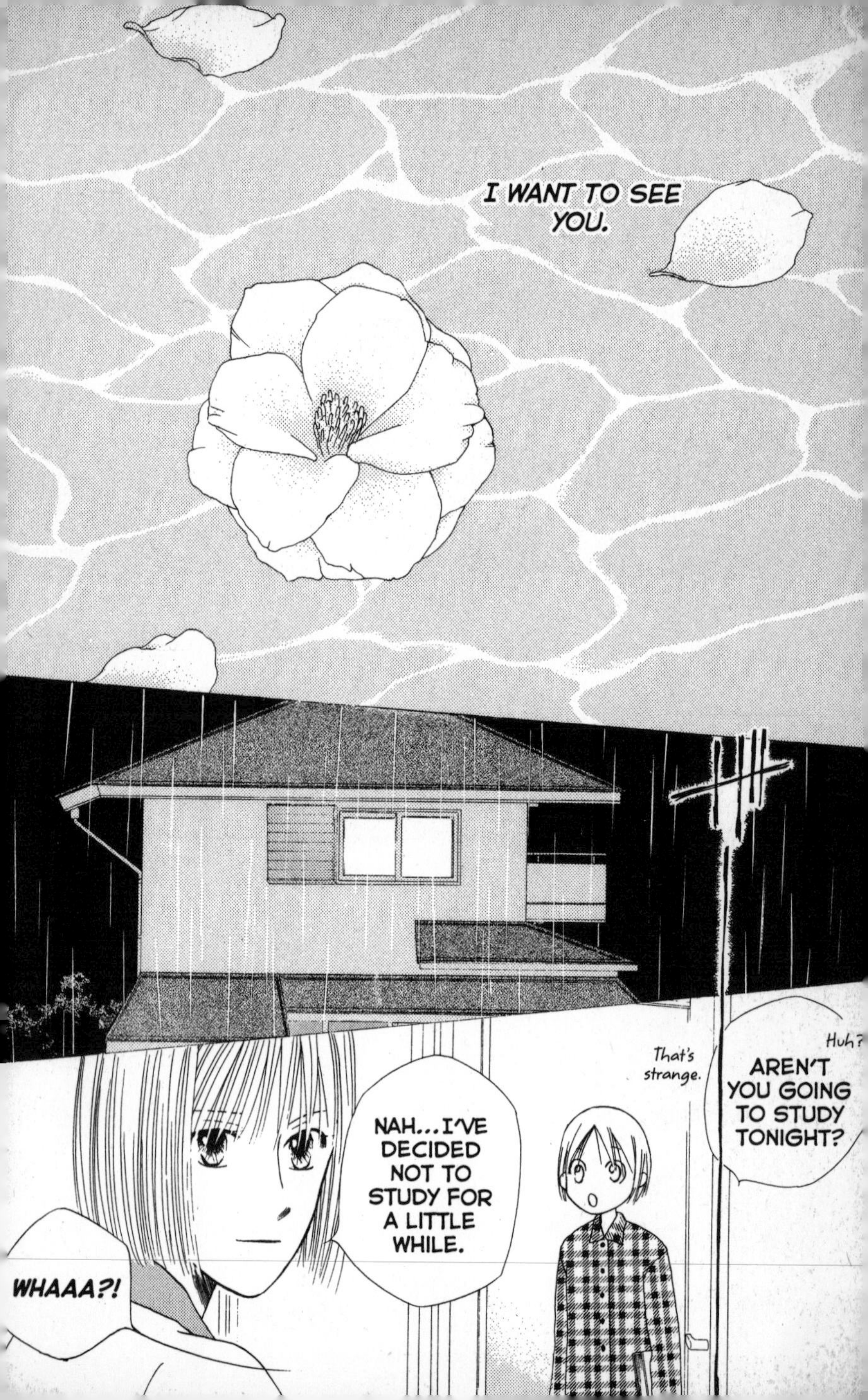
I WANT TO SEE YOU.
Huh?
AREN'T YOU GOING TO STUDY TONIGHT?
That's strange.
NAH...I'VE DECIDED NOT TO STUDY FOR A LITTLE WHILE.
WHAAA?!

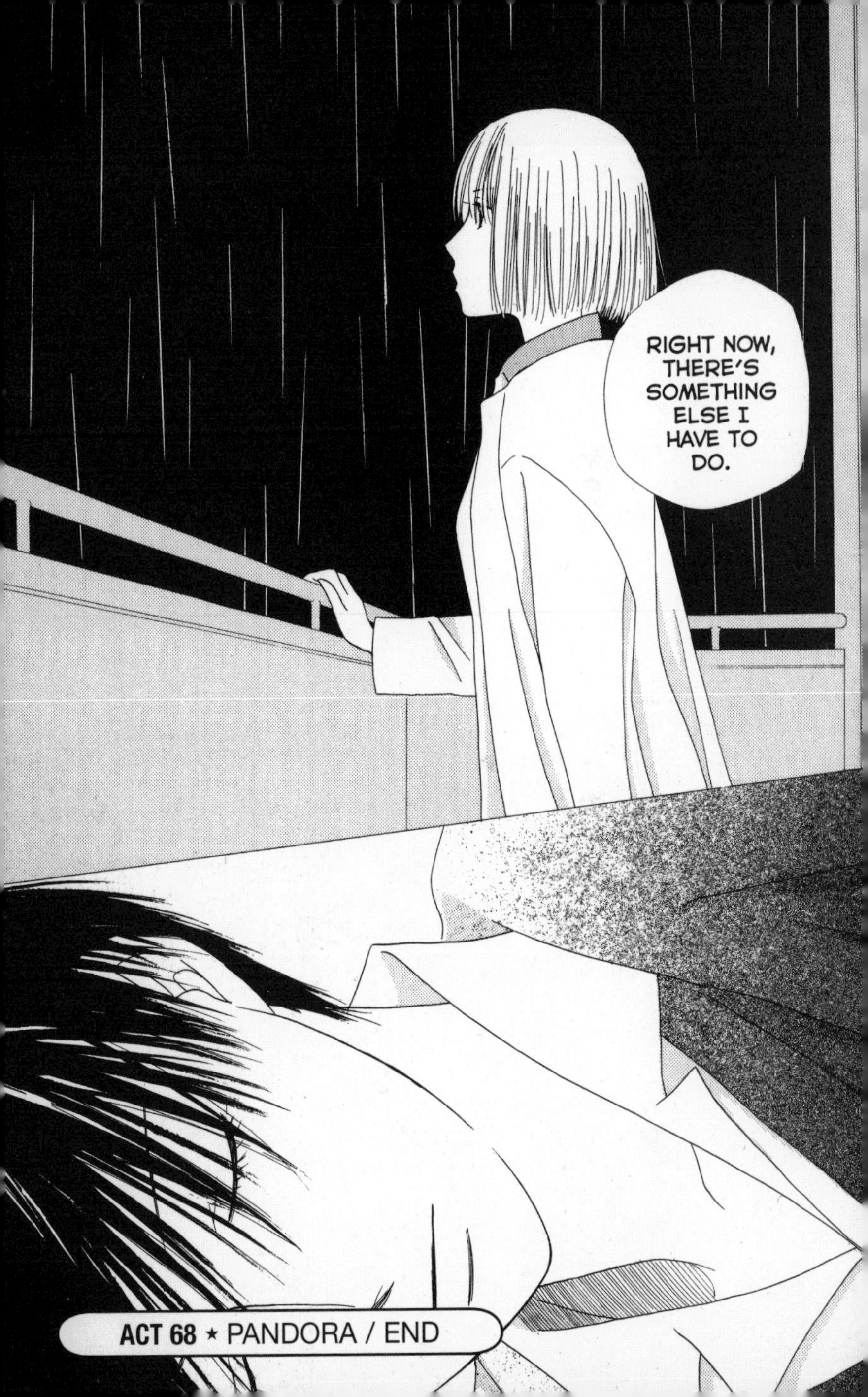
RIGHT NOW, THERE'S SOMETHING ELSE I HAVE TO DO.
ACT 68 ★ PANDORA / END

Tsuda Diary

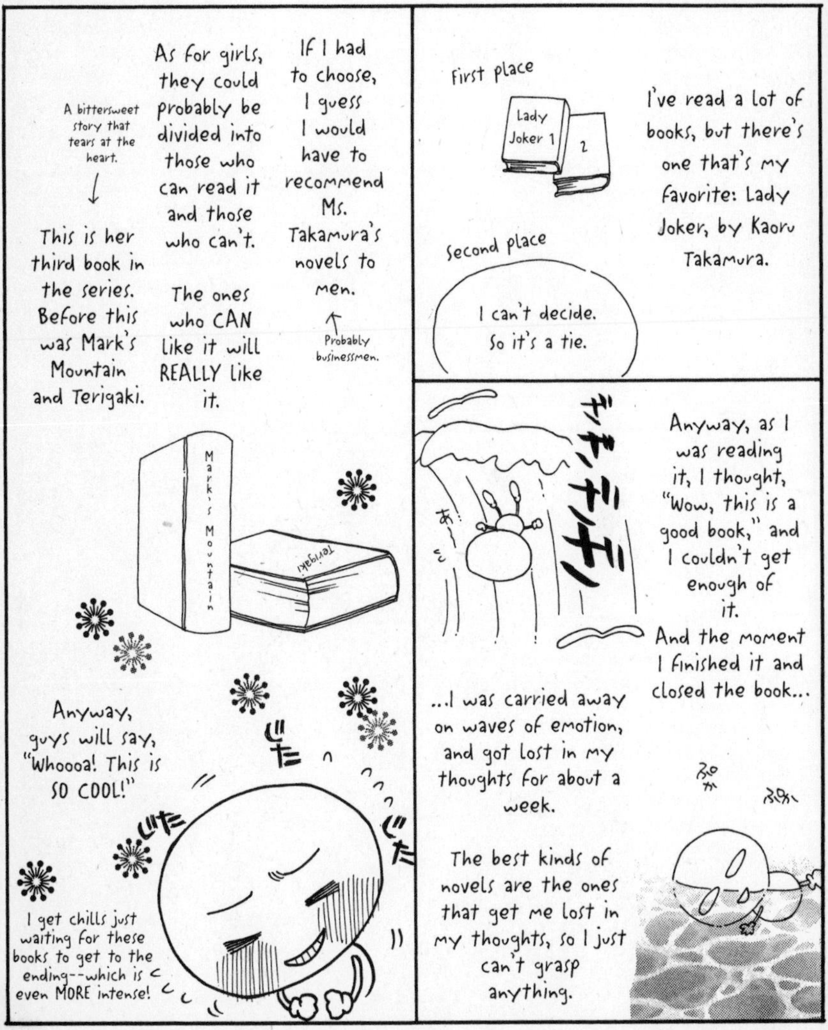
I've read a lot of books, but there's one that's my favorite: Lady Joker, by Kaoru Takamura.
First place
Lady Joker 1
2
Second place
I can't decide. So it's a tie.
Anyway, as I was reading it, I thought, "Wow, this is a good book," and I couldn't get enough of it.
And the moment I finished it and closed the book...
...I was carried away on waves of emotion, and got lost in my thoughts for about a week.
The best kinds of novels are the ones that get me lost in my thoughts, so I just can't grasp anything.
ぷか
ぷか
If I had to choose, I guess I would have to recommend Ms. Takamura's novels to men.
Probably businessmen.
As for girls, they could probably be divided into those who can read it and those who can't.
The ones who CAN like it will REALLY like it.
A bittersweet story that tears at the heart.
This is her third book in the series. Before this was Mark's Mountain and Terigaki.
Mark's Mountain
Terigaki
じた
じた
じた
Anyway, guys will say, "Whoooa! This is SO COOL!"
I get chills just waiting for these books to get to the ending--which is even MORE intense!

On Cyberculture

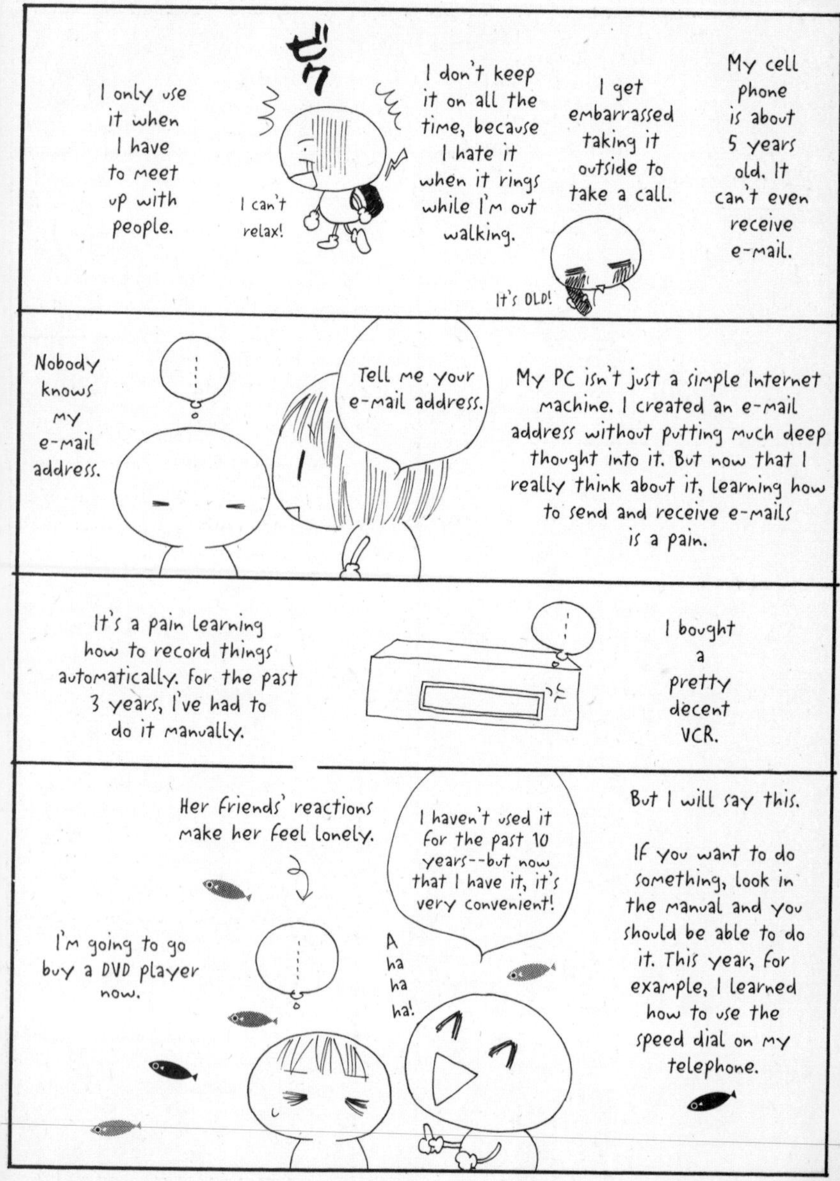
My cell phone is about 5 years old. It can't even receive e-mail.
It's OLD!
I get embarrassed taking it outside to take a call.
I don't keep it on all the time, because I hate it when it rings while I'm out walking.
ビク
I can't relax!
I only use it when I have to meet up with people.
My PC isn't just a simple Internet machine. I created an e-mail address without putting much deep thought into it. But now that I really think about it, learning how to send and receive e-mails is a pain.
Tell me your e-mail address.
Nobody knows my e-mail address.
I bought a pretty decent VCR.
It's a pain learning how to record things automatically. For the past 3 years, I've had to do it manually.
But I will say this.
If you want to do something, look in the manual and you should be able to do it. This year, for example, I learned how to use the speed dial on my telephone.
I haven't used it for the past 10 years--but now that I have it, it's very convenient!
A ha ha ha!
Her friends' reactions make her feel lonely.
I'm going to go buy a DVD player now.

Able Readers

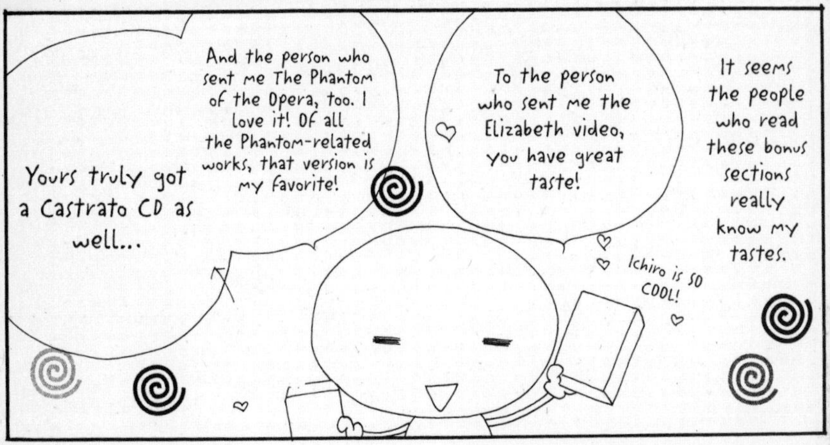
It seems the people who read these bonus sections really know my tastes.
To the person who sent me the Elizabeth video, you have great taste!
Ichiro is SO COOL!
And the person who sent me The Phantom of the Opera, too. I love it! Of all the Phantom-related works, that version is my favorite!
Yours truly got a Castrato CD as well...

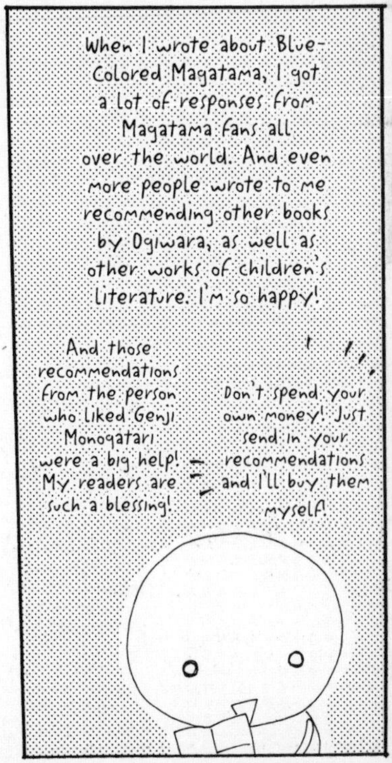
When I wrote about Blue-Colored Magatama, I got a lot of responses from Magatama fans all over the world. And even more people wrote to me recommending other books by Ogiwara, as well as other works of children's literature. I'm so happy!
Don't spend your own money! Just send in your recommendations and I'll buy them myself.
And those recommendations from the person who liked Genji Monogatari were a big help! My readers are such a blessing!

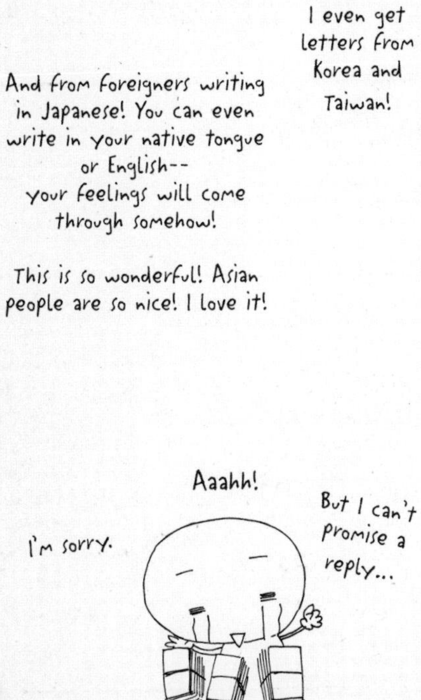
I even get letters from Korea and Taiwan!
And from foreigners writing in Japanese! You can even write in your native tongue or English-- your feelings will come through somehow!
This is so wonderful! Asian people are so nice! I love it!
But I can't promise a reply...
Aaahh!
I'm sorry.

Oh--and I certainly appreciate letters that simply give me your impressions of the story.

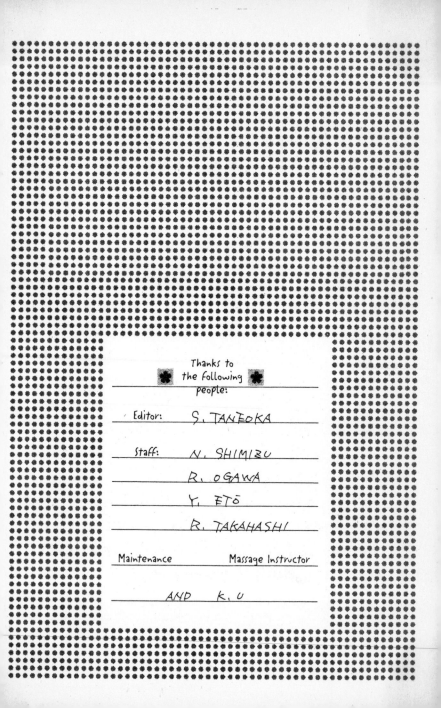

Thanks to
the following
people:

Editor: S. TANEOKA

Staff: N. SHIMIZU

R. OGAWA

Y. ETŌ

R. TAKAHASHI

Maintenance   Massage Instructor

AND   K. U

coming soon

kare kano

his and her circumstances

volume fifteen

Soichiro's meetings with his birth mother continue to be a secret from everyone... especially Yukino. When his adoptive parents find out, they want him to be open with them, but how can he tell anyone about his memories of an abusive childhood? Instead, Soichiro turns to his best friend Asaba for support, while continuing to shut Yukino out. Desperate, Yukino goes to confront him. Will Soichiro finally tell Yukino the truth...or will it destroy them both?

TOKYOPOP SHOP

SOKORA REFUGEES™

Kana thought life couldn't get any worse—behind on her schoolwork and out of luck with boys, she is also the only one of her friends who hasn't "blossomed." When she falls through a magical portal in the girls' shower, she's transported to the enchanted world of Sokora—wearing nothing but a small robe! Now, on top of landing in this mysterious setting, she finds that her body is beginning to go through some tremendous changes.

Preview the manga at:
www.TOKYOPOP.com/sokora

TEEN
AGE 13+

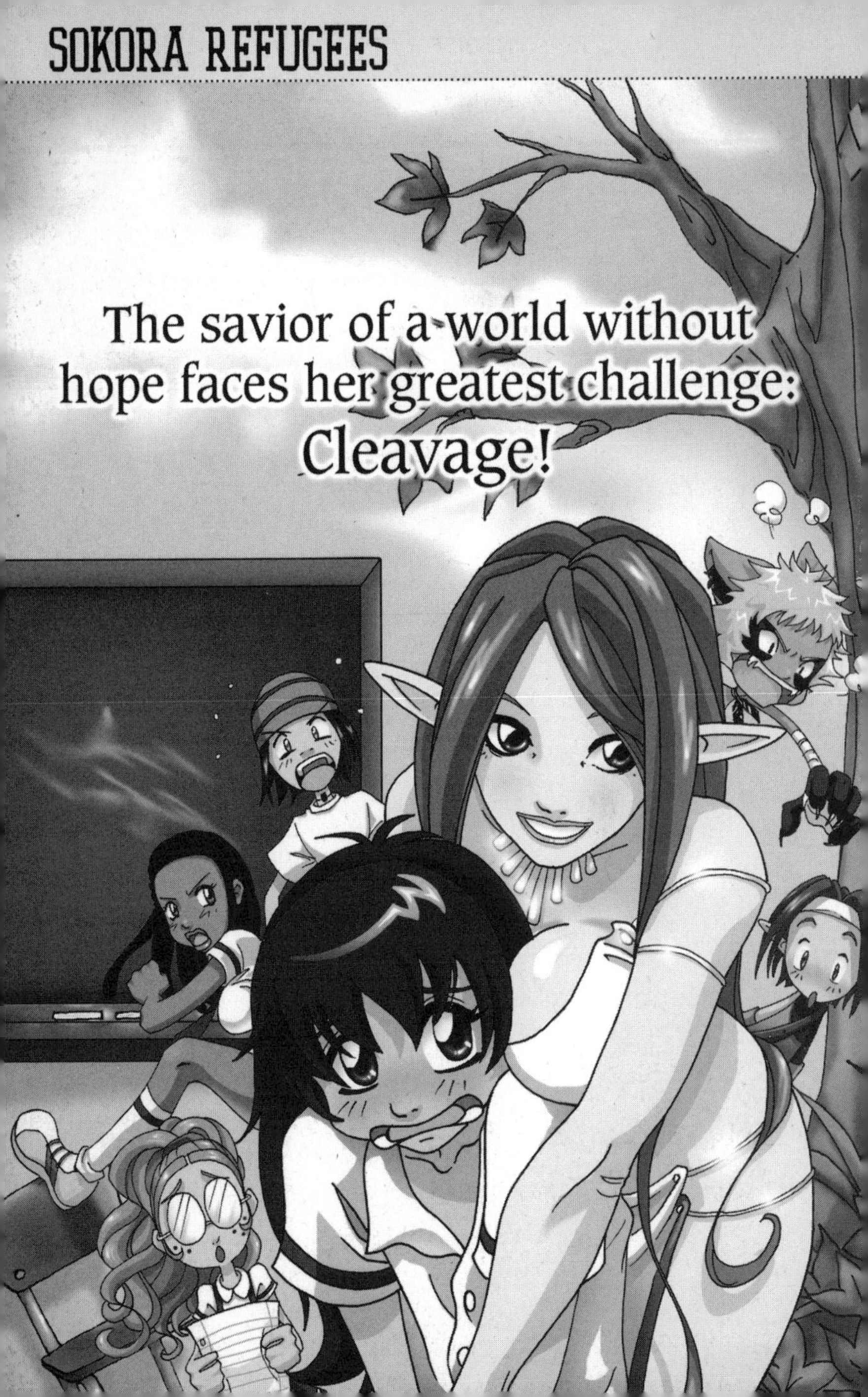
SOKORA REFUGEES
The savior of a world without
hope faces her greatest challenge:
Cleavage!

EDITORS' PICKS

TOKYOPOP MANGA SUPPLEMENT

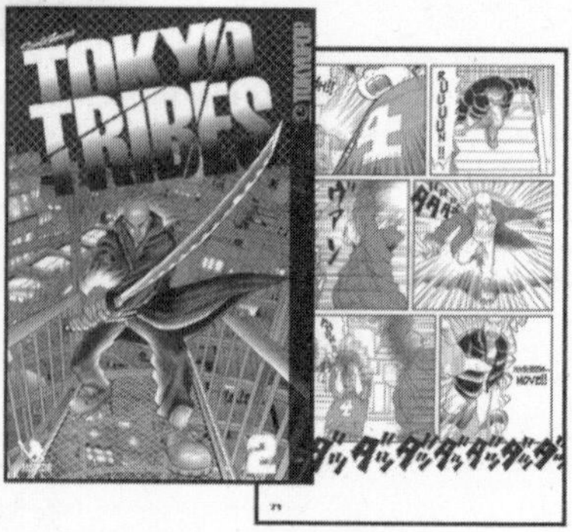
TOKYO TRIBES
2

BY SANTA INOUE

TOKYO TRIBES

Tokyo Tribes first hit Japanese audiences in the sleek pages of the ultra-hip skater fashion magazine *Boon.* Santa Inoue's hard-hitting tale of Tokyo street gangs battling it out in the concrete sprawl of Japan's capital raises the manga storytelling bar. Ornate with hip-hop trappings and packed with gangland grit, *Tokyo Tribes* paints a vivid, somewhat surreal vision of urban youth: rival gangs from various Tokyo barrios clash over turf, and when the heat between two of the tribes gets personal, a bitter rivalry explodes into all-out warfare.

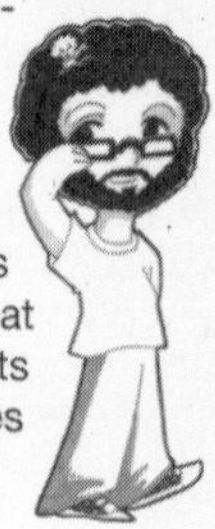

~Luis Reyes, Editor

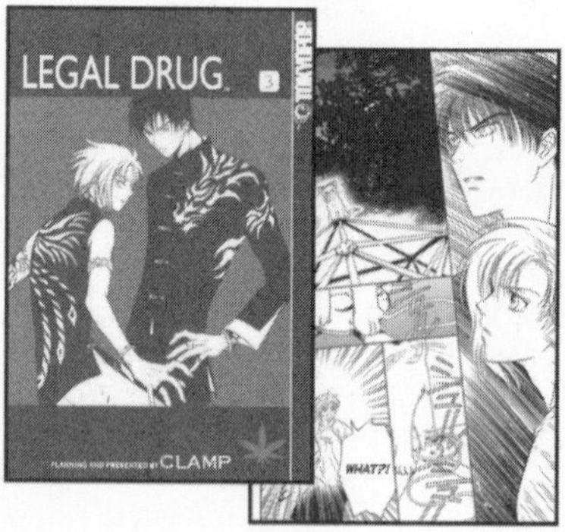
LEGAL DRUG
3
CLAMP
WHAT?!

BY CLAMP

LEGAL DRUG

CLAMP is the four-woman studio famous for creating much of the world's most popular manga. For the past 15 years they have produced such hits as the adorable *Cardcaptor Sakura,* the dark and brooding *Tokyo Babylon,* and the sci-fi romantic comedy *Chobits.* In *Legal Drug,* we meet Kazahaya and Rikuou, two ordinary pharmacists who moonlight as amateur sleuths for a mysterious boss. *Legal Drug* is a perfect dose of mystery, psychic powers and the kind of homoerotic tension for which CLAMP is renowned.

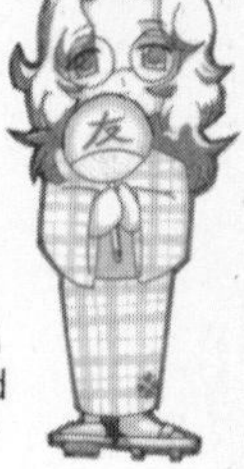

~Lillian Diaz-Przybyl, Jr. Editor

EDITORS' PICKS

TOKYOPOP MANGA SUPPLEMENT

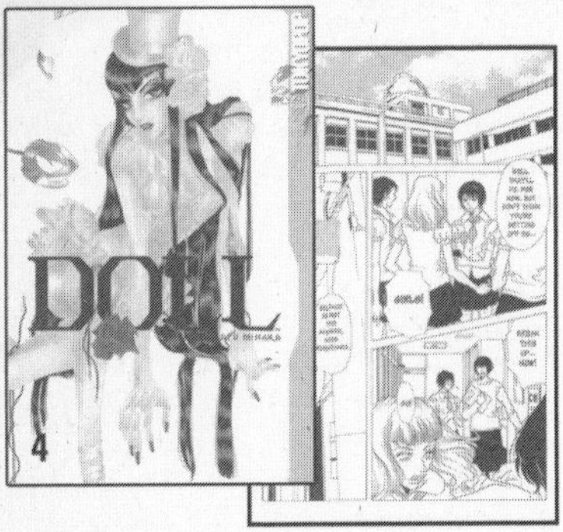
DOLL
4

BY MITSUKAZU MIHARA

DOLL

Mitsukazu Mihara's haunting *Doll* uses beautiful androids to examine what it means to be truly human. While the characters in *Doll* are draped in the chic Gothic-Lolita fashions that made Mihara-sensei famous, the themes explored are more universal—all emotions and walks of life have their day in *Doll*. *Doll* begins as a series of 'one-shot' stories and gradually dovetails into an epic of emotion and intrigue. It's like the *Twilight Zone* meets *Blade Runner!*

~Rob Tokar, Senior Editor

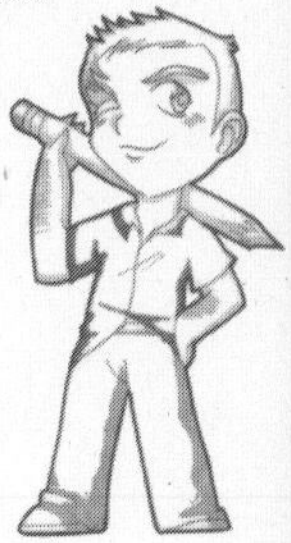

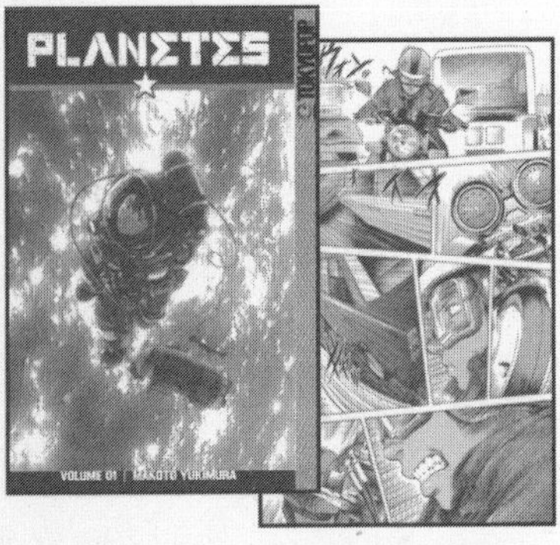
PLANETES
VOLUME 01 | MAKOTO YUKIMURA

BY MAKOTO YUKIMURA

PLANETES

Makoto Yukimura's profoundly moving and graphically arresting *Planetes* posits a near future where mankind's colonization of space has begun. Young Hachimaki yearns to join this exciting new frontier. Instead, he cleans the glut of orbital junk mankind's initial foray into space produced. He works with Fee, a nicotine-addict beauty with an abrasive edge, and Yuri, a veteran spaceman with a tragic past in search of inner peace. *Planetes* combines the scope of Jules Verne (*Around the World in Eighty Days*) and Robert Heinlein (*Starship Troopers*) with the philosophical wonder of *2001: A Space Odyssey.*

~Luis Reyes, Editor

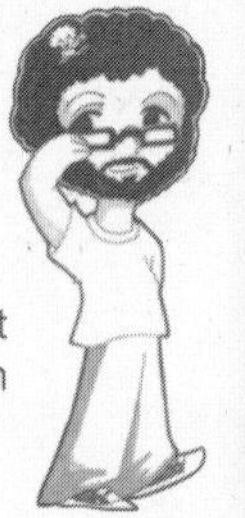

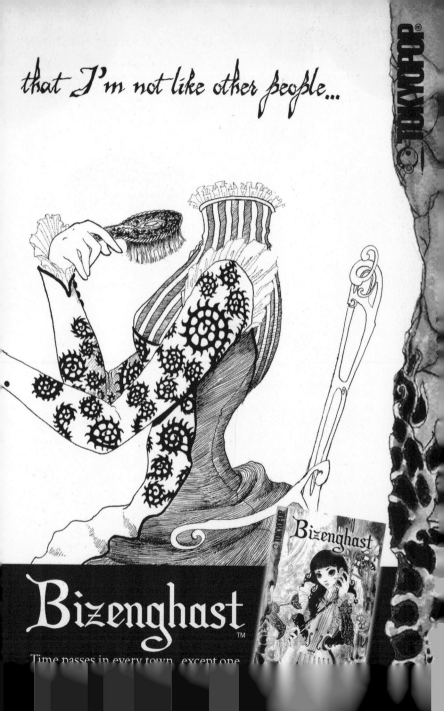

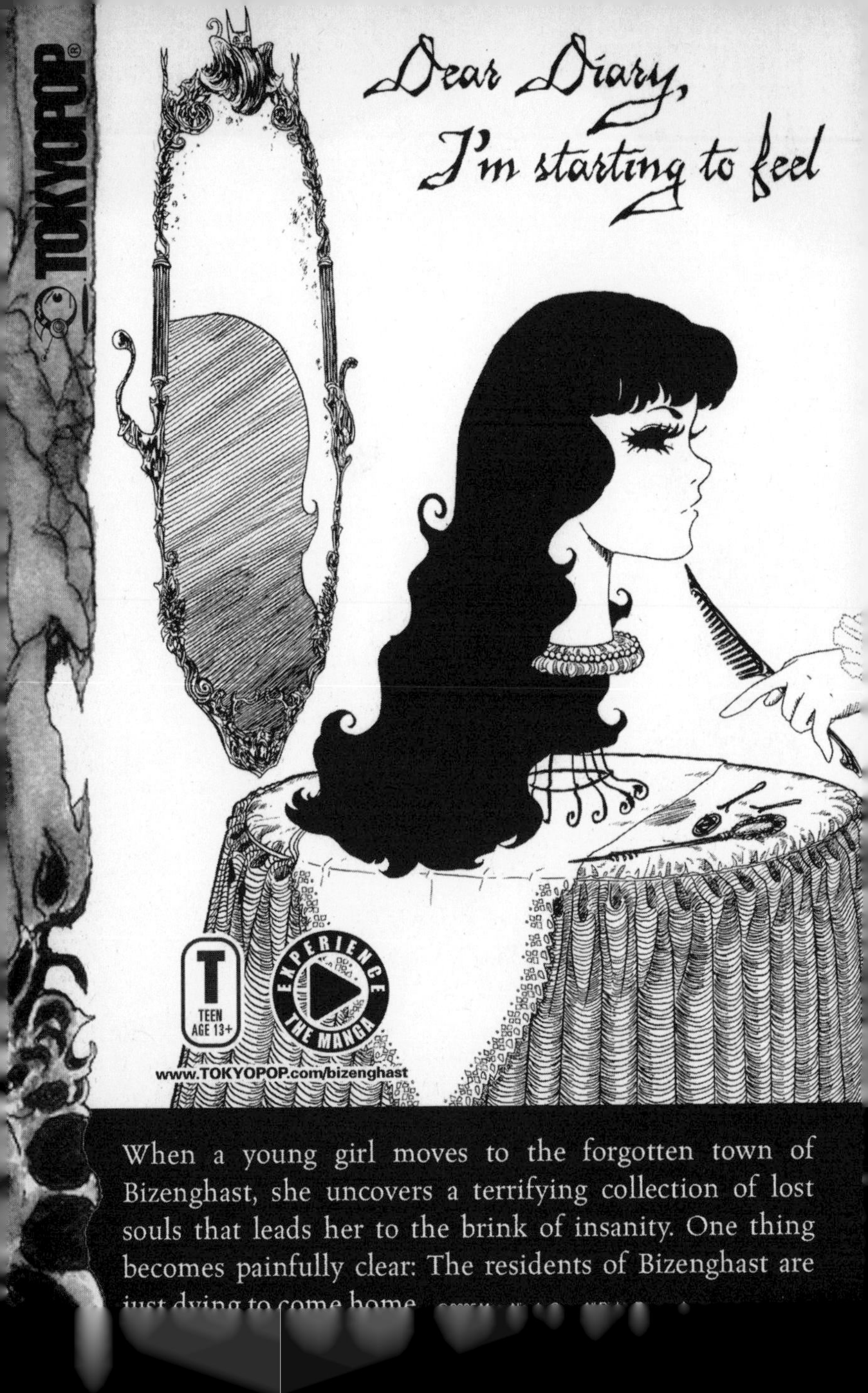
TOKYOPOP®
Dear Diary,
I'm starting to feel
T
TEEN
AGE 13+
EXPERIENCE
THE MANGA
www.TOKYOPOP.com/bizenghast

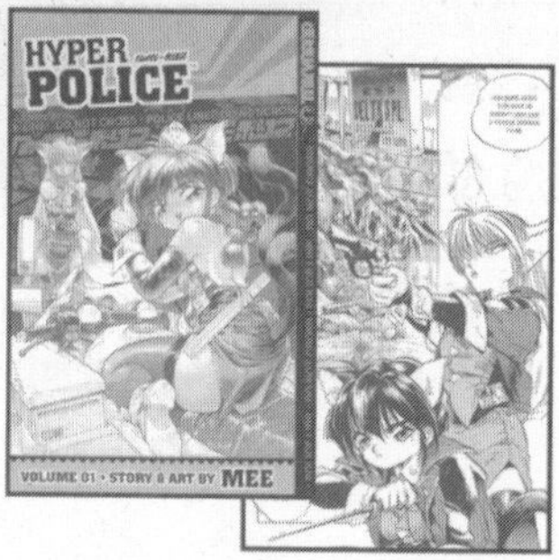
HYPER POLICE
VOLUME 01 • STORY & ART BY MEE

HYPER POLICE

BY MEE

In a future rife with crime, humans are an endangered species—and monsters have taken over! Natsuki is a cat girl who uses magical powers to enforce the law. However, her greatest threat doesn't come from the criminals. Her partner Sakura, a "nine-tailed" fox, plots to eat Natsuki and gobble up her magic! In this dog-eat-dog world, Natsuki fights to stay on top!

OT OLDER TEEN AGE 16+

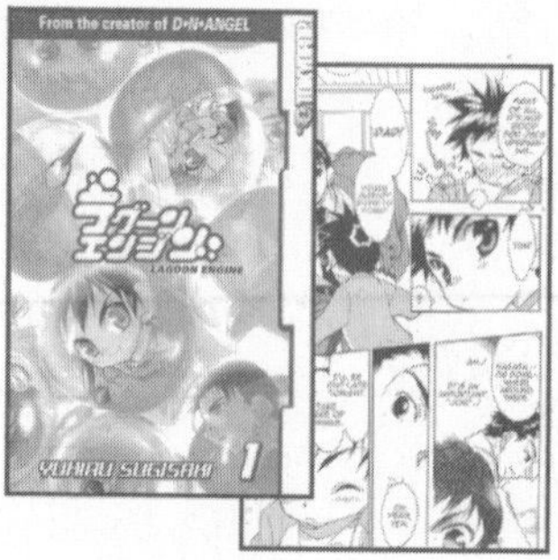
From the creator of D•N•ANGEL
LAGOON ENGINE
YUKIRU SUGISAKI 1

LAGOON ENGINE

BY YUKIRU SUGISAKI

From the best-selling creator of *D·N·Angel!*

Yen and Jin are brothers in elementary school—and successors in the Ragun family craft. They are Gakushi, those who battle ghosts and evil spirits known as "Maga" by guessing their true name. As Yen and Jin train to join the family business, the two boys must keep their identities a secret...or risk death!

T TEEN AGE 13+

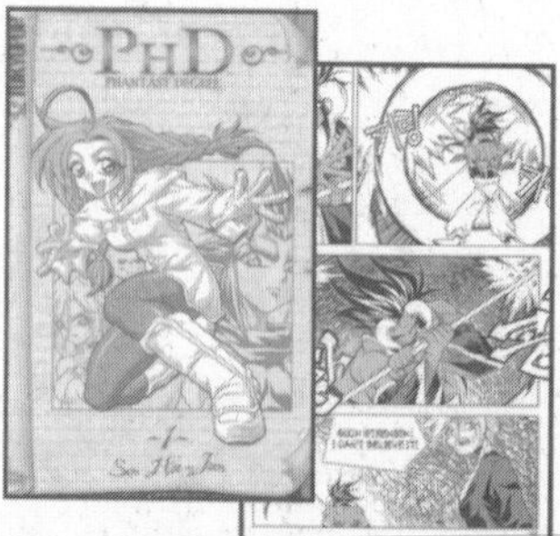
PHD
PHANTASY DEGREE

PHD: PHANTASY DEGREE

BY HEE-JOON SON

Sang is a fearlessly spunky young girl who is about to receive one hell of an education...at the Demon School Hades! She's on a mission to enroll into the monsters-only class. However, monster matriculation is not what is truly on her mind—she wants to acquire the fabled "King's Ring" from the fiancée of the chief commander of hell!

T TEEN AGE 13+

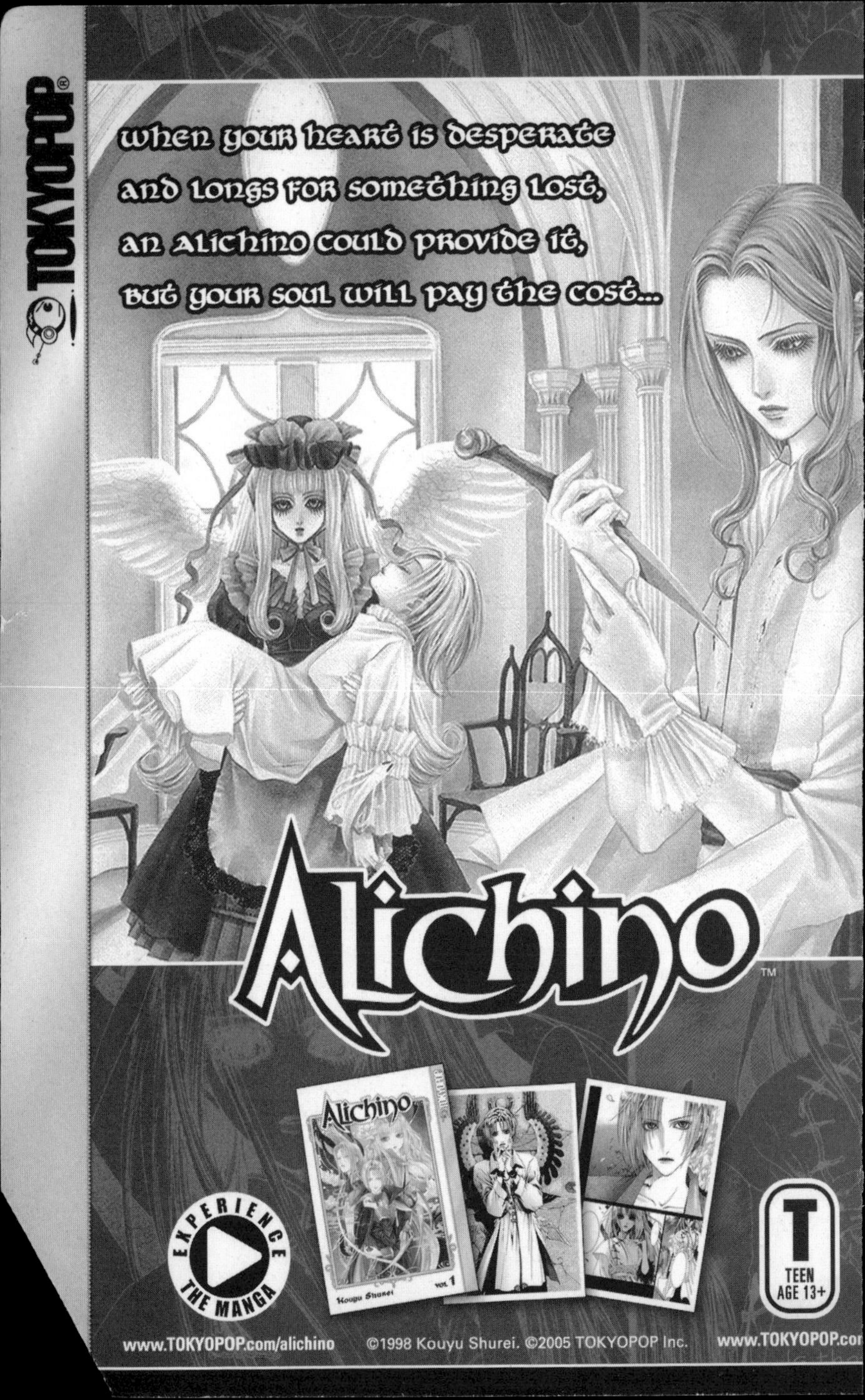
TOKYOPOP®
when your heart is desperate
and longs for something lost,
an alichino could provide it,
but your soul will pay the cost...
Alichino™
Alichino
Kouyu Shurei
VOL. 1
EXPERIENCE THE MANGA
T
TEEN
AGE 13+
www.TOKYOPOP.com/alichino
©1998 Kouyu Shurei. ©2005 TOKYOPOP Inc.
www.TOKYOPOP.com

STOP!

This is the back of the book.
You wouldn't want to spoil a great ending!

This book is printed "manga-style," in the authentic Japanese right-to-left format. Since none of the artwork has been flipped or altered, readers get to experience the story just as the creator intended. You've been asking for it, so TOKYOPOP® delivered: authentic, hot-off-the-press, and far more fun!

DIRECTIONS

If this is your first time reading manga-style, here's a quick guide to help you understand how it works.

It's easy... just start in the top right panel and follow the numbers. Have fun, and look for more 100% authentic manga from TOKYOPOP®!

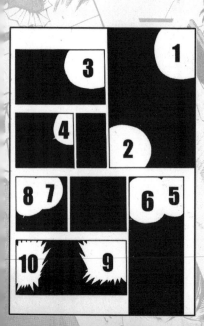